The Autobiography of Lorenzo de' Medici The Magnificent

A Commentary on My Sonnets

translated with an introduction

by

JAMES WYATT COOK

together with the text of
Il Comento
in the critical edition of
Tiziano Zanato

Arizona Center for Medieval and Renaissance Studies
Tempe, Arizona
2000

© Copyright 1995
Center for Medieval and Early Renaissance Studies
State University of New York at Binghamton

Second Printing
© Copyright 2000
Arizona Board of Regents for Arizona State University

Library of Congress Cataloging-in-Publication Data

Medici, Lorenzo de', 1449–1492.
　[Comento. English]
　The autobiography of Lorenzo de' Medici the Magnificent : a commentary on my sonnets / translated with an introduction by James Wyatt Cook.
　　　p. cm. — (Medieval & Renaissance texts & studies ; v. 129)
　Includes bibliographical references and index.
　ISBN 0–86698–136–5
　1. Medici, Lorenzo de', 1449–1492—Criticism and interpretation. I. Cook, James Wyatt, 1932– . II. Title. III. Series.
PQ4630.M3C62 1994
851'.2—dc20   94–11190
　　　　　　　　　　　　　　　　　　　　　　　　　　　　　　　　　　　CIP

This book is made to last.
It is set in Bembo
and printed on acid-free paper
to library specifications

Printed in the United States of America

The Autobiography of Lorenzo de' Medici The Magnificent

A Commentary on My Sonnets

Medieval and Renaissance Texts and Studies

Volume 129

Table of Contents

List of Abbreviations	ix
Introduction	1
Chronology of the Life of Lorenzo de' Medici	25
Prologue	31
[Sonnet]	
1	58
2	60
3	66
4	70
[New Argument]	72
5	80
6	84
7	88
8	92
9	96
10	102
11	106
12	110
13	118
14	124
15	132
16	140
17	144
18	150
19	154
20	162
21	166
22	170
23	180
24	186
25	190
26	194
27	198
28	200
29	206

[Sonnet]
30	210
31	216
32	220
33	226
34	232
35	236
36	242
37	248
38	252
39	256
40	260
41	266
Index of First Lines of Poems	273
Appendix A	276
Bibliography	281
List of Abbreviations	285
Index	287

Acknowledgments

Many persons and institutions have, in various ways, made possible my preparation of this translation. I am indebted particularly to the Albion College Faculty Development Committee and the Hewlett-Mellon Faculty Development Fund whose generosity enabled me to consult two of the Florentine manuscripts of the *Comento* and gave me a block of time to complete a first draft. I am also obliged to the staffs of the Newberry Library, and of the Biblioteche Medicea Laurenziana and Riccardiana for their splendid assistance. Professor Tiziano Zanato of the University of Venice provided me with most useful advice about the state of the text and with proof copies of his new critical edition, and Professors Paula Backscheider of Auburn University, Peter Wiggins of William and Mary College, and James Diedrick of Albion College provided helpful feedback on early drafts of the introduction. Ms. Jennifer McMullen entered most of the text into a computer and assisted me in comparisons between the critical texts of Bigi and Zanato. Mr. Brian John Smith read a subsequent draft of the English aloud to me while I followed in the Italian—a process which caught many places where text had inadvertently been lost to eyeskips during revision, and Professor Konrad Eisenbichler of the University of Toronto made many invaluable suggestions for textual emendations. I am also grateful to Professor Germaine Warkentin of Victoria University in the University of Toronto for having first suggested this project to me, to the late Professor Armando de Gaetano of Wayne State University, who taught me my first Italian, and to the anonymous readers of MRTS for their careful and helpful criticism. Thanks too to Ms. Lori Vandermark for her careful supervision of this book's production.

The introduction to the translation is especially indebted to the participants in three quintocentennial, international conferences sponsored by Brooklyn College, by The Warburg Institute and the University of Warwick, and by Villa I Tatti and the Istituto Nazionale di Studi sul Rinascimento. The names of those whose ideas seemed relevant for inclusion in my discussion appear along the way, but I wish to express my special appreciation to the University of Hull's Dr. Judith Bryce, whose suggestions catalyzed my thinking about *il Comento*, and to Professor Nicolai Rubinstein, the general editor of Lorenzo's *Lettere*, for his advice.

Most especially, I appreciate the loving support of my wife Barbara, who cheerfully soldiered on while I worked in Florence, at the Newberry, and in London.

List of Abbreviations

Aen. = Virgil, *Aeneid*.
Bigi = Bigi, Emilio ed. *Scritti Scelti di Lorenzo de' Medici*. Turin: UTET, 1965.
Canz. = canzone.
Comento = Zanato, Tiziano, ed. *Lorenzo de' Medici, Comento de' Miei Sonetti*, Florence: Leo S. Olschki, 1991.
Comento a Inf. = Landino, Cristofero. *Comento a Inferno*.
Conv. = Alighieri, Dante. *Il Convivio* 2d. ed. 2 vols. Ed. Antonio Enzo Quaglio, G. Busnelli, and G. Vandelli (Florence: Le Monnier), 1964.
De an. = Aristotle, *De animalium generatione*.
Dec. = Boccaccio, Giovanni. *Decameron*. Trans. John Payne Berkeley: Univ. of California Press, 1982.
De vulg. elo. = Alighieri, Dante. *De vulgari eloquentia*.
Ep. Rac. = Poliziano, Agnolo. "Epistola," in Medici, Lorenzo de'. *Raccolta aragonese*.
FC = Jayne, Sears Reynolds, trans. "Marsilio Ficino's Commentary on Plato's *Symposium*," in *The University of Missouri Studies* 29, 1, 1944 (119–247).
Inf. = Alighieri, Dante. *Inferno*.
In Phil. com. = Ficino, Marsilio. "Commentary on the 'Philebus'," 44 and 45, in In Platonem, *Opera*.
Jackson = *Dante's Convivio*. Trans. William Walrond Jackson. Oxford: Clarendon Press, 1909.
L. = Lorenzo de' Medici
Met. = Ovid, *Metamorphoses,* 2 vols. Trans. Frank Justus Miller. New York: G. P. Putnam's Sons, 1916.
Par. = Alighieri, Dante. *Paradiso*.
Pol. = Aristotle, *Politics*
Problematum = Aristotle, *Problematum ineditorium*. Ed. Didot.
Rep. = Plato, *Republic*. In *Plato with an English Translation,* 2 vols, trans. R. G. Bury, London: William Heinemann, 1926
Rvf = Petrarch, Francesco. *Rerum vulgarium fragmenta: Petrarch's Canzoniere*. Trans. James Wyatt Cook. Binghamton, N. Y.: Center for Medieval and Renaissance Texts. (Forthcoming).
SA = Ficino, Marsilio. *Sopra lo amore*. In *Opere*.

Saggio = Zanato, Tiziano. *Saggio sul "Comento" di Lorenzo de' Medici*. Florence: Olschki, 1979.

Som. Scip. = Petrarca, Francesco. *Somnium Scipionis*.

Sul Testo = Zanato, Tiziano. "Sul Testo del 'Comento' Laurenziano," *Studi di Filologia Italiana* 38 (1980): 71–152.

Theol. Plat. = Ficino, Marsilio. *Theologiae Platonicae* IV, in *Opera Omnia*, 2 vols. Turin: Bottega D'Erasmo, 1962.

Tr. M. = Petrarch, Francesco. "Triumph of Death." In *The Triumphs of Petrarch*. Trans. Ernest Hatch Wilkins Chicago: Univ. Chicago Press, 1962.

Tusc. Disp. = Cicero, Marcus Tullius. *Tusculan Disputations*. Trans. J. E. King. Cambridge, Mass.: Harvard Univ. Press, 1971.

Un Nuovo Codice = Zanato, Tiziano. "Un Nuovo Codice del 'Comento' Laurenziano, *Studi di Filologia Italiana* 39 (1981): 29–55.

Vita coel. = Ficino, Marsilio, *Vita coelestis*. In *Opere* 1.

VN = Alighieri, Dante. *The Vita Nuova and Canzoniere of Dante Alighieri*. Trans. Thomas Okey and Philip H. Wicksteed. London: J. M. Dent and Sons, 1933.

Introduction

History remembers Lorenzo de' Medici the Magnificent as ruler of Florence and her dependencies, as heir to a far-flung banking and commercial empire, as benefactor of the University of Pisa, as patron of the arts, and as statesman and diplomat. Italians remember him popularly as one of history's few inheritors of a great patrimony who was intellectually, morally, and temperamentally equipped to do it justice. North Americans, however, have until recently remembered less well Lorenzo's stature among his contemporaries and successors as thinker, as poet, and as literary critic. He is perhaps least well remembered outside Italy for his unfinished *Comento de' miei sonetti*, a text only once before entirely translated into English, and then privately published.[1] Yet this often neglected document is important, even crucial, to our growing understanding of the mind, the art, the political and dynastic ambitions, and the personality of Lorenzo. First, it constitutes an interior autobiography. Second, in conducting an intimate discourse about ideas with Lorenzo's friends and associates in the Florentine intellectual community as it circulated among them in draft, the *Commentary* positions Lorenzo's thinking at the intersection of a partly shared, yet nonetheless idiosyncratic, set of literary, philosophical, and religious coordinates. Finally, it erects the theoretical framework for a Laurentian political manifesto, albeit one that perhaps Lorenzo never successfully implemented.

The composition of the "Comento"

According to Tiziano Zanato, editor of the authoritative critical text of the *Comento*, Lorenzo developed the work through a series of revisions that involved at least three major stages. The Medicean grandee initially conceived his commentary's general outline around 1473, but continually

---

[1] M. L. Marshall, trans. *The Comment of Lorenzo de' Medici, the Magnificent on some of his sonnets* (Washington: The Marshalls, 1949). Jon Thiem has included a partial revision of Marshall's translation of portions of Il Comento in his recent *Lorenzo De' Medici: Selected Poems and Prose* (University Park, Pa.: Penn State Univ. Press, 1992); and Angelo Lipari translated extended portions of the work in his *The Dolce Stil Novo According to Lorenzo De' Medici* (New Haven: Yale Univ. Press, 1936).

revised it as he composed more and more of the poems that finally appear in it, and as his thinking shifted under the influence of the writings of members of his literary circle. In a brilliant piece of literary-historico detective work too complex to detail here, Zanato responds to, corrects, and expands the arguments of Emilio Bigi, Raffaella Castagnola Leporatti, and Mario Martelli, establishing connections between Lorenzo's shifting thinking and growing knowledge on the one hand and, on the other, his acquaintance with particular documents. These include both documents that he authored and those of others. As a result, Zanato establishes a series of dates representing the earliest moments at which Lorenzo might have reasonably composed particular portions of the commentary. Zanato alludes to a very early version, composed between 1473 and 1478, as "phase A." He then posits an intermediate stage, "phase B," which Lorenzo developed largely between 1484 and 1486 (particularly 1485–86), and, finally, "phase C," the version which has come down to us, traceable to as late as 1490–91.[2] Certainly, a version was circulating among Lorenzo's acquaintance as early as July 15, 1484, for in a letter of that date Giovanni Pico della Mirandola alludes to the document, calling it a "paraphrase" of his own thought. In October, 1486, Lorenzo received a letter from Ser Piero da Bibbiena mentioning "il vostro *Commento de' Sonetti.*"[3] Nineteenth-century romantic views of the author as lonely genius may sometimes have called Lorenzo's authorship of the *Commentary* into question, but in the swirls and eddies of fifteenth-century Florentine intellectual life, the ideas of Lorenzo and his circle were in constant interchange, and, indeed, the mutual exchange and development of ideas in writing was a characteristic mode for the expression of friendship. We can, of course, attribute specific ideas within the densely intertextual *Comento* to one or another of Lorenzo's contemporaries, but to my knowledge no serious reason exists to call his authorship of *il Comento* or his other works into question. Indeed, in view of the many urgent civic, political, and mercantile matters that competed with composition for his time and attention, the scope of Lorenzo's literary production was remarkable. His surviving lit-

---

[2] For an exhaustive discussion of the proposed chronology of Lorenzo's composition of the commentary, see Tiziano Zanato, *Saggio sul "Comento" di Lorenzo De'Medici* (Florence: Olschki, 1979), 285–321, and *Lorenzo de' Medici: Comento de' Miei Sonetti*, Istituto Nazionale Di Studi Sul Rinascimento, Studi e Testi 25 (Florence: Olschki, 1991), 123–29. See also, Mario Martelli, *Studi laurenziani* (Florence: Olschki, 1965) and "Questioni di cronologia laurenziana," *Lettere italiane* 18 (1966): 249–61; and see Emilio Bigi, ed. *Scritti Scelti di Lorenzo de' Medici* (Turin: UTET, 1965) 1ff.

[3] See Zanato, *Comento*, 127.

erary *opera* occupy two substantial volumes in the series *Scrittori d'Italia*.[4] Beyond this, two *novelle*, *Giacoppo* and *Ginevre*, were discovered among the Medici papers in 1864 and subsequently attributed definitively to Lorenzo.[5] The great majority of his works, however, are in vernacular verse and include sonnets, ballate, canzone, and carnival songs. Only the *Comento*, however, gives us at once extensive samples of Lorenzo's poetry and of his careful, dialectical prose.

Lorenzo's Commentary: An interior autobiography

More than anything else that Lorenzo wrote, *il Comento* approaches autobiography—indeed, I suggest, it *is* an autobiography, if not of the man Lorenzo was, then certainly of the man he wished others to see, and perhaps of the man he sought to become.[6] But Lorenzo's *Commentary* does not belong to that species of autobiography typified by Goethe's *Dichtung und Wahrheit* or by *The Education of Henry Adams*, in which the writer seeks principally to lay out for the reader the interactive strands of history—both his own and his country's—that compose him. Neither does it belong to the species of autobiography that Karl Joachim Weintraub calls *res gestae*—records of deeds done or chronicles of events.[7] Thus, it does not recount that Lorenzo was Born to Piero di Cosimo and Lucrezia Tornabuoni de' Medici on January 1, 1449, or that he succeeded to the patriarchy of the Medici family following the deaths of his grandfather Cosimo in 1464, and of his father in 1469. It does not tell us that a year earlier he had been betrothed to, or—as he notes in his diary—had had "given to him," the Roman noblewoman Clarice Orsini, whom he married by proxy and who, in due course, bore him seven children. Nor does it recount the way in which he met the putative lady of the sonnets, Lucrezia Donati, when both she and Lorenzo were twelve, that he wrote some precocious love poems addressed to her or that, like Dante's Beatrice

---

[4] Attilio Simioni, ed., *Scrittori d'Italia*, vol. 54, 2 tomes (Bari: Laterza, 1913–14).

[5] See Bigi, 605.

[6] Others before me have called attention to the autobiographical aspects of Il Comento, notably William J. Kennedy in his "Petrarchan Figurations of Death in Lorenzo de' Medici's Sonnets and Comento," in *Life and Death in Fifteenth Century Florence*, eds. Marcel Tetel, Ronald G. Witt, and Rona Goffen (Duke Univ. Press: Durham and London, 1989), 46–68; Andre Rochon in *La Jeunesse de Laurent de Medicis (1449–1478)* (Paris: Les Belles Lettres, 1963); and Giancarlo Massacurati, in "Storia e funzione della poesia lirica nel Comento di Lorenzo de' Medici," *Modern Language Notes*, 104:1 (Jan. 1989): 48–67.

[7] Karl J. Weintraub, "Autobiography and Historical Consciousness," *Critical Inquiry* 1 (1975): 822.

or Petrarch's Laura, Lucrezia married someone else, the older Nido Artinghelli.

Instead Lorenzo's work contains a remarkably stylized, idealized, and abstract record of things thought, writers, and subjects studied and learned, sufferings and joys experienced, poems created, spiritual growth and aspiration, and, perhaps, thinly disguised political theorizing, all filtered through the mind and sensibility of a person of extraordinary genius and feeling and, with respect to the prose portions, largely couched in an almost scholastic form of dialectic *questiones*. The text unfolds the story of how the sum total of Lorenzo's intellectual, moral and, especially, his emotional experience has formed him *within*—*informed* him in the Renaissance sense of that term. It reveals to us the way a confessed melancholiac with a propensity for jealousy, one who has undergone a traumatic series of unspecified familial and political disasters, has sought for and, to a degree, has *found* solace and happiness in two ways. He has loved a woman, never named in the text, who, unlike Petrarch's Laura, has both reciprocated his feeling and actively participated in helping him accomplish a spiritual and moral reformation. By implication, he has also found a modicum of happiness in friendship and in shared intellectual and artistic pursuits. He makes this clear in the *Comento*, when he observes: "I have been much persecuted by men and by fortune so that some little solace ought not to be denied me, and this I have only found in loving ardently and in composing and commenting upon my verses." In its tracking of the elements that have contributed to such happiness as Lorenzo has experienced, the *Commentary*, in its final revision at least, is the autobiography of the interior man. Like many autobiographies of this sub-genre, as Weintraub's classic study "Autobiography and Historical Consciousness (1975)" suggests, *il Comento* in its final form seems to take its impetus from changes that Lorenzo perceived in himself—changes brought on in significant measure, I think, by the psychological readjustments Lorenzo had to make in order to cope with the traumatic events surrounding the loss of his father and grandfather, the assassination of his brother Giuliano, and the near loss of his own life in the Pazzi conspiracy of 1478.

Men and fortune continued to hound Lorenzo intermittently throughout his life, and, since the fifteenth century, historians and biographers have recounted repeatedly the disasters that afflicted him. Following the dual loss of father and grandfather, he was the object of several conspiracies against his life. Of these the most dangerous was that involving members of the Pazzi family in 1478—a conspiracy to which Lorenzo alludes in the text and one that succeeded in wounding Lorenzo himself, that took the life of his brother Giuliano, and that produced armed strife, Florence's falling under papal interdict, and Lorenzo's personal excommunication. The

persecutions continued intermittently almost to the moment of his death, for in one account of Lorenzo's passing, the Dominican Friar Girolomo Savonarola is said to have intruded upon his last moments and perhaps to have misrepresented them to history.[8] Clearly, as Maurice Rowden observes, being the ruler of Florence "was not an easy life, particularly after a youth spent discussing the future civilization based on that 'perfect man' of the Jews and that other 'perfect man' of the Greeks" (155). Fortune had afflicted him with hereditary gout, and after frequent and increasingly debilitating attacks of the disease throughout his adulthood, on April 8, 1492, Lorenzo died from complications arising from the ailment at the family villa at Careggi.

In the course of the lengthy preamble to his *Commentary*, Lorenzo sets out his own sense of the place of his literary work in the amorous vernacular tradition that he both continues and expands. As a practicing poet, Lorenzo perceived himself to be—as indeed he was—the principal literary heir to the tradition of the *tre corone* of Italian vernacular writing and their precursors. For him, this tradition begins with Guido Guinizelli, founder of the school of the "sweet new style"—the *dolce stil novo*—and continues through Guido Cavalcanti, to the triple crowns of Italian letters, Dante, Petrarch, and Boccaccio. In very significant ways, as Angelo Lipari (1936) has argued, Lorenzo continues the traditions of the *stilnovisti*. But that is not, as Lipari seems to imagine, the whole story. Lorenzo's literary thinking is as eclectic as his scientific erudition, and, as Giancarlo Mazzacurati has so clearly recognized, that thinking is regularly innovative.[9] Though we often find Lorenzo depending on Dante for literary argument, he sometimes takes issue with the earlier poet. On the matter of style, for example, Lorenzo differs with his great literary forebear about the relative

---

[8] See Hugh Ross Williamson, *Lorenzo the Magnificent* (New York: G. Putnam's Sons, 1974), 266. According to Maurice Rowden, in *Lorenzo the Magnificent* (London: Weidenfeld and Nicolson) 217–18, two accounts exist of Savonarola's final visit to Lorenzo. The more likely of the two suggests that Lorenzo called for the Friar and the less likely that Savonarola came unbidden. According to Poliziano's eyewitness account, written some two months after the fact, Savonarola, responding to a request that he come, urged Lorenzo to "hold fast the faith, (*tenere la fede*)" and to swear to lead the purest of lives thenceforward. Lorenzo assured him that his faith was unshaken and that he would strive to lead a pure life and face death courageously and asked for Savonarola's blessing, after which the two prayed together. According to the account of Fra Silvestro, Savonarola's amanuensis, the Friar came unbidden, and reproved and castigated the moribund Lorenzo, insisting that he restore his ill-gotten wealth and that he restore liberty to Florence.

[9] Mazzacurati, 51. Mazzacurati conducts a fascinating discussion of the way in which Lorenzo's Comento contributes to the formation of a new critical idiom and a new set of genres and critical norms for Italian literature.

nobility of the sonnet and the canzone. Unlike Dante, Lorenzo considers the shorter form the nobler because there is greater difficulty in treating important matters within its formal constraints. Often too, Lorenzo concurs in the literary assessments made by members of his intellectual circle, like Cristoforo Landino or Agnolo Poliziano, but *Il Magnifico*[10] disagrees with them in his favorable evaluation of Boccaccio's work. In what we may regard as one of the first instances of Italian literary criticism, Lorenzo assigns Boccaccio to the highest rank of literary genius by judging him master of the high style as well as of the medium and low. Lorenzo also admires Petrarch and emulates his images. Indeed, Lorenzo's sonnets contain a complex and pervasive network of allusion to the *Rerum vulgarium fragmenta*, but while Petrarch's obsession with Laura led that poet into a psychological and spiritual labyrinth from which no sure escape ever comes, Lorenzo's love for his *donna* is directly responsible for the poet's progress up the rungs of the *scala amoris*—the ladder of love that, in the view of Renaissance amatory theory, led toward such perfection as was humanly possible.

Consciously modeled, first, upon Dante's *la Vita Nuova* and *il Convivio*, and second, particularly in the sonnets, upon the example of Petrarch in the *Rerum vulgarium fragmenta*, in his *sonnetiere*, Lorenzo, like Petrarch, retrospectively sets in new order 41 of his own sonnets and, like Dante, conducts an exposition of them, mentioning in passing two poems that are not included in the text, but that appear here as "Appendix A." Before beginning that exposition, Lorenzo first discusses in a long preamble the reasons that have moved him to undertake this work. In the preamble, he defends himself against a series of accusations that he anticipates his critics might use to reprove him for wasting his valuable time in this sort of enterprise. Using many of the same arguments that Dante employed in his *Convivio*,[11] Lorenzo defends his choice of the vernacular and asserts Tuscan's suitability to the expression of his (or any) thought.

Dependent, then, as the *Comento* undeniably is on antecedent texts, it establishes that dependency not as slavish imitation but rather as a courtly acknowledgment of the influence of its models, as a form of intellectual discourse with them and with the ideas of Lorenzo's contemporaries, and as a starting point from which to move forward. Considering particularly the structures of *La Vita Nuova*, and the *Rerum vulgarium fragmenta*, with

---

[10] The title, Il *Magnifico*, though retrospectively attached almost exclusively to Lorenzo, the magnificent, was in his own time an honorific of address regularly applied to grandees of Lorenzo's class.

[11] See Zanato, *Saggio*, 12.

their divisions between poems during the lives, and, later, after the deaths of their ladies, Lorenzo's *sonnetiere* reveals telling originality in at least two respects. First, the collection celebrates not one but two ladies. The first of them was probably Simonetta Cattaneo, reputed mistress of his brother Giuliano. The Lorenzo persona in *il Comento* participates in the general sorrow evoked by her untimely death.[12] The first four sonnets are addressed to her "pneuma," that is, to her liberated soul that survives her physical death and becomes stellified.[13] The second formal innovation that Lorenzo achieves involves his beginning from the death of Simonetta and proceeding to the new life that his participation in the partly conventional, partly idiosyncratic *itinerarium* of the true lover calls forth in him. This decision to invert the direction of the tradition within which he perceives himself working and to proceed from death to life, however, *Il Magnifico* feels obliged to justify as a potentially blameworthy departure from the norms of an emerging vernacular literature. Yet that very justification also serves to emphasize the novelty of his treatment of his material, and *novità* was a positive value for creative persons in Lorenzo's Florence. But these two innovations by no means exhaust Lorenzo's resources for shaping his material in new ways and, in the process, for shaping himself as well.

Everywhere in the *Commentary*, as Tiziano Zanato has so clearly recognized, appears evidence that Lorenzo regularly tested the validity of borrowed ideas and judgments by the demanding standards of his own intellect, taste, and experience.[14] The thinking of others that stands the test—such

---

[12] Simonetta died on April 26, 1476, at the age of 22. She is pictured by Botticelli as the auburn-haired young woman holding Venus' cloak in his Birth of Venus. See Williamson, 97.

[13] Lorenzo and his circle were much interested in Aristotle's doctrine of the pneuma, which the philosopher describes as the seat of the nutritive and sensitive souls and the physiological locus of *phantasia* and is "analogous to that element of which the stars are made" (*de gen. anim.* 736 b 27ff.). In Porphyry, whom Lorenzo also had studied, the pneuma is closely connected with the irrational soul, which in Augustine's citations from the *de regressu animae* is called "*anima spiritualis.*" Cited in Proclus: *The Elements of Theology*, trans. E. R. Dodds (Oxford: The Clarendon Press, 1933), 315 and 318.

[14] See Zanato, *Saggio* 67: "Love and Beauty, erotic theory and aesthetic concept are wed in an atmosphere of the art and taste of Medicean Florence, finding adepts among painters, poets, and philosophers"; or again, "Lorenzo, in the *Comento*, uses different cultural sources in almost every one of his assertions: his page is never a landing at strange harbors, original philosophic acquisitions, but instead a recovery and redeployment of the most varied knowledge of others in an entirely personal mixture; the originality of the Magnificent is not so much measured in his content, but rather in his extraordinary reinterpretative ability thanks to which each step, every moment of the works allow one to perceive, with clarity, precious and multiplex presences, and at the same time raising [them]

as the Ficinian and stilnovistic views of the purifying effects of mutual love on the human heart—he makes his own. Views that he cannot verify, however, like Ficino's assertion that touching one another produces malefic effects on the relationship of pure lovers, Lorenzo rejects. In place of Ficino's idea, Lorenzo substitutes his own experience of the beneficial effect of his lady's touch in ennobling his life. When he has no experience on which to base his own opinion or against which to test that of his authorities, Lorenzo cites them evenhandedly in the manner of medieval dialectical argument. He explains, for instance, that the Peripatetics, following Aristotle, have one explanation for the phenomenon of sight, the Academics, following Plato, another. Whichever is correct, Lorenzo has tested in his own life the effects that follow from the phenomenon and has confirmed for himself both the views of Ficinian Neoplatonism and the stilnovistic explanation of the participation of the sense of sight in the lover's spiritual progress.

Although in *il Comento* he never names the *donna* responsible for his progress, she seems, again like Beatrice and Laura, to have become for him the *figura* upon whom he focussed his poetic, moral, philosophical and, perhaps, his religious aspirations. Likewise, his regular habit of combining personifications of emotions, thoughts, and even objects, with definitions that raise them by at least one order of tropological magnitude beyond that which they expressly name, seems further to invite the reader to construct a self-consistent allegory. A case in point occurs in the commentary on sonnet 38, when he instructs the reader that he is referring to elevated and perfected minds when he uses the phrase "noble hearts." At least one interpreter, Angelo Lipari, has accepted with exceptional ingenuity the frequent invitations to allegorize, concluding, finally, that the ladies celebrated in the sonnets were not ladies at all, but rather the embodiment of Italian literature itself. Certainly, though Lipari's identification is open to serious question, it is fair to say that the ladies, whatever their relationship to the author may have been in real life, do become, in these poems and in the accompanying commentary, literary constructs that, like Dante's Beatrice and Petrarch's Laura, clearly transcend mere history, even if they have some historical basis. Like all the *donne* in the refined amorous tradition of the poets of the sweet new style, or of Petrarch after them, or of

---

toward a new, original equilibrium. An extremely rich prose reveals a highly skilled artist, exactly the opposite of the dilettantish image of the Medicean lord that even today certain critics drag out and tiresomely repeat" (*Saggio* 88, trans. mine). To Professor Zanato's patient and brilliant comparison of all the known mss. and of the early printed versions of the *Comento*, we owe his new critical text and edition of the *Comento* (Florence: Olschki, 1991).

the Provençal and perhaps the Sufi Muslim poets before them, Lorenzo's women become subordinate to their emblematic value for the poet; they become representatives of the poet's own goals and aspirations as those have been shaped by his Christian, Neoplatonic and amorous vernacular education. In keeping with the conventions of the genre, the lover exchanges hearts with the lady, and in her keeping and under her discipline, both his heart, one of several personified aspects of himself, and he are ennobled. He ascends the ladder of love. In the process, his sensibility, his morals, and his Christian virtues become refined as he strives to emulate the lady and, in doing so, to achieve both a sort of secular perfection and, in what I take to be an autobiographical application of the norms of the vernacular poetic tradition, an evanescent and occasional happiness of the sort we observe in the twelfth sonnet, "When after my lucky heart was overcome."

The evidence that the death of Simonetta Cattaneo Vespucci provided Lorenzo with the literary occasion for composing some and for revising other portions of his previously planned *sonnetiere* seems clear.[15] Her surviving portraits depict Simonetta as a woman of extraordinary vivacity and beauty—someone who very well might make a significant impression on a man like Lorenzo, especially if she were involved with a person close to him. We know also, however, that Lorenzo was away from Florence when she died, and that the account he gives of her cortege is second hand. At the very least, then, his account of her death is fictionalized and subordinated to his literary agenda. If what I have said above about the writing of *il Comento*'s being an act of self-definition is accurate, then the death of Simonetta—associated as she was with Giuliano and with the relatively care-free days of Lorenzo's early youth—may be thought of as the moment from which Lorenzo at least fictively dates the search for a new identity more or less forced upon him by the inexorable march of family disasters detailed above.

As *il Comento* underwent successive revisions, Lorenzo, I am convinced, used it to bring together his developing thought on a host of subjects and to situate within the matrix of that thinking what he perceived to be the several emotional foci of his life. His treatment of the death and stellification of Simonetta Cattaneo in the first four sonnets and in their accompanying commentary, for example, tempts a reader to discover a sort of artistic and emotional distancing from his grief at the death of his brother Giuliano, an event so dramatic and, given the threat to his own life as well

---

[15] Zanato (*Saggio*, 285ff.) proposes the probable stages of composition through which il Comento passed. Certainly the sonnets dedicated to Simonetta antedate her death.

as the loss of his brother's, so traumatic for Lorenzo, that it must have been among the most important in his emotional life. I find it notable that Giuliano's assassination on April 26, 1478 occurs two years to the day after the death of Simonetta—April 26, 1476. In view of the coincidence of the death date of the two lovers, it seems to me at least arguable that Lorenzo retrospectively used the death of Simonetta as a mechanism for distancing himself from the grief and trauma associated with Giuliano's assassination, and as an opportunity to reflect upon the fact of death itself. Then, by examining the fictive event's religious, philosophical, and aesthetic implications in that context, he inferentially confronts what theologian Paul Tillich has termed the "ontological shock"—the emotional, as opposed to the intellectual, recognition of the inevitability of one's own death. In thus ritualizing loss, he finds some solace for grief. That solace in turn enables him to renew his interest in, and commitments to, continuing human enterprise—though he is never totally free from a morbid melancholia that sometimes makes him find the idea of death attractive.

A second crucial emotional focus for Lorenzo's partly retrospective, partly dynamic view of his own artistic, intellectual and emotional history was surely his precocious love for Lucrezia Donati. His relationship with Donati was for Lorenzo a source of genuine if ephemeral happiness, and the possibilities for human happiness that life can hold constitutes, as I have already suggested, the central issue that Lorenzo addresses in *il Comento*. His essentially Neoplatonic treatment of the lover's progress along an emotionally rocky *itinerarium* toward ennoblement and toward affectionate mutuality with the beloved effectively links the familiar amorous program of the poets of the sweet new style with Marsilio Ficino's insistence that the aim of human existence is the achievement of such happiness as human beings can aspire to in an imperfect world.

Dismissing all speculation about Lucrezia Donati as unlikely, by contrast, Hugh Ross Williamson thinks that the lady of the last 37 sonnets is entirely fictive and simply provides Lorenzo with an occasion for writing Neoplatonic love poems.[16] A certain circumstantiality in the commentary, however, as well as a long tradition of supporting archival scholarship, makes me think that the lady—Donati or not—nevertheless is real and not exclusively a convenient fiction for Lorenzo's literary and self-fashioning programs. Several of Lorenzo's accounts of interactions between himself and the lady suggest an autobiographical basis: for example, she sends him a gift of violets. These might, of course, be emblematic too, like those of John Donne in the first lines of "The Ecstasy," but the way in which

---

[16] Williamson, 138.

Lorenzo uses them to discuss the fortune that brought these particular violets to the lady's hand suggests a real gift on a real occasion. Also, the unconscious misogyny of passages in which he declares her to be gifted beyond what is useful in a woman, but not on that account a "know-it-all," suggests that there was once a real woman at least in the back of Lorenzo's mind. To be weighed in the balance against this, however, is the fact, pointed out to me by Doctor Judith Bryce of the University of Hull, that such remarks were almost proverbial in the discussion of women in Lorenzo's time. I personally find his allusion to his lady's singing songs composed by him to be compelling evidence for a real woman.

Undeniably though, real, fictive, or both at once, the lady of Lorenzo's sonnets is a woman who has been thrust into the stylized, even stereotypical roles demanded both by an amorous literary tradition and by a philosophical regimen whose ultimate shared objective is the elevation of the male lover to a state of multidimensional grace and beatitude through the intercession, and one might even say the mothering, of women idealized almost past human recognition. In that process, the lady of Lorenzo's sonnets becomes transmuted for him into Lady Philosophia, thus invoking a tradition as old as Boethius' *Consolation of Philosophy*; she also becomes Lady Poesia, and, near the end, in the company of the three cardinal Christian virtues of Faith, Hope, and Charity, she becomes Lady Gratia as well.[17] This progress, one in which the author, ennobled by the lady's efforts, represents himself as having participated, makes me agree with Zanato that, though *il Comento* remains unfinished, its argument is essentially complete and that the outcomes of the *Commentary*, subject to the human limitations on happiness that Lorenzo recognized so well, are essentially positive. Lorenzo did not think that life could bring total happiness, as is illustrated by his retelling the story about Jove's pouring mixed fortune and misfortune on those whom he *favors*. But, Lorenzo insists, such happiness as may be available he has experienced.

Among other emotional issues inherent in Lorenzo's composition of *il Comento*, his evident pleasure in writing and in scientific, philological and theological reflection and speculation also regularly reveals itself in the prologue to the work and in the commentary on the sonnets, and implicit in that appearance, I feel sure, is a kind of anticipatory pleasure at his friends' expected approbation of this work—an approbation that was indeed forthcoming. Finally in this connection, I would feel remiss if I failed to call

---

[17] This sort of tropological overlay is perfectly in keeping with the sort of patristic exegesis expounded by Cristofero Landino in his *Commentary on the Divine Comedy of Dante Alighieri*, which Lorenzo knew well.

attention to the intense pleasure, reflected both in the *Comento* and in his other works, that Lorenzo clearly took in nature and its works. While his treatment of flowers and trees and watercourses has demonstrable poetic antecedents in Petrarch, we know that, like Petrarch, Lorenzo genuinely loved the countryside, and both his preference for country living and his nature poems reveal that affection both in tone and image. His treatment of the noble racehorse, though modeled on earlier discussions, nevertheless conveys Lorenzo's passionate interest in (not to say his professional expertise about) the subject, and we know that he loved animals. He owned a horse that is reputed to have refused food after a race unless fed from Lorenzo's own hand.[18] He also owned a tame giraffe that is sometimes pictured in paintings depicting Lorenzo's court. Just as the Queen of England is sometimes said never to smile naturally except when looking into the face of a horse, it may well be that a person in Lorenzo's position, inundated with requests for patronage and constrained always to assess the motives and agendas of people around him, was able to find in the company of some animals a pleasure untrammeled by cynicism or suspicion.

All these sources of happiness Lorenzo treats either directly or implicitly in his development of the *Commentary*. In considering that development, William J. Kennedy sees the composition of *il Comento* as the construction of "an unabashed autobiographical platform on which to shape and reshape the events of his life as he wants his Florentine audience to perceive them, a work of masterful rhetoric in the disputative, controversialized sense inscribed by Renaissance humanists [in whose] practice language displaces combat, and rhetoric becomes a weapon of aggression."[19] With much of this view and with much else in Kennedy's careful analysis, I essentially agree. Nevertheless, I would insist that, though undeniably shaped in part for public purposes, the *Commentary* nevertheless remains principally the autobiography of the interior and private man.

Certainly, the face that Lorenzo puts on in *il Comento* is a public face. He did not intend his text for private consumption only. Not only did it circulate in manuscript, but also, given the propensity of the entire Medici dynasty for public image-building and their penchant for using various sorts of patronage, propaganda and spectacle to give carefully structured accounts and impressions of themselves, I cannot but suppose that something of what Kennedy suggests pervades Lorenzo's *Commentary* as well.

---

[18] According to Richard Mallett, in a lecture, "Horse Racing and Politics: The Role of Lorenzo's Stable," at Warburg Institute of Univ. London Conference on Lorenzo. Warwick, May 31, 1992.

[19] Kennedy, 49.

But beyond those indisputably important political purposes that I shall recur to below, the composition and, until the end of his life, the ongoing revision of the *Comento* seems also to constitute an act of self-exploration and self-definition. As Kennedy suggests, the text assuredly served as Lorenzo's self portrait—the Lorenzo he wanted the world to conceive of and remember. And, as Alison Brown makes clear in her study "Guicciardini and Lorenzo," that portrait contrasts markedly with the reality of Lorenzo's anger, intolerance, suspiciousness, apparent cruelties and vindictiveness, his nocturnal pursuit of women, and his extravagance—all traits which Brown has thoroughly documented in sources contemporary with Lorenzo.[20] At the same time, I think, he strove to trace in himself the ideas and feelings that had made him what he ideally perceived himself to be, despite the disjuction between his idealized, interior pursuit of perfection and the profligate behavior which Brown believes contributed to his early demise. I believe he needed to unravel some of the complexities that accompanied his unprecedented position as the uncrowned—and sometimes, more importantly, unfunded—ruler of a world at once and often indistinguishably political, intellectual, literary, philosophical and theological. Even near the end of his life, the Lorenzo whom his tutor, Gentile Becchi, and his mother, Lucrezia Tornabuoni de' Medici, had encouraged throughout his childhood to excel at everything, had still to excel at understanding and fashioning himself.

Kennedy seems to think, however, that Lorenzo's purposes are unidimensionally propagandistic and manipulative, if not wholly cynical. Drawing almost exclusively upon the text of the sonnets to support his views, Kennedy argues that Lorenzo's motives are merely political. He properly envisions a Lorenzo in political trouble, casting about for support at any level he can gain it: "readers," Kennedy asserts, "may not support Lorenzo's political goals [but] all might share in his amatory misfortunes. Lorenzo seeks an audience of lovers who have experienced Love's torments. He seeks Petrarch's audience."[21] I concur in Kennedy's view concerning Lorenzo's desire to capture Petrarch's audience, but perhaps Kennedy overemphasizes amatory *suffering* as the point with which Lorenzo expects that audience to identify. Although Lorenzo certainly suffers in his quest for his lady, his positive reformation under her living influence transcends his suffering and contributes materially to his achieving such happiness as a constitutional melancholiac can manage in an imperfect world, whereas Petrarch remains forever lost in the labyrinths of ambiguity.

---

[20] Paper given at Warwick University conference on Lorenzo, May 30, 1992.

[21] Kennedy, 49.

Thus, though I agree that Petrarch's audience is among the readers whom Lorenzo wishes to address, in addition to desiring to enlist the attention and sympathy of those who "know love's ways by trial" (*Rvf*, 1, 7), and who read Petrarch, Lorenzo surely is casting his nets wider.

Beyond those tormented by Love's cruelty and beyond readers of amatory verse, he also addresses those who know philosophy, who know the ancients, who know the Bible, the church fathers, and their exegesis, who know the scholastic models of systems of government, and those who deeply and regularly think about such matters. That audience, with whose members Lorenzo was in constant contact and with many of whom he was on the best of terms, would surely have perceived and been offended by any hint of the disingenuousness that Kennedy discerns. Indeed, I think they would have found it particularly offensive in so serious and, until near its stopping point, so carefully crafted a document as *il Comento*. Just as Lorenzo selects the sonnet as the form he thinks noblest for publicly celebrating his interior development, so he selects the form of the commentary precisely because, as he says in his prologue, ordinarily, commentaries "are reserved for matters of theology or of philosophy, and for consequential and significant concerns, [for] the edification and consolation of our minds, or the benefit of the human race." True, Lorenzo makes this claim in the context of defending himself, with perhaps ironic good humor, against those who might reprove him for having thought about and written verses on so light a subject as amorous passion at all, and, just as bad, for commenting on them. Despite his suggestion that his own work might be an exception from this gravity of purpose, Lorenzo's disclaimer nevertheless establishes his readers' expectations for the seriousness of the matter treated in the commentary. It also heightens the probability that Lorenzo's *Commentary* will, despite his disclaimer, meet those expectations.

Lorenzo's Education and his Literary Circle

The readers whom I have particularly in mind—readers not only of Lorenzo's poetry, but especially of his prose—are, of course, the members of his intellectual circle whose thought is so richly represented in the text of the *Commentary*, and who, recognizing in Lorenzo's composition of the *Commentary* an act of friendly literary intimacy and even collaborative thinking, approvingly read drafts of *il Comento*, congratulated Lorenzo on it, and urged him to get busy and finish it. Principally, this part of Lorenzo's intended audience included the Neoplatonist philosopher, Marsilio Ficino; the polymath and syncretist, Giovanni Pico della Mirandola; the exegete, allegorist and professor of literature, Cristoforo Landino; the humanist and Lorenzo's closest friend, Angelo Poliziano; Lorenzo's former

tutor, the Bishop of Arezzo, Gentile Becchi; and, though the *Commentary* may have been a little rarified for his coarser tastes, Lorenzo's early companion, Luigi Pulci. Beyond this group, the audience would also have included others whom I mention below. That the friendship and company of these people mattered much to Lorenzo is a fact so well established that it requires no argument here. And *il Comento* pays tribute to at least some of Lorenzo's friends in its frequent employment of their ideas and works.

William Kent, in a lecture delivered at the Warburg Institute/University of Warwick Conference, "Lorenzo the Magnificent: Culture and Politics in Medicean Florence," on May 29, 1992, offered a composite picture of a young Lorenzo who was, in a sense, both a child prodigy as a learner and, according to contemporary accounts, an impatient and supremely self-confident young man driven to excel at everything he set his hand to. The education of this gifted youngster and that of his brother, Giuliano, was principally in the hands of the Humanist scholar, Gentile Becchi (d. 1497). Through Medici patronage, Becchi eventually became both an ambassador and the bishop of Arezzo (1473). It was this gentle and learned priest whom Piero di Cosimo made responsible for moral, spiritual and intellectual education of his sons. According to Kent, Becchi was a careful teacher, a loving guide, and a devoted taskmaster who, together with Lorenzo's deeply influential, assertive, and gifted mother, Lucrezia Tornabuoni, imparted to the scion of the Medici dynasty a taste for learning and mastering a broad range of subjects that included both classical and vernacular letters. This nurtured taste was coupled with a natural and passionately intense interest in everything he undertook. As a result, Lorenzo became not the dilettantish master of the city of Florence that some of his biographers have rather tiresomely represented as dabbling in intellectual pursuits and in the arts but instead, as I have remarked, a genuine polymath who appeared in the advance guard of the philosophic and literary movements of his time—not merely as an observer, but as a full-fledged participant, and often as the prime mover.

Becchi aside, Lorenzo remained in almost daily close contact with the leading intellectual lights of Florence practically from infancy. His literary circle was far too extensive to permit comment here on even all the major figures who belonged to it. Following the lead, however, of Mario Martelli in his *La cultura letteraria al tempo di Lorenzo*,[22] I do wish to mention at least those who seem preeminently influential on Lorenzo's literary development. The influences these persons exercised were overlapping,

---

[22] Lecture given at the Warburg Institute, Univ. of Warwick conference on Lorenzo. London, May 27, 1992.

and Lorenzo remained close to most of them throughout his career, but at different periods in his literary development, Martelli suggests, one or the other of them became predominantly influential.

Earliest among these, one finds the brothers Pulci, Lucca and, most particularly, Luigi. Luigi Pulci was a witty poet—sometimes scandalously so—who worked in the popular idiom of Florence, and whom Lucrezia Tornabuoni commissioned to write the heroic epic *Morgante Maggiore*, which was a prototype of the Italian mock heroic epic. Pulci and Lorenzo were boon companions who crawled the taverns and wenched together. They were also, however, poetic companions who wrote carnival songs, sonnets, canzoni, strambozzi—literary productions typical of Florentine popular culture. But Lorenzo's carefree days were not destined to last long, and after the death of his grandfather, Cosimo, and his father Piero, and particularly after the Pazzi conspiracy and the death of Giuliano, Lorenzo's literary taste shifted away somewhat from the forms that Pulci continued to prefer. From at least the time of the *Raccolta Aragonese*—a collection of Italian vernacular poems sent in 1468 by Lorenzo to Don Federigo of Aragon in which Lorenzo had included some of his own work—Lorenzo had been increasingly interested in the work of his great trecento literary forbears. As that interest developed into a desire to emulate them, the influence of the humanist scholar Agnolo Poliziano—who was to become and remain Lorenzo's best friend—and of Cristoforo Landino, author of a commentary on the works of Dante and a very considerable poet and literary critic in his own right, came to predominate. Landino and Poliziano were classical scholars with a harder taste and, at least as time went on, with a more serious spirit than Luigi Pulci, and perhaps under their influence Lorenzo conceived his two major literary projects—emulating Petrarch by collecting a canzoniere of his own work in the spirit, if not the genre, of the *Rerum vulgarium fragmenta*, and emulating Dante's *Vita Nuova*, in *il Comento* itself. Supplementing and overlaying the influence of Poliziano and Landino, the Neoplatonist thought of Marsilio Ficino and, at least from 1484 onwards, that of Giovanni Pico della Mirandola appears everywhere in Lorenzo's literary production. Ficino had been a member of Lorenzo's circle since Cosimo's time, and had founded a Florentine academy. This academy has come down to us as "the Florentine Platonic Academy," but as James Hankins has recently shown, it is likely that the representation of Ficino's academy as a reinstitution of Plato's, and the assertion of Lorenzo's regular and central role in its deliberations, are the post-Laurentian artifacts of early historians.[23]

---

[23] James Hankins, "Lorenzo and the Invention of the Platonic Academy," paper given

In the 3rd week of January, 1474, Ficino sent Lorenzo a letter containing Ficino's *de Amore*, his commentary on the *Symposium* of Plato. Of this influence there is ample evidence everywhere in the text of *il Comento* itself, for, philosophically, Lorenzo's text relies most heavily upon the *de Amore* for its blend of Neoplatonic and stilnovistic doctrine. Plato, Aristotle and Pliny contribute scientific ideas, and Lorenzo makes it abundantly clear that he has done his homework. During this period, too, Lorenzo—perhaps influenced by Ficino's earlier translation of Dante's *De Monarchia* [1468]—became intensely interested in the glorious emergence of the Italian vernacular in the hands of Dante, Petrarch, and Boccaccio. The same sort of influence, though perhaps at another level, of the work of Giovanni Pico della Mirandola appears as well. Pico firmly believed that all systems of thought contained truth and that all were finally reconcilable with each other and with Christianity in the unity of the ground of being of the universe. With some minor differences, Ficino shared this conviction, and the resulting syncretism is a prominent feature of Lorenzo's thought in his *Commentary*. In the last two years of his life, Martelli proposes, Lorenzo, like the rest of Florence, comes increasingly under the influence of Friar Girolomo Savaranola, the Dominican friar who, after the fall of the Medici, was to castigate Florence with the rod of his religious zeal. It was, assuredly, during this period that Lorenzo attempts what is for him a new genre, a *sacre rappresentazione di San Pietro e Paolo*, a religious morality play in *ottava rima*, which was performed at his son Piero di Lorenzo's confraternity of San Giovanni Evangelista very much in the manner of all school plays—with a part of some sort for every child.[24]

This characterization of periods of influence in Lorenzo's life is perhaps somewhat too schematic. Lorenzo's friendships continue and periods of influence overlap. We have clear evidence that Lorenzo's interest in theology was not merely coeval with the appearance of Savanarola, for example, but that it continued as a steady current throughout his intellectual life. Jill Kraye tells us, for instance, that on the 23rd of June, 1489—the eve of the feast of St. John the Baptist—Dominicans and Franciscans staged a heated debate concerning theodicy at the *duomo*.[25] Was Adam's sin the greatest of all sins in the universe, or was God ultimately responsible? So gripping,

---

at "Lorenzo il Magnifico and his World, International Conference." Florence, June 13, 1992.

[24] For this characterization, I rely gratefully on the work of Professor Nerida Newbigin of the University of Sydney, "The Politics of the 'sacra rappresentazione' in Lorenzo's Florence," lecture presented at Univ. of Warwick Conference on Lorenzo, May 31, 1992.

[25] Jill Kraye, "Lorenzo and the Philosophers," lecture presented at the Warburg Institute Conference on Lorenzo, May 28, 1992.

apparently, did the discussion become that, at Lorenzo's invitation, it was continued in the Medici Palace in the Via Larga (today's Via Cavour) the following week on June 30. Present at that discussion as principals, Kraye continues, we find the Thomist Domenican Scotist Nicholas Mirabilis (whom some thought [rather heretically] to be the reincarnation of St. Thomas himself). We also find the Franciscan, Giorgio Benigno Salviati; the physician-philosopher Domenico Bianchelli; the mathematical logician of the Merton school, and the physician and humanist Bernardo Torni; Ficino, Poliziano, Giovanni Pico della Mirandola; and, of course, Lorenzo himself. According to Kraye, Lorenzo raised a question about the degree to which Lucifer's corrupt will might be considered responsible for the fall. In conducting a fascinating prosoprographic discussion of those present and of their ideas, Kraye reminds us that the central unifying interest of the members of Lorenzo's circle was theological. It serves well, I think, to bear this often overlooked truth firmly in mind as one reads Lorenzo's *Commentary*. The final vision at which the text arrives is one of the lady surrounded by personifications of the cardinal Christian virtues of Faith, Hope and Charity.

The essential originality of the *Commentary*, then, is to be found in its idiosyncratic synthesis of everything Lorenzo has read and thought about and lived through and, finally, discovered to be crucial—a synthesis produced by the brilliant, morally attractive, and actively analytic mind of a polymath who has thoroughly mastered the subjects that interest him and who has managed to apply them all pragmatically to the management both of his interior life and of the Florentine body politic.

Theorizing a polity—the quality of "gentilezza"

In connection with that Florentine polity, the care with which Lorenzo stipulatively defines his ennobled heart's central attribute of *gentilezza* as a kind of nobility based on the capacity to do the job for which divine providence and a person's proclivities have destined him reveals the degree to which Lorenzo recognized that in this text he was carving out for himself a linguistic and political niche that the world had, perhaps, never before exactly encountered. As a republic, Florence offered Lorenzo at least the ostensible model of private citizen. Certainly that was a role he often chose to adopt. He used it to temporize when it suited his diplomatic purposes, arguing often that he could not make important decisions without referring them to the appropriate Florentine committee. The problem with the republican model, of course, was its inefficiency, and in a state whose very survival often depended upon the nimble-footedness of its leader in making decisions and taking action based on them, it must have often seemed to him frustrating and ill suited.

Opposed to the model of the republican private citizen was the model of the *gran signore*, of hereditary rule. But Florentine history had dealt hard with its seigneury, marginalizing its members and doing its best to break their power and influence. Unquestionably, Lorenzo had imperial aspirations for Florence, and equally unquestionably he entertained dynastic ambitions for his family. Both he and the Florentine state, however, were beset with enemies. At the period that saw the composition of *il Comento*, the dangerous political environment in which he found himself and Florence made the seignorial model untenable and required the development of a compromise. The concept of *gentilezza*, as I think, served the turn nicely. In his exposition of the etymology of the word *gentile*, Lorenzo first establishes the term as a paranym for the ancient Romans. "Gentiles," he explains, was what the Jews called the citizens of Rome, and the nobility of the Romans' works thus became associated with the word. This association, evoking as it did national myths both republican and imperial, Lorenzo must have considered a master stroke. That to which the word *gentile* could be applied was anything aptly, even ideally, suited for its function in the world. It could equally well be applied to a noble racehorse, a useful farm implement, the Italian vernacular in which Lorenzo composed, the role of Florentine diplomacy in the Italian peninsula, or, by a not too demanding extension, to the role that Lorenzo carved for himself as competent *capo della bottega*, master or foreman of the shop, who was good at what he did and survived and prevailed by his abilities in the role for which Providence and, very significantly, his own capacities had selected him. The Florentine state, too, perennially weak militarily, had to survive by mercantile and financial activity, by its native genius, and by astute diplomacy. The Florentine empire for which Lorenzo hoped would necessarily be an unprecedented enterprise.

It may be that, ultimately, Lorenzo abandoned this most innovative of his political hopes—creating a new sort of state with a new sort of leader. It may be that, unable to institutionalize the political vision one infers from the *Commentary*, he increasingly felt obliged to fall back upon the more familiar models of hereditary titles in trying to assure his own and his family's continued ascendancy.[26] Finally, of course, he secured a cardinal's hat for his son, Giovanni, who eventually became Pope Leo X. This coup led in due course to a Medici *Gran Duca* in the Florentine seat of power

---

[26] Alison Brown in a paper "Guicciardini and Lorenzo" delivered May 30, 1992, at the Warburg-Univ. of Warwick Conference on Lorenzo, explored the possibility that Lorenzo, had he lived longer, would have made himself Lord of Florence, perhaps by becoming Gonfaloniere for life.

and to a more regressive model of government. For a moment, nevertheless, as Giancarlo Mazzacurati has so convincingly argued with respect to Lorenzo as an innovator in literary genre, for a moment a kind of Bakhtinian interstice opened in the fabric of expectation for modes of government.[27] Into that space Lorenzo's imagination projected a possibility, and in the *Commentary*, I believe, in his careful, stipulative definition of *gentilezza*, he begins laying the theoretical ground for its future realization.

Style and the modern reader

The style of the *Commentary* is not necessarily one that a modern reader will find instantly congenial, and this fact may have dissuaded some scholars from discovering its very real treasures. In the original, the leisurely pace of Lorenzo's periodic sentences and the tangled referentiality of his pronouns are unfamiliar to the modern reader—even of Italian. The sentences are intentionally convoluted and, as Emilio Bigi remarked, the entire work is "Neoplatonic," "stilnovistic,... and ostentatiously erudite."[28] One can and should demur from the harshness of Bigi's "ostentatious," but sometimes the self-referential, syllogistic precision of the prose can seem overwrought. Also, the intense and repetitive focus upon the eyes and hand of his lady and on their effects upon his developing moral character may seem tedious to some. Any tedium, however, is regularly relieved, first, by insights into Lorenzo's character, second and especially by the sonnets themselves, which are regularly charming and sometimes brilliant, and then by passages that bring together classical philosophy, physiognomy, psychology and theology with Renaissance love theory. Beyond this, one finds interesting if sometimes fanciful etymologies, and one discovers those frequent passages that can be construed as covert invitations to allegorical reading.

Text and Translation

The text of the *Comento* survives in seven known manuscripts in Italian Libraries and one in Seville, but none of them seems to be an autograph.[29] I have translated the text of Tiziano Zanato's new critical edition

---

[27] Mazzacurati, 48–67.

[28] In Bigi, 295–96.

[29] For a complete description of the mss. and a detailed comparison of their readings with one another and with the principal printed editions as well, see Tiziano Zanato, "Sul Testo del 'Comento' Laurenziano," *Studi di Filologia Italiana* 38 (1980): 71–152; and "Un

of the *Comento De' Miei Sonetti*.[30] Working from Zanato's page proofs, I have followed all his suggested emendations save one—a hypothetical insertion of a maxim from Epictetus. I found Zanato's argument for Lorenzo's intention to include the maxim convincing, but I preferred to incorporate in a footnote Zanato's speculation about exactly which maxim it might be. Occasionally, I have also included in brackets clarifying phraseology in English. To the best of my knowledge, this translation accurately represents the latest and most carefully edited critical text available.

Among the many perplexities and difficulties with which Lorenzo's *Comento* presents the translator, a continuing challenge arises from considering the way one can or ought to render *"gentilezza"* and *"gentile"* into English. The words are crucial, and no contemporary English word exactly captures their implications across the range of contexts in which Lorenzo employs them. My one predecessor in Englishing the whole of the *Comento*, M. L. Marshall, employs "gentility" and "genteel."[31] But at least the second of these terms carries undercurrents of opprobrium in English that are utterly foreign to Lorenzo's meaning. The solution, however, employed by Angelo Lipari, (1935) who translated extended portions of the text, was exactly right—for speakers of Middle English. Lipari proposed and indeed tried resurrecting the Chaucerian *"gentilesse"* to express Lorenzo's central concept. Though at first tempted to emulate Lipari in this, I finally decided against it, since in any case the word would remain opaque without explanation. By *"gentilezza"* Lorenzo meant, as I have said, a quality that, in an observer's opinion, peculiarly characterized as admirably suited to its proper employment or purpose the person to whom or object to which it was applied. In the case of human beings, he meant by *"gentilezza"* a particular nobility of character, mind, and spirit—not inherited titles. It is a combination of Aristotelian magnanimity and that sort of nobility of spirit, derived from Divine grace, enjoyed by Griselda in Boccaccio's tenth tale of the tenth day and emphasized both by Petrarch and Chaucer in their versions of the story. Lorenzo himself is at great pains to define the quality, treating its (false) etymology at comparatively great length. This search for the precise meaning of this term, I suggest, as well as theorizing a polity, may also well be considered an integral aspect of

---

Nuovo Codice del 'Comento' Laurenziano," *Studi di Filologia Italiana* 39 (1981): 29–55. On the possibility that Ms. Riccardiano 2726 may be an autograph, see Mario Martelli, "L'autografo laurenziano del 'Comento dei Sonetti,' " *La Bibliofilia* 68 (1966) 233–71.

[30] Zanato, 1991.
[31] Marshall, 1946.

Lorenzo's search for self. Lorenzo's status as a ruler without formal title who exercises the responsibilities of a prince without corresponding office and emolument from the public purse, as *primus inter pares* in a city whose republican origins and whose inexact locatability in the scholastic discourse concerning six sorts of government, must have left Lorenzo perplexed and searching for an apt description. Finding this word in the emergent vernacular he so admired, a word susceptible of stipulative definition, he makes of it an adjective and a noun that adequately defined his political, social, and intellectual status. As I have already suggested, a political and linguistic "space" had opened. Lorenzo stepped in to fill both. I have therefore opted throughout to use "nobility" to translate this concept (though not always the word, since occasionally Lorenzo also uses the same term to mean a quality of gentleness in the modern English sense). But I always employ it with the caveat that the translation always means "nobility" in the stipulated Medicean sense.

Beyond this, the principles of the translation have been these: I have been at pains to be accurate, using etymological dictionaries and, through multiple drafts, querying persons with a better command of Lorenzo's Florentine idiom than I possess. I have tried to preserve the tone, as I perceive it, both of Lorenzo's poetry and of his prose. My critical reading of the *Commentary* is *ex post facto*—that is, I did not undertake the translation with a preconceived notion about Lorenzo's objectives or accomplishment; thus I feel certain that I have avoided shaping my English version in a way that represents either my prejudices or my critical conclusions. At the same time, whatever principles a translator enunciates, pragmatism must always play a central role. I have tried, therefore, to do what works well, and I hope that Lorenzo, were he able to read these pages, would find them in his sense *gentile*.

Because Italian tolerates, while English resists, long suspensions between subject and verb and pronominal references to distant nouns, I have been obliged sometimes to rearrange the order of clauses and phrases, but I have restricted these liberties to seeking idiomatic English equivalents for Lorenzo's Italian. At the unanimous suggestion of all who reviewed an early version of my manuscript, I have modified the punctuation to approximate more closely a modern English standard. I have also adopted the perhaps somewhat archaic English convention of beginning each line of verse with a capital. Finally, I have tried to convey a sense of the poetic values of the poems by rendering them in blank verse sonnets—a form rare but not unknown in English and particularly suited to moving from a language whose rhyming resources are so much greater than those of English. While not being driven always by what Milton called the "vexation, hindrance

and constraint," of the "jingling sound of like endings,"[32] I have recognized that one does not lightly abandon the familiar rhyming form of the Italian sonnet. I have therefore made no effort to repress occurrences of accidental rhyme.

---

[32] Cf. John T. Shawcross, ed., *The Complete English Poetry of John Milton* (Garden City, New York: Doubleday and Company, 1963), 221. Robert Lowell's *History* (New York: Farrar Strauss and Giroux, 1973), is an entire collection of contemporary free and blank verse sonnets, and Edmund Spenser's translations from Petrarch in Van Der Noodt's *Theatre* were in blank verse.

Chronology of the Life of Lorenzo de' Medici

1449

January 1: Lorenzo born to Piero di Cosimo de' Medici and Lucrezia Tornabuoni.

1464

Death of Lorenzo's grandfather Cosimo, the father of his country.

1469

February 7: Lorenzo's joust—thought to have been held in honor of the beauty of Lorenzo's mistress, Lucrezia Donati, and celebrated in a poem, "La Giostra di Lorenzo de' Medici," by Luigi Pulci.

June 4: Marriage to Roman noblewoman Clarice Orsini.

December 2: Death of Piero and Lorenzo's reluctant accession to his father's role as uncrowned prince of Florence.

1472

Sack of Volterra—a decision that Lorenzo regretted. His policy of military suppression of a riot in the dependency of Volterra resulted in rapine and pillage. Lorenzo personally distributed relief, but the outcome of his policy troubled him until his dying day.

Lorenzo revives the University of Pisa by making it a branch of the University of Florence and endowing it.

1474–75

This early, Lorenzo decides to collect his literary work in an organic corpus in the manner of Petrarch. "Phase A" of the *Commentary* under development (Zanato, *Comento*, 123).

1475

The joust of Lorenzo's brother, Giuliano, celebrated in verse by Agnolo Poliziano. Officially held to mark Florence's alliance with Venice, but in fact held to celebrate the beauty of Simonetta Cattaneo Vespucci, Giuliano's mistress and presumably the dead lady of the *Comento*.

1476

Raccolta Aragonese—a manuscript collection of Italian poetry compiled by Lorenzo for Don Federigo. It includes poems by Lorenzo himself, suggesting that he views himself as continuing the tradition of Guinizelli, Petrarch, and Dante.

April: Mission to Rome, ostensibly to sign an agreement with Pope Paul II concerning the alum mines at Tolfe, but really to enlist papal support for continuation of the Sforza dynasty as Dukes of Milan.

April 26: Death of Simonetta Cattaneo Vespucci.

1478

April 26: Assassination of Giuliano and attempt on the life of Lorenzo during high mass at the Duomo. The Pazzi conspiracy whose aftermath included Lorenzo's excommunication, a papal interdict against Florence and a war in which Pope Sixtus IV, Naples, Calabria, and others opposed Florence.

1479–80

Lorenzo travels to Naples to persuade King Ferrante to break off his alliance with Pope Sixtus IV—Lorenzo's most successful diplomatic accomplishment.

1480–83

Lorenzo composes many of the verses appearing in the *Comento*.

1484

Giovanni Pico della Mirandola joins the Medicean coterie.

July 15: Giovanni Pico alludes to a version of the *Comento*, calling it a "paraphrase" [of his own thought]. "Phase B" of the *Comento* in progress.

1486

October: Letter to Lorenzo from Ser Piero da Bibbiena that mentions "il vostro *Commento de' sonetti*."

1488

July: Sudden death of Clarice

1489

Lorenzo successfully negotiates a Cardinalate for his 14–year–old son, Giovanni, later Pope Leo X.

1490

Revisions of *Comento* continue.

1491

December 29: Attack of gout leading to Lorenzo's death. He was working on the *Comento* at least this late in his life.

1492

April 8: Death of Lorenzo from hereditary disease of gout.

COMENTO DE' MIEI SONETTI

[Critical text edited by
Tiziano Zanato
and reprinted here with his permission.]

[Proemio]

Assai sono stato dubbioso e sospeso se dovevo fare la presente interpetrazione e comento delli miei sonetti, e, se pure qualche volta ero più inclinato a farlo, le infrascritte ragioni mi occorrevano in contrario e mi toglievano da questa opera. Prima, la presunzione nella quale mi pareva incorrere comentando io le cose proprie, così per la troppa extimazione che mostravo fare di me medesimo, come perché mi pareva assumere in me quello iudicio che debba essere d'altri, notando in questa parte l'ingegni di coloro alle mani de' quali perverranno li miei versi, come poco sufficienti a poterli intendere. Pensavo, oltre a questo, potere essere da qualcuno facilmente ripreso di poco iudicio, avendo consumato il tempo e nel comporre e nel comentare versi, la materia e subietto de' quali in gran parte fussi una amorosa passione; e questo essere molto più repransibile in me per le continue occupazioni e publiche e private, le quali mi dovevano ritrarre da simili pensieri, secondo alcuni non solamente frivoli e di poco momento, ma ancora perniziosi e di qualche preiudicio così all'anima nostra come all'onore del mondo. E, se questo è, il pensare a simili cose è grande errore, metterle in versi molto maggiore, ma il comentarle non pare minore difetto che sia quello di colui che ha fatto uno lungo e indurato abito nelle male opere; *maxime* perché e comenti sono riservati per cose teologiche o di filosofia e importanti grandi effetti, o a edificazione e consolazione della mente nostra o a utilità della umana generazione. Aggiugnesi ancora a questo, che forse a qualcuno parrà repransibile, quando bene la materia e subietto fussi per sé assai degno, avendo scritto e fattone menzione in lingua nostra materna e vulgare, la quale, dove si parla et è intesa, per essere molto comune non pare decline da qualche viltà, e in quelli luoghi dove no n'è notizia non può essere intesa, e però a questa parte questa opera e fatica nostra pare al tutto vana e come se non fussi fatta.

Queste tre difficultà hanno insino a ora ritardato quello che più tempo fa avevo proposto, cioè la presente interpetrazione. Al presente ho pure deliberate, vinto, al mio parere, da migliore ragione, metterla in opera, pensando che, se questa mia poca fatica sarà di qualche extimazione e grata a qualcuno, sarà bene collocata e non al tutto vana; se pure arà poca grazia,

Prologue

I have been very doubtful and uncertain about whether or not I ought to prepare the present interpretation of and commentary upon my sonnets, and if, nevertheless, I was sometimes more inclined to do it, the arguments listed below dissuaded me and cut me off from this work. First, by commenting myself on my own works, I seemed to risk presumption, both by showing that I esteemed myself too highly and by seeming to usurp the judgment that ought to belong to others, suggesting in this way that the intellect of those into whose hands my verses fall is inadequate to enable them to understand. Besides this, I thought someone could easily reprove me for poor judgment in having wasted my time composing and commenting on verses whose material and subject had for the most part been an amorous passion. And this might seem much more reprehensible in me because of the continual business, both public and private, which obliged me to turn away from such thoughts—thoughts that, according to some, were not only frivolous and of little importance, but even pernicious and rather harmful, and as dangerous to our souls as to our earthly reputation. And, if this is so, not only is thinking about such things a great error, but putting them into verses is a far greater one, and commenting on them seems no less a failing than is the fault of someone who has made a long and hardened habit of evil deeds—especially since commentaries are reserved for matters of theology or philosophy, and for consequential and significant concerns, or for the edification and consolation of our minds, or for the benefit of the human race. Besides, it may seem reprehensible to someone, perhaps, though the material and subject were themselves very worthy, that writing and uttering them in our mother tongue, which, by being very commonplace where it is spoken and understood, may not seem to avoid some base expression. In those places where our language is unknown, it cannot be understood, and thus in that region this work and our pains will seem all in vain and as if they had not been accomplished.

These three difficulties have until now delayed what I have for a long time proposed, that is, the present interpretation. At present, persuaded as it seems to me by the best of arguments, I have indeed decided to undertake the work, thinking that, if this little effort of mine is of some value and welcome to someone, it will be worthwhile and not entirely in vain. If it finds little favor, then, it will be little read and reproached by few,

sarà poco letta e da pochi vituperata, e, non essendo molto durabile, poco durerà ancora la reprensione nella quale possa incorrere.

E, rispondendo al presente alla prima ragione e a quelli che di presunzione mi volessino in alcuno modo notare, dico che a me non pare presunzione lo interpetrare le cose mie, ma più presto tòrre fatica ad altri; e di nessuno è più proprio officio lo interpetrare che di colui medesimo che ha scritto, perchè nessuno può meglio sapere o elicere la verità del senso suo: come mostra assai chiaramente la confusione che nasce della varietà de' comenti, nelli quali el più delle volte si segue più tosto la natura propria che la intenzione vera di chi ha scritto. Né mi pare per questo fare argumento che io tenga troppo conto di me medesimo o tolga ad altri el giudicarmi: perché credo sia officio vero d'ogni uomo operare tutte le cose a benificio degli uomini, o proprio o d'altri; e perché ognuno non nasce atto o disposto a potere operare quelle cose che sono reputate prime nel mondo, è da misurare sé medesimo e vedere in che ministerio meglio si può servire all'umana generazione, e in quello essercitarsi, perché e alla diversità delli ingegni umani e alla necessità della vita nostra non può satisfare una cosa sola, ancora che sia la prima e più excellente opera che possino fare gli uomini: anzi, pare che la contemplazione, la quale sanza controversia è la prima e più excellente, pasca minore numero delli uomini che alcuna delle altre. E per questo si conclude non solamente molte opere d'ingegno, ma ancora molti vili ministerii concorrere di necessità alla perfezzione della vita umana, et essere vero officio di tutti gli uomini, in quel grado che si truovono o dal cielo o dalla natura o dalla fortuna disposti, servire alla umana generazione. Io arei bene desiderato potermi essercitare in maggiore cose; né voglio però per questo mancare, in quello che sopporta lo ingegno e forze mie, a qualcuno, se non a molti, e quali, forse più tosto per piacere a me che perché le cose mie satisfaccino a'lloro, me hanno confortato a questo: l'auttorità e grazia delli quali vale assai appresso

and, if it is not very durable, the reprehension into which it may fall will likewise last only a little while.

And, responding now to my first argument[1] and to those who would be pleased to accuse me of presumption in some form, I say that it does not seem to me presumption to interpret my own work, but rather eagerness to free others from the task. And I insist that for no one is interpretation a more appropriate office than for that same person who has composed. For no one can better know or elucidate the truth of his meaning. This clearly appears in that confusion which breeds from the variety of comments that, most of the time, follow their own agendas rather than the true intention of the one who has written. Neither does it seem to me that in making this argument I take too great account of myself or take judging me away from others. For I believe it is the true office of every man to carry out all things to men's benefit, either one's own or that of others. And because not everyone is born capable of doing or disposed to do those things that are reputed foremost in the world, it is up to the individual to take stock of himself and to see in what calling he can best serve the human race and to work in it. For one calling alone, owing both to the diversity of human intelligence and to the necessities of our life, does not suffice, even if it is the premier and most excellent work that men are capable of doing. Rather, it seems that contemplation, which unquestionably is the first and most excellent [vocation], nourishes a smaller number of men than some of the others.[2] And from this one concludes that not only many works of talent, but even many low occupations by necessity combine to produce the perfection of human life. And it must be the true office of all men to serve the human race in whatever degree they find themselves placed, either by heaven or by nature or by fortune. I should certainly have desired to be able to labor in major affairs. In view of this, therefore, in whatever my intelligence and my powers make possible, I do not wish to fail any person, let alone many persons, whose authority and

---

[1] I.e., the fear of being thought presumptuous. In this argument, Lorenzo follows with some modifications Dante's defense of himself in *Convivio* 1, 2. All *Conv.* references are to *Dante Alighieri, Il Convivio* 2nd. ed. 2 vols., eds., Antonio Enzo Quaglio, G. Busnelli, and G. Vandelli (Florence: Le Monnier, 1964). English translations unless otherwise noted are from *Dante's Convivio*, trans. William Walrond Jackson (Oxford: Clarendon Press, 1909), cited as "Jackson."

[2] The motif of the necessary variety of human occupation appears in Dante, *Par.* 8, 118–48 and in *Conv.* 4, 4, 1–2, which in its turn derives from Aristotle, *Pol.* 1, 2 and *De An.* 11, 19. Cited by Bigi, 299. At this point in the text of all mss. save one a lacuna occurs. Here Zanato interpolates the unique reading of Ms. Seville 7.1.33 (formerly AA. 141. 44), cited in Tiziano Zanato, "Un Nuovo Codice del 'Comento' Laurenziano," *Studi di Filologia Italiana* 39 (1981) 29–55.

di me. E se non potrò fare altra utilità a chi leggerà li versi miei, almanco qualche poco di piacere se ne piglierà, perché forse qualche ingegno troverranno proporzionato e conforme al loro; e se pure qualcuno se ne ridessi, a me sarà grato che tragga de' versi miei questa voluttà, ancora che sia piccola; parendomi, massimamente publicando questa interpetrazione, sottomettermi più tosto al giudicio degli altri, conciosiacosa che se da me medesimo avessi giudicato questi miei versi indegni d'essere letti, arei fuggito il giudicio degli altri, ma comentandogli e publicandogli fuggo, al mio parere, molto meglio la presunzione del giudicarmi da me medesimo.

Ora, per rispondere alle calunnie di quelli che volessino accusarmi avendo io messo tempo e nel comporre e nel comentare cose non degne di fatica o di tempo alcuno, per essere passione amorose etc., e maxime tra molte mie necessarie occupazioni, dico che veramente con giustizia sarei dannato quando la natura umana fussi di tanta excellenzia dotata, che tutti gli uomini potessino operare sempre tutte le cose perfette; ma perché questo grado di perfezzione è stato concesso a molti pochi, e a questi pochi ancora molto rare volte nella vita loro, mi pare si possa concludere, considerata la imperfezione umana, quelle cose essere migliori al mondo nelle quali interviene minore male. E giudicando piu tosto secondo la natura comune e consuetudine universale degli uomini, se bene non l'oserei affermare, pure credo l'amore tra gli uomini non solamente non essere repressibile, ma quasi necessario, e assai vero argumento di gentilezza e grandezza d'animo, e sopra tutto cagione d'invitare gli uomini a cose degne et excellenti, et essercitare e riducere in atto quelle virtù che in potenzia sono nell'anima nostra. Perche, chi cerca diligentemente quale sia la vera diffinizione dello amore, trova non essere altro che appetito di

grace count very much with me and who, perhaps, rather to please me than because my works were satisfying to them, have encouraged me in this one.[3] And if I can do nothing else useful for those who will read my verses, at least they may take some little pleasure from them because they may perhaps find some wit proportionate to and consonant with them. And even if someone should laugh at them, it will please me that he draws even this little delight from my verses. Indeed, it especially seems to me that in publishing this interpretation I submit myself rather more to the judgment of others. Because if I had myself judged these verses of mine unworthy of being read, I should have fled the judgment of others, but by commenting on them and publishing them, it seems to me, I flee far better the presumption of making my own judgment of myself.

Now, to respond to the calumny of those who would wish to accuse me of having invested time both in composing and in commenting upon things not worth the pains nor worth any time because of being amorous passions and so forth—especially given my many necessary occupations—I say that truly I could with justice be condemned, if human nature were endowed with such great excellence that all men could always produce all things perfectly. But because this degree of perfection has been granted to very few, and to those few, moreover, only on very rare occasions in their lives, one can conclude, it seems to me—human imperfection considered—that in the world those things are best into which the least harm obtrudes. And judging rather according to the common nature and universal custom of men, although I would not dare to affirm it, still I believe that in mankind love is not only not reprehensible, but an almost necessary and very true test of nobility and greatness of soul. And above all [love is] the cause that leads men to worthy and excellent endeavors, and leads them to practice and to turn into action those virtues that are potentially in our soul.[4] Therefore, whoever diligently seeks the true definition of love, finds it to be nothing other than an appetite for beauty.[5] And if it is

---

[3] Perhaps especially Pico della Mirandola who called the *Comento* his "paraphrase." See Pico's letter of 15 July 1484 in E. Garin, *Prosatori latini del Quattrocento* (Milan: Riccardo Ricciardi, 1952) 797–805.

[4] Lorenzo here re-echoes the stilnovistic conceit of the identity of love with nobility of soul, and particularly of Guinizelli's canzone, "Al cor gentil rempaira sempre Amore" (Love always comes soonest to the noble heart). See also Sears Reynolds Jayne, trans. "Marsilio Ficino's Commentary on Plato's *Symposium*," (hereafter cited as *FC*) in *The University of Missouri Studies*, 29, 1, 1944 (119–247), especially 1, 3, (125–29).

[5] This definition is that of Ficinan Platonism; see *FC*, 1, 3 (128): "the nature of Love is . . . that it attracts to beauty. . . .", and 2, 9, (146): "for love is the desire of enjoying beauty."

bellezza; e, se questo è, tutte le cose deforme e brutte necessariamente dispiacciono a chi ama. E mettendo per al presente da parte quello amore el quale, secondo Platone, è mezzo a tutte le cose a trovare la loro perfezzione e riposarsi ultimamente nella suprema bellezza, cioè Dio; parlando di quello amore che s'extende solamente ad amare l'umana creatura, dico che, se bene questa non è quella perfezzione d'amore che si chiama "sommo bene," almanco veggiamo chiaramente contenere in sé tanti beni et evitare tanti mali, che secondo la comune consuetudine della vita umana tiene luogo di bene: *maxime* se è ornata di quelle circunstanzie e condizioni che si convengono a uno vero amore, che mi pare sieno due: la prima, che si ami una cosa sola; la seconda, che questa tale cosa si ami sempre. Queste due condizioni male possono cadere se il subietto amato non ha in sé, a proporzione dell'altre cose umane, somma perfezzione, e se, oltre alle naturali bellezze, non concorre nella cosa amata ingegno grande, modi e costumi ornati e onesti, maniera e gesti eleganti, destrezza d'accorte e dolci parole, amore, constanzia e fede; e queste cose tutte necessariamente convengono alla perfezione dello amore. Perché, ancora che il principio d'amore nasca dagli occhi e da bellezza, nondimeno alla conservazione e perseveranza in esso bisognano quell'altre condizioni; perché se, o per infermità o per età o altra cagione, si scolorissi il viso e mancassi in tutto o in parte la bellezza, restino tutte quell'altre condizioni, non meno grate allo animo e al cuore che la bellezza agli occhi. Né sarebbono ancora queste tali condizioni sufficienti, se ancora in colui che ama non fusse vera cognizione di queste condizioni, che presuppone perfezzione di iudicio nello amante; né potrebbe essere amore della cosa amata verso colui che ama, se quello che ama non meritassi essere amato, presupposto lo infallibile iudicio della cosa amata. E però, chi propone uno vero amore, di necessità propone grande perfezzione, secondo la comune consuetudine degli uomini, così nello amato come in chi ama; e come adviene in tutte le altre cose perfette, credo che questo tale amore sia suto al mondo molto raro: che tanto più arguisce l'excellenzia sua. Chi ama una cosa sola e sempre,

this, all deformed and ugly things necessarily displease one who loves. I set aside for the moment that love which, according to Plato, is the means whereby all things find their perfection and ultimately rest in the Supreme Beauty, that is, in God. And speaking of that love that is proffered solely for loving the human creature, I say that, although this is not that perfection of love that one calls "the highest good," at least we see clearly that it contains in itself so many benefits and that it avoids so many evils that, according to the common customs of human life, it is considered to be good. This is especially so if it is adorned with those circumstances and conditions that are appropriate for a true love, which seem to me to be two: the first, that a person love one beloved only; and the second, that a person love this same beloved always. It is difficult for these two conditions to be fulfilled if the beloved does not have in herself, in proportion with other human qualities, the highest perfection, and if, beyond those natural beauties there do not come together in the beloved great liveliness of mind, graceful and chaste behavior and habits, an elegant manner and actions, wise adroitness and sweet words, and love, constancy, and faith. And these things all necessarily combine in the perfection of love. Therefore, although the beginning of love springs from the eyes and from beauty,[6] nevertheless in its conservation and continuation those other conditions are necessary. Because, if either by infirmity or through old age or through some other cause, the face were to lose its color, and beauty were partly or wholly to disappear, all those other conditions would remain, no less pleasing to the mind and heart than beauty is to the eyes. Nor still would those same conditions be sufficient if there were not in him who loves, moreover, a true recognition of these conditions, which [recognition] presupposes perfection of judgment in the lover. Neither could there be love for the beloved in the lover if the lover were not himself worthy to be loved, presupposing the infallible [good] judgment of the beloved. And therefore whoever posits true love of necessity posits great perfection, according to the common usage of men, both in the beloved and in the lover. And, as is the case with all other perfect things, I believe that such love as this occurs but very rarely in the world. And this [rarity] argues its excellence even more. Whoever loves one thing only and

---

[6] According to stilnovistic theory, renewed and re-echoed by Ficino, love springs from the eyes and from beauty in this way: "The appearance of a man, which because of an interior goodness graciously given him by God, is beautiful to see, frequently shoots a ray of his splendor, through the eyes of those looking at him, into their souls," FC, 62,2, (183); and cf. 7,1 (216–17), where the Cavalcantian doctrine of falling in love is recapitulated; see also the subtle analyses of the role of the eyes in amorous bewitchment in 7,4–5, (221–25).

di necessità non pone amore ad altre cose, e però si priva di tutti gli errori e voluttà nelle quali comunemente incorrono gli uomini; e amando persona atta a conoscere e cercando in ogni modo che può di piacerli, bisogna di necessità che in tutte le opere sue cerchi degnificarsi e farsi excellente tra gli altri, seguitando opere virtuose, per farsi più degno che può di quella cosa che lui stima sopra all'altre degnissima; parendogli che, e in palese e in occulto, come la forma della cosa amata sempre è presente al cuore, così sia presente a tutte l'opere sue, le quali laudi o reprenda secondo la loro convenienzia, come vero testimonio e assistente giudice non solo delle opere, ma de' pensieri. E così, parte colla vergogna reprimendo el male, parte con lo stimolo del piacerli excitando il bene, se pure questi tali perfettamente non operano, almanco fanno quello che al mondo è reputato manco male: la quale cosa, rispetto alla imperfezzione umana, al mondo per bene si elegge.

Questo adunque è stato il subietto de' versi miei. E se, pure con tutte queste ragioni, non risponderò alle obtrettazioni e calunnie di chi mi volessi dannare, almanco, come disse il nostro fiorentino Poeta, apresso di quelli che hanno provato che cosa è amore, «spero trovare pietà, non che perdono»: il giudicio de' quali è assai a mia satisfazzione. Perché, se gli è vero, come dice Guido bolognese, che amore e gentilezza si convertino e sieno una cosa medesima, credo che agli uomini basti e solamente sia expetibile la laude degli alti e gentili ingegni, curandosi poco degli altri, perché è impossibile fare opera al mondo che sia da tutti gli uomini laudata; e però chi ha buona elezione si sforza acquistare laude apresso di quelli che ancora loro sono degni di laude, e poco cura la oppinione degli altri. A me pare si possa poco biasimare quello che è naturale; nessuna cosa è più naturale che l'appetito d'unirsi con la cosa bella, e questo appetito è suto ordinato dalla natura negli uomini per la propagazione della umana generazione, cosa molto necessaria alla conservazione della umana spezie. E a questo la vera ragione che ci debba muovere non è né nobilità di

always, of necessity does not give love to other things, and therefore is free of all the errors and sensuality into which men commonly fall. And in loving a suitable person, by knowing and by searching in every way for that which can please him, one must of necessity in all his works seek to make himself worthy and to make himself excellent among the others, pursuing virtuous works, in order to make himself as worthy as he can for that one whom he considers most worthy above all others. For just as it seems to him that, both in public and in private, the form of the beloved is always present in his heart, so it is present in all his works, which are praised or reproved according to their suitability, as true witness and as attending judge not only of his works, but of his thoughts as well.[7] And thus, partly reproving evil with shame and partly encouraging the good with the stimulus of pleasure, those two parties [true lovers], if they do not achieve perfection, at least achieve what the world considers less bad—which, given human imperfection, in the world is considered good.

This then has been the subject of my verses. And if, even with all these arguments, I have not responded to all the accusations and calumnies of those who would wish to condemn me, at least, as our Florentine poet said in the company of those who had proved what love is, "I hope to find compassion, not just forgiveness."[8] His judgment meets very much with my approval. If it is true, therefore, as Guido of Bologna says,[9] that love and nobility convert into each other and are one in the same thing, I believe that for men only the praise of high and noble talents is sufficient and desirable, and I care little for the opinion of the others, because it is impossible to do work in the world that is praised by all men. And therefore whoever has good judgment is constrained to obtain praise in the company of those who are indeed worthy of praise, and to regard little the opinion of others. It seems to me that one can little blame that which is natural. Nothing is more natural than the desire for uniting oneself with the beautiful, and this desire has been ordained by nature in men for the propagation of the human race, a most necessary thing for the preservation of the human species.[10] And the true reason that must move us to this is

---

[7] Besides those named above, L. is indebted for this conceit of love as an element of reciprocal moral purification to the *stilnovisti* and still more to Ficino: see *FC*, 1, 4, (131): "if two people love each other, they watch each other constantly, and also try to please each other ... they abstain from all evil ... so that they may not appear contemptible in the eyes of the beloved, but may seem worthy of an exchange of love."

[8] Petrarch, Francesco, *Rerum vulgarium fragmenta* (hereafter *Rvf*) 1, 8.

[9] Guido Guinizelli (1240–1276), usually considered the founder of the stilnovistic school.

[10] See *FC*, 2,7, (143). "But the power of generation in us, which is the second Venus,

sangue, né speranza di possessioni, di ricchezza o d'altra conmodità, ma solamente la elezzione naturale, non sforzata o occupata da alcuno altro rispetto, ma solamente mossa da una certa conformità e proporzione che hanno insieme la cosa amata e lo amante, affine della propagazione dell'umana spezie. E però sono sommamente da dannare quelli e quali l'appetito muove ad amare sommamente le cose che sono fuori di questo ordine naturale e vero fine già proposto da noi, e da laudare quelli e quali, seguitando questo fine, amano una cosa sola diuturnamente e con somma constanzia e fede.

A me pare che assai copiosamente sia risposto a tale obietto. E, dato che questo amore, come di sopra abbiamo detto, sia bene, non pare molto necessario purgare quella parte che in me parebbe forse più reprensibile, per le diverse occupazioni publiche e private: perché, s'egli è bene, il bene non ha bisogno d'alcuna excusazione, perché non ha colpa. E se pure qualche scrupoloso iudicio non volessi ammettere queste ragioni, almanco conceda questa piccola licenzia alla età iuvenile e tenera, la quale non pare tanto obligata alla censura e iudicio degli uomini e nella quale non pare tanto grave qualunque errore, *maxime* perché è più stimulata a declinare dalla via retta e per la poca experienzia manco si può opponere a quelle cose che la natura e comune uso delli uomini persuadono. Questo dico in caso che pure fussi stimato errore amare molto, con somma sincerità e fede, una cosa, la quale sforza per la perfezzione sua l'amore dello amante: la quale cosa non confesso essere errore. E, se questo è, o per le ragioni dette o avuto rispetto alla età, né il comporre né il comentare miei versi fatti a questo proposito mi può essere imputato a grave errore. E dato che fussi vero che non si convenissi comento a simile materia, per essere piccola e poco importante o a edificazione o a contento della mente nostra, dico che, se questo è, la fatica di questo comento convenirsi massimamente a me, acciò che altro ingegno di più excellenzia che il mio non abbia a consumarsi o mettere tempo in cose sì basse; e se pure la materia è alta e degna, come pare a me, el chiarirla bene e farla piana e intelligibile a ciascuno essere molto utile: e questo, per quello che ho detto di sopra, nessuno il può fare con più chiara expressione del vero senso che io medesimo. Né io sono stato il primo che ho comentato versi importanti simili

not nobility of blood, nor the hope for possessions, for wealth or for other commodities, but only natural choice, not compelled by or preoccupied with any other consideration, but only moved by a certain conformity and proportion that the lover and the beloved have for each other to the end of propagating the human species. And therefore I strongly support condemning those whose appetite moves them to love excessively those things that are outside the natural order and this true end, intended for us. And indeed, [I strongly support] praising those who, pursuing this end, love only one person continually and with firm constancy and faith.

To me it seems I have answered very copiously to such an objection. And given that this love, as we have said above, is good, it does not seem very necessary to eliminate that part of me that would perhaps seem more reprehensible because of my various private and public occupations. For, if that part is good, the good has no need of any apology since it has no fault. And even if some scrupulous critic should not wish to accept these arguments, at least permit this little license to tenderness and youth, which does not seem under much obligation to the censure and prudence of men, and in which any errors do not seem as serious, especially since youth is more inclined to stray from the right path, and through the lack of a little experience cannot even resist those things that nature and the common practice of men persuade one [not to do]. I say this in case it were considered an error to love greatly with the highest sincerity and faith someone who compels by her perfection the lover's love for the beloved—a thing that I do not confess to be an error. And if this is so, either on account of the arguments stated or on account of age, neither composing nor commenting upon my verses, done with this intention, can be considered a grave error in me. And given that it were true that commenting on a subject like this is improper owing to its being slight and of little importance either to the edification or to the pleasure of our mind, in that case I say that the effort of this commentary agrees particularly with me, so that another intellect of greater excellence than mine will not have to consume itself wasting time on things so low. And even if the subject is elevated and worthy, as it seems to me, clarifying it well and making it plain and intelligible to each person is very useful. And this, because of what I have said above, no one can do with a clearer expression of its true sense than I myself. Nor have I been the first to comment on verses treat-

---

desires to create another form like this. Therefore there is a love in each case; in the former it is the desire of contemplating beauty; and in the latter, the desire of propagating it; both loves are honorable and praiseworthy, for each is concerned with the divine image."

amorosi subietti, perché Dante lui medesimo comentò alcuna delle sue canzone e altri versi; e io ho letto il comento di Egidio romano e Dino Del Garbo, excellentissimi filosofi, sopra a quella subtilissima canzona di Guido Cavalcanti, uomo al tempo suo reputato primo dialettico che fussi al mondo, e inoltre in questi nostri versi vulgari excellentissimo, come mostrano tutte le altre sue opere e *maxime* la sopra detta canzona, che comincia *Donna mi prega* etc., la quale non importa altro che il principio come nasce ne' cuori gentili amore e gli effetti suoi. E se pure alla purgazione mia non sono sufficienti né le sopra scritte ragione, né gli essempli, la compassione almeno mi doverrà giustificare, perché, essendo nella mia gioventù stato molto perseguitato dagli uomini e dalla fortuna, qualche poco di refriggerio non mi debbe essere dinegato, el quale solamente ho trovato e in amare ferventemente e nella composizione e comento de' miei versi, come piu chiaramente faremo intendere quando verremo alla exposizione di quello sonetto che comincia *Se tra gli altri sospiri che escono di fore*. Quale sieno sute le mie maligne persecuzioni, per essere assai publiche è assai noto; qual sia suta la dolcezza e refriggerio che 'l mio dolcissimo e constantissimo amore ha dato a queste, è impossibile che altri che io lo possi intendere, perché, quando bene l'avessi ad alcuno narrato, così era impossibile a lui lo intenderlo come a me referirne il vero. E però torno al sopra detto verso del nostro fiorentino Poeta, che, «dove sia chi per pruova intenda amore» (così questo amore che io ho tanto laudato, come qualche particulare amore e carità verso di me), «spero trovare pietà, non che perdono».

Resta adunque solamente rispondere alla obiezzione che potessi essere fatta avendo scritto in lingua vulgare, secondo il giudicio di qualcuno non capace o degna d'alcuna excellente materia e subietto. E a questa parte si risponde alcuna cosa non essere manco degna per essere più comune, anzi

ing of similar amorous subjects, because Dante himself commented upon some of his canzoni and other poems.[11] And I have read the commentary of Egidio the Roman and Dino del Garbo,[12] very excellent philosophers, on that very fine canzone of Guido Cavalcanti, a man reputed in his time to be the foremost dialectician in the world, and furthermore very excellent in these our vernacular poems, as all his works show and especially the above mentioned canzone that begins: *A lady entreats me...* etc., which concerns nothing else than the principle of the way that love is born in noble hearts and its effects.[13] And if neither the arguments set forth above nor the examples are sufficient to clear me, compassion at least must justify me because, having in my youth been much persecuted by men and by fortune,[14] some little solace ought not to be denied me, and this I have only found in loving ardently and in composing and commenting upon my verses, as we shall demonstrate more clearly when we come to the exposition of that sonnet that begins: "Sometimes among the sighs that from my breast...," etc. [10]. Such terrible persecutions as I have undergone are very well known because they are public knowledge. And what the sweetness and solace has been that my sweetest and most constant love has given for these, it is impossible that anyone other than I could understand, because, until I had clearly recounted these things to someone, understanding them would have been as impossible for him as referring to the truth about them for me. Accordingly, I return to the above-mentioned verse of our Florentine poet that, "where there may be someone who understands love by trial" (both this love that I have so greatly praised, and some particular love and charity toward me), "I hope to find compassion, not just forgiveness."

All that remains to do is to answer to the objection that could be made to my having written in the vernacular that, according to the judgment of some, has neither the capacity nor the merit for certain excellent material and subjects.[15] And to this view one responds: some things are not less worthy because they are more common, rather one proves every good to

---

[11] In *Conv.* and *VN*.

[12] Egidio Colonna romano (1246–1316), a theologian and author, and Dino del Garbo (d. 1327) a Florentine physician and philosopher.

[13] Bigi calls attention to similar and more detailed appreciations of Guido in Poliziano's dedicatory *"epistola"* to Lorenzo's *Raccolta aragonese* (which also pays homage to Egidio); in Boccaccio's *Decameron* 6,9; and in *FC*, 7.

[14] Here and elsewhere the persecutions of men and fortune allude to the conspiracy of the Pazzi (1478) during which Lorenzo was attacked and his brother Giuliano killed, and to the subsequent period of political difficulties and warfare.

[15] Bigi, 306 cites analogues to this defense of the vernacular in *Ep. Rac.* and in *Conv.* I.

si prova ogni bene essere tanto migliore quanto è più comunicabile e universale, come è di natura sua quello che si chiama "sommo bene": perché non sarebbe sommo se non fussi infinito, né alcuna cosa si può chiamare infinita, se non quella che è comune a tutte le cose. E però non pare che l'essere comune in tutta Italia la nostra materna lingua li tolga dignità, ma è da pensare in fatto la perfezzione o imperfezzione di detta lingua. E, considerando quali sieno quelle condizioni che danno dignità e perfezzione a qualunque idioma e lingua, a me pare sieno quattro, delle quali una o al più dua sieno proprie e vere laude della lingua, l'altre più tosto dependino o dalla consuetudine e oppinione degli uomini o dalla fortuna.

Quella che è vera laude della lingua è lo essere copiosa e abundante e atta a exprimere bene il senso e concetto della mente. E però si giudica la lingua greca più perfetta che la latina, e la latina più che la ebrea, perché l'una più che l'altra meglio exprime la mente di chi ha o detto o scritto alcuna cosa.

L'altra condizione che più degnifica la lingua è la dolcezza e armonia, che resulta più d'una che d'un'altra; e benché l'armonia sia cosa naturale e proporzionata con la armonia dell'anima e del corpo nostro, nondimeno a me pare, per la varietà degli ingegni umani, che tutti non sono bene proporzionati e perfetti, questa sia più presto oppinione che ragione: conciosicosa che quelle cose che si giudicano secondo che comunemente piacciono o non piacciono, paiono più tosto fondate nella oppinione che nella vera ragione, *maxime* quelle, el piacere o dispiacere delle quali non si prova con altra ragione che con l'appetito. E, non obstanti queste ragione, non voglio però affermare questa non potere essere propria laude della lingua; perché, essendo l'armonia (come è detto) proporzionata alla natura umana, si può inferire il giudicio della dolcezza di tale armonia convenirsi a quelli che similmente sono bene proporzionati a riceverla, el giudicio de' quali debba essere acettato per buono, ancora che fussino pochi: perché le sentenzie e iudicii degli uomini più presto si debbono ponderare che numerare.

L'altra condizione che fa più excellente una lingua è quando in una lingua sono scritte cose subtili e gravi e necessarie alla vita umana, così alla mente nostra come alla utilità degli uomini e salute del corpo: come si può dire della lingua ebrea, per li ammirabili misterii che contiene, accomodati, anzi necessarii alla ineffabile verità della fede nostra; e similmente della lingua greca, contenente molte scienzie metafisiche, naturali e morali

be greatly better the more it is communicable and universal, as is that which by its nature is called the "highest good." For it would not be the highest if it were not infinite, neither could any thing be called "infinite" if not that which is common to all things. And therefore it does not seem that being common to all Italy takes dignity away from our mother tongue, but one should consider in fact the perfection or the imperfection of this language. And, considering what the conditions are that give dignity to any idiom or tongue, they seem to me to be four, among which one, or at most two, are rightly and truly advantages of a language. The others rather depend either on the customs and opinions of men or on fortune.

That which is truly an advantage of a language is its being copious and abundant and suited to express well the sense and the concept of the mind. And therefore one judges the Greek language to be more perfect than the Latin and the Latin more than the Hebrew, because one more than the other better expresses the mind of whoever has either spoken or written something.

The other circumstance that most renders a language fitting is the sweetness and harmony that results more from one than from another. And although harmony is a natural matter and proportional with the harmony of our body and our mind, it nevertheless seems to me, because of the variety of human talent, that all are not well proportioned and perfect, [and that] this is more properly a matter of opinion than reason. For those things that are judged according to whether they commonly please or disappoint seem founded rather in opinion than in true reason, especially those whose pleasing or displeasing are not proved with other arguments than preference.[16] And, these arguments not withstanding, I do not therefore wish to affirm that this cannot be an advantage belonging to a language. Because since harmony, as one says, is proportionate to human nature, one infers the judgment of the sweetness of such harmony to be appropriate for those who are likewise well proportioned to receive it [and] whose judgment must be accepted as good, even though they may be few—because the opinions and judgments of men must more readily be weighed than counted.

The other condition that makes a language very excellent occurs when subtle and serious matters are written in it—matters necessary to human life, both to our minds and to the use of men and to the health of the body—as can be said of the Hebrew language, for the admirable mysteries that it contains, suitable, or rather necessary to the ineffable truth of our faith. And likewise [this can be said] of the Greek language, which ex-

---

[16] Ital. *appetito*.

molto necessarie alla umana generazione. E quando questo adviene, è necessario confessare che piu presto sia degno il subietto che la lingua, perché il subietto è fine e la lingua è mezzo. Né per questo si può chiamare quella lingua più perfetta in sé, ma più tosto maggiore perfezzione della materia che per essa si tratta; perché, chi ha scritto cose teologiche, metafisiche, naturali e morali, in quella parte che degnifica la lingua nella quale ha scritto pare che più presto reservi la laude nella materia, e che la lingua abbi fatto l'officio d'instrumento, el quale è buono o reo secondo el fine.

Resta un'altra sola condizione che dà reputazione alla lingua, e questo è quando il successo delle cose del mondo è tale, che facci universale e quasi comune a tutto il mondo quello che naturalmente è proprio o d'una citta o d'una provincia sola. E questo si può più presto chiamare felicità e prosperità di fortuna che vera laude della lingua, perché l'essere in prezzo e assai celebrata una lingua nel mondo consiste nella oppinione di quelli tali che assai la prezzono e stimono, né si può chiamare vero e proprio bene quello che depende da altri che da sé medesimo: perché, quelli tali che l'hanno in prezzo potebbono facilmente sprezzarla e mutare oppinione, e quelle condizioni mutarsi per le quali, mancando la cagione, facilmente mancherebbe ancora la degnità e laude di quella. Questa tale degnità d'essere prezzata per il successo prospero della fortuna è molto apropriata alla lingua latina, perché la propagazione dello Imperio Romano l'ha fatta non solamente comune per tutto il mondo, ma quasi necessaria. E per questo concluderemo che queste laude externe e che dependono dall'oppinione degli altri o dalla fortuna non sieno laude proprie.

E però, volendo provare la degnità della lingua nostra, solamente dobbiamo insistere nelle prime condizioni e vedere se la lingua nostra facilmente exprime qualunque concetto della nostra mente; e a questo nessuna migliore ragione si può introducere che l'experienzia. Dante, il Petrarca e il Boccaccio, nostri poeti fiorentini, hanno, nelli gravi e dolcissimi versi e orazioni loro, mostro assai chiaramente con molta facilità potersi in questa lingua exprimere ogni senso. Perché, chi legge la *Comedia* di Dante vi troverrà molte cose teologiche e naturali essere con grande destrezza e facilità expresse; troverrà ancora molto attamente nello scrivere suo quelle tre generazioni di stili che sono dagli oratori laudati, cioè umile, mediocre e alto; e in effetto, in uno solo, Dante ha assai perfettamente absoluto quello che in diversi auttori, così greci come latini, si truova. Chi negherà nel Petrarca trovarsi uno stile grave, lepido e dolce, e queste cose amorose con tanta gravità e venustà trattate, quanta sanza dubio non si truova in Ovidio, Tibullo, Catullo, Properzio o alcuno altro latino? Le

presses many natural, moral and metaphysical sciences, very necessary to the human race. And when this is the case, it must be sooner confessed that the subject rather than the language is worthy, because the subject is the end and the language is the means. Also because of this one cannot call that language more perfect in itself, but rather of greater perfection owing to the material treated by it. Because whoever has written of theological, metaphysical, moral, and natural matters dignifies to that degree the language in which he has written, it seems that the praise ought sooner be accorded the matter and that the language has performed the office of instrument, which is good or wicked according to its objective.

There remains only one other condition that gives a language its reputation, and this occurs when the result of worldly events is such that it makes universal and almost common to all the world that [language] that is naturally characteristic either of a single city or of a province. And this can more readily be called felicity and prosperity of fortune than a true advantage of the language, because a language's being valued and highly celebrated in the world consists in the opinion of those who prize and esteem it. Neither can that good be called true or characteristic that depends on others rather than upon itself—since those who prize it could easily disdain it and change their opinions, and those conditions could change by which, if the occasion were lacking, the dignity and praise of the language could easily also be lacking. Such a dignity as this of being prized for a felicitous event of fortune is very applicable to the Latin language, because the expansion of the Roman Empire not only made it common through all the world, but also almost necessary. And owing to this we conclude that these extrinsic advantages and those that depend on the opinions of others or on fortune are not inherent advantages.

And therefore, if we wish to prove the dignity of our language, we need only insist on the principal condition that our language easily express any concept of our minds; and for this one can introduce no better argument than that from experience. Dante, Petrarch and Boccaccio, our Florentine poets, have, in their profound and very sweet verses and discourses, shown very clearly with what great ease every meaning can be expressed in this language. Therefore, whoever reads the *Commedia* of Dante will find many theological and natural matters expressed there with great adroitness and facility. He will find very aptly [expressed] in his writing those three sorts of style that are praised by rhetoricians, that is the low, the middle, and the high. And in effect Dante has very perfectly performed in only one [work] that which one finds in several authors, both Greek and Roman. Who will deny that in Petrarch one finds a style at once serious, sprightly, and sweet, and finds those amorous matters treated with gravity and stylistic grace—as much, indubitably, as one finds in Ovid,

canzone e sonetti di Dante sono di tanta gravità, subtilità e ornato, che quasi non hanno comparazione. In prosa e orazione soluta, chi ha letto il Boccaccio, uomo dottissimo e facundissimo, facilmente giudicherà singulare e sola al mondo non solamente la invenzione, ma la copia et eloquenzia sua; e considerando l'opera sua del *Decameron,* per la diversità della materia, ora grave, ora mediocre e ora bassa, e contenente tutte le perturbazioni che agli uomini possono accadere, d'amore e odio, timore e speranza, tante nuove astuzie e ingegni, e avendo a exprimere tutte le nature e passioni degli uomini che si trovano al mondo, sanza controversia giudicherà nessuna lingua meglio che la nostra essere atta a exprimere. E Guido Cavalcanti, di chi di sopra facemmo menzione, non si può dire quanto commodamente abbi insieme coniunto la gravità e la dolcezza, come mostra la canzona sopra detta e alcuni sonetti e ballate sue dolcissime. Restono ancora molti altri gravi et eleganti scrittori, la menzione de' quali lasceremo più tosto per fuggire la prolissità, che perché non ne sieno degni. E però concluderemo più tosto essere mancati alla lingua uomini che la essercitino, che la lingua agli uomini e alla materia; la dolcezza e armonia della quale, a chi per essersi assuefatto con essa ha con lei qualche consuetudine, veramente è grandissima e atta molto a muovere.

Queste, che sono e che forse a qualcuno potrebbono pure parere proprie laude della lingua, mi paiono assai copiosamente nella nostra. E per quello che insino a ora *maxime* da Dante è suto trattato nella opera sua, mi pare non solamente utile, ma necessario, per li gravi e importanti effetti, che li versi suoi sieno letti, come mostra lo essemplo per molti comenti fatti sopra la sua *Comedia* da uomini dottissimi e famosissimi, e le frequenti allegazioni che da santi et excellenti uomini ogni dì si sentono nelle loro publiche predicazioni. E forse saranno ancora scritte in questa lingua cose subtili e importante e degne d'essere lette, *maxime* perchè insino a ora si può dire essere l'adolescenzia di questa lingua, perché ogni ora più si fa

Tibullus, Catullus, and Propertius or some other Latin author? The songs and sonnets of Dante are of such seriousness, refinement, and adornment that they have almost no equal. In prose and in discourse, whoever has read Boccaccio, a very learned and productive man, will easily discern that not only is his invention unique and remarkable, but also that his fluency and eloquence are as well. And, if one considers his work in the *Decameron*, for the diversity of the material, now profound, now ordinary, and now low, considers the way it contains all the difficulties of love and hate, fear and hope, so many new artful dodges and contrivances,[17] and its having to express all the personalities and passions of the people that one finds in the world, without controversy one will judge no language better suited than our own for expressing them. And Guido Cavalcanti, of whom we made mention above—one cannot readily say how well he has joined together gravity and sweetness, as the above-mentioned canzone ["A lady entreats me..."] and some of his very sweet sonnets and ballads reveal. There still remain many serious and elegant writers whose mention we shall pass over rather to avoid prolixity than because they are undeserving of note.[18] And therefore we conclude that the persons who employ the language are in short supply, rather than that the language is unsuitable for the people or the subject matter. The sweetness and harmony of the language are truly very great and suited to be very moving for anyone who, by being accustomed to it, has some practice in it.

These, which are the advantages—and which perhaps could even seem to some the inherent advantages—of language, seem to me to be very abundant in our tongue. And because of what until now has been treated principally by Dante in his works,[19] it seems to me not only useful, but also necessary because of its serious and important concerns, that his poetry be read, as the example of many comments made upon his *Commedia* by very learned and very famous men reveals,[20] as do the frequent allusions that one hears every day from holy and excellent men in their public sermons. And perhaps there are also written in this tongue refined and important matters worthy of being read, particularly because, up until now, this language can be said to be in its adolescence, because it is always

---

[17] Ital. *astuzie e ingegni*.

[18] Here L. is more generous than his model, *Ep. Rac.*, which notes a great difference between Dante and Petrarch and all the others. See Bigi, 7.

[19] Especially the *Convivio*. Like Dante, Lorenzo here considers the famous *questione della lingua*—the debate concerning the worthiness of the vernacular tongue to express elevated subject matter and feeling.

[20] Among whom principally Cristoforo Landino (1424–98), a Neoplatonic commentator and interpreter of the *Commedia* and a frequent visitor at the Medici court.

elegante e gentile; e potrebbe facilmente, nella iuventù e adulta età sua, venire ancora in maggiore perfezzione, e tanto più aggiugnendosi qualche prospero successo e augumento al fiorentino imperio: come si debbe non solamente sperare, ma con tutto l'ingegno e forze per li buoni cittadini aiutare; pure, questo, per essere in potestà della fortuna e nella voluntà dello infallibile iudicio di Dio, come non è bene affermarlo, non è ancora da disperarsene. Basta, per al presente, fare questa conclusione: che di quelle laude che sono proprie della lingua, la nostra ne è assai bene copiosa; né giustamente ce ne possiamo dolere. E per queste medesime ragioni nessuno mi può riprendere se io ho scritto in quella lingua nella quale io sono nato e nutrito, *maxime* perché e la ebrea e la greca e la latina erono nello tempo loro tutte lingue materne e naturali, ma parlate o scritte più accuratamente e con qualche regola o ragione da quelli che ne sono in onore e in prezzo, che generalmente dal vulgo e turba populare.

Pare con assai sufficienti ragioni provato la lingua nostra non essere inferiore ad alcuna delle altre; e però, avendo in genere dimostro la perfezzione d'essa, giudico molto conveniente ristrignersi al particulare e venire dalla generalità a qualche proprietà, quasi come dalla circumferenzia al centro. E però, sendo mio primo proposito la interpetrazione de' miei sonetti, mi sforzerò mostrare, tra gli altri modi delli stili vulgari e consueti per chi ha scritto in questa lingua, lo stile del sonetto non essere inferiore o al ternario o alla canzona o ad altra generazione di stile vulgare, arguendo dalla difficultà: perché la virtù, secondo e filosofi, consiste circa el difficile.

È sentenzia di Platone che il narrare brevemente e dilucidamente molte cose non solo pare mirabile tra gli uomini, ma quasi cosa divina. La brevità del sonetto non comporta che una sola parola sia vana, e il vero subietto e materia de' sonetti, per questa ragione, debba essere qualche acuta e gentile sentenzia, narrata attamente e in pochi versi ristretta, fuggendo la obscurità e durezza. Ha grande similitudine e conformità questo modo di

becoming more elegant and noble. And both in its youth and its adulthood, it could still easily reach major perfection, and much more so if some propitious event and the growth of the Florentine empire as well join forces with it—as one must not only hope, but also must strive for with all one's talent and strength on behalf of the good citizens. Since this growth, however, is in the power of Fortune and at the option of the infallible judgment of God, it is good neither to affirm it, nor yet to despair of its happening. It is enough, for the present, to draw this conclusion: that of those advantages that are inherent in a language, ours is very abundantly and well supplied, and we cannot justly complain about it. And for these same reasons, no one can reprove me if I have written in that language in which I have been born and nurtured, especially since Hebrew, Greek, and Latin were in their time all natural and vernacular mother tongues, but tongues spoken or written more accurately and with some rule or reason by those who are honored and esteemed, rather than more generally by the common masses and crowd.

It seems that I have proved with very sufficient arguments that our language is not inferior to any of the others. And therefore, having demonstrated its perfection in general, I consider it very fitting to limit myself to particulars and to come from generality to certain properties, almost as from the circumference to the center. And therefore, the interpretation of my sonnets being my first objective, I shall be obliged to show, among the other modes of the vernacular styles and customs of whoever has written in this language, that the style of the sonnet is not inferior to tercets[21] or to the canzone or to some other genre of vernacular style, arguing from [the point of view of its] difficulty—because merit, according to the philosophers, keeps company with the difficult.[22]

It is the judgment of Plato that recounting many things briefly and lucidly not only seems admirable among men, but almost something divine. The brevity of the sonnet does not allow even one word to be wasted, and the true subject and material of sonnets, for this reason, must be some pointed and noble wisdom, aptly narrated and compressed into a few lines, [and] avoiding obscurity and dissonance. This sort of style has a

---

[21] L. uses Ital. "*ternario*" (tercet) for the extended terza rima of Dante's *Commedia*. L. does not mean a poem written in a trisyllabic line with a metrical pattern like the nursery rhyme "to màrket/to màrket," which Dante in *De vulg. elo.* 2, 12, 8, found little adapted to the tragic style.

[22] See Plato, *Rep.* 2, 364a, and *Laws*, 4, 718e where he cites Hesiod: "In front of goodness the immortal gods/ Have set the sweat of toil, and thereunto/ Long is the road and steep, and rough withal/ The first ascent. . ." in *Plato with an English Translation*, 2 vols, trans. R. G. Bury (London: William Heinemann, 1926) 2: 303.

stile con lo epigramma, quanto allo acume della materia e alla destrezza dello stile, ma è degno e capace il sonetto di sentenzie più gravi, e però diventa tanto più difficile. Confesso il ternario essere più alto e grande stile, e quasi simile allo eroico; né per questo però più difficile, perché ha il campo più largo, e quella sentenzia che non si può ristrignere in due o in tre versi sanza vizio di chi scrive, nel ternario si può ampliare. Le canzone mi pare abbino grande similitudine con la elegia; ma credo, o per natura dello stile nostro o per la consuetudine di chi ha scritto insino a qui canzone, lo stile della canzona non sanza qualche poco di pudore ammetterebbe molte cose non solamente leggieri e vane, ma troppo molle e lascive, le quali comunemente si trovano scritte nelle latine elegie. Le canzone ancora, per avere più larghi spazii dove possino vagare, non reputo tanto difficile stile quanto quello del sonetto; e questo si può assai facilmente provare con la experienzia, perché chi ha composto sonetti e s'è ristretto a qualche certa e subtile materia, con grande difficultà ha fuggito la obscurità e durezza dello stile; et è grande differenzia dal comporre sonetti in modo che le rime sforzino la materia, a quello che la materia sforzi le rime. E' mi pare ne' versi latini sia molto maggiore libertà che non è ne' vulgari, perché nella lingua nostra, oltre a' piedi, che più tosto per natura che per altra regola è necessario servare ne' versi, concorre ancora questa difficultà delle rime; la quale, come sa chi l'ha provato, disturba molte e belle sentenzie, né permette si possino narrare con tanta facilità e chiarezza. E che il nostro verso abbia e suoi piedi si prova perché si potrebbono fare molti versi contenenti undici sillabe, sanza avere suono di versi o alcun'altra differenzia dalla prosa. Concluderemo per questo il verso vulgare essere molto difficile, e, tra gli altri versi, lo stile del sonetto difficillimo, e per questo degno d'essere in prezzo quanto alcuno degli altri stili vulgari. Né per questo voglio inferire li miei sonetti essere di quella perfezzione che ho detto convenirsi a tal modo di stile; ma, come dice Ovidio di Phetonte, per al presente mi basta avere tentato quello stile che appresso e vulgari è più excellente, e se non ho potuto aggiugnere alla perfezzione sua o conducere questo curro solare, almanco mi sia in luogo di laude lo ardire d'avere tentato questa via, ancora che con qualche mio mancamento le forze mi sieno mancate a tanta impresa.

great similarity to and conformity with the epigram, as far as the insight of its material and the dexterity of its style are concerned, but the sonnet is worthy and capable of the most serious pronouncements and therefore becomes vastly more difficult. I confess *terza rima* to be a higher and grander style, and almost like the heroic. Not for this reason, however, is it more difficult because it has a larger scope, and that pronouncement that a writer cannot compress into two or three lines without defect, he can expand in *terza rima*. It seems to me that canzoni are very much like the elegy. But either because of the nature of our style or of the usage of those who until now have written canzoni, I think that the style of the canzone would, not without a little shame, admit many matters not only light and vain, but matters too soft and lascivious, which one often finds written in Latin elegies. The canzone, moreover, by having wider spaces in which to wander, is not considered as difficult in style as the sonnet. And this one can very easily demonstrate from experience, because whoever has composed sonnets and been restricted to some certain and subtle material, has with great difficulty escaped obscurity and harshness of style. And there is a great difference between composing sonnets in a way in which the rhymes control the material, and in a way in which the material controls the rhymes. And there seems to me to be much greater freedom in Latin lines than in the vernacular, because in our language, besides the metrical feet that, rather by nature than by other rules, one must preserve in the lines, this difficulty of rhyme also occurs. [This difficulty], as anyone who has tried it knows, not only interferes with many a beautiful sentiment, but it also does not allow one to be able to narrate with great facility and clarity. And that our verse has its own meter is proved because many lines can be composed containing eleven syllables without having the sound of verses or of being any different from prose. From this we conclude vernacular verse to be very difficult, and, among the other genres, the style of the sonnet the most difficult, and therefore worthy of being as highly regarded as any of the other vernacular styles. I do not wish to infer from this that my sonnets are of that perfection that I have said belongs to such a stylistic genre; but, as Ovid said of Phaeton, for the present it is enough to have attempted that one that is the most excellent among the vernacular styles, and if I have not been able to achieve his [Phaeton's] perfection or to drive this solar chariot, at least I may deserve a place of merit for having attempted this way, even if among my failings I lack the strengths for such a great enterprise.[23]

---

[23] In his defense of the sonnet against the ode, L. disagrees with Dante. In *De vulg. elo.*, 2,3,2–6 and 4,1, Dante consigns the sonnet to the middle style.

Parrà forse suto questo nostro proemio e troppo prolisso e maggiore preparazione che non è in sé lo effetto. A me pare non sanza vera necessità essere suto alquanto copioso, e, considerando la inezzia di questi miei versi, ho giudicato abbino bisogno di qualche ornamento, el quale si conviene a quelle cose che per loro natura sono poco ornate; né si conveniva minore excusazione alle colpe che forse mi sarebbono sute attribuite. E però, absoluta questa parte, verremo alla exposizione de' sonetti, fatto prima alquanto di argumento, che pare necessario a questi primi quattro sonetti.

[Argumento]

Forse qualcuno giudicherà poco conveniente principio a' versi miei cominciando non solamente fuora della consuetudine di quelli che insino a qui hanno scritto simili versi, ma, come pare *prima facie*, pervertendo quasi l'ordine della natura, mettendo per principio quello che in tutte le cose umane suole essere ultimo fine; perché li primi quattro sonetti furono da me composti per la morte d'una donna, che non solo extorse questi sonetti da me, ma le lacrime universalmente dagli occhi di tutti gli uomini e donne che di lei ebbono alcuna notizia. E però, non obstante che paia cosa molto absurda cominciando io dalla morte, a me pare principio molto conveniente, per le ragioni che diremo appresso.

È sentenzia de' buoni filosofi la corruzzione d'una cosa essere creazione d'un'altra e il termine e fine d'uno male essere grado e principio d'un altro. E questo di necessità adviene, perché, essendo la forma e spezie, secondo e filosofi, inmortale, di necessità conviene sempre si muova sopra la materia; e di questo perpetuo moto necessariamente nasce una continua generazione di cose nuove, la quale essendo sanza intermissione di tempo alcuno e con una brevissima presenzia dello essere delle cose e dello stato

Perhaps this introduction of ours will seem too prolix and a greater introduction than the text itself. To me it seems truly necessary for it to have been thus copious, and, considering the inconsequentiality of these verses of mine,[24] I decided they had need of some ornament, which suits those things that by their nature are little ornamented, and neither were minor apologies adequate for the faults that perhaps might have been attributed to me. And therefore, as this part is completed, we shall pass on to the exposition of the sonnets, having first made whatever argument seems necessary to these first four.

[Argument]

Perhaps someone will deem the beginning of my verses to be unfitting by commencing not only outside the usual practice of those who have until now written similar verses, but, as it seems *prima facie,* one almost perverting the order of nature, in placing at the beginning that which in all human things is usually the ultimate end. For I wrote the first four sonnets about a lady's death,[25] which not only wrung these sonnets forth from me, but universally drew tears from the eyes of all the men and women who had any knowledge of her. And therefore, notwithstanding that my beginning with death seems very absurd, it seems to me a very fitting beginning for the reasons that we shall give hereafter.

It is the judgment of good philosophers that the corruption of one thing is the creation of another, and the termination and end of one bad thing, to be the first step and the beginning of another.[26] And this comes to pass of necessity, because, since, according to the philosophers, form and species are immortal, by necessity it is proper for them always to pass through matter. And from this perpetual motion is necessarily born a continual generation of new things, which occurs without the intermission of any time and with such a very brief presence of the existence of the thing

---

[24] Here Lorenzo imitates Petrarca, who calls his vernacular poems *nugae*—trifles. See Francesco Petrarca, *Letters on Familiar Matters,* trans., Aldo Bernardo, 3 vols., (Baltimore: The Johns Hopkins Press, 1985), 3: 86.

[25] Traditionally thought to be Simonetta Cattaneo, born at Genoa about 1453 and married in 1468 to Marco di Piero Vespucci of Florence. Pictured in Botticelli's *Birth of Venus* as the holder of Venus' cloak, and perhaps in his *Primavera* as one of the three graces, and portrayed by Piero di Cosimo, Simonetta was rumored to be the Mistress of Lorenzo's brother Giuliano, she died on the 26th of April, 1476. Lipari, 62, preferring an allegorical reading of the *Commentary,* questions this identification.

[26] On the immortality of matter and its continual transformation into new things, see Marsilio Ficino, *Theologiae Platonicae* IV, in *Opera Omnia,* 2 vols. (Turin: Bottega D'Erasmo, 1962) 1: 152 (132), ff.

d'esse in quella tale qualità o forma, bisogna confessare il fine d'una cosa essere principio d'un'altra; e, secondo Aristotile, la privazione è principio delle cose create. E per questo si conclude nelle cose umane fine e principio essere una medesima cosa: non dico già fine e principio d'una cosa medesima, ma quello che è fine d'una cosa, *inmediate* è principio d'un'altra. E, se questo è, molto convenientemente la morte è principio a questa nostra opera. E tanto più, perché chi essamina più sottilmente troverrà il principio della amorosa vita procedere dalla morte, perchè chi vive ad amore muore prima all'altre cose; e se lo amore ha in sé quella perfezzione che già abbiamo detto, è impossibile venire a tale perfezzione se prima non si muore quanto alle cose più imperfette. Questa medesima sentenzia pare che abbino seguito Omero, Virgilio e Dante, delli quali Omero manda Ulisse apresso alli inferi, Virgilio Enea, e Dante lui medesima perlustra lo inferno, per mostrare che alla perfezzione si va per questa via. Ma è necessario, dopo la cognizione delle cose imperfette, quanto a quelle morire: perché, poi che Enea è giunto a' campi elisii e Dante condotto in paradiso, mai più si sono ricordati dello inferno; e arebbe Orfeo tratto Euridice dello inferno e condottola tra quelli che vivono, se non fussi rivoltosi verso lo inferno: che si può interpetrare Orfeo non essere veramente morto, e per questo non essere agiunto alla perfezzione della felicità sua, di avere la sua cara Euridice. E però il principio della vera vita è la morte della vita non vera; né per questo pare posto sanza qualche buono respetto la morte per principio de' versi nostri.

Morì, come di sopra dicemmo, nella città nostra una donna, la quale se mosse a compassione generalmente tutto il popolo fiorentino, non è gran maraviglia, perchè di bellezze e gentilezze umane era veramente ornata quanto alcuna che inanzi a·llei fussi suta; e, infra l'altre sue excellenti dote, aveva così dolce e attrattiva maniera, che tutti quelli che con lei avevono qualche domestica notizia credevono da essa sommamente essere amati. Le donne ancora e giovane sue equali non solamente di questa sua excellenzia tra l'altre non avevono invidia alcuna, ma sommamente essaltavono e

and of its state of being in that particular quality or form, that one must confess the end of one thing to be the beginning of another. And, according to Aristotle,[27] deprivation is the beginning of created things. And from this one concludes that in human affairs the end and the beginning are the same thing. I do not say indeed that they are the end and the beginning of the same thing, but that what is the end of one thing is *immediately* the beginning of another. And, if this is the case, death is most fittingly the beginning for this work of ours. And much more so because, whoever considers it very subtly will find that the beginning of the amorous life proceeds from death, because whoever is alive to love first dies to other things.[28] And if love has in itself that perfection of which we have already spoken, it is impossible to come to such perfection without first dying to the more imperfect things. This same wisdom it seems, was followed by Homer, Virgil and Dante, among whom Homer sent Ulysses among the shades, Virgil sent Aeneas, and Dante himself explored the inferno, to show that one must go toward perfection by this path. But it is necessary, after recognizing some imperfect things, to die with respect to them; because, after Aeneas arrived at the Elysian Fields, and Dante was led to Paradise, never more do they remember the underworld. And Orpheus would have drawn Eurydice forth from hell and led her among the living, if he had not turned back toward the underworld. For Orpheus can be interpreted to be not truly dead, and because of this not to have arrived at the perfection of his happiness, of having his dear Eurydice. And therefore the principle of real life is the death of the life that is unreal. Because of this, employing death as the beginning of our verses seems not without some merit.

There died in our city,[29] as we said above, a lady, whose death moved to compassion generally the entire Florentine people. It is not a great marvel, because she was truly endowed with as much beauty and human nobility as anyone who had lived before her. And, among her other excellent gifts, she used to have such a sweet and attractive manner, that all those who had any familiar dealing with her believed themselves exceedingly loved by her. Matrons and young women of her own age as well not only did not envy, among other [qualities], this her most excellent virtue, but they exalted and praised exceedingly her beauty and nobility—in such

---

[27] Cf. *Physics*, vol. I, 9.

[28] See *FC*, 2,8, 143: "Plato calls love 'something bitter' and correctly so, because whoever loves dies....for his consciousness, oblivious of himself is devoted exclusively to the loved one."

[29] Illustrating his own principle of beginning the exposition of his sonnets with death, Lorenzo chooses as the first word of this section, "*Morì*."

laudavono la biltà e gentilezza sua: per modo che impossibile pareva a credere che tanti uomini sanza gelosia l'amassino e tante donne sanza invidia la laudassino. E se bene la vita sua, per le sue degnissime condizioni, a tutti la facessi carissima, pure la compassione della morte, e per la età molto verde e per la bellezza che, così morta, forse più che mai alcuna viva mostrava, lasciò di lei uno ardentissimo desiderio. E perché da casa al luogo della sepoltura fu portata scoperta, a tutti che concorsono per vederla mosse grande copia di lacrime: de' quali, in quelli che prima n'avevono alcuna notizia, oltre alla compassione nacque ammirazione che lei nella morte avesse superato quella bellezza che, viva, pareva insuperabile; in quelli che prima non la conoscevano, nasceva uno dolore e quasi rimordimento di non avere conosciuto sì bella cosa prima che ne fussino al tutto privati, e allora conosciutola per overne perpetuo dolore. Veramente in lei si verificava quello che dice il nostro Petrarca: «Morte bella parea nel suo bel volto».

Essendo adunque questa tale così morta, tutti e fiorentini ingegni, come si conveniva in tale publica iattura, diversamente e si dolsono, chi in versi e chi in prosa, della acerbità di questa morte, e si sforzorono laudarla, ciascuno secondo la facultà del suo ingegno; tra li quali io ancora volsi essere e accompagnare le lacrime loro con li infrascritti sonetti, de' quali il primo comincia così:

I

O chiara stella, che coi raggi tuoi
togli alle tue vicine stelle il lume,
perché splendi assai più che 'l tuo costume?
Perché con Phebo ancor contender vuoi?
    Forse i belli occhi, quali ha tolti a noi
Morte crudel, che omai troppo presume,
accolti hai in te: adorna del lor nume,
il suo bel carro a Phebo chieder puoi.
    O questo o nuova stella che tu sia,
che di splendor novello adorni il cielo,
chiamata essaudi, o nume, i voti nostri:
    leva dello splendor tuo tanto via,
che agli occhi, che han d'eterno pianto zelo,
sanza altra offensïon lieta ti mostri.

a fashion that it seemed impossible to think that so many men could love her without jealousy and that so many women could praise her without envy. And although her life, by its most worthy circumstances made her very dear to everyone, yet when she died thus, because of her youth and her beauty, the pity of her death showed that perhaps more than anyone who had ever lived, she left a most ardent yearning behind her. And because she was borne uncovered from her house to the place of her burial, all those who gathered to see her were moved to shed an abundance of tears. In those of them who had known her earlier, beyond compassion, admiration was born that in death she had surpassed that beauty that in life seemed unsurpassable. Those who had not known her before felt such a sorrow and almost a remorse at not having known such a beautiful person before everyone had been deprived of her, and then at having known her only to suffer eternal sorrow because of it. Truly verified in her was what our Petrarch says: "Death seemed lovely in her lovely face."[30]

As she was thus dead, then, all the Florentine wits, as is fitting for such a public loss, variously mourned, some in verses and some in prose, for the bitterness of this death, and each one felt compelled to praise her according to his ability and talent. Among these, I also set about doing it and about joining my tears with theirs in the sonnets written below, the first of which begins thus:

1

O brilliant star, which with your rays make fade
The light of all your neighboring stars, why now
Do you shine brighter than your custom is?
Why do you wish with Phoebus to contend?
  Those lovely eyes, perhaps, which cruel Death,
Who until now presumes too much, has reft from us
You've welcomed to yourself: decked with their glory,
From Phoebus his fair car you can demand.
  If this, or if a new star you've become,
Which with fresh glory so adorns the heavens,
When called upon, o saint, please grant our prayers:
  Abate your splendor, so to eyes that yearn
To weep eternally for you, without more harm
You, joyful, can reveal yourself to us.

---

[30] *Tr. M.*, 1, 172.

Era notte e andavamo insieme parlando di questa comune iattura uno carissimo amico mio e io; e così parlando, et essendo il tempo molto sereno, voltavamo gli occhi a una chiarissima stella, la quale verso l'occidente si vedeva, di tanto splendore certamente, che non solamente di gran lunga l'altre stelle superava, ma era tanto lucida, che faceva fare qualche ombra a quelli corpi che a tale luce s'opponevono. E, avendone di principio ammirazione, io, vòlto a questo mio amico, dissi: — Non ce ne maravigliamo, perché l'anima di quella gentilissima o è transformata in questa nuova stella o si è coniunta con essa; e, se questo è, non pare mirabile questo splendore. E però, come fu la bellezza sua, viva, di gran conforto agli occhi nostri, confortiamogli al presente con la visione di questa chiarissima stella; e se la vista nostra è debole e frale a tanta luce, preghiamo el nume, cioè la divinità sua, che li fortifichi, levando una parte di tanto splendore, per modo che sanza offensione degli occhi la possiamo alquanto contemplare. E per certo, essendo ornata della bellezza di colei, non è presuntuosa volendo vincere di splendore l'altre stelle, ma ancora potrebbe contendere con Phebo e domandarli il suo carto, per essere auttrice lei del giorno. E, se questo è, che sanza presunzione questa stella possi fare questo, grandissima presunzione è suta quella della morte, avendo manomessa tanta excellentissima bellezza e virtù.—

—Parendomi questi ragionamenti assai buona materia a uno sonetto, mi parti' da quello amico mio e composi il presente sonetto, nel quale parlo alla sopra detta stella.

II

Quando il sol giù dall'orizzonte scende,
rimiro Clyzia pallida nel vólto,
e piango la sua sorte, che li ha tolto
la vista di colui che ad altri splende.
Poi, quando di novella fiamma accende
l'erbe, le piante e' fior' Phebo, a noi vòlto,
l'altro orizzonte allor ringrazio molto
e la benigna Aurora che gliel rende.
Ma, lasso, io non so già qual nuova Aurora
renda al mondo il suo Sole! Ah, dura sorte,
che noi vestir d'eterna notte volse!
O Clyzia, indarno speri vederlo ora!
Tien' li occhi fissi, infin li chiugga morte,
all'orizzonte extremo che tel tolse.

It was night and a very dear friend of mine and I were walking together and speaking of this common loss. And as we spoke thus, and as the weather was very clear, we turned our eyes to a most brilliant star, which was seen toward the west [shining] with such a great splendor, certainly, that not only did it far surpass the other stars, but it was so luminous that it cast some shadow on those bodies that opposed themselves to such a light. And from the first marvelling at it, I, turning to this friend of mine, remarked: "There is nothing for us to marvel at, because the soul of that most noble lady either has been transformed into this new star or has been joined with it. And, if this is the case, this splendor does not seem marvelous. And therefore, as her beauty, while she lived, was of great comfort to our eyes, at present we comfort them with the sight of this exceedingly brilliant star. And if our sight is weak and frail in such great light, we implore her pneuma, that is, her divinity, that it may strengthen our eyes, diminishing a part of such great splendor, so that, without harming our eyes, we may contemplate her for a while. And certainly, since it is adorned with her beauty, its wishing to outdo the other stars in glory is not presumptuous, for she could even contend with Phoebus and demand his chariot from him in order to be the authoress of the day. And, if it is the case that the star can do this without presumption, it has been a very great presumption on the part of death to have wasted such exceptional beauty and virtue."

As these discourses seemed to me very good material for a sonnet, I parted from that friend of mine and composed the present sonnet in which I address the above mentioned star.

2

When, from the far horizon, sinks the sun,
I gaze again on Clytie's pallid face,
And I lament the fate that snatched away
From her the sight of one who elsewhere shines.
    When with new flame, then, Phoebus, back with us,
Sets grass and plants and flowers all alight,
The alternate horizon much I thank,
And thank kind Dawn who gives him back again.
    But, woe! I know not what new Dawn can give
The world its sun again! Ah, cruel fate,
Which wished to clothe us in eternal night!
    O Clytie, vain your hope to see him now:
Until death close your eyes, fix them upon
The far horizon that took him away.

Morì questa excellentissima donna del mese d'aprile, nel quale tempo la terra si suole vestire di diverse colori di fiori, molto vaghi agli occhi e di grande recreazione all'animo. Mosso io da questo piacere, per certi miei amenissimi prati solo e pensoso passeggiavo, e, tutto occupato nel pensiero e memoria di colei, pareva che tutte le cose reducessi a suo proposito. E però, guardando tra fiore e fiore, vidi tra gli altri quello piccolo fiore che vulgarmente chiamiamo "tornalsole" e da' Latini detto *clytia;* nel quale fiore, secondo Ovidio, si transformò una ninfa, Clyzia chiamata, la quale amò con tanta veemenzia e ardore il sole, che così, conversa in fiore, sempre al sole si rivolge e tanto quanto può questo suo amato vagheggia. Rimirando io adunque questo amoroso fiore, pallido come è natura degli amanti e perché veramente il fiore è di colore pallido, perché è giallo e bianco, mi venne compassione della sorte sua; perché, essendo già vicino alla sera, pensavo che presto perderebbe la dolcissima visione dello amato suo, perché già il sole s'apressava al nostro orizzonte, che privava Clyzia della sua amata vista; el dolore della quale era ancora maggiore, perché quello che era negato a'llei era comune a molti altri, cioè agli occhi di coloro che sono chiamata "antipodi," a' quali splende il sole quando noi ne siamo privati e la notte de' quali a noi fa giorno. Da questo pensiero entrai in uno altro: che, se bene lei per una notte perdeva questa diletta visione, almanco la mattina seguente gli era concesso el rivederla, perché, come l'orizzonte occidentale gliele toglie, l'orientale gliele rende, e la benigna Aurora, piatosa allo amore di Clyzia, di nuovo gliele mostra; e io ancora ringrazio per questo l'orientale orizzonte che gliel rende, perché è cosa molto naturale e umana avere compassione agli afflitti, *maxime* a quelli che hanno qualche similitudine d'afflizzione con noi. Questa sorte di Clyzia, diversa e alterna, mi fece dipoi pensare quanto era più dura e

This most excellent lady died in the month of April, in which time the earth is customarily clothed in various colors of flowers, very appealing to the eyes and very restorative to the mind. Moved by this pleasure, I went walking alone and lost in thought[31] through certain of my very agreeable meadows, and, entirely occupied with thoughts and memories of her, it seemed that everything was reduced to her.[32] And therefore, looking from flower to flower, I saw among the others that little flower that in the vernacular we call "sunflower" and by the Latins called "*clitia.*" Into that flower, according to Ovid,[33] was transformed a nymph named Clytie, who loved the Sun with such great vehemence and ardor, that, transformed thus into a flower, she always turned toward the sun, and in so far as she was able always gazed fondly upon this her beloved. As I was gazing then upon this amorous flower, pale as is the nature of lovers and because truly, since it is yellow and white, the flower is a pallid color, I felt pity for its fate. For, since it was already almost evening, I thought that soon she would lose the very sweet sight of her beloved, for already the sun was approaching our horizon that was depriving Clytie of her beloved view. The sorrow of this was already great, for that which was denied to her was granted to many others, that is to the eyes of those who are called "antipodeans,"[34] among whom the sun shines when we are deprived of it, and whose night is our day. From this thought I entered into another—that, although she was losing this delightful vision for one night, on the following morning, at least, she would be permitted to see it again, because, as the western horizon takes it from her, the eastern gives it back to her, and kind Dawn, pitying Clytie's love, shows [the Sun] to her again. And I also give thanks for this eastern horizon that brings him back to her, because it is very natural and human to have compassion for the afflicted,[35] especially for those that have some affliction like our own. This fate of Clytie,

---

[31] See *Rvf.*, 36,1. "Alone in thought... I wander...."

[32] Ital. *proposito*. I am grateful to Tiziano Zanato for this clarification.

[33] Ovid, *Metamorphoses*, trans., Frank Justus Miller (New York: G. P. Putnam's Sons, 1916) 2 vols., 2, IV, lines 169–270.

[34] Renaissance moral geography divided the world into eastern and western hemispheres with the east, the direction of the earthly paradise and heaven, at the top. Jerusalem was at the center of the world, and the pillars of Hercules the western extremity. From a European perspective, the antipodes were in the opposite hemisphere, where people necessarily walked with heads upside down and where it was day while in Europe it was night.

[35] Here L. alludes to the opening words of Boccaccio's *Decameron*, "Human it is to have compassion for the afflicted...," trans., John Payne (Berkeley: Univ. of California Press, 1982), 3.

iniqua sorte quella di colui che desidera assai vedere la cosa, il vedere della quale necessariamente gli è interdetto, non per una notte, ma per sempre. Veggo quale Aurora rende a Clyzia il suo sole, ma non so quale altra Aurora renda al mondo questo altro Sole, cioè gli occhi di colei; e se questo Sole non può tornare, di necessità agli occhi di quelli che non hanno altra luce bisogna sia sempre notte, perché non è altro la notte che la privazione del lume del sole; e però durissima sorte è quella di colui che con assai desiderio aspetta quello che non può avere. Né questo tale può avere altro refriggerio che ricordarsi e tenere gli occhi della mente sua fissi a quello che ha più amato e che gli è suto più caro; perché, come credo avenga a Clyzia, che la sera resta vòlta col viso allo orizzonte occidentale, che è quello che gli ha tolta la visione del sole, insino che la mattina el sole la rivolta all'oriente, così questo novello Clyzia non può avere maggiore refriggerio che tenere la mente e il pensiero vòlto all'ultime impressioni e più care cose del suo Sole, che sono a similitudine dello orizzonte occidentale, ché lo hanno privato della sua amata visione. Possiamo ancora dire questo ultimo orizzonte intendersi la morte di questa gentilissima, perché «orizzonte» non vuole dire altro che l'ultimo termine, di là dal quale gli occhi umani non possono vedere: come diciamo, se 'l sole tramonta, quell'ultimo luogo di là dal quale il sole non si vede più, e, quando si leva, il primo luogo dove il sole appare. E però convenientemente possiamo chiamare la morte quell'orizzonte che ne tolse la vista degli occhi suoi; al quale questo nuovo Clyzia, cioè lo amatore degli occhi suoi, debbe tenere gli occhi fissi e fermi, venendo in considerazione che ciascuna cosa mortale, ancora che bella et excellentissima, di necessità muore. E questa tale considerazione suole essere grande et efficace remedio a consolare ogni dolore e a mostrare agli uomini che le cose mortali si debbono amare come cose finite e sottoposte alla necessità della morte. E chi considera questo in altri, può facilmente conoscere questa condizione e necessità in sé medesimo, servando quello sapientissimo detto che nel tempio d'Appolline era scritto, «Nosce te ipsum», perseverando in questo pensiero infino che la morte venga; la quale renderà il Sole suo a questo nuovo Clyzia, come l'Aurora lo rende a Clyzia già convertita in fiore, perché allora l'anima, sciolta dal corpo, potrà considerare la bellezza dell'anima di costei, molto più bella che quella la quale era prima visibile agli occhi: perché la luce degli occhi umani è come ombra respetto alla luce dell'anima. E cosi come la morte di colei è stata orizzonte all'occaso del sole degli occhi suoi, così la morte di questo nuovo Clyzia sarà l'orizzonte orientale che renderà a·llui il suo Sole, come l'Aurora lo rende a Clyzia già conversa in fiore.

strange and different, made me then think how much harder and how unjust was that fate for one who very much desired to see something whose sight was necessarily forbidden him, not for one night, but forever. I see what Dawn gives Clytie back her sun, but I don't know what other Dawn gives back to the world this other sun, that is, her eyes. And, of necessity, if the sun cannot return, it must always be night to the eyes of those who have no other light, because night is nothing other than the absence of the light of the sun. And thus the hardest fate is that of someone who awaits with very great desire that which he cannot have. Neither can someone like this have any solace other than remembering and holding the eyes of his mind fixed on what he has loved most and what has been most dear to him. Because, just as I believe it happens with Clytie, that in the evening she remains turned with her face toward the western horizon, which is the one that has bereft her of the sight of the sun, until the morning sun turns her back again toward the east, so this new Clytie [*i.e.*, the lady's lover] cannot but receive the greatest solace from holding his mind and thought turned toward his dearest concerns with his sun and toward his final impressions, which are like the western horizon, and which have deprived him of his beloved vision. We can also say that this last horizon stands for the death of this most noble lady, since "horizon" means nothing more than the ultimate terminus, beyond which human eyes cannot see, as we say, when the sun sets, the last place from which the sun is seen no more and, when it rises, the first place where the sun appears. And therefore we can fitly call death that horizon that took from us the sight of her eyes, for which this new Clytie, that is the lover of her eyes, must hold his eyes fixed and firm, taking into consideration that every mortal thing, even though it be beautiful and most excellent, of necessity dies. And such a consideration as this usually is a great and efficacious remedy for consoling every sorrow and for showing men that mortal things must be loved as things finite and subject to the necessity of death. And whoever considers this in others can easily understand this condition and necessity in himself, observing that very wise saying that was written in the temple of Apollo, "know thyself," [and] persevering in this thought until death comes, which will restore his sun to this new Clytie, as the Dawn restores [it] to [that] Clytie already converted to a flower. For then the soul, released from the body, will be able to consider the beauty of her spirit, much more lovely than that which before was visible to the eyes, because the light of human eyes is like a shadow with respect to the light of the soul. And so as her death has been the horizon at the setting azimuth of the sun in her eyes, so the death of this new Clytie will be the eastern horizon that will restore his sun to him, as the Dawn restores him to Clytie already transformed into a flower.

Questo pensiero adunque parendomi fussi assai conveniente materia da mettere in versi, feci il presente sonetto.

III

Di vita il dolce lume fuggirei
a quella vita che altri "morte" appella,
ma morte è sì gentile oggi e sì bella,
ch'io credo che morir vorran li dèi.
    Morte è gentil, poich'è stata in colei
che è or del ciel la più lucente stella;
io, che gustar non vo' dolce poi che ella
è morta, seguirò questi anni rei.
    Piangeran sempre gli occhi, e 'l tristo core
sospirerà del suo bel sol l'occaso,
lor di lui privi, e 'l cor d'ogni sua speme.
    Piangerà meco dolcemente Amore,
le Grazie e le sorelle di Parnaso:
e chi non piangeria con queste insieme?

È comunemente natura degli amanti e pasto della amorosa fame pensieri tristi e malinconici, pieni di lacrime e sospiri, e questo comunemente è nella maggiore allegrezza e dolcezza loro. Credo ne sia cagione che lo amore che è solo e diuturno procede da forte inmaginazione, e questo può male essere se l'umore malencolico nello amante non predomina, la natura del quale è sempre avere sospetto e convertire ogni evento, o prospero o adverso, in dolore e passione. Se questa è propria natura degli amanti, certamente il dolore loro è maggiore che quello delli altri uomini quando a questa proptietà naturale si aggiugne accidente per sé doloroso e lacri-

This thought then seeming to me to be material very fitting to be put into verses, I made this sonnet.

3

I would escape the sweet light of my life
To that life which by others is called "death,"[36]
But death's today so noble and so fair
That I believe the gods must wish to die.

Death has grown noble since it's been in her,
For she is now the brightest star of heaven;
Not wishing sweetness, now that she is dead,
I shall live out these wicked years of mine.

My eyes will ever weep, my sad heart sigh
Because their lovely sun has set; bereft
Of it are they, my heart of every hope.

How sweetly Love will weep with me, as will
The Graces, the Parnasan sisters too;
And in such company who would not weep?

It is commonly the nature of lovers and the repast of those hungry for love [to have] sad and melancholy thoughts, full of tears and sighs, and this commonly happens amidst their greatest joy and sweetness. The cause of this I believe to be that a love that is exclusive and long lasting proceeds from a strong imagination, and this can be bad unless the melancholic humor[37] does not predominate in the lover, whose nature is always to be suspicious and to convert every event whether favorable or adverse, into sorrow and passion. If this is the very nature of lovers, certainly their sorrow is greater than that of other men when to this natural propensity are added events that in themselves are sorrowful or pitiful. And no one

---

[36] See Francesco Petrarca, "The Triumph of Death," 1, 171–2, in *The Triumphs of Petrarch*, trans., Ernest Hatch Wilkins (Chicago: Univ. Chicago Press, 1962), 60: "And that which is called 'death' by foolish folk/ Was a sweet sleep upon her Lovely eyes. . . ."

[37] "The psychology of antiquity . . . deduced the principal temperaments from the predominance in the organism of one of the four humors: yellow bile, phlegm, blood and black bile, . . ." (Greek, melaina cholos; hence "melancholy"). "The four elements, the cardinal points [of the compass], the divisions of the day and of human life correspond to those four liquids of the organism." See Ioan P. Couliano, *Eros and Magic in the Renaissance*, trans., Margaret Cook (Chicago: Univ. Chicago Press, 1987), 46–48. Two sorts of melancholy occurred, however. One, "cold" melancholia, arising from a person's natural predisposition, and the other "hot" or sanguinary melancholia, resulting from overheating the blood. It was the second sort which afflicted lovers and of which Lorenzo complains.

moso; e nessuna cosa può accadere allo amante degna di più dolore e lacrime, che la perpetua privazione della cosa amata. Di qui si può presummere quanto dolore dessi la morte di colei a quelli che sommamente l'amavono, che ragionevolmente fu el maggiore che possi provare uno uomo.

È natura de' melancolici, come abbiamo detto essere gli amanti, nel dolore non cercare altro rimedio che accumulazione di dolore e avere in odio e fuggire ogni generazione di refriggerio e consolazione. E però, se qualche volta per rimedio di questo acerbissimo dolore si poneva inanzi agli occhi la morte, in quanto era fine di questa dolorosa passione era odiata da me; e tanto più doveva essere odiata, quanto la morte, per essere stata negli occhi di colei, si poteva stimare più dolce e più gentile, perché essendosi comunicata a una cosa gentilissima, di necessità participava di quella qualità che tanto copiosa aveva trovato in lei. E, pensando quanto per questo fussi fatta gentile la morte, credevo gli iddei inmortali dovere mutare sorte e ancora loro volere gustare la gentilezza della morte. E, se questo era, io, per mia natura desiderando solamente dolore e non gustare alcuna cosa dolce, per più mio dolore eleggevo seguitare questi rei anni della vita, acciò che 'l mio dolore fussi più diuturno e che gli occhi potessino più tempo piangere e il cuore più lungamente sospirare l'occaso, cioè la morte, del mio sole, gli occhi privati della loro dolcissima visione e il cuore d'ogni sua speranza e conforto; piangendo e sospirando in compagnia d'Amore, delle Grazie e delle Muse, a' quali è così conveniente il pianto e il dolore, come agli occhi e al cuore mio. Perché, come gli occhi e 'l cuore hanno perduto quello fine al quale da Amore erono suti ordinati e destinati, così Amore debba ancora lui piangere, perché aveva posto lo imperio e fine suo negli occhi di costei, e le Grazie tutti e doni e virtù loro nella sua bellezza, le Muse la gloria del loro coro in cantare le sue dignissime laude. Adunque convenientemente el pianto a tutti questi conviene; e chi non piangessi con questi, bisogna sia uomo al tutto sanza parte o d'amore o di grazia. E però ciascuno debba piangere, alcuni per non essere, altri per non parere almeno rebelli da tanta gentilezza.

Questi affetti arei voluto exprimere nel presente sonetto.

thing can befall a lover that merits more sorrow and tears than the perpetual absence of the person beloved. From this one can presume how much sorrow her death aroused in those who loved her exceedingly—sorrow that was arguably the greatest a man could stand.

It is the nature of the melancholy, as we have said lovers to be, not to seek any other remedy for sorrow but the accumulation of sorrow [itself] and to hate and to flee every kind of solace and consolation. And, therefore, if sometimes as a remedy for this very bitter sorrow, death was set before my eyes, in so far as it was an end for this dolorous passion, I hated it. And the more one ought to have hated death, the more death, by having been in her eyes, could be thought most sweet and most noble, because, by having been communicated to a most noble creature, of necessity Death had participated in that quality that had been very abundantly found in her.[38] And, thinking how noble death had been made by this, I believed that the immortal gods must alter fate, and that they too [must] desire to taste the nobility of death. And, if this was the case, by my nature desiring only sorrow and not wanting to taste anything sweet, for my greater sorrow I chose to endure these wicked years of life, so that my sorrow would be more lasting and that my eyes could weep a longer time and my heart sigh longer for her setting,[39] that is for the death of my sun, with my eyes deprived of their sweetest sight and my heart of its every hope and comfort—weeping and sighing in the company of Love,[40] of the Graces, and of the Muses, to whom weeping and sorrow are as fitting as they are to my eyes and heart. In fact, as the eyes and the heart have lost that end for which they had been destined and ordained by Love, so Love must also weep himself, because he had established his empire and objective in her eyes, and the Graces all their gifts and their virtues in her beauty, [and] the Muses the glory of their choir in singing her most worthy praises. Then fittingly the tears of all these come together. And whoever would not weep with these must be a man entirely without any trace either of love or grace. And therefore each one must weep, some for not being, others for not seeming at least rebels from such nobility.

These sentiments I wished to express in the present sonnet.

---

[38] Cf. *The Vita Nuova and Canzoniere of Dante Alighieri*, trans., Thomas Okey and Philip H. Wicksteed (London: J. M. Dent and Sons, 1933), 80–81, (canz. 23, lines 72–74): "Dolcissima Morte ... tu dèi essere gentile, in tal parte se' stata." ("Sweetest Death ... [thou] must needs ... have become gentle, in such place has thou been!")

[39] Ital. *occaso*, a poetic word for the setting of the sun.

[40] See *Rvf.*, 25,1: "Love wept and I wept with him too."

IV

    In qual parte andrò io, ch'io non ti truovi,
trista memoria? In quale obscuro speco
fuggirò io, che sempre non sia meco,
trista memoria, che al mio mal sol giovi?
    Se in prato lo qual germini fior' nuovi,
se all'ombra d'arbuscei verdi m'arreco,
veggo un corrente rivo, io piango seco.
Che cosa è, ch'e miei pianti non rinnuovi?
    S'io torno all'infelice patrio nido,
tra mille cure questa in mezzo siede
del cor, che come suo consume e rode.
    Che debb'io fare omai, a che mi fido?
Lasso, che sol sperar posso merzede
da morte, che oramai troppo tardi ode!

    Non si maraviglierà alcuno, il cuore del quale è suto acceso d'amoroso fuoco, trovando in questi versi diverse passioni e affetti molto l'uno all'altro contrarii, perché, non essendo amore altro che una gentile passione, sarebbe più presto maraviglia che uno amante avessi mai punto di quiete o vita uniforme. E però, se ne' nostri e negli altrui amorosi versi spesso si troverrà questa varietà e contradizione di cose, questo è privilegio degli amanti, sciolti da tutte qualitati umane, perché alcuna ragione non se ne può dire, né trovare modo o consiglio in quelle cose che solo la passione regge. Pare il presente sonetto molto contrario al precedente, perché come quello fugge ogni generazione di consolazione e pare si pasca e del presente dolore e della speranza d'averlo ancora maggiore, questo mostra avere cerco diverse ragioni di consolazione, e, se bene indarno, molte cose avere provato perché questa acerbissima memoria della morte di colei fuggissi dall'animo; e in fine mostra qualche desiderio della morte, dal quale el precedente è in tutto alieno.
    Chi sente excessivo dolore, comunemente in due modi fa pruova di mitigarlo, cioè o che qualche cosa amena, dolce e piacevole adolcisca il dolore, o che qualche pensiero grave e importante lo cacci; e comunemente s'elegge prima quello rimedio che è più facile e dolce. E però, sentendo io l'acerbità di questa memoria, andavo cercando o qualche luogo solitario e ombroso o l'amenità di qualche verde prato (come ancora

4

>Where shall I go that I don't find you there,
>Sad memory? To what dark cavern shall
>I flee so you aren't always there with me,
>Sad memory, sole treatment for my ill?
>   If to the meadow where new flowers spring,
>If to the shade of green trees I'm induced,
>And see a flowing stream, I weep it dry:
>What is it that will not renew my tears?
>   If to my sad paternal seat I go,
>Among a thousand cares, this in the midst
>Of my heart sits and gnaws, consumes its own.
>   What must I do now? In whom place my trust?[41]
>Alas! for I can only hope for grace
>From Death, who hates now much too late.

No one whose heart has been burned by amorous fire will be surprised to find in these verses various passions and sentiments very contrary to one another, because, since love is nothing other than a noble passion, it would sooner be a marvel that a lover ever had a quiet moment or a regular life. And therefore, if in our amorous verses and in those of others is often found this variety and contradiction of things, this is a privilege of lovers, set free from every human quality,[42] because neither can any reason be given for it, nor any order or reason be in those things that only passion rules. This sonnet seems much opposed to the preceding one because, just as that one flees every kind of consolation and seems to feed on present sorrow and on the hope of having it greater still, this one appears to have sought various reasons for consolation, and, although in vain, has tried many things to make this very bitter memory of her death flee from the mind. And at last it shows some desire for death, toward which the preceding sonnet is entirely disinclined.

Whoever feels excessive sorrow commonly tries to diminish it in two ways, that is either that some agreeable, sweet and pleasing thing may assuage the sorrow, or that some serious and important thought may drive it away. And commonly that first remedy is chosen since it is easier and more sweet. And therefore, as I was feeling the bitterness of this memory, I went seeking either some place solitary and shady, or the amenity of

---

[41] See *Rvf.* 268,1: "Che debb'io far . . ." ("What must I do. . . .")

[42] See *Rvf.*, 15, 12–14: "Do you not recollect/ That this a privilege of lovers is/Set free from all their human attributes?"

testifica il comento del secondo sonetto), o mi poneva presso a qualche chiara e corrente acqua o all'ombra di qualche verde arbuscello. Ma ‹a me› interveniva come a quello che è agravato d'infermità, el quale, avendo corrotto il gusto, se bene diverse spezie di delicati cibi gli sono amministrati, di tutti cava un medesimo sapore, che converte la dolcezza di que' cibi in amaritudine. Così, quanto più letizia dovevano porgere al cuore mio queste cose diverse e amene, perché il gusto mio era corrotto e l'animo disposto a lacrime, tutte multiplicavono il dolore mio; e la memoria di colei, che in ogni luogo e tempo era presente, mi mostrava con molto maggiore amatitudine che l'ordinario tutte quelle cose. E se bene questa memoria era durissima e molesta, pure, come abbiamo detto dello infermo, el quale se bene e cibi tutti rapportono al gusto amaritudine, pure lo nutriscono e sono cagione che viva, così di questo amarissimo cibo della memoria sua si sostentava la mia vita. E, in effetto, contro a questo male nessuno migliore antidoto o rimedio si trovava che 'l male medesimo; né si poteva vincere quel pensiero se non col medesimo pensiero, perché altra dolcezza non restave al cuore che questa amarissima memoria: e però sola questa giovava al mio male. Essendo adunque necessario ricorrere al secondo rimedio, fuggivo di questi dilettevoli luoghi nel freto e tempesta delle civili occupazioni. Questo rimedio ancora era scarso, perché avendo quella gentilissima preso el dominio del mio cuore e una volta fattolo suo, tra tutti gli altri pensieri el pensiero e memoria di lei stava nel mezzo del cuore, e, a dispetto di tutte l'altre cure, come sua cosa se lo consumava: perché «cura» non vuole dire altro se non quella cosa che arde e consuma 'il cuore. E però, non potendo né con l'uno né con l'altro modo levarmi da tanta amaritudine e acerbità, non mi restava altro rimedio e speranza che quella della morte; la quale troppo tardi ode: che si può interpetrare così per non avere voluto prima udire e prieghi di tanti che a·llei desideravono la vita, come perché l'afflizzione sentita dopo la morte sua, non avendo altro rimedio che la morte, era sì grande, che ogni indugio e dilazione della morte, ancora che piccolo, pareva insopportabile.

[Nuovo Argumento]

Avendo absoluto la exposizione de' quattro precedenti sonetti et essendo quelli che seguono molto differenti, pare necessario, per maggiore

some green meadow (as the commentary on the second sonnet testifies); either I placed myself near some clear and running water or in the shadow of some lovely green tree. But I was like someone burdened with infirmity, who, although various sorts of delicate food are administered to him, because his taste has been ruined, extracts the same flavor from everything, which converts the sweetness of those victuals into bitterness. Thus, though the various and agreeable things ought to have offered my heart more gladness, because my taste was spoiled and my mind disposed to tears, they all magnified my sorrow. And the memory of her, which was present in every place and time, displayed for me all those things with much greater bitterness than ordinarily. And although this memory was extremely hard and troubling, nevertheless, as we have said of the infirm person, although all foods taste bitter to him, nonetheless they nourish him and are the cause of his living, so did this very bitter food of her memory sustain my life. And, in effect, against this ill no better antidote or remedy could be found than the illness itself. Nor could that thought be overcome except by the same thought, because no other sweetness remained in my heart except this very bitter memory, and therefore only this helped my malady. As it was then necessary to recur to the second remedy, I fled from those delightful places into the narrow seas and storms of civic life. This remedy also proved inadequate, because, as this most noble lady had seized the dominion of my heart and at once made it hers, among all those other thoughts, the thought and memory of her stayed in my heart, and, despite all the other cares, like property of its own, that thought consumed my heart. In fact, "care" means nothing except "that thing that burns and consumes the heart."[43] And therefore, not being able either in the one fashion or in the other to draw away from such great bitterness and sourness, there remained no remedy or hope other than that of Death, which too late pays heed. For Death's not having wished at first to hear the prayers of many who desired life for her can be thus interpreted, because the affliction felt after her death, not having any remedy other than death, was so great that every delay and postponement of death, no matter how small, seemed insupportable.

[New Argument]

As I have completed the exposition of the four preceding sonnets and as those which follow are very different, it seems necessary, for their

---

[43] Bigi notes and Zanato concurs that here L. follows the etymology of Varro: "care, that which gnaws the heart" (*De lingua latina* 6, 46).

dilucidazione, fare prima uno nuovo argumento, il quale sia comune a tutti li seguenti sonetti, acciò che si verifichi quello che di sopra abbiamo detto, cioè che la morte sia stata conveniente principio a questa nuova vita, come mi sforzerò di mostrare appresso.

Nascono tutti gli uomini con uno naturale appetito di felicità, e a questo, come a vero fine, tendono tutte le opere umane. Ma perché è molto difficile a conoscere che cosa sia felicità e in che consista, e se pure si conosce non è minore difficultà el poterla conseguire, dagli uomini per diverse vie si cerca. E però, dapoi che in genere e in confuso gli uomini questo si hanno proposto per fine, cominciano chi in uno e chi in uno altro modo a cercare di trovarlo; e così, da quella generalità ristrignendosi a qualche cosa propria e particulare, diversamente s'affaticano, ciascuno secondo la natura e disposizione sua: onde nasce la varietà delli studii umani e l'ornamento e maggiore perfezzione del mondo per la diversità delle cose, simile all'armonia e consonanzia che resulta di diverse voce concorde. E a questo fine forse Colui che mai non erra ha fatto obscura e difficile la via della perfezzione. E così si conosce l'opere nostre e la intelligenzia umana avere principio dalle cose più note, venendo da quelle alle manco note; né è dubio alcuno essere di più facile cognizione le cose in genere, che in spezie e particulate: dico, secondo il discorso dell'umana intelligenzia, la quale non può avere vera diffinizione d'alcuna cosa, se prima non procede la notizia universale di quella.

Fu adunque la vita e morte di colei che abbiamo detto, a me notizia universale di amore e cognizione in confuso che cosa fussi amorosa passione; per la quale universale cognizione divenni poi alla cognizione particulare della mia dolcissima e amorosa pena, come diremo appresso. Imperò che, essendo morta la donna che di sopra abbiamo detto, fu da me e laudata e deplorata nelli precedenti sonetti come publico danno e iattura comune, e fui mosso da uno dolore e compassione che molti e molti altri mosse nella città nostra, perché fu dolore molto universale e comune. E se bene nelli precedenti sonetti sono scritte alcune cose che più tosto paiono da privata e grande passione dettate, mi sforzai, per meglio satisfare a me medesimo e a quelli che grandissima e privata passione avevono della sua morte, propormi inanzi agli occhi di avere ancora io perduto una carissima

greater clarification, first to compose a new argument, which is common to all the following sonnets, so that what we have said above will be verified, that is that death has been a suitable beginning to this new life, as I try to demonstrate next.

All men are born with a natural appetite for happiness,[44] and toward this, as toward a true end, all human acts are bent. But because it is very difficult to know what happiness is and in what it consists, and because—even if one knows—being able to achieve it is no minor difficulty for men, they seek happiness by diverse paths. And therefore, seeing that men have generally and confusedly proposed this as their objective, one will begin in one way and one in another to seek to find it. And so, from that generality, focussing on something appropriate and particular, they are variously employed, each according to his nature and disposition. From this springs the variety of human studies and the ornament and major perfection of the world through the diversity of things, like the harmony and consonance that results from blending different voices.[45] And to this end, perhaps, He who never errs, has made the way of perfection dark and difficult. And thus we know that our works and human intelligence start from those things that are better known and from them move on toward the less known. Neither is there any doubt that it is easier to recognize things in general than in species and particularities—I mean according to the discourse of human intelligence, which cannot have a true definition of anything, unless the universal knowledge of it comes first.

The life and death of her about whom we have spoken, then, was for me a universal knowledge of love and a recognition in the midst of confusion of what constituted amorous passion. Through this universal knowledge I moved then to the particular knowledge of my very sweet and amorous pain, as we shall shortly say. Nevertheless, that the lady about whom we have spoken above was dead, I both celebrated and deplored in the preceding sonnets as a public harm and a common misfortune, and I was moved by a sorrow and a compassion that moved many, many others in our city, because it was a most universal and common sorrow.[46] And although in the preceding sonnets I have written some things that rather seem spoken from a great and private distress, I was compelled, so that I could better satisfy both myself and those who had a private and exceeding distress on account of her death, to set before my eyes [the fact that] I too

---

[44] Cf. Ficino, *Theol. Plat.* 14, 2, in *Opera*, p. 307 (337).

[45] Bigi cites Dante, Par. 6, 124–6: "Diverse voices make sweet music...," in *The Divine Comedy*, trans., Charles Singleton (Princeton: Princeton Univ. Press, 1977), 67.

[46] See *Rvf.* 3,8: "When midst the common sorrow came my woe."

cosa, e introdurre nella mia fantasia tutti gli affetti che fussino atti a muovere me medesimo, per potere meglio muovere altri. E, stando in questa immaginazione, cominciai meco medesimo a pensare quanto fussi dura la sorte più di quelli che assai avevono amato questa donna, e cercare con la mente se alcuna altra ne fussi nella città degna di tanto amore e laude. E, stimando che grandissima felicità e dolcezza fussi quella di colui, el quale o per ingegno o per fortuna avessi grazia di servire una tale donna, stetti qualche spazio di tempo cercando sempre e non trovando cosa che al giudicio mio fussi degna d'uno vero e constantissimo amore; et essendo già quasi fuora d'ogni speranza di poterla trovare, fece in uno punto più el caso che in tanto tempo non aveva fatto la exquisita diligenzia mia; e forse Amore, per mostrare a me meglio la sua potenza, volle celarmi tanto bene in quello tempo che io più lo cercavo e disideravo, e concederlo a quello tempo quando al tutto me ne pareva essere disperato. Facevasi nella città nostra una publica festa, dove concorsono molti uomini e quasi tutte le giovane nobile e belle. A questa festa, quasi contro a mia voglia, credo per mio destino, mi condussi con alcuna compagni e amici miei, perché ero stato per qualche tempo assai alieno da simili feste, e, se pure qualche volta m'erono piaciute, procedeva più presto da una certa voglia ordinaria di fare come gli altri giovani, che da grande piacere che ne traessi. Era tra l'altre donne una agli occhi miei di somma bellezza e di sì dolci e attrattivi sembianti, che cominciai, veggendola, a dire: «Se questa fussi di quella dilicatezza, ingegno e modi che fu quella morta che abbiamo detta, certo in costei e la bellezza e vaghezza e forza degli occhi è molto maggiore». Dipoi, parlando con alcuno che di lei aveva qualche notizia, trovai molto bene rispondere gli affetti, non così a ciascuno comuni, a quello che la bellezza sua, e *maxime* gli occhi, mostravano; nelli quali si verificava molto ‹bene› quello che dice Dante in una sua canzona parlando degli occhi della donna sua: «Ella vi reca Amore come a suo loco». Veramente quando la natura gli creò, non fece solamente due occhi, ma il vero luogo dove stessi Amore e insieme la morte, o vero vita e ‹'n›felicità degli uomini che fiso

had lost someone very dear, and to introduce into my fantasy all those affections that were apt to move me, in order to better move others. And, remaining in this fantasy, I began within myself to consider how much harder the fate was of those who had so greatly loved this lady, and to search with my mind [to see] if there was not some other woman in the city worthy of such great love and praise. And, concluding that the greatest happiness and sweetness was his who, either on account of talent or fortune, had the grace to serve such a lady, I remained for a certain length of time always seeking and not finding anyone that in my judgment was worthy of a true and most constant love. And just when I was already almost beyond any hope of being able to find someone, all at once chance accomplished more than my most scrupulous diligence had done in so much time. And perhaps Love, the better to show me his power, wanted to conceal so much good from me during that time when I most sought and desired it, and to confer it at that time when all to me seemed hopeless. In our city a public festivity is celebrated where many men and almost all the lovely and noble young women gather together. To this festivity,[47] almost against my will, I was conducted, by my destiny as I believe, with some of my companions and friends, for I had for some time been very estranged from similar celebrations, and, even if they sometimes pleased me, that proceeded more readily from a certain ordinary desire to act like the other young men, than from being drawn to it for great enjoyment. There was among the other ladies[48] one[49] who in my eyes was of such extraordinary beauty and of such sweet and attractive appearance that, seeing her, I began to say: "If this one were of that delicacy and wit and had the manners of that dead lady about whom we have spoken, certainly the beauty in her and the attractiveness and the power of her eyes is much greater." Afterward, speaking with someone who had some knowledge of her, I found his sensations, though we did not share each one, to accord very well with what her beauty and especially her eyes showed forth. By these [eyes] is clearly proved what Dante says in his canzone, speaking about the eyes of his lady: "There she carries Love as if in his own place."[50] Truly, when nature created them, it did not only make two eyes, but the true place where love and death stood together, or truly

---

[47] Perhaps the feast of San Giovanni or *carnivale*.

[48] See *Rvf.* 13,1: "When midst the other ladies now and then."

[49] Probably Lucrezia Donati.

[50] *Conv.* 3, *canz.* 2, l. 58. Busnelli and Vandelli in *Il Convivio*, 2nd. ed., 2 vols. (Florence: Le Monnier, 1964) 1: 254, give the line as, "*che le vi reca Amor com'a suo loco.*" Lorenzo's ms. copy of the *Convivio*, Tiziano Zanato has told me, gives the line as: "*ch'ella vi reca. . . .*"

gli riguardassino, secondo che da loro fussino amati o odiati. Cominciai adunque in quel punto ad amare con tutto il cuore quella apparente bellezza; e di quello che non appariva, la oppinione e indizio che ne dava tanto dolce e peregrino aspetto mi fece nascere uno incredibile desiderio. E dove prima mi maravigliavo non trovando cosa che io giudicassi degna d'uno sincero amore, cominciai 'avere maggiore ammirazione, avendo veduto una donna che tanto excedesse la bellezza e grazia della sopra detta morta. E in effetto, tutto del suo amore acceso, mi sforzai diligentemente investigare quanto fussi gentile e accorta e in parole e in fatti; e in effetto trovai tanto excellente tutte le sue condizioni e parti, che molto difficilmente conoscere si poteva qual fussi maggiore bellezza in lei, o del corpo o dell'ingegno e animo suo.

Era la sua bellezza, come abbiamo detto, mirabile: di bella e conveniente grandezza; il colore delle carni bianco e non smorto, vivo e non accesso; l'aspetto suo grave e non superbe, dolce e piacevole, sanza leggerezza o viltà alcuna; gli occhi vivi e non mobili, e sanza alcuno segno o d'alterigia o di levità. Tutto il corpo sì bene proporzionato, che tra l'altre mostrava degnità, sanza alcuna cosa rozza o inetta; e nondimeno, e nello andare e nel ballare e nelle cose che è lecito alle donne d'operare il corpo, e in effetto in tutti li suoi moti, era elegante e avenente. Le mani, sopra tutte le altre che mai facessi natura, bellissime, come diremo sopra alcuni sonetti alli quali le sue mani hanno dato materia. Nello abito e portamenti suoi molto pulita e bene a proposito ornata, fuggendo però tutte quelle fogge che a nobile e gentile donna si sconvengono e servando la degnità e gravità. Il parlare dolcissima veramente, pieno d'acute e buone sentenzie, come faremo intendere nel processo, perché alcune parole e sottili inquisizioni sue hanno fatto argumento a certi delli miei sonetti. Parlava a tempo, breve e conciso, né si poteva nelle sue parole o disiderare o levare; li motti e facezie sue erono argute e salse ⟨e⟩, sanza offensione però d'alcuno, dolcemente mordente. Lo ingegno veramente maraviglioso, assai più che a donna non si conviene; e questo però sanza fasto o presunzione, e fuggendo uno certo vizio che si suole trovare nella maggiore parte delle donne, alle quali parendo intendere assai, diventano insopportabili, volendo giudicare ogni cosa, che vulgarmente le chiamiamo "saccente." Era prontissima d'ingegno, tanto che molte volte o per una sola parola o per uno

the life and infelicity of the men who regarded them steadily, according to whether they [the men] were loved or despised by them [the eyes]. I began then in that instant to love with all my heart that visible beauty. And as to that invisible [beauty], the belief and the evidence that gave me such a sweet and rare view of it made spring up in me an incredible desire. And whereas before I was marvelling at not finding a person whom I could judge worthy of a sincere love, I began to marvel more greatly, having seen a woman who greatly exceeded the beauty and grace of the dead lady spoken of above. And in effect, all aflame with love for her, I felt compelled to investigate diligently what might be noble and wise both in words and in deeds. And in effect I found all her circumstances and parts very excellent, for it was very difficult to be able to know what her greatest beauty was, whether of her body or of her talent or of her mind.

Her beauty was, as we have said, marvelous:[51] she was of attractive and appropriate size; the color of her complexion white but not pallid, fresh but not red; her bearing serious but not haughty, sweet and pleasing, without any lightness or vulgarity; her eyes lively but not shifty, without any sign of arrogance or of levity. Her entire body was well proportioned, for among the others she displayed dignity without anything uncouth or inept. And, all the same, in walking and in dancing and in those things at which it is proper for women to exert their bodies, and in effect in all her motions she was elegant and charming. Her hands were beautiful beyond all others that nature ever made, as we shall say in some sonnets to which her hands have given subjects. In her dress and her carriage she was very elegant and well and appropriately adorned, avoiding, however, all those fashions that are unfitting for noble and courtly ladies, and maintaining her gravity and dignity. Her speech was truly exceedingly sweet, full of keen and good judgment, as we shall understand in due course, since some words and dainty requests of hers have been the subject in certain of my sonnets. She spoke with relevance, brevity and concision, and one could wish no more nor any less from her words; her pleasantries and jests were quick-witted and sharp, and sweetly biting without, however, offending anyone. Her intelligence was truly marvelous far beyond what was appropriate to a woman. But this was so, however, without ostentation or presumption, and she avoided a certain defect that one usually finds in most women who, in seeming to understand a great deal, become unbearable by wishing to judge every matter, and who are commonly called "know-it-alls." She was very perceptive, so much so that many times by a single word or by a little gesture she understood the mind of someone else. In

---

[51] What follows is a conventional courtly catalogue of the lady's charms.

piccolo cenno comprendeva l'animo altrui; nelli modi suoi dolce e piacevole oltre a modo, non vi mescolando però alcuna cosa molle o che provocassi altri ad alcune poco laudabile effetto; in qualunque sua cosa saggia e accorta e circunspetta, fuggendo però ogni segno di callidità o di duplicità, né dando alcuna suspizione di poca constanzia o fede. Sarebbe più lunga la narrazione di tutte le sue excellentissime parti che il presente comento; e però con una parola concluderemo il tutto e veramente affermeremo nessuna cosa potersi in una bella e gentil donna desiderare, che in lei copiosamente non fussi.

Queste excellentissime condizioni m'avevono in modo legato, che no avevo o pensiero o membro più che fussi in sua libertà. E posso dire, quanto agli occhi miei, che quella morta di chi abbiamo detto fussi la stella di Venere, da' Latini *Lucifer* chiamata, la quale, precedendo il sole, venendo poi quello maggiore lume, cede e al tutto si spegne, quasi come se fussi ordinata per advertire gli uomini che il sole viene, e non per dare luce al mondo. Muore e spegnesi questa stella sopravenendo lo splendore del sole, e nondimeno è chiamata *Lucifer,* che vuol dire una cosa che porta seco luce, la quale luce non porta nel mondo se non quando si spegne la luce sua; parve adunque ancora a' Latini la morte di questa stella vita e principio della luce del giorno. Adunque con queste auttorità ancora si verifica la morte di quella essere suto conveniente principio a questo giorno, che fece agli occhi miei el nuovo sole degli occhi di colei; la quale se bene abbiamo molto laudata, le laude non aggiungono però alla excellenzia e meriti suoi. Mostrommi il morto *Lucifer* che presto doveva venire questo mio novello sole, e, come abbiamo detto, scòrse el cammino mio cieco alla visione di questo tanto splendore; e, poi che ebbe assuefatti gli occhi miei a vedere lo splendore della sua stella, cioè splendore celeste, sentendo il sole sopravenire si spense, e io, che per lei avevo cominciato a voltare gli occhi in cielo, con manco offensione della vista mia gli pote' traducere dal lume della stella allo splendore del sole.

V

Lasso a me!, quando io son là dove sia
quello angelico, altero e dolce volto:
il freddo sangue interno al core accolto

her manners she was extraordinarily sweet and pleasing, not mixing therewith, however, any sensuality or anything that would provoke in others some less laudable sensation. In whatever she did, she was wise and shrewd and circumspect, avoiding, however, any sign of craftiness or duplicity, and arousing no suspicion of little constancy or faith. The narration of all her very excellent attributes would be longer than this commentary. And therefore we conclude everything with one word, and we affirm that, truly, there was nothing that one could desire in a beautiful and noble woman that was not abundantly in her.

These very excellent attributes had bound me in such a way that I had neither a thought nor a limb that was any longer at its liberty. And I can say that, in my eyes, that dead one about whom we have spoken was the star of Venus, called *Lucifer* by the Latins, which precedes the sun. Then when that greater light comes, it yields and is completely extinguished for everyone, almost as if it had been appointed to notify men that the sun is coming but not to give light to the world. This star dies and is extinguished, overcome by the splendor of the sun, and nevertheless it is called Lucifer, which means that which carries the light with it, but it does not carry light to the world except when its own light is put out. The death of this star, then, seemed to the Latins to be also the life and the beginning of the light of the day. With this authority, therefore, one proves the death of that one to have been the fitting beginning of this day, which, in my eyes, was brought forth by the new sun of the eyes of that lady, whose praises, although we have much praised her, nevertheless do not approach her excellence and merits. The death of *Lucifer* showed me that soon this new sun of mine had to come, and, as we have said, it directed my blind pathway to the sight of this great glory.[52] And, after my eyes had become accustomed to the glory of the star, that is to celestial splendor, feeling the sun arrive upon the scene, [the star] was extinguished, and I, who on account of it had begun to turn my eyes toward heaven, with less harm to my sight could transfer my eyes from the light of the star to the splendor of the sun.

5

Ah woe is me! when I am in the place
Where rests that lofty, sweet, angelic face,
My cold blood rushes inward to my heart

---

[52] Bigi, 330, glosses the "blind pathway" as that by which the heart flees from the breast of the poet toward the eyes of the lady.

        lascia sanza color la faccia mia.
          Poi, mirando la sua, mi par sì pia,
che io prendo ardire e torna il valor tolto:
Amor, ne' raggi de' belli occhi involto,
mostra al mio tristo cor la cieca via.
          E parlandoli allor dice: —Io ti giuro
pel santo lume di questi occhi belli,
del mio stral forza e del mio regno onore,
        ch'io sarò sempre teco, e te assicuro
esser vera pietà che mostran quelli.
Credeli, lasso!, e da me fugge il core.

    Era, come abbiamo detto, il mio cuore tutto acceso e infiammato della biltà e gentilezza di questa mia donna, e se alcuna parte restava in me che non consentisse coll'altre, ne era cagione il dubbio che avevo che con tanta bellezza e gentilissimi modi non fusse congiunta qualche durezza e poca pietà; perché sapevo già quanto era grande il disio, e aspettavone grandissima passione e insopportabile tormento quando in questa mia gentilissima non fussi stata pietà. Questo sospetto teneva ancora in me il mio cuore, né lo lasciava assicurare al partire. E però se mi trovavo alla presenza di lei, el viso suo, veramente angelico, pareva al cuore dolce e altero: dolce perché così veramente era, altero gliele faceva parere el dubbio già detto della poca pietà. E però prima diventavo tutto pallido, perché el cuore, essendo già acceso e avendo il dubbio che di sopra abbiamo detto, non poteva fare che sommamente non temessi. Di questo suo timore nasceva in lui affanno, e però li spiriti vitali, correndo per soccorrere al cuore, lasciavono la faccia mia sanza colore, pallida e smorta; e insieme con li spiriti, come ha ordinato la natura, assai copia di sangue intorno al cuore conveniva. Questo generava in quel luogo caldo assai più che l'usato; né potendo tanto caldo essalare, per essere piccolo lo spazio a tanta quantità, ne nasceva quasi una suffocazione di quelli spiriti e sangue: onde era constretto, non

>And leaves my countenance all colorless.
>   On hers I gaze then; so devout it seems[53]
>That I take heart and valor fled returns:
>Love, in the rays of those fair eyes entwined,
>The blind path to my woeful heart reveals.
>   And, speaking to my heart, Love says: "I swear
>Upon the sacred light of those fair eyes—
>My arrow's strength, the honor of my realm—
>   That I'll be always with you, and be sure,
>It is true piety those eyes show forth."[54]
>My heart believes him, woe! and flees from me.

As we have said, my heart was all kindled and inflamed by the beauty and nobility of this my lady, and if any part remained in me that would not agree with the others, the cause of it was the fear that I felt that some hardness and little pity would be mixed with such great beauty and such exceedingly noble manners. For I already knew how great was my desire, and I expected from it a very great passion and unbearable torment in case there had been no pity in this my most gentle lady. This suspicion was still holding my heart in me, and the suspicion did not permit my heart to declare its departure. And therefore if I found myself in her presence, her face, truly angelic, seemed to my heart sweet and aloof—sweet because so it truly was—aloof [because] my already mentioned fear of little pity made her [face] seem so to my heart. And therefore, first I became all pale, because my heart, already aflame and harboring the above mentioned fear, could do other than fear exceedingly. Because of my heart's fear, palpitations sprang up in it, and therefore the vital spirits,[55] racing to rescue my heart, left my face pallid and colorless. And together with the spirits, as nature has ordained, a great abundance of blood came and surrounded the heart. This generated in that place much more heat than usual. And when so much heat was unable to escape, being so great a quantity in so small a space, the spirits and blood almost produced suffocation. Unable to rise

---

[53] L. intends "devout" to be taken in its several senses: compassionate, pious, loving, etc.

[54] By "*pietà*" L. means both piety and pity of the sort a lady feels for a man tormented by love for her.

[55] Bigi, 331, cites Ficino's definition of vital spirits which is also a stilnovistic tradition and is based upon Aristotelian physiology: vital spirits are "a certain very thin and clear vapor created through the heat of the heart from the purest part of the blood," which, "... diffused through all the parts ... receives the powers (*virtù*) of the soul and communicates them to the body" and "also receives through the instruments of the senses the images of external bodies...." *FC*, 6, 6, 189.

potendo essalare, il sangue a mortificarsi e raffredarsi, come mostra la experienzia in quelli che per paura muoiono, alli quali si truova intorno al cuore quantità di sangue coagulato e freddo, ancora che nell'altre sue membra resti qualche qualità di caldo. Ma poi, rimirando la faccia sua, parendomi vi fussi tanti segni di pietà, il cuore poneva da parte la paura e ripigliava qualche ardire; e per questo li spiriti vitali ritornavano al luogo onde prima erono partiti, e con loro tornava il valore e colore prima perduto. E tanto più, perché, guardando negli occhi suoi, vedevo Amore involto ne' raggi di quelli belli occhi e mostrandoli la via come potessi fuggire da me nelli occhi della donna mia; la quale via si può dire cieca, perché il cuore non aveva però certezza alcuna se non per le parole d'Amore, e però camminava per tenebre e in dubbio di sé medesimo: ‹e› tanto più, perché Amore, el quale era sua scorta a quello cammino, ancora lui si dipigne cieco. E acciò che 'l mio cuore gli dessi più fede, giura per li occhi della mia donna essere vera la pietà che quelli mostran di fuora, e oltre a questo di stare sempre in compagnia del cuore mio, perché dove concorre pietà e amore non può essere sospetto o timore al cuore mio. E giurando Amore per li occhi di colei, non può fare più efficace giuramento, perché «giuramento» non è altro che producere per testimonio di quello che tu affermi quella cosa per la quale giuri: perché, chi giura, *verbi gratia,* per Giove, vuole che Giove sia testimonio e quasi fideiussore della observanzia di quella cosa, e chi rompe uno sacramento e diventa periuro, offende la prima cosa e vilipende qaello per chi ha giurato. Avendo adunque Amore giurato per li occhi della donna mia, e subiungendo che gli occhi suoi sono l'onore e forza sua, doveva il cuore credere ad Amore, perché non è da presummere volessi ingannare o provocarsi inimici quelli occhi, nelli quali era posto l'onore e forza sua. E però non errò il cuore mio credendogli: e abbandonatamente lasciò el mio petto e se n'andò in quelli splendidissimi e amorosa occhi.

VI

Spesso mi torna a mente, anzi già mai
si può partir della memoria mia,
l'abito e il tempo e il loco dove pria
la mia donna gentil fiso mirai.
    Quel che paressi allora, Amor, tu il sai,
che con lei sempre fusti in compagnia:
quanto vaga, gentil, leggiadra e pia,
né si può dir né imaginare assai.

from there, the blood was constrained to mortify itself and to cool itself, as experience demonstrates in those who die from fear, inside whose hearts is found a quantity of coagulated and cold blood, although in their other [organs and] limbs some quality of heat remains. But then, looking at her face again, as there seemed to me to be many signs of pity, my heart put its fear aside and once again found some courage. And at this the vital spirits returned to the place from which they had first departed, and with them returned the prowess and the color formerly lost. And even more, because, looking in her eyes, I saw Love intertwined among the rays of those lovely eyes, and he showed my heart the way it could flee from me into the eyes of my lady. That way one can call blind, because the heart still had no certainty except for the words of Love, and therefore it wandered through the dark and among doubts within itself—all the more, because Love, who was its guide upon that road, still is depicted as blind himself. And in order that my heart might be roused to greater faith, Love swore by the eyes of my lady that the pity they showed forth was true, and beyond this that he would always remain in the company of my heart, for, where pity and love concur, my heart can feel neither suspicion nor fear. And since Love had sworn by her eyes, there could not be a more efficacious oath, because "swearing" is nothing but producing as a witness to that which you affirm the thing by which you swear. For, whoever swears, for example, by Jove, wishes that Jove will witness and almost be guarantor of the fulfillment of that thing, and whoever breaks an oath and becomes a perjurer offends against the first [that which one affirms] and dishonors that by which he has sworn. Love having therefore sworn by the eyes of my lady, and adding to that the fact that her eyes are his honor and power, my heart had to believe Love, because it is not to be presumed he would wish to deceive or provoke the enmity of those eyes, in which was his place of honor and his power. And therefore my heart did not err in believing him. And with utter abandon it left my breast and went from it into those most splendid and amorous eyes.

6

How often to my mind returns—or yet,
From memory can never parted be—
The dress, the time and place, where first I gazed
Intently on my noble lady fair.
What she then seemed, Love, well you know, for you
Were always with her, keeping company:
How lovely, gentle, graceful, and devout
Cannot be spoken nor imagined well.

> Quando sopra i nivosi et alti monti
> Apollo spande il suo bel lume adorno,
> tali e crin' suoi sopra la bianca gonna.
> El tempo e 'l loco non convien ch'io conti,
> ché dove è sì bel sole è sempre giorno
> e paradiso ove è sì bella donna.

Sogliono le prime impressioni nelle menti degli uomini essere molto veemente, e pare cosa molto conforme alla ragione che così sia. Perché, essendo la mente nostra per natura ordinata a ricevere diverse impressioni e con questo naturale appetito di non stare vacua, fa come uno assetato, el quale spegne la sete con la prima cosa che gli occorre atta ad extinguerla, e tanto più volentieri lo fa, quanto è più quella tal cosa dolce al gusto; per questa ragione, secondo Platone, quelli che sono di tenera età hanno più tenace memoria, perché quelle cose che loro imparano, come prime e nuove impressioni meglio si riservano nella memoria.

Essendo adunque già assicurato da Amore il mio cuore e già da me fuggito, nessuna cosa molesta restave nel pensiero, parendomi già vedere indizii assai certi della futura pietà nella donna mia. Questo generava in me grandissima speranza e dolcezza; e perché naturalmente s'appetisce quello che piace, quando non può essere presente la memoria e il pensiero ce lo rappresenta, e più volentieri quelle cose che sono sute prime, come principio e cagione di quello bene che sente la mente. Erano adunque nella memoria mia quasi perpetualmente presenti lo abito, del quale era adorna la mia donna, e il luogo e 'l tempo quando prima fiso mirai negli occhi suoi, cioè quando, già acceso dello amore suo, con somma delettazione la guardai: perché il mirar fiso non procede se non da due cagioni, cioè o per conoscere bene quella tale cosa che si guarda, o per grande delettazione che si piglia guardandola. Cessava in me la prima cagione, perché già conoscevo la bellezza e forza degli occhi suoi; restava adunque solamente il diletto, cagione del mio mirare fiso. E io, se bene per altri tempi avevo veduto gli occhi suoi, non avendo ancora avuto grazia di conoscerli, non gli avevo mirati fiso; e quando prima gli mirai fiso fu dopo la cognizione di tanto bene, dopo la quale *inmediate* e necessariamente tutto di loro m'accesi: perché prima procede la cognizione e poi lo amore. Quello che paressi agli occhi miei era a me molto difficile o inmaginare o referire, perché le bellezze sue, come dice Dante, «soverchiono lo nostro intelletto, come raggio di sole in fraile viso»; e però quello che era impossibile a me

> When over high and snowy mountaintops
> Apollo spreads his lovely, comely light,
> So seemed her hair above her snow white gown.
> I need not tell the time and place, for where
> A sun so lovely is, it's always day,
> And paradise where such a lady fair.

The first impressions in the minds of men are usually very powerful, and it stands to reason that this should be so. Because our mind is ordered by nature to receive diverse impressions, and with its natural appetite for not remaining empty, it behaves like a thirsty person who slakes his thirst with the first thing that happens to be suited to quench it, and the sweeter something is to his taste, the more willingly he does so. For this reason, according to Plato, those who are of a tender age have a more tenacious memory, because those things that they learn as first and new impressions are better kept in the memory.[56]

My heart having thus been already assured by Love, and having already fled from me, nothing disturbing remained in my thought, for I already seemed to see very certain indications of future pity in my lady. This generated in me exceedingly great hope and sweetness. And because we naturally hunger for what we like, when it can't be present our memory and thought represent it to us, and more willingly those things that have been first, like the principle and cause of that good that the mind perceives. There were almost perpetually present in my memory, then, the dress that had adorned my lady, and the place and the time when first I had gazed intently into her eyes, that is when, already kindled by her love, with exceeding delight I looked on her. Because gazing intently proceeds from nothing other than two causes, which are either from recognizing as good what one looks upon, or from the great delight that one receives from looking at it. The first cause was diminishing in me because I already knew the beauty and the power of her eyes. There remained then only the delight, the cause of my intent gazing. And I, although on other occasions I had seen her eyes, not having yet had the grace of knowing them, I had not yet gazed on them intently. And when I first gazed intently on them, it was after the knowledge of such a great good, after which I was *immediately* and necessarily entirely kindled by them—because knowledge goes before and then comes love. That which appeared to my eyes was for me very difficult either to imagine or recount, because her beauties, as Dante says,[57] "overcome our intellect as the sun's ray does weak sight."[58] And

---

[56] See Plato, *Rep.*, II, 377b.
[57] In *Conv.* II, 59–60.

lasciai' Amore, il quale, stando sempre con lei e abitando (come abbiamo detto) negli occhi suoi, e meglio conoscere e più absolutamente exprimere poteva tanta excellenzia. E, oltre a questo, proponendo io che la sua bellezza, leggiadria, gentilezza e pietà erono cose impossibile o a narrare o a inmaginare, e parendo questo a chi legge mirabile e quasi impossibile, pare molto conveniente producere in fede di questo uno testimonio autentico; e nessuno è migliore testimonio che Amore, *maxime* sendo suto presente, e ancora merita essere creduto da quelli almanco che li sono stati subietti, e quali, come nel proemio dicemmo, bisogna che sieno animi alti e gentili, appresso li quali basta simili amorosi miracoli avere fede; e se fuora di questo numero non fussino creduti, non è bene che e cuori rozzi e villani e rebelli da Amore gustino tanta gentilezza.

Avendo adunque in genere detto della excellenzia di costei e quanto nel primo aspetto paressi bella, gentile e pia, parve da fare menzione delle tre cose proposte nel principio del sonetto, cioè l'abito e 'l tempo e 'l loco. E però, quanto allo abito, ancora che sia minore la comparazione che la excellenzia di lei, essendo vestita tutta di bianco e mostrando in su quel campo e suoi aurei capelli, mi parve conveniente assimigliarli a' raggi del sole quando si spandono sopra a uno monte di candida neve, perché né meno candida cosa coprivano e capelli che sia la neve, né manco splendore avevono e capelli che li raggi del sole; e se capelli erono tanto lucenti, molto più erono gli occhi. E però, quanto al tempo, non è dubbio che era giorno, el quale almeno faceva il sole degli occhi suoi. E, dato che questo fussi, il luogo di necessità era paradiso, perché dove era tanto splendore, bellezza e pietà, certamente si può dire paradiso; el quale paradiso, chi vuole rettamente diffinire, non vuole dire altro che uno giardino amenissimo, abundante di tutte le cose piacevoli e dilettevoli, d'arbori, di pomi, di fiori, e acque vive e correnti, canti d'uccelli, e in effetto di tutte le amenità che può pensare el cuore dell'uomo. E per questo si verifica che paradiso era ove era sì bella donna, perché quivi era copia d'ogni amenità e dolcezza che uno gentile cuore può disiderare.

VII

Occhi, voi siate pur dentro al mio core
e vedete il tormento ch'ei sostiene

therefore what was impossible for me I left to Love, who by being always with her and dwelling, as we have said, in her eyes, was better able to know and to express more definitely such great excellence. And beyond this, I affirm that her beauty, grace, nobility, and piety were things impossible either to recount or to imagine, and as this will seem marvelous and almost impossible to a reader, it seems very fitting to produce in support of this an authentic witness. And no one is a better witness than Love, especially since he was present, and he also deserves to be believed by those at least who have been his subjects, and who, as we said in the prologue, must have high and noble minds, among which minds it suffices to have faith in similar amorous miracles. And if outside this band they are not believed, it is not a good thing that either rough and ill-bred hearts or rebels against love should taste such nobility.

Having then in general spoken of her excellence and of how beautiful, noble, and pious she appeared at first sight, it seemed that mention needed to be made of three things proposed in the beginning of the sonnet, that is the dress, the time and the place. And therefore, as regards her dress—although that is a very slight matter in comparison with her own excellence—she was dressed all in white and showing above that field her golden hair—[so that] it seemed to me fitting to compare it to the sun's rays when they are spread above a mountain of pure white snow, because nothing less white than snow did her hair cover, nor did her hair possess less splendor than the rays of the sun. And if the hair was shining thus brightly, much more so were her eyes. And therefore, as regards the time—there is no doubt that it was day, which at least made of her eyes the sun. And, given that this was the case, of necessity, the place was paradise, because wherever there was such great splendor, beauty, and piety certainly can be called paradise. For, whoever wishes correctly to define "paradise," means nothing other than a most agreeable garden, abounding with pleasant and delightful things, with trees, with apples, with flowers, with fresh and flowing waters, songs of birds, and in effect with all the amenities that the heart of a man can think of. And thus it is proved that paradise was where such a lovely lady was, because here was an abundance of every amenity and sweetness that a noble heart can desire.

7

Eyes, you are certainly within my heart,
And look upon the torment it sustains

---

[58] See also *Par.* 30, 25–27.

 e la sua intera fé: dunque, onde adviene
che madonna non cura il suo dolore?
  Tornate a·llei, e con voi venga Amore,
testimone ancor lui di tante pene;
dite che resta al cor sol questa spene
de' prieghi vostri, e se invan fia, si more.
 Portate a·llei i miseri lamenti.
Ma, lasso, quanto è folle il mio disio,
chè 'l cor non vive sanza gli occhi belli!
  O occhi, refrigerio a' miei tormenti,
deh, ritornate al misero cor mio!
Amor sol vadi, e lui per me favelli.

 Era già per li occhi miei discesa al cuore la imagine della bellezza di costei, e gli occhi suoi avevono fatto in esso tale impressione, che sempre gli erono presente; e Amore, il quale abbiamo detto sempre con loro abitava, se n'era ancora lui in compagnia di quelli occhi venuto. Il cuore per questo era di tante fiamme circundato, che li pareva impossibile a·ssopportare lo affanno che dal suo ardente desiderio nasceva; e, pensando quale migliore remedio potessi a questo male opporre, nessuna cosa gli occorse di maggiore efficacia che fare intendere la sua dolorosa condizione e miserabile stato alla donna mia, la quale sola poteva, come sola cagione di tanta pena, sollevarlo. Pareva in questo caso necessario eleggere nunzio e messaggero che avessi due condizioni: una, che fussi grato a colei a cui era mandato, perché avendo a riportare grazia, più facilmente si poteva per mezzo di graziosa persona; l'altra, che chi andava, oltre a essere bene informato della miseria in che si trovava il cuore, fussi creduto da·llei, acciò che la verità della pena più facilmente movessi la pietà. E però fece il cuore concetto di pregare gli occhi della donna mia, e quali, essendo in lui, vedevano il suo grande tormento, che andassino a referirlo a·llei; e in compagnia di loro Amore, acciò che, multiplicati li intercessori e il numero de' testimoni del male suo, più facilmente s'impetrasse grazia per questa graziosi messi: perché nessuno doveva essere alla donna mia o più grato o più creduto che Amore e gli occhi suoi medesimi. Erono testimoni quelli occhi, e Amore con loro, della pena del cuore e ancora della intera sua fede, non superata dalla grandezza de' martirii, e credeva per questo il cuore che a·llei dovessi essere noto lo stato suo; e, come nel processo del sonetto si vede, era in grande errore, perché non potendo vivere il cuore sanza quelli occhi et essendo vivo quando mandava questi nunzii, per le parole sue medesime si comprende che quelli occhi mai s'erano partiti dal

    And on its utter faith; how is it then,
    My lady pays no heed to all its woe?
       Go back to her, and with you let Love come—
    A witness too of so much pain—and tell
    Her that my heart's one hope is in your prayers,
    And if this be in vain, my heart will die.
       Please bear to her my wretched plaints. But, woe,
    How great a madness this desire of mine;
    My heart without those lovely eyes can't live.
       O eyes, the solace for my torment, Ah!
    Come back again unto my wretched heart;
    Let Love alone go; let him speak for me.

The image of her beauty had already descended through my eyes into my heart, and her eyes had made such an impression that they were always present. And Love, who we have said above always lived in them, also had himself come with her in company with those eyes. On account of this my heart was surrounded by such great flames that it seemed impossible for it to support the suffering that was born from its ardent desire. And, thinking what better remedy might be employed against this, nothing of greater efficacy occurred to it to do than to make known to my lady its sorrowful and miserable condition that she alone, as the sole cause of so much pain, could relieve. It seemed necessary in this case to select a herald and a messenger that could meet two conditions: the first was that he be pleasing to her to whom he was sent, because, having to beg grace, it could most easily be done by means of a gracious person. The other was that whoever went, beyond being well informed about the wretched state in which my heart found itself, must be believed by her, so that the truth about my pain might more easily move her to pity. And therefore my heart prepared the conceit of praying to the eyes of my lady, which, being within it, saw its great torment, and went to report that to her. And in their company went Love, that is, by increasing the intercessors and the number of witnesses to [my heart's] ill, grace might be more easily obtained by these gracious means—for no one should have been either more welcome to my lady or more credible than Love and her own eyes. Those eyes and Love with them were witnesses of the pain of my heart and of its utter faith, not surpassed by the excesses of its suffering, and my heart believed that because of this she must take note of its condition. And, as one sees in the development of the sonnet, that [sending the eyes] was a great error because, since the heart was unable to live without those eyes and since it was alive when it sent these messengers, by its very own words one understood that those eyes were never to be separated from my heart.

cuore mio. E però, quando il cuore dice: «Tornate a·llei», presupponendo quasi che altre volte si fussino partiti, si vede che il cuore per la passione erra; come ancora mostra maravigliandosi lui che madonna non curi il suo dolore, presupponendo gli sia noto. Prega adunque il cuore questi due nunzii che vadino a placare la durezza della donna mia, come unico refugio e sola speranza della sua salute. E chi legge bisogna presupponga che già gli occhi e Amore erano in cammino per partirsi, quando il cuore, accortosi dello errore suo e che impossibile gli era a vivere sanza quegli occhi, gli richiamò indrieto, pregandogli che restino con lui e commettendo che Amore solo andassi e pregassi per lui.

Una passione amorosa in dua modi si può levare dal cuore, cioè o con dimenticare la cosa amata o col placarla. Tentò il cuore mio l'una e l'altra via; e volendo cacciare da sé gli occhi di colei, fece experienzia di metterla in oblivione, perché non è nel cuore quella cosa di che altri non si ricorda. Tentò questo remedio invano, e però ricorse al secondo, cioè di placarla; questo non si può fare se non per mezzo d'Amore, né poteva nascere pietà nella donna mia se Amore non era con lei insieme con la certezza della pena e fede del cuore, perché l'amore, la pena e la fede sono quelle cose che muovono la pietà.

Parla adunque il presente sonetto agli occhi della donna ‹mia›, che erano continui assistenti al cuore.

VIII

Quel che il proprio valore e forza excede,
folle è sperare o disïar d'avere.
Se alcun tien l'occhio fisso per vedere
il sol, né quel né altra cosa vede.
    Se gli è vero il pensier d'alcun che il crede,
l'alta armonia delle celeste spere
vince i mortali orecchi; né volere
si dee quel che altri con suo danno chiede.
    Ah, folle mio pensier!, perché pur vuole
giugner pietate alle bellezze oneste
della mia donna, agli occhi, alle parole.
    Suo parlar men che l'armonia celeste
non vince, o il guardo offende men che il sole:
or pensa se pietà si aggiugne a queste!

Adviene spesse volte agli uomini che desiderano quello che sarebbe loro gravissimo danno e sperano ottenere quelle cose che sono impossibili a conseguire, mossi da presunzione e ignoranzia, la quale secondo e filosofi

And therefore, when my heart says: "Go back to her," presupposing almost that other times [the eyes] had departed, one sees that the heart is straying for passion. This also appears in its marvelling that my lady doesn't heed its sorrow, when it presupposes that she knows it. My heart then begs these two messengers, who are going, to allay the severity of my lady, as the only solace for and sole hope of its well being. And the reader must suppose that the eyes and Love were already about to depart when the heart, becoming aware of its error and of how impossible it was for it to live without those eyes, called them back again, begging them to remain with it, and trusting that Love would go and pray for it.

In two ways can an amorous passion be lifted from the heart, that is either by forgetting the beloved person or by appeasing the passion. My heart attempted both one way and the other. And, wishing to drive her eyes out of itself, it made the experiment of placing her in oblivion, because nothing is in the heart that is not remembered. It tried this remedy in vain, and therefore recurred to the second, that is to appease the passion. This it could not do except by means of Love, nor could pity be born in my lady if Love were not with her, together with the certainty of the heart's pain and faith, because love, pain, and faith are those things that move pity.

This sonnet then speaks to the lady's eyes, which were the continual assistants of the heart.

8

What folly to hope for or desire to have
That which exceeds one's proper worth or strength.
If one holds fixed his eye to see the sun,
He'll not see that nor any other thing.
    And if that thought believed by some is true,
That the celestial spheres' high harmony
Will vanquish human ears, wish not to have
What someone else to his undoing craves.
    Ah, my mad thought! why do you even wish
That pity, with my lady's beauties chaste,
And with her eyes and words might be conjoined?
    No less than heaven's harmony her speech
Will win; her glance no less than sun will harm:
Now think if pity were conjoined with these!

It often times happens with men that they desire what could very gravely injure them and that they hope to obtain those things that are im-

[93]

è madre di tutti e mali. Questo difetto più spesso si ritruova in quelli che sono posti in maggiore desiderio e passione, nelli quali la afflizzione e la pena è sì grande, che ogni desperate via tentano per liberarsene. Questo tale errore si nota per lo sopra scritto sonetto, el quale prima propone quanto sia grave inconveniente o desiderare o sperare di avere quelle cose che excedono le forze nostre e alle quali la natura nostra non è proporzionata, per essere assai inferiore e meno degna, subiungendo due essempli in confermazione di questa verità. El primo contro a quelli occhi che presumono guardare verso il sole, e quali non solamente non lo possono vedere, ma pèrdono per quello la visione dell'altre cose; l'altro essemplo è degli orecchi, e quali non sono sufficienti a potere udire l'armonia delle spere celesti. E per chiarire meglio questa parte è da intendere essere suto oppinione di alcuni filosofi, la quale mette Cicerone nel suo libro intitolato *De somnio Scipionis,* che il moto delle celeste spere generi diverse voci secondo la diversità de' moti, più veloce o più tarda, e di tutti insieme una dolcissima armonia, di tanta grande voce e suono, che gli orecchi umani non sono sufficienti a udire, come gli occhi mortali non possono vedere il sole; dando per essemplo che quelli uomini e quali nascono vicini alle cateratte del Nilo, cioè dove quello grande fiume d'altissimi monti cade in basso, per lo strepito e romore grande tutti sono sordi. Questa oppinione, non essendo molto aprovata, ancora da me non è messa per certa, e però dissi: «Se gli è vero il pensiero d'alcun che ‹il› crede». Da queste comparazioni degli occhi e degli orecchi umani non proporzionati a potere vedere il sole o udire l'armonia predetta, vengo poi a mostrare lo errore degli occhi e degli orecchi miei, e quali sono suti presuntuosi, gli occhi a guardare il sole della donna mia, gli orecchi a udire l'armonia dolcissima delle parole sue. E, se questo è grave errore, molto maggiore è quello del pensiero mio e molto maggiore presunzione, desiderando che s'agiunga pietà, cioè tanto maggiore forza, alle bellezze della donna mia; le quali se erano insopportabili alli miei frali e umili sensi sanza questa pietà, si può pensare quanto el pensiero mio desideri contro a sé, volendo agiugnere forza alla offesa sua.

Pare molto conveniente alla presente materia fare intendere la cagione

possible to achieve, moved by presumption and ignorance, which according to the philosophers is the mother of all evils.[59] This defect one finds most often in those who are trapped in overwhelming desire and passion, in whom affliction and suffering are so great that they attempt every desperate means to free themselves from them. Such an error as this is noted by the sonnet written above, which first proposed something that is very unsuitable, either to desire or to hope to have those things that exceed our strength and to which our nature is not proportioned by being very much inferior and less worthy, and I submitted two examples in confirmation of this truth. The first was about those eyes that presume to look toward the sun, but that not only cannot see it, but lose on that account the sight of other things. The other example concerns the ears, which are inadequate to be able to hear the harmony of the celestial spheres. And to better clarify this part one must understand that it was the opinion of some philosophers, which Cicero puts in his book entitled *On the Dream of Scipio*, that the motion of the celestial spheres generates various sounds, according as the variety of the motion is faster or slower, and from all together [proceeds] a harmony most sweet, of such great resonance and sound that human ears are inadequate to listen, just as mortal eyes cannot look at the sun. And it gives as an example that those men who live near the cataract of the Nile, that is where that great river falls from very high mountains into the depths, are all deaf because of the din and the great noise.[60] This opinion, not being shared by many, I also do not put forward as a certainty, and therefore I said: "And if that thought believed by some is true." From these comparisons about human eyes and ears' being ill adapted to be able either to see the sun or to hear the aforesaid harmony, I go on then to demonstrate the error of my eyes and ears, which have been presumptuous, the eyes by looking upon the sun of my lady, and the ears by listening to the very sweet harmony of her words. And, if this is a grave error, much greater is that of my thought and overweening presumption in desiring that pity, which is a much greater power, be added to the beauties of my lady. And if those beauties were unbearable by my frail and humble sense without this pity, it can be imagined how much this thought of mine was inimical to itself by wishing to add power to what harmed it.

It seems very fitting that this material make clear the reason why one

---

[59] Bigi cites Ficino, "Commentary on the 'Philebus'," 44 and 45, in *In Platonem, Opera*, 1266 (2: 262): "ignorantia et confidentia sui nacta quidem potentiam terribilis est."
[60] See *Som. Scip.* 5, and *Rvf.* 48, 9–10: "Perhaps, just as the Nile falls from on high/And deafens with its roar its neighbors round...."

per che si fa solamente menzione del pensiero, degli occhi e degli orecchi, e non d'altra forza o senso; e però diremo apresso da che cagione mossi abbiamo fatto questo. Secondo li Platonici tre sono le spezie della vera e laudabile bellezza, cioè berezza d'anima, di corpo e di voce. Quella dell'anima può solamente conoscere e appetire la mente, quella del corpo solamente diletta gli occhi, quella della voce gli orecchi; e diletta degli altri sensi fuora di questi, come vili e non convenienti ad animo gentile, sono repudiate. Pel pensiero adunque s'intende la mente, la quale ha per obietto la bellezza dell'anima, la quale consiste nella perfezzione che dalla virtù gli viene; et è più e manco bella, e di più e manco bellezza è ornata, secondo che è accompagnata da più virtù, così in numero come in quantità e perfezzione d'esse. La bellezza del corpo e grazia d'esso pare che proceda dall'essere bene proporzionato, di grazioso aspetto, e in effetto da una certa venustà e leggiadria, la quale qualche volta piace non tanto per la perfezzione e buona proporzione del corpo, quanto per una certa conformità che ha con li occhi ai quali piace, che dal cielo o dalla natura procede: e tutto questo è obbietto e iudizio degli occhi. La terza bellezza, della voce, consiste quando di più voce concorde resulta uno concento che si chiama armonia; e questo può procedere così da diverse voce, come è detto, come da una dolcezza e suavità di parole insieme bene connesse e accomodate, le quali ancora non possono essere così composte sanza armonia. Tutta questa bellezza solamente agli orecchi si riferisce. E per questo solamente questi tre modi abbiimo posti a conoscere la donna mia: imperò che per quella pietà che 'l mio pensiero desiderava in lei bisogna intendere la bellezza delle virtù e dote dell'anima della donna mia, desiderate dalla nostra mente (perché la pietà è opera degnissima dell'anima mossa da iustizia, perché, essendo posta in anima ragionevole, sanza qualche parte di merito non si muove); per li occhi suoi la bellezza del corpo, dagli occhi miei amata; per le parole sue, che vincono l'armonia celeste, si tocca la terza bellezza, della voce e dell'armonia, alla quale solo gli orecchi miei stavono intenti. Perché copiosamente queste tre bellezze erano in questa gentilissima, bellissima e dolcissima donna, la quale è a me cara sopra ogni cosa.

IX

Occhi, io sospiro come vuole Amore
e voi avete per mio mal diletto;
sempre ardo, né già mai giugne allo effetto
qual più disia lo inveterato ardore.
    Ma voi sentite ben pel mio dolore,

mentions only the thought, the eyes, and the ears, and not some other ability or sense. And therefore we say in connection with this argument that we were moved by this. According to the Platonists, the species of true and laudable beauties are three: that is, beauty of spirit, of body, and of voice. That of the spirit can only be known and yearned for by the mind, that of the body only delights the eyes, and that of the voice the ears. And the delights of the other senses beyond these are repudiated as being low and unsuitable to a noble mind. For the thought, then, one must understand the mind, which has as its object the beauty of the soul, which consists in the perfection that comes to it from virtue, and which is more or less beautiful, and more or less adorned with beauties according as it is accompanied by more virtue, both more in number and more in magnitude and perfection. The beauty of the body and its grace seem to proceed from being well proportioned, [from being] of graceful aspect, and in effect from a certain loveliness and winsomeness, which sometimes pleases not as much by the perfection and good proportion of the body as by a certain conformity that it has with the eyes that it pleases, [a conformity] that proceeds from heaven or from nature. And all this is the object and the judgment of the eyes. The third beauty, of the voice, exists when a concert results from the concord of many voices, which is called harmony. And this can proceed from diverse voices, as has been said, and from a sweetness and smoothness of words well connected together and suitable, which cannot yet be thus composed without harmony. All this beauty applies only to the ears. And only in these three ways have we gone about knowing my lady. For this reason, the pity that my thought desired in her must be understood to be the beauty of my lady's virtue and the gifts of her spirit desired by our mind (because pity is a most worthy work of the spirit moved by justice, because, being located in the rational soul, without some portion of merit [pity] is not moved). By her eyes [one understands] the beauty of her body [desired] by my enamored eyes. With her words, which overcome celestial harmony, one touches upon the third beauty, of the voice and of harmony, upon which only were my ears intent. Therefore these three beauties were copiously in this most noble, most lovely, and sweetest lady who, beyond every other thing, is dear to me.

9

O eyes, I sigh as Love wants me to do,
And you in my affliction take delight.
I always burn, but never reach the goal
My long established ardor most desires.
    But you are well acquainted with my woe,

> perché mirate il più gentile obietto
> che aver possiate: al vostro ben perfetto
> vi conduce la doglia di me, cuore.
> Se pur piangete, io son quel che distillo
> alquanto del mio mal per la via vostra;
> né il ben vi toglie il cor, quando si duole.
> Pregate meco Amor che sia tranquillo,
> qual se benigno il chiaro obietto mostra,
> quanto sarà più bello il vostro sole!

Se gli è vera quella diffinizione d'amore che nel proemio abbiamo detto, molto bene ancora si verifica il proposito e intenzione del presente sonetto, la quale è di provare per evidente ragioni che il cuore acceso d'amore già mai ha pace, e gli occhi dello inamorato tanto sono più felici, quanto il cuore ha maggiore tormento. La diffinizione che abbiamo detta d'amore è che amore sia desiderio di bellezza; e, se questo è, molto veramente si può dire amore non possedere quella bellezza che desidera, perché se la possedessi el desiderio d'essa sarebbe invano, perché non si può desiderare quello di che altri ha copia. E però diremo altra cosa essere amore, altra cosa essere il fine che lo muove, perché lo amore desidera et è mosso da uno fine che si chiama felicità e beatitudine, la quale consiste nel congiugnersi con quella bellezza che lo amore appetisce e con essa inseparabilmente stare; e insino a tanto che a questo fine di beatitudine non si perviene, amore non solamente non è bene, anzi è pena e tormento insopportabile, più e manco secondo la grandezza dello amore. E però, presupponendo che il cuore non sia pervenuto alla perfezione di questa beatitudine e dolcezza, bisogna confessare il cuore sia gravemente tormentato, perché il cuore ha per obbietto quella beatitudine della quale è privato. Ma gli occhi, l'officio de' quali è vedere, tanto sono più felici, quanto veggono cosa più bella, e ciascuna cosa tanto pare agli occhi più bella, quanto è maggiore lo amore, cioè il desiderio del cuore; perchè se lo amore è grande, necessariamente conviene che la bellezza o sia o paia agli occhi grande, altrimenti non sarebbe amore, cioè il desiderio della bellezza. Adunque si conclude per una medesima cagione gli occhi essere tanto più felici quanto il cuore è più misero: pigliando questi termini largamente, cioè il cuore come sede e luogo della concupiscibile, cioè nel quale

> Because you gaze on the most noble thing
> That you could have: this pain of mine conducts
> You, Heart of mine, to your most perfect good.
>
> If yet you weep, I rather, from my grief
> Distill those tears by way of you, nor does
> The heart's lamenting take away your good.
>
> Pray Love with me that I may be at peace,
> So, if your object bright some kindness shows,
> By that much more your sun will lovely be.

If the definition of love that we have given in the prologue is true, extremely well confirmed is the aim and the intention of this sonnet, which is to prove by evident arguments that the heart that burns with love never has peace, and the eyes of the lover are much happier than the heart that suffers greater torment. The definition that we have given of love is that love is the desire for beauty. And, if it is this, it can be said very truly that love does not possess that desired beauty, because, if it possessed it, the desire for it would be in vain, because that which one has in abundance cannot be desired.[61] And therefore we speak of love's being one thing, and of the end that moves it being another, because love desires and is moved by an end that one calls "felicity" and "beatitude," which consists in being united with that beauty for which love hungers and in being inseparable from it. And until this end of beatitude is attained, love not only is not a good, it is rather a torture and an unbearable torment, which is greater or less according to the magnitude of the love. And therefore, presupposing that the heart has not achieved the perfection of this beatitude and sweetness, one must confess that the heart is gravely tormented, because the heart has as its object that beatitude of which it is deprived. But the eyes, whose office it is to see, are far happier insofar as what they behold is lovelier, and each thing seems much lovelier to the eyes insofar as the love, that is the desire of the heart, is greater. Because, if the love is great, it necessarily follows that the beauty either is great or seems so to the eyes, otherwise it would not be love, that is, the desire for beauty. For the same reason one concludes, then, that the eyes are as much happier as the heart is more wretched—taking these terms broadly, that is, taking the heart as the seat and the location of the concupiscible spirits,[62] that is

---

[61] Bigi cites Socrates in Plato, *Symposium*, where Socrates reports what Diotima has taught him about love, in *Plato with an English Translation* (London: William Heinemann, 1925) 5:200–209, and FC 6,2, (183–4), and 6,7, (189–92).

[62] Those spirits which communicate to the body the desire of the soul for that which is pleasing. Plato locates them between the heart and the navel, see *Timaeus*, 70 d: "And

nascono tutti e desideri, e gli occhi non in quanto sono senso, perché come senso proprio et exteriore non possono giudicare la bellezza d'una cosa o d'un'altra; e però bisogna per li occhi intendere l'operazione dell'anima nostra, che opera mediante gli occhi, e quel contento e piacere che sente per mezzo dello strumento degli occhi, quando per rapporto loro giudica una cosa bella e piglia per questo consolazione e conforto.

Parla adunque nel presente sonetto il cuore agli occhi miei, mostrando l'afflizzione e miseria in che si truova, come vuole Amore, e il diletto che pel male suo sentono gli occhi, mostrarldo prima il male suo e poi il loro diletto. La miseria del cuore è questa: che lui sempre desidera quello che non possiede, né agiugne a quello effetto e fine il quale lui più brama e desia d'uno desio antiquo e inveterato. Ma gli occhi non solamente veggono l'obbietto loro, cioè gli occhi e la bellezza della donna mia, ma veggono la più bella et excellente cosa che possino vedere, cioè la donna mia, perché nessuna cosa può tanto desiderare il cuore quanto lei; e dal desiderio suo nasce la maggiore bellezza della donna mia, la quale è tanto più bella e perfetta, quanto è maggiore la doglia del cuore, cioè il desiderio d'essa, per le cagione che abbiamo dette. Risponde dipoi a una tacita contradizione che li potria essere fatta, cioè che gli occhi qualche volta ancora loro piangono, e questo pare contro alla felicità la quale il cuore afferma essere negli occhi; e però dice che, se pure gli occhi piangono, questo non procede per cagione d'alcuna pena loro, ma dal dolore e desiderio del cuore, il quale per la via delle lacrime sfoga una parte del suo dolore. Poi, rivoltatosi a'lloro, gli priega che loro prieghino Amore che faccia pietosa la donna mia; e a questo gli debbe muovere non solamente la compassione della miseria del cuore, ma ancora la speranza di maggiore bene degli occhi, perché, agiugnendosi pietà nella donna mia, Amore sarà tranquillo, cioè il desiderio della bellezza già sarà adempiuto, né più molesterà il cuore; e in questo caso il sole, cioè gli occhi e bellezza della donna mia, sarà molto più bello agli occhi, e tanto più bellezza vedranno quanto la pietà la farà maggiore.

Pare molto conveniente, in confermazione di quello che abbiamo detto, che il cuore sia cagione delle lacrime, narrare come naturalmente le lacrime procedino più tosto dal cuore che dagli occhi e intendere che cagione muove le lacrime, come diremo appresso. Secondo e fisici, nel cuore nascono tutte le perturbazioni, d'allegrezza, di dolore, d'ira, di speranza e

where all desires are born, and taking the eyes not in their capacity as sensory organs, because really as external sense organs, they cannot judge the beauty of one thing or another. And therefore the eyes must be understood to mean the operation of our soul, which works through the eyes, and [to mean] that contentment and pleasure [the soul] feels by means of the instrument of the eyes when through their report it judges a thing beautiful and takes consolation and comfort from this.

In this sonnet [above], then, my heart is speaking to my eyes, explaining the affliction and misery in which it finds itself, as Love wishes, and the delight that the eyes feel by means of that ill, showing first the heart's ill, and then the eyes' delight. The misery of the heart is this: that it always desires that which it does not possess, nor can it achieve that end and effect it yearns for and desires as an ancient and ingrained desire. But the eyes not only perceive their object, that is my lady's eyes and her beauty, but they also see the loveliest and most excellent thing that it is possible for them to see, that is my lady, because the heart can desire nothing more than it desires her. And from its desire is born the greater beauty of my lady, who is as much more beautiful and perfect as the suffering of the heart, that is, its desire for her, is greater, for the reasons we have indicated. The sonnet next replies to a tacit contradiction that can be remarked there, which is that the eyes sometimes still weep, and this seems contrary to the felicity that the heart affirms to be in the eyes. And therefore it says that, even if the eyes do weep, this does not occur because of any pain of theirs, but because of the sorrow and desire of the heart, which by means of the tears vents a part of its sorrow. Then, addressing them [the eyes], it prays that they will beg Love to make our lady pitying, and not only would compassion for the heart's misery move them to this, but also the hope of greater good for the eyes, because, if pity in my lady is also achieved, Love will be peaceful, that is the desire for beauty will be fulfilled, and the heart will no longer be troubled. And in this case the sun, that is the eyes and beauty of my lady, will be greatly more beautiful to my eyes, and they will see more beauty insofar as pity will make it greater.

It seems very fitting, in confirmation of our having said that the heart is the cause of the tears, to recount how the tears naturally proceed from the heart rather than from the eyes, and to understand what causes tears as we shall say next. According to physicians, in the heart are born all the

---

all that part of the Soul which is subject to appetites for foods and drinks, and all the other wants that are due to the nature of the body, they planted in the parts midway between the midriff and the boundary at the navel...." In *Plato* (Cambridge: Harvard Univ. Press, 1952) 7:183.

di timore, e qualunque altra passione; le quali tutte, così nate nel cuore, per una certa conleganzia e conformità che è tra il cuore e il cervello, subito al cervello sono comunicate. Onde adviene che quando si comunica con lui o dolore o letizia, el cervello, oppresso o vero compresso da alcuna di queste passione, quasi in sé medesimo si ristringe; et essendo per natura umido e ristringendosi in guisa d'una spugna piena d'acqua, distilla per li occhi una parte di quella umidità, e così genera lacrime, le quali sono più abundante in uno che in un altro, secondo che il cervello è più o manco umido o secco. È cosa manifesta che ancora si piange così per allegrezza come per dolore; ma, secondo Aristotile, questa differenzia hanno le lacrime che procedono da letizia da quelle che vengono da dolore, che le lacrime liete sono fredde, le dolorose più calde; e ne assegna questa ragione: l'allegrezza e il dolore, per essere diverse passione, fanno molti diverse effetti, perché l'allegrezza dilata e fa più rari li spiriti vitali, il dolore gli ristrigne; dove concorre maggiore numero di spiriti, di necessità è maggiore copia di caldo, e così *e contra;* onde nasce la differenzia delle lacrime calde e fredde, che nascono o da dolore o da letizia. Concludesi per questo le lacrime avere due cagioni, l'una la passione del cuore, l'altra la distillazione della umidità che fa il cervello, e per questo gli occhi più tosto essere via che cagione delle lacrime.

X

Se tra li altri sospir' che escon di fore
del petto, come vuol mia dura sorte,
Amor qualcun ne mischia, par che porte
dolcezza alli altri e riconforti il core.
    Quel viso, che col vago suo splendore
ha già li spirti e le mie forze extorte
più volte delle avare man' di morte,
ancora aiuta l'alma, che non more.
    Fortuna invìda vede quel sospiri
che manda Amor dal core, e li comporta,

disturbances of joy, of sorrow, of wrath, of hope and of fear, and whatever other passions. All of these, being thus born in the heart, are immediately communicated to the brain by a certain linkage and conformity that exist between the heart and the brain. Because of this it happens that when either sorrow or delight are communicated to it, the brain, oppressed, or truly, compressed by some of these passions, is almost squeezed into itself. And being by nature moist and compressible like a sponge full of water, it distills through the eyes a part of that moisture, and so are generated tears, which are more abundant in one than in another according as the brain is more or less moist or dry.[63] It is evident that one can as well weep for joy as for sorrow. But, according to Aristotle, tears that result from joy have this difference from those that come from sorrow: joyful tears are cold, sorrowful ones hot.[64] And this reason accounts for it: joy and sorrow, by being different passions, produce very different effects, because joy dilates the vital spirits and makes them more rarified, but sorrow compresses them. Where a greater number of spirits come together there is of necessity a greater abundance of heat, and *vice versa*. From this is born the difference between hot and cold tears, which are born either from sorrow or from joy. From this we conclude that tears have two causes. The one is the passion of the heart, the other the distillation of moisture that the brain produces, and for this reason the eyes are rather the means than the cause of tears.

10

If midst the sighs that from my breast escape,
Just as my cruel fate desires, Love with
Them mixes some, it seems to offer to
Those others sweetness that revives my heart.
    That face, which with its lovely splendor has
Already torn my spirits and my force
So often from the greedy hand of death,
Assists my soul so that it does not die.
    Envious Fortune sees those sighs that Love
Sends from my heart and lets them pass,

---

[63] This explanation for the origin of tears comes from Aristotle, *Problematum ineditorium*, 2, 2, (ed. Didot), cited in Zanato, *Saggio*, 118, and in Bigi, 344, n. 2.
[64] Bigi (344) notes and Zanato (*Saggio* 118) concurs that Aristotle's discrimination in *Problematum* 31, 23 is between hot tears produced by spiritual sorrow and cold tears produced by physical ills. Lorenzo's discrimination above is either his own (Bigi) or an infidelity (Zanato) to his source.

> credendo che si arroga a' miei martìri.
> Così la inganno e fòlla manco accorta,
> se advien che Amore a lacrimar mi tiri;
> nè sa quanta dolcezza il pianto porta.

Promettemmo nel proemio, quando venissimo alla exposizione del presente sonetto, narrate quanto fussi grande e maligna la persecuzione che io sopportai in quel tempo e dalla fortuna e dagli uomini; e nondimeno, sono in disposizione passarmene molto brievemente, per fuggire el nome di superbo e vanaglorioso, imperò che il narrare e proprii e gravi pericoli difficilmente si fa sanza presunzione o vanagloria. E questo credo proceda ché, quando uno legno di turbolentissima tempesta dopo molti pericoli e paure si riduce nella tranquillità del porto, el più delle volte el nocchiere e governatore d'esso più tosto alla proprio virtù lo atribuisce che ad alcuna benignità della fortuna; e acciò che la virtù sua paia tanto maggiore, accresce tanto più il pericolo passato, e spesse volte fuora della verità, acciò che della virtù sua ancora si creda più che non è il vero. Questo medesimo essemplo seguitando, li medici della età nostra sempre fanno il pericolo dello infermo assai maggiore ch'e' non è, mettendo spesse volte dubbio di morte in quelli nelli quali la salute quasi manifesta si vede: perché, sopravenendo pure la morte, la colpa sia più tosto della natura che della cura; venendo la salute, la cura e opera si mostri tanto più efficace. E però, brevemente, diremo la persecuzione essere suta gravissima, perché li persecutori erano uomini potentissimi, di grande auttorità e ingegno e in disposizione e proposito fermo della mia intera ruina e desolazione, come mostra avere tentato tutte le vie possibili a nuocere a uno. Io, contro a chi venivano queste cose, ero giovane, privato e sanza alcuno consiglio o aiuto se non quello che dì per dì la divina benignità e clemenzia mi ministrava. Ero redutto a quello che, essendo a uno medesimo tempo nell'anima con excomunicazione, nelle facultà con rapine, nello stato con diversi ingegni, nella famiglia e figliuoli con nuovo trattato e macchinazione, nella vita con frequenti insidie persequitato, mi saria suto non piccolo grazia la morte, molto minor male allo appetito mio che alcuno di quelli altri. Essendo adunque in questa obscurità di fortuna posto, tra tante tenebre qualche

> Believing they will swell my sufferings.
> Thus I deceive her, make her notice less,
> If, as it happens, Love leads me to weep;
> Nor does she know what sweetness, too, tears bring.

We promised in the prologue that when we came to the exposition of this sonnet, we would tell how great and wicked was the persecution that I bore at that time both from Fortune and from men. But nevertheless I am disposed to pass over this very briefly, to avoid being called proud or vainglorious, since reporting both one's own and serious dangers can hardly be done without presumption or vainglory. And I believe this happens because, when a ship, after many dangers and fears of extremely turbulent storms, has once again gained the tranquillity of the harbor, most of the time its pilot and helmsman attributes that [success] to his own ability rather than to the benevolence of fortune. And in order that his abilities will seem the greater, he very much increases the dangers past, and often times exceeds the truth, so that more about his ability is believed than is true. Pursuing this same example, the physicians of our age make the danger to the ill person appear to be much greater than it is, often times putting the fear of death into those whose health one almost self-evidently sees—because, if death indeed occurs, the blame is rather nature's than the cure's. If health is restored, their cure and work show themselves to have been that much more efficacious. And therefore we shall briefly say that the persecution had been very serious, because the persecutors were most powerful men of great authority and intelligence, and they purposed and were firmly disposed to accomplish my utter ruin and desolation, as demonstrated by their having attempted in every way possible to harm me. I, against whom these actions were taken, was a young private person without any counsel and with no help except for that which from day to day Divine benevolence and clemency administered to me. I was reduced to a state such that, being at one in the same time afflicted in my soul with excommunication,[65] in my mental powers with rapine, in my government with diverse stratagems, in my family and children with new treachery and machinations, and in my life with frequent and persistent plots, death would have been no small grace for me, being much less an evil to my taste than any of those other things. Being then placed by Fortune in

---

[65] Pope Sixtus IV had been an accessory to the attempt of the Pazzi on Lorenzo's life as had the Florentine Archbishop Salviati. The enraged Florentine citizenry hanged Salviati along with other conspirators. In reprisal, Sixtus arrested all Florentine citizens in Rome, put Florence and her dependencies under an interdict, and excommunicated Lorenzo himself (Williamson, 177).

volta pure luceva lo amoroso raggio, talora gli occhi, talora il pensiero della donna mia; la quale dolcezza e refriggerio traeva la vita mia delle mani della morte, ancora che la fortuna non s'accorgesse di questo mio refriggerio, perché non discerneva bene gli amorosa sospiri da quelli che procedevano da lei. E però dico che, quando Amore mescolava alcuno de' suoi sospiri tra quelli che mi dava la mia adverse fortuna e dura sorte, gli amorosa adolcivono e mitigavono quelli altri e riconfortavono il cuore; e se adveniva qualche volta che vedessi il viso della donna mia, come altre volte aveva extorto delle mani avare di morte li spiriti e forze mie, al presente ancora difendeva contro alla morte l'anima mia. Et «extorta» non vuole dire altro che una cosa che è tolta a uno a suo dispetto; e la morte è veramente avara, perché maggiore avarizia non può essere che di colui il quale vuole il tutto per sé, come la morte vuole ogni mortal cosa. Subiunge poi che, veggendo la fortuna, inimica e invidiosa d'ogni mio bene, quelli sospiri che Amore mandava dal cuore, non gli conosceva per, amorosi, ma, credendo procedessino dalla mia mala sorte e persecuzione predetta, gli comportava, non credendo mi portassino dolcezza, ma che si arrogessi tanto più al mio male e che la pena mia fussi tanto maggiore. E io, accorgendomi dello inganno della fortuna, per ingannarla tanto meglio, qualche volta, come Amore voleva, piangevo e mi lamentavo, e tanto manco poteva intendere la fortuna la dolcezza e de' sospiri e de' pianti miei. Con questa arte adunque, per virtù di quelli belli occhi e d'Amore, qualche volta sentivo qualche refriggerio e dolcezza, la quale non arei sentita se·lla fortuna se ne fussi accorta.

XI

Se il fortunato cor, quando è più presso
a voi, madonna mia, talor sospira,
non s'incolpi di ciò disdegno o ira
o päura o dolor, lo qual sia in esso;
    ma la dolcezza che Amor li ha concesso
ciascun spirto disvia e a sé il tira,
tal che alcun refrigerio più non spira
al cor, che arde oblïato di sé stesso.
    Amor vede, se presto non soccorre,
per soverchia dolcezza il cor perire,
e i vaghi spirti al suo soccorso chiama.
    Ciascun per obedirlo pronto corre:
così crëan talor qualche sospire,
per refrigerio a quel che morir brama.

this darkness, among such great shadows, sometimes the amorous ray, now of the eyes, now of the thought of my lady, brought light. Her sweetness and solace drew my life from the hand of Death, even though Fortune was not aware of this solace of mine, because she could not well separate the amorous sighs from those that proceeded from her. And therefore I say that, when Love was mixing some of his sighs among those given me by my adverse fortune and cruel fate, the amorous ones sweetened and mitigated those others and revived my heart. And if it sometimes happened that I saw the face of my lady, as it had other times torn my spirits and my powers from the greedy hand of Death, at present it also defended against the death of my soul. And "torn from" means nothing other than a thing that is stolen from someone despite him. And Death is truly greedy, because greater avarice is not possible than his who wants everything for himself as Death wants every mortal thing. It follows that, Fortune, inimical to and envious of my every good, seeing those sighs that Love sent forth from my heart, did not recognize them as amorous, but, believing they proceeded from my evil fate and the aforementioned persecution, she tolerated them, not thinking that they brought me sweetness, but that they would very much exacerbate my distress and that then my pain would be much greater. And, perceiving this deception of Fortune, in order to deceive her much better, sometimes, as Love desired, I wept and lamented, and Fortune was very much less able to understand the sweetness either of my sighs or of my complaints. With these ruses then, by the power of those lovely eyes and of Love, sometimes I felt some solace and sweetness, which I would not have felt if Fortune had been aware of it.

11

> If when my heart so fortunate sometimes,
> My lady, near you sighs, accuse it not
> Of that disdain or wrath, that sorrow or
> That fear that it may have within itself;
> The sweetness, though, that Love has granted it,
> Diverts each spirit, draws it to itself,
> So that the heart, which burns forgotten by
> Itself, cannot breathe any coolness more.
> Love sees that, lacking prompt relief, the heart,
> Through overwhelming sweetness, soon will die
> And calls the wandering spirits to its aid.
> Each hurries quickly to obey his call;
> Such sighs as these are thus created as
> A solace for a man who yearns to die.

Io vorrei avere o tal forza di parole o tanta fede apresso degli uomini, che potessi bene exprimere e fare credere la excellenzia della donna mia, perché a'llei sarebbe onore e io fuggirei qualche pericolo d'essere stimato poco veritiero; ma non potendo né exprimere né mostrare gli occhi e le bellezze sue, perché, secondo il comune uso, forse quello che è virtù a incarico sarebbe atribuito, almanco mi sforzerò in qualche parte mostrare la gentilezza dello ingegno suo, narrando alcuno delli suoi motti, e questi, al mio parere, molto più alti e sottili che a donna non si conviene. E perché dinanzi abbiamo detto che le parole e quesiti suoi qualche volta hanno dato argumento a' nostri versi, el presente sonetto è uno d'essi, come faremo intendere apresso.

Ero assai vicino agli occhi suoi, per modo che da presso e quelli e l'altre bellezze potevo vedere; e guardando fiso in essi, tutto acceso già di speranza e pieno di dolcezza, qualche volta con profondi sospiri sospiravo. Questa gentilissima, alla quale già era noto il desiderio e stato del cuore mio, con dolcissime parole mi domandò come io ero contento e come stavo; e rispondendo io che più contento non poteva essere, né il cuore in maggiore dolcezza, ella subiunse:—Donde procedono adunque questi tuoi sospiri?—Io, e per timidità e perché e la bellezza e le parole avevono quasi trattomi di me stesso, non potei per allora rispondere altro; ma, partitomi dipoi da lei, feci il presente sonetto, nel quale mi sforzai mettere le cagioni naturali onde procedono e sospiri. È fatto questo sonetto in risposta di quella gentilissima donna: e però parla alla donna mia e dice che se 'l mio cuore fortunato, cioè felice e contento (perché «fortunato» non vuole dire altro che quello el quale ha prospera fortuna), sospira in quel tempo quando è più presso alla donna mia, cioè agiunto alla sua beatitudine, non n'è cagione alcuna perturbazione o cosa che l'offenda, come sarebbe sdegno, ira, dolore o paura; ma, volendo intendere meglio il vero, ne è cagione la dolcezza che lui sente, la quale è sì grande, che tiene occupate tutte le forze e spiriti vitali e gli svia dal loro officio naturale alla fruizione di quella dolcezza. Essendo adunque tutti li spiriti attenti a questo, bisogna cessino le operazioni naturali che per mezzo loro si fanno. Tra l'altre operazioni naturali è ancora il respirare, o vogliamo dire alitare, el quale ancora s'intermette per quello abbiamo detto; di qui nasce che al cuore manca el suo usato refriggerio, perché, essendo el cuore di natura caldo, e

I should like to have either such a power of language or such great faith in men, that I could well express and make people believe in the excellence of my lady, because it would do her honor and I would flee some danger of being esteemed untruthful. But as I am unable either to describe or to figure forth her eyes and her beauties, according to the common use, lest that which is a virtue be perhaps thought blameworthy, I am at least in some measure obliged to demonstrate the nobility of her intelligence by recounting some of her pleasantries, and these, as it seems to me, are much more elevated and refined than is appropriate to a woman. And because we have said before that her words and enquiries have sometimes given our verses their argument, this sonnet, as we shall soon understand, is one of those verses.

I was very close to her eyes, so that I could see both them and her other beauties from near at hand. And looking intently into them, already kindled by hope and filled with sweetness, sometimes I breathed forth profound sighs. This most gentle lady, who had already taken note of my desire and the state of my heart, with very sweet words asked me if I were happy and how I was. And when I answered that I could not be happier nor my heart in greater sweetness, she remarked: "Whence, then, proceed these sighs of yours?" I, for timidity and because both her beauty and her words had almost drawn me from myself, by then could not answer further; but, taking my leave of her, then, I made this sonnet in which I made myself put down the natural causes from which sighs proceed. This sonnet is composed in answer to this very gentle lady. And therefore it speaks to my lady and says that, if my fortunate heart, that is happy and content (because "fortunate" means nothing other than what fortune has prospered), sighs in that time when it is nearest to my lady, that is, when it arrives at its beatitude, it is not the result of any disturbance or thing that harms it, like disdain, wrath, sorrow, or fear would be. But, if she wishes to know the truth, the sweetness that it [my heart] feels is the cause of the sighs, which sweetness is so great that it keeps all my powers and vital spirits occupied, and misleads them from their natural offices to the enjoyment of that sweetness.[66] When the spirits, then, are all attentive to this, the natural operations performed by their means must cease. Among the other natural operations is also respiring [*respirare*], or, as we mean, breathing [*alitare*], which also is mediated by that about which we have spoken. From this it comes to pass that the heart lacks its accustomed cool-

---

[66] Bigi (348, n.2) notes this as a typical stilnovistic theme. See also *FC*, 6, 9, (194): "to whatever the serious attention of the soul is directed, to that also fly the spirits, which are the chariots or vehicles of the soul."

ancora per el concorso delli spiriti molto più acceso, si suffocherebbe e morrebbe se non si rinfrescassi per mezzo di quella aria, la quale aria per quello alito continuamente si rinuova e rinfresca. Di questo nasce che Amore, veggendo el cuore mio in tanto pericolo, chiama in soccorso e suoi spiriti vitali; e veramente Amore gli muove, perché la natura, amatrice della conservazione della vita, subitamente pigne in ogni passione del cuore li spiriti vitali: e quali spiriti, per ubbidire a questo amore della natura, con prontitudine e velocità corrono in soccorso suo. Di questo nasce che, se prima il cuore aveva bisogno di respirare e refriggerarsi, molto più ne ha bisogno sopravenendo tanti spiriti, e quali di natura loro sono caldi; e però necessariamente bisogna tirare dentro al petto più quantità d'aria, per ristorare l'ordinario officio dello alito, quale era intermesso. E di qui nasce il sospiro, e quinci si rinfresca il cuore; el quale, avendo già dimenticato sé stesso, per sé non si curava di morire, anzi bramava sì dolce e sì felice morte. Possiamo adunque dire el sospiro procedere da ogni passione di mente e da ogni fatica del corpo, pur che la passione della mente sia efficace in modo che diverta o intermetta le operazioni naturali dell'ordinario alitare, che appresso a' Latini propriamente *refocilare* si chiama, o vogliamo dire *respirare;* la fatica e agitazione del corpo, come in uno che corra o facci qualche forte essercizio, ancora genera sospiri, perché il caldo naturale si excita e accende, né potrebbe il corpo in quella fatica perseverare, se el cuore non si refrigerassi e spesso respirassi.

Vorrei avere potuto meglio exprimere questo mio concetto, perché così si conveniva a tanto degno e gentile quesito; e nondimeno ho eletto più tosto che al sonetto manchi ornamento e la vera expressione di questo senso, che in me manchi una pronta volunta di satisfare a quello che vuole Amore.

XII

Poscia che il bene adventurato core,
vinto dalla grandezza de' martìri,
mandando innanzi pria molti sospiri,
fuggì dello angoscioso petto fore,
    stassi in quei due belli occhi con Amore;
e perché loro, ove che Amor li giri,

ing, because, since the heart is hot by nature, and also much more kindled by the running together of the spirits, it would suffocate and die unless it were recovered by means of that air that is continually renewed and refreshed by breathing. From this it comes to pass that Love, seeing my heart in such danger, calls its vital spirits to the rescue. And truly Love moves them, because Nature, a lover of the preservation of life, in every passion of the heart immediately thrusts the vital spirits on. And these spirits, in order to obey this love according to their nature, with promptitude and speed run to its [the heart's] assistance. It follows from this that, if the heart at first needed to breathe and cool itself, it has much greater need of that [cooling] after so many spirits, whose nature is hot, suddenly arrive. And therefore necessarily it must draw into the breast a greater quantity of air to restore the ordinary function of breathing that was interrupted. And from this issues the sigh, and the sigh cools the heart, which, having already forgotten itself, by itself could not have been saved from dying, rather it desired such a sweet and such a happy death. We can then say that the sigh proceeds from every passion of the mind and from every effort of the body, provided that the passion of the mind functions in a way that diverts or interrupts the natural operations of ordinary breathing, which according to the Latins is properly called *refocilare,* or as we say, "respiring" [*respirare*].[67] The effort and agitation of the body, as in one who runs or performs some vigorous exercise, also generates sighs because the natural heat is excited and kindled, neither could the body continue in that effort if the heart did not cool itself and often breathe.

I would wish to have been better able to express this conceit of mine because it was so suitable to such a worthy and noble inquiry. And nevertheless I have rather chosen that the sonnet lack ornament and the true expression of this meaning, than that a prompt will be lacking in me to satisfy that which Love wished.

12

When after my lucky heart was overcome
By the intensity of all its pain,
It first sent many sighs ahead and then
It fled forth from my anguished, stricken breast,
    It stayed in those two lovely eyes with Love;
And since wherever Love caused them to turn,

---

[67] See Zanato, *Saggio,* 132 for Lorenzo's understanding of the etymologies of these words.

fan gentile ogni cosa che·llà miri,
degnato hanno ancor lui a tanto onore.
    Il cor, dagli occhi a questo bene eletto,
fatto è per lor virtù tanto gentile,
che più cosa mortal non brama o prezza;
    e benché abbin cacciato fòr del petto
quelli occhi ogni pensier vulgare e vile,
né torna a me, né brama altra bellezza.

Come nel precedente sonetto abbiamo narrato, già el cuore, assicurato da Amore, era da me fuggito, e di questo convenientemente séguita volere intendere e in che luogo arrivassi e in che stato si trovassi. Le quale cose si narrano nel presente sonetto, la sentenzia del quale è questa: che dapoi che il cuore mio, bene adventurato (e questo si vede per la conclusione del sonetto, perché «adventurato» si può chiamare quello che è gentile e perfetto, come dimosterremo nella diffinizione infrascritta della gentilezza; e però non dice bene adventurato per essere suto vinto dalla grandezza de' martirii, ma pel bene che glien'è seguìto), dico adunque che, dapoi che questo cuore, vinto dai martirii, molto sospirò, finalmente si partì del petto mio. Li martirii suoi non erano altro che lo acceso desiderio della bellezza della donna mia. Così adunque fuggito, giunse agli occhi suoi e da loro graziosamente fu ricevuto: che si può interpretare che il cuore mio si pasceva e della bellezza di quelli occhi e della speranza che aveva della futura pietà; la quale speranza gli dava Amore, che era ancora lui in quelli occhi, el quale non è mai sanza pietà. Questo dolcissimo ricetto, per la virtù di quelli occhi, fece gentile el mio cuore; perché, se gli è vero che quelli occhi, mossi da Amore, faccino gentile ogni cosa che e' guardano, molto più dovevono fare il mio cuore degno di tanto onore, cioè della gentilezza, il quale cuore sempre in loro abitava. E, per exprimere meglio il vero e verificare quanto è detto, diremo in questo modo: farsi gentile le cose che sono vedute da quelli occhi, quando Amore gli muove; per li occhi suoi si presuppone una singulare bellezza, per Amore pietà; e dove concorrono queste due cose, nasce nel cuore di chi vede gran dolcezza e amore, el quale, secondo che abbiamo detto, non è mai sanza gentilezza. Né possono quelli occhi mossi da Amore, cioè con affezzione, guardare cosa che non sia o in potenzia o in atto gentile, perché l'affezzione non si extende se non a quello che piace, né può piacere se non quella cosa la quale abbi qualche conformità con noi; e però, presuposto la gentilezza di quelli occhi, si verifica che e' non possono con amore guardare cosa che non

> There they ennobled all they looked upon,
> My heart they deigned to honor greatly too.
> Selected for this blessing by those eyes,
> My heart was made so noble by their power,
> That no more could a mortal crave or prize.
> And though those eyes have driven from my breast
> Each vulgar thought and low, my heart to me
> Returns not, nor for other beauty yearns.

As we explained in the preceding sonnet, already my heart, assured by Love, had fled from me, and from this fittingly follows the desire to know both in what place it had arrived and in what condition it found itself. These things are recounted in the sonnet above, the meaning of which is this: that, after my lucky heart (and this one sees in the conclusion of the sonnet, because one can call something "lucky" that is noble and perfect, as we shall demonstrate in the definition of nobility written below. And therefore it does not say "lucky" because it was overcome by the intensity of its torments, but because of the blessing for it that followed from them). I say then that, after this heart that was overcome by torments had sighed a great deal, finally it left my breast. Its torments were none other than the kindled desire for the beauty of my lady. Thus fled, then, it arrived in her eyes and they graciously received it. For one can understand that my heart nourished itself both on the beauty of those eyes and on the hope that it had for future pity. This hope, Love, who was also in those eyes and who is never without pity, gave to it. This very sweet shelter made my heart noble by the power of those eyes. Because, if it is true that those eyes, moved by Love, made everything noble that they looked upon, they must have made my heart, which always dwelt in them, much more worthy of such an honor, that is of nobility. And to better express the truth and to confirm what we say, we shall speak in this fashion. The things that are seen by those eyes are made noble when Love moves them. By her eyes I mean a singular beauty, by Love, pity. And where these two things concur there is born in the heart of whoever watches great sweetness and love, which, as we have said, is never without nobility. Neither when they are moved by Love, that is by affection, can those eyes see anything that is not noble either in its potential or in its deeds, because affection does not extend to that which does not please it, nor can anything please except what has some conformity with us.[68] And therefore, presupposing the nobility of those eyes, one confirms that they cannot look with love on

---

[68] See, FC, 2,8, (146): "Likeness generates love."

faccino gentile. El cuore mio adunque, eletto, cioè non per alcuno merito suo ma per liberalità e grazia della donna mia assunto a questo grado di gentilezza, già si stimava tanto e in tale perfezzione gli pareva essere venuto, che non estimava alcuna cosa vile o mortale. E perché non paia questo contradica a quello abbiamo detto, che sanza qualche merito non possa alcuna cosa ricevere da quelli occhi il grado di questa gentilezza, avendo io detto che il mio cuore sanza merito a questo fu eletto, dico, confermando la sentenzia sopra detta, che possiamo chiamare uno "gentile" o in atto o in potenzia, cioè veramente gentile e con tutte le parte che vengono da gentilezza, o atto a potere essere gentile: come diremo d'un fabro, el quale avendo il ferro sanza alcuna certa forma, si può dire abbi in mano una spada, una zappa o quello instrumento il quale è sua intenzione di comporre di quel ferro. Era il mio cuore prima questo ferro rozzo, ma atto a essere quello che volevano quelli occhi; e perché in loro potenzia era o lasciarlo così rozzo o fame una o un'altra cosa, per elezione del fabro fu fatto gentile cosa: e, quanto alla elezione, sanza merito; quanto allo essere disposto e atto a essere gentile, non sanza qualche merito; e così si absolve questa parte. Io, veggendo il mio cuore tanto gentile, cominciai ad amarlo più e desiderare che tornassi a me; e per muoverlo a questo, purgai la mente e il petto mio d'ogni cosa vile e vulgare per mezzo pure di quelli occhi, la perfezzione de' quali, portata in me dagli occhi miei, si restò nella inmaginazione. Né sarebbe restata quella gentilissima forma in mezzo di tutti i miei pensieri, se i miei pensieri fussino suti vili e vulgari; e però, come di natura fa il bene, «così» prima spogliò el petto mio d'ogni male. E, non obstante questa purgazione, non voleva tornare il cuore mio a me, né desiderava altra bellezza che quella di quelli occhi ove lui era; e così di necessità bisogna fussi, sendo quelli occhi bellissimi e 'l

anything that is not thus ennobled. My heart, then, although not for any merit of its own, but, through the liberality and grace of my lady, chosen and elevated to this degree of nobility, already rated itself so highly and seemed to have arrived at such perfection that it could not esteem anything mortal or low. And therefore this does not seem to contradict what we have said, that without some merit something cannot receive from those eyes this degree of nobility, though I have said that my heart without merit was chosen for this. I say, confirming the above stated meaning, that we can call one "noble" either in deed or in potential, that is truly noble and having all the attributes that proceed from nobility, or capable of becoming noble—just as a smith who is holding some iron without any certain form can be said to have in his hand a sword, a mattock or whatever instrument it is his intention to fashion from that iron. My heart was at first this rough iron, but capable of being that which those eyes desired. And because it was in their power either to leave it thus rough or to make something other of it, by the choice of the smith it was made into something noble. And, as regards the choice, it was unmerited. As regards being disposed and apt to be noble, [it was] not without some merit. And so this part is done. I, seeing my heart so noble, began to love it more and to want it to return to me. And, to move it to this, I cleansed my mind and breast of everything low and common, even by means of those eyes whose perfection, carried inside me by my eyes, remained in my imagination.[69] Neither, if my thoughts had been low and common, would that most noble form have remained in the midst of all my thoughts. And therefore, as it naturally produces the good, [so] it first stripped every evil from my breast. But, this cleansing notwithstanding, my heart did not wish to return to me, nor did it desire any beauty other than that of the eyes where it was. And of necessity it had to be so, since those eyes were most

---

[69] We see here the process by which, according to the stilnovists and to Ficino, the individual is ennobled by love. Note also the literalness of "imagination,"—the actual imprinting of the image of the beloved on the heart of the lover. See *FC*, 6, 6 (189): "the spirit receives through the instruments of the senses the images of external bodies; these images cannot be communicated directly to the soul, because incorporeal substance, which is more excellent than bodies, cannot be given form by them through the reception of images.... But ... the soul ... easily sees the images of bodies shining in it as though in a mirror.... While it sees these images, it conceives in itself by its own strength images like them but much purer. Conception of this kind we call imagination and fancy; the images conceived here are kept in the memory." Lorenzo's discussion here suggests that he was engaged in a program whose object was the cleansing of his own pneuma. See Ficino, *Vita coelestis* 4: "It [the spirit] becomes heavenly if it is scrupulously purged of its filth and everything tainted by it—purged of everything dissimilar to its heavenly essence." Cited in Couliano, 131.

cuore già fatto gentile, come meglio faremo intendere nella exposizione di quel sonetto che comincia *Candida, bella e dilicata mano.*

Pare solamente al presente necessario, perché spesse volte nelli nostri versi si truova questo vocabulo di "gentilezza" e "gentile," diffinire una volta per sempre quello che sia gentilezza secondo la mia oppinione. Né arei presunto di fare questo se Dante, clarissimo poeta, in quella canzona dove si diffinisce la gentilezza, non si fussi ristretto alla diffinizione della gentilezza dell'uomo, la quale lui chiama quasi «nobilità». Ma essendo questo vocabulo, secondo il vulgare uso, quasi comune a tutte le cose, non mi pare inconveniente dire quello che ne intendo; *maxime* perché, nella significazione che si usa, è vocabulo nuovo e al tutto vulgare, del quale non può essere né per diffinizione né per lo uso degli antichi alcuna certa proprietà. Pare adunque a me che questo vocabulo "gentile" sia nato da quelli che "gentili" furono chiamati, cioè e Romani, e quali e dalli ebrei teologi e da' cristiani furono chiamati "gente," e dipoi "gentili," come per molti essempli si può provare. E perché e gentili, cioè e Romani, in queste cose che il mondo onora e pregia furono reputati excellentissimi, credo si cominciassi ‹a› chiamare "gentile" ogni cosa che avessi tra le altre qualche excellenzia, quasi opera fatta da' gentili o che alla excellenzia loro convenissi. Lo uso dipoi ha allargato la significazione del vocabulo, tanto che la diffinizione è molto difficile; perché si dirà, *verbi gratia,* uno "gentile" avorio o uno "gentile" ebano, che l'uno è tanto più bello quanto è più candido, l'altro quanto è più nero è più stimato: cose molto contrarie l'una all'altra, e nondimeno expresse dal medesimo vocabulo. Diremo adunque "gentile" essere quella cosa la quale è bene atta e disposta a fare perfettamente l'officio che a'llei si conviene, accompagnata da grazia, la quale è dono di Dio. E, per essemplo, chiameremo "gentile" un cavallo corridore, el quale corra più velocemente che gli altri, e oltre a questo vi

beautiful and my heart was already made noble, as we could best understand in the exposition of that sonnet [13] that begins: "O pure white, delicate and lovely hand."

Because often times in our verses these words "nobility" [*gentilezza*] and "noble" [*gentile*] are found, it only seems necessary now to define once and for all what in my opinion nobility is. Nor would I have presumed to do this if Dante, the very famous poet, in that ode where nobility is defined,[70] had not limited the definition of the nobility [*gentilezza*] of man to what he almost calls "magnanimity" [*nobilitá*]. But because this word, according to vernacular use, is almost applied to everything, it does not seem inappropriate to tell what I understand by it, especially because, in the meaning that is used, it is a new word and completely vernacular, and so there cannot be either through the definition or the usage of the ancients any established meaning. It seems then to me that this word "noble" [*gentile*] issued from those who were called "the noble ones" [*gentili*], that is the Romans,[71] who were called first "people" [*gente*], and afterwards "gentiles" [*gentili*] both by Hebrew and by Christian theologians, as can be proved by many examples. And because the gentiles, that is the Romans, were reputed most excellent in those things that the world honors and prizes, I believe that people began to call "noble," [*gentile*], every thing that had some excellence beyond the others, almost works that the "nobles" had done or that suited their excellence. Usage has since broadened the meaning of the word so that its definition is very difficult. For one will say, for example, a "noble" ivory or a "noble" ebony, because the one is as much more esteemed because it is whiter as is the other because it is blacker—things very contrary to each other, but nevertheless expressed by the same word. We say then that a certain thing is "noble" that is well adapted and disposed to perform perfectly the office to which it is suited, accompanied by grace that is a gift of God.[72] And, for example, we call "noble" a race horse that runs faster than the others.

---

[70] See Dante, *Conv.* 4, the ode beginning, "The dulcet rimes of love that I was wont." (Jackson, 190), and the accompanying commentary in sections 16 (250–252) and 19 (Jackson, 258–60), where "gentilezza" is understood as nobility of the mind.

[71] Bigi (353, n. 1) says that *gentile* in the meaning of "noble" comes directly from the Latin *gentilis*, meaning "of good stock." The rest of Lorenzo's explanation, however, is false etymology. What is perhaps most important here is that Lorenzo does not argue the case for hereditary nobility, but rather for nobility of attribute.

[72] Compare Dante, *Conv.* 4, 16, 4, (251): "this word, nobility signifies in each thing the perfection of nature peculiar to it." Zanato (*Saggio*, 133) observes that the most significant part of the etymology is original with Lorenzo, but also notes as a parallel example Landino's definition in *Comento a Inf.* 2, 94.

agiugneremo la bellezza, che agli occhi lo facci grato. Perché, oltre al correre forte, non sarebbe gentile s'e' non corressi levato e ben partito e con poca dimostrazione di fatica o d'affanno; né sarebbe gentile se e' non fussi bello, né avessi piccola testa e asciutta, larghe le nare del naso, gli occhi di conveniente grandezza e vivi, piccoli orecchi, collo sottile e svelto, non molto petto ma raccolto, el piè di buon colore e forte, alti e larghi calcagni, giuntato corto; le gambe né grosse né sottile, ma asciutte, le quali equalmente eschino delle spalle; abbi assai, a proporzione del resto, dalla punta della spalla al guidalesco; schiena non molto lunga, doppio di lombi, poco corpo e non pendente, e lungo più di sotto che nella schiena, le lacche buone, le falce di drieto diritte, piccolo coda; mantello che sia grato agli occhi, con qualche buono segno: come sarebbe un cavallo, *verbi gratia,* tutto morello, col piè di drieto sinistro balzano e un poco di stella in fronte. Chi volessi laudare con queste parte uno corsiere da guerra, errerebbe, perché ha a fare officio molto diverso. E però la gentilezza è quasi una distinzione iudiciale di tutte le cose.

Volendo adunque vedere quello che era il mio cuore già fatto gentile, è necessario intendere l'officio del mio cuore, el quale, avendo per obbietto gli occhi e bellezza della donna mia, a me pare avessi tre officii: l'uno conoscere, l'altro amare, il terzo fruire e godere quella bellezza. E se questa bellezza è grande, come abbiamo detto, grande perfezzione bisognava fussi quella del cuore a conoscerla, ad amarla e a fruirla. Non diremo più di questa parte per al presente, perché nelli sonetti seguenti explicheremo molto meglio questa materia e mosterremo chiaramente perché il cuore già fatto gentile non può bramare altra bellezza che quella della donna mia.

XIII

Candida, bella e dilicata mano,
ove Amore e Natura poser quelle

And beyond this we add its beauty, which makes it pleasing to the eyes. Because, apart from strong running, it would not be noble if it did not run with a proper gait and stride and with small evidence of effort or fatigue. Nor would it be noble if it were not handsome nor unless it had a small, shapely head, large nostrils, eyes of suitable size and brightness, small ears, a fine, smooth neck, a chest not large but compact, the feet of good color and strong, high and large hock points, short tendoned; the legs should come forth evenly from the shoulders, neither thick nor thin but firm. From the point of the shoulders to the withers he must be very well developed in proportion with the rest of his body; his spine not very long, double the loins, of little belly and not drooping, and longer beneath than in the spine, the buttocks sound, the hocks straight behind, a short tail; a coat pleasing to the eyes with some good marking—as a nearly all black horse would be, for example, with a white band on the left back foot and a little star on his forehead.[73] Whoever would wish to praise these attributes in a war horse would be mistaken because it has a very different office.[74] And therefore nobility is almost a judgmental distinction in all things.

Wishing then to see what had made my heart noble, it is necessary to understand the office of my heart, which, having as its object the eyes and beauty of my lady, seemed to me to have three functions: the first to know, the second to love, and the third to use and enjoy that beauty. And if this beauty is great, as we have said, it must have been great perfection for the heart to know it, to love it, and to enjoy it. We shall not say more about this part for the present, because in the sonnets following we shall explain this material much better and we shall clearly show why the heart, already made noble, cannot yearn for any other beauty than that of my lady.

13

O pure white, delicate and lovely hand,
Where love and nature placed those graceful sweets,

---

[73] There is an Italian proverb that an all black horse is sure to be vicious, so these markings suggest a horse of good temper.

[74] Lorenzo's expert judgment concerning horses and his energetic interest in them communicates itself as one of most charming passages of L's *Commentary*. To document Lorenzo's originality in this discussion, Zanato (*Saggio*, 126–8) provides a point-by-point comparison of Lorenzo's text with its sources and analogues: Dante, *Conv.* 1, 5, 11; two widely-known, pre-15th c. tracts on horsemanship by Giordano Ruffo and by Dino di Piero Dini, appearing in Riccardiana codices 2934 and 1684, and cited as Laurentian sources by M. Martelli in "Il Sonetto del cavallo perfetto," *Rinascimento* 2, 6, 1966, 57–77; the anonymous "sonnet of the perfect horse," itself; and Luigi Pulci's *Morgante*.

>   leggiadrie dolci, sì gentili e belle,
> che ogni altra opera lor par fatta invano,
>   tu träesti del petto il cor pian piano
> per la piaga che fèr le vaghe stelle,
> quando Amor sì piatose e dolce felle;
>   tu drieto a·lloro entrasti a mano a mano;
>   tu legasti il mio cor con mille nodi;
> tu 'l formasti di nuovo; e poi che fue
> gentil fatto per te, rompesti e lacci.
>   S'egli è fatto gentil, non convien piùe
> cercar per rilegarlo nuovi modi
> o pensar che altra cosa mai li piacci.

Abbiamo detto quelle cose potersi chiamare "gentile," le quale perfettamente e con grazia fanno quello a che sono ordinate; e per questo parrebbe, *prima facie,* che qualunque cosa fatta una volta gentile non avessi bisogno d'alcuna altra cosa alla perfezzione sua: che pare contro a quello che dice il presente sonetto. La conclusione del quale è che la mano gentilissima della donna mia, avendomi tratto il cuore del petto, lo abbi fatto gentile avendolo formato di nuovo; el quale cuore già era suto fatto gentile dagli occhi suoi, come mostra il sonetto già exposto che comincia *Poscia che 'l bene adventurato core.* E però, prima che più particularmente vegnamo alla exposizione del sonetto, per concordare questa apparente contradizione diremo così. Che se·lla gentilezza è quello che abbiamo detto, tante cose possono essere gentili quanto sono e fini a che tendono le cose; come si vede per experienzia in uno uomo, perché lo chiameremo nella sua tenera e puerile età un "gentile" fanciullo, dipoi un "gentile" garzone, un "gentile" giovane, un "gentile" uomo, etc., secondo che l'età e la natura gli mostra diversi fini: perché diverse cose convengono a diverse età. E però, quando el mio cuore si fuggì negli occhi della donna mia, dalli quali fu fatto gentile, si può intendere che allora il cuore aveva per obiecto solamente gli occhi della donna mia e le altre aparenti bellezze, e solamente di quello si pasceva per mezzo della visione degli occhi miei; e a questo fu fatto gentile, cioè a intendere, contemplare e fruire solamente per mezzo degli occhi quella bellezza. Ma dipoi, essendo quella mano candidissima entrata nel petto e trattone il cuore, pare che questo fussi absunto a più degno officio, perché questo mostra la iurisdizione che aveva la donna mia sopra 'l mio cuore et expressamente chiarisce che già lei lo reputava suo; et essendo sua cosa per elezzione di lei, di necessità lo amava. E questo mostra più chiaramente lo averlo cominciato a fare gentile con li occhi, cioè fattoli questo benifizio, perché quelle cose si amano più che l'altre,

> So noble and so lovely that it seems
> That all their other works are made in vain,
> > You gently drew my heart forth from my breast,
> Out through the wound the lovely stars had made
> When Love made them so pious and so sweet;
> You entered in behind them, bit by bit,
> > And with a thousand knots you bound my heart.
> You formed it new; and when you afterward
> Had made it noble, you broke all its bonds.
> > Since it is made noble, it won't do
> To longer seek to bind it with new knots,
> Or ever think it pleased by something else.

We have said that those things can be called noble that perfectly and with grace perform that for which they are ordained. And from this it would seem, *prima facie,* that whatever had been once made noble would not need anything else for its perfection—which seems counter to what the sonnet above says. Its conclusion is that the very noble hand of my lady, having drawn my heart from my breast, had made it noble by having formed anew that heart that had already been made noble by her eyes, as the sonnet, already explained, shows that begins: "When after my lucky heart...." [12] And therefore, before we more particularly come to the exposition of the sonnet, in order to resolve this apparent contradiction, we shall speak thus. For if nobility is what we have said, as many things can be noble as there are ends toward which those things tend. We see this from experience in a man, because we call him in his tender and puerile age a "noble" little fellow, and then a "noble" lad, and then a "noble" young man, and "noble" man, etc., according as his age and nature reveal different ends for him. Because different things are suited to different times of life. And therefore, when my heart was fled into the eyes of my lady, by which it was made noble, one can understand that then the heart had as its object only the eyes of my lady and her other associated beauties, and only on those was it nourished by means of the sight of my eyes. And for this was it made noble, that is, to understand, to contemplate and to enjoy that beauty only by means of the eyes. But after that whitest of hands entered into my breast and drew the heart from it, it seemed that it would be elevated to a very worthy office, because this demonstrates the jurisdiction that my lady exercised over my heart, and it expressly clarifies that she already considered it hers. And being her own by her own choice, of necessity she loved it. And this appears most clearly in my heart's having begun to be made noble by the eyes, that is by their having done it this kindness, because those things are loved more than others that we account

le quale noi reputiamo nostre e, come nostre, abbiamo cominciato a benificarle. Altro era adunque l'officio del cuore prima che la donna mia facessi segno alcuno d'amore verso di lui, altro è questo che doveva fare dopo tante benigne dimostrazione; e però, come a nuovo officio e fine, di nuovo bisognò farlo gentile, perché non solamente aveva per obbietto la bellezza sua, ma ancora lo amore della donna mia: tanto più degna cosa, quanto più spirituale e manco corporea, e non di manco o meno desiderabile bellezza al cuore mio che gli occhi suoi agli occhi miei. Era adunque necessario, come è detto, di nuovo farlo gentile e formarlo per questo nuovo obbietto, e questo officio a nessuno pare che più si convenissi che alla mano della donna mia. La quale bisogna intendere fussi la mano sinistra, la quale, partendo dal cuore, ⟨appariva⟩ come più certo nunzio e testimonio della intenzione del cuore della donna mia: perché si dice nel dito anulario, cioè quello che è allato al dito che vulgarmente chiamiamo "mignolo," è una vena che viene *inmediate* dal cuore, quasi un messo della intenzione del cuore. Veggiamo adunque di necessità el cuore di nuovo bisognava essere riformato e fatto gentile a questo nuovo e più degno fine, e che la vera ministra a questo effetto era la mano sinistra, per le sopra dette ragioni.

Ora verremo a più particulare exposizione del sonetto. Certamente, tra l'altre gentilissime bellezze della donna mia, le mani sue non parevono cose umane; e benché ambo fussino belle, pure el presente sonetto, come di sopra dicemmo, parla alla mano sinistra, la quale chiama candida, bella e dilicata non perché comprenda tutte le bellezze di quella mano, ma, narrandone una parte, vuole che chi legge comprenda ogni essatta perfezzione che si convenga a una mano. E che questo sia vero, lo mostra subiungendo poi che l'amore e la natura gli avevono in modo contribuito ogni loro gentilezza, leggiadria e dolcezza, e in effetto ogni generazione d'ornamento, che pareva ogni altra opera loro fatta invano, quanto a comparazione di queste bellezza. Qui è da notare che tutte le cose che piacciono, per due rispetti piacciono, cioè o per essere perfettamente belle o per essere molto amate e desiderate, perché spesso adviene che s'ama una cosa che non è reputata bella; e però, dove si unisce colla bellezza naturale lo amore, nessuna cosa può piacere tanto. Per questo si dice che l'amore e la natura avevono posto in quella mano ogni ornamento: che si può interpetrare la perfezzione della bellezza naturale e lo amore grande, che non lasciava mancare alcuna, ancora che piccola parte di bellezza a quella mano. Questa mano tanto bella, adunque, entrò nel petto mio, el quale trovò aperto per la ferita che prima avevono fatta gli occhi, drieto alli quali subitamente entrò e ne trasse el mio cuore. Ebbono grazia gli occhi miei, prima, di conoscere la bellezza degli occhi suoi, e poi, come spesso

to be our own and that, as our own, we have begun to treat kindly. Moreover, these were the offices of my heart before my lady had given it any sign of love. Then too, it was this that it was obliged to do after so many demonstrations of kindness. And therefore, as for a new office and end, it needed to be made noble again, because it not only had her beauty as its object, but also the love of my lady—a thing as much more worthy as it was more spiritual and less corporeal, and her beauty was no less wanting nor less desirable to my heart than were her eyes to mine. It was then necessary, as has been said, to make my heart noble again and to shape it for this new object, and for this function nothing seemed better suited than the hand of my lady. This must be understood to have been the left hand, which, in departing from my lady's heart, [appeared] like a more certain messenger and witness of its intention. For it is said that in the ring finger, that is the one next to the finger that in the vernacular we call "the little finger," is a vein that comes *directly* from the heart, almost a messenger of the heart's intention. Of necessity we see then that my heart again had to be reformed and made noble to this new and worthier end, and that the true officer to this effect was her left hand for the reasons stated above.

Now we shall proceed to a more particular exposition of the sonnet. Certainly, among the other very noble beauties of my lady, her hands did not seem merely human. And since both were lovely, this sonnet really, as we said above, speaks about the left hand, which it calls white, lovely, and delicate not because it encompasses all the beauties of that hand, but because, in talking about one attribute, it wants the reader to understand every exact perfection that is appropriate to a hand. And that this is true is shown by saying in addition that Love and Nature have in a way given to it their every nobility, grace, and sweetness, and in effect every sort of adornment, so that it seemed that every other work of theirs had been made in vain in comparison with these beauties. Here it must be noted that all things that please do so in two respects, that is either by being perfectly beautiful or by being greatly loved and desired, because it often happens that a thing is loved that is not accounted beautiful; and therefore where love is united with natural beauty, nothing can please so much. For this reason I say that Love and Nature had placed every adornment in this hand—which can be interpreted to be the perfection of natural beauty and the great love that left nothing lacking, however small, which was suited to the beauty of that hand. This hand so lovely, then, entered into my breast, which it found open because of the wound that her eyes earlier had given it, after which her hand immediately entered and drew my heart forth from it. My eyes had been graced before by knowing the beauty of her eyes, and then, as often happens, either while dancing or in some

adviene, o ballando o in altro simile onesto modo fui fatto ancora degno di toccare la sua sinistra mano: perché sulla scala d'amore si monta di grado in grado. Ebbe tanta forza questa mano così da me tocca, che mi tolse di me lo intero dominio e, come abbiamo detto, trasse el cuore del mio petto; el quale, preso da questa mano, fu di principio legato molto stretto, dipoi reformato di nuovo e fatto gentile da quella mano, perché il formare è proprio officio delle mani. Et essendo così reformato e fatto gentile, quella mano sciolse tutti e lacci e misse il mio cuore in libertà, perché essendo fatto gentile non poteva amare se non gentile cose, nè avere altro che gentilissimo obbietto; e nessuno più gentile ne poteva trovare che la donna mia, anzi la vera gentilezza. E però non bisognava dubitare che mai più si partissi da lei, perché già stava sanza essere legato; né ancora si poteva dubitare che altra bellezza gli potessi piacere, perché se quella cosa piace più la quale è o pare più bella che l'altre, nessuna più bella se ne poteva trovare che la donna mia: della quale si può veramente dire, per essere gentile e bella, quello che dice Dante:

«Di costei si può
dire gentile in donna ciò che in lei si truova,
e bello è tanto quanto lei simiglia».

XIV

O mano mia, suavissima e decora!
«Mia» perché Amor, quel giorno che ebbe a sdegno
mia libertà, mi dette te per pegno
delle promesse che mi fece allora.
   Dolcissima mia man, con quale indora
Amor li strali onde cresce il suo regno,
con questa tira l'arco, a cui è segno

other likewise chaste fashion,[75] I was also made worthy to touch her left hand—because on the ladder of love one climbs step by step. When I touched it in this way, this hand had such great power that it seized entire dominion over me and, as we have said, drew forth from my breast my heart. Taken by this hand, my heart was in the beginning very tightly bound, then reformed again and made noble by that hand, because the appropriate office of hands is shaping. And when my heart had been so reformed and ennobled, that hand struck all the fetters and set my heart at liberty, because once it had been ennobled it could not love any except noble things, nor have other than a most noble object. And no one could be found for it nobler than my lady, or rather, than true nobility. And therefore one need not doubt that my heart never after parted from her, for it had already been unbound, nor should one doubt that no other beauty could please it, because if that pleases most that is or seems more beautiful than the others, nothing more beautiful could be found for my heart than my lady—about whom, for being noble and lovely, once can truly say that which Dante says:

> Of her one can say:
> What's noble in a lady is what one finds in her,
> And beautiful what most resembles her.[76]

14

> O my own gentlest, loveliest of hands!
> "My own," for Love, that day when he denied
> My liberty, gave you to me, a pledge
> For promises that he then made to me;
>   O sweetest hand of mine, with which Love gilds
> The arrows that make his dominion grow,
> With you he draws his bow, which makes a mark

---

[75] Among Lorenzo's many accomplishments, that of choreographer has been little noted, but, in fact, Lorenzo choreographed at least two dances: Lauro, (Lorenzo's nickname), a dance for two, and *Venus*, a dance for three dancers. Both these choreographies appear in F. Zambrini, *Scelta di Curiositá letterarie inedite or rare*, vol. 131, Bologna, 1873, 65–68. In a lecture with performance, "A Choreography by Lorenzo in Botticelli's *La Primavera*" at an international conference on Lorenzo, Brooklyn, May 1, 1992, Emily Jayne (to whom I am indebted for the Zambrini reference) argued convincingly that *Venus* is the dance performed by the three graces in Botticelli's *Primavera*. See Emily Jayne, "Tuscan Dancing Figures in the Quattrocento," diss., Princeton Univ., 1990, for a discussion of the connection between Lorenzo's dance and Botticelli's painting.

[76] *Conv.* 3, 49–50, (1:254). Translation mine.

        ciaschedun cor gentil che s'innamora.
          Candida e bella man, tu sani poi
        quelle dolci ferite, come il telo
        facea (come alcun dice) di Pelide.
          La vita e morte mia tenete voi,
        eburnee dita, e il gran disio ch'io celo,
        qual mai occhio mortal vedrà, né vide.

Come nel precedente sonetto abbiamo detto, la natura e lo amore danno ogni perfezzione e ornamento. Questo medesimo conferma il sonetto presente, el quale, parlando pure a quella mano gentilissima, la chiama suavissima e decora: decora per li ornamenti e bellezze naturali, suavissima per lo amore e desiderio d'essa, perché se non fussi questo amore e desiderio non potrebbe essere suave, ancora che bellissima. Oltre a queste due proprietà, è da notare che io la chiama mia; e perché questo pareva arroganzia, perché di sì bella e gentile cosa non ero degno, replico questo vocabulo «mia» *inmediate* nel secondo verso, e giustifico se così la chiama mostrando esserne cagione Amore, el quale me la dette per pegno della promessa pietà della donna mia. È comune e antiqua consuetudine tra gli uomini in ogni patto e transazzione, per più efficace segno del cuore e voluntà nostra, toccare con la mano destra propria la destra di colui con chi si fa il patto, e comunemente s'usa quando si perviene a pace dopo qualche guerra e ingiuria seguìta; similmente, quando in tali o in altri casi si piglia giuramento alcuno, la destra mano è lo instrumento e ministra. Credo questa tale consuetudine sia suta introdotta dalla cagione che diremo apresso. Qualunque pace o simile patto e fede data che fussi interrotta o non observata, bisogna che sia così rotta da qualche nuova ingiuria, della quale il più delle volte suole essere principio e ministra la mano destra, che è quella che percuote e nella maggiore parte degli uomini è più expedita e pronta alla offesa; e però, usandosi la destra nelle convenzioni sopra dette come testimonio e confermazione di quello che è fatto, pare che si oblighi quella cosa la quale prima e più facilmente può violare il patto. Dettemi adunque Amore questo pegno delle promesse sue quel giorno che ebbe a sdegno la mia libertà, cioè quello dì che mi legò. E qui è da notare che questo pare contro alla verità, perché quel giorno che quelli occhi mi legorono, ancora non avevo tocca questa gentilissima mano. Ma bisogna intendere in uno

Of every noble heart that falls in love.
　White hand and beautiful, those injuries
So sweet you then heal up as did the spear
Of Peleus (as some are wont to say).[77]
　You, ivory fingers, hold my life and death,
And hold the great desire that I conceal,
Which mortal eye has never seen nor shall.

　As we have said in the preceding sonnet, nature and love gave [her hand] every perfection and grace. This same the present sonnet confirms, which even speaks of that hand as most noble and calls it gentlest and loveliest—loveliest because of its graces and natural beauties; most gentle because of its love and desire, because if there were not this love and desire it would not be able to be gentle, much less most lovely. Beyond these two attributes, it is to be noted that I call it "my own" hand. And because this seems arrogant, because I was unworthy of such a noble and lovely thing, *immediately* in the second line, I repeat this phrase[78] "my own," and I justify my naming it thus by showing Love to be the cause of that, [Love] who gave it to me as a pledge of my lady's promised pity. It is a common and ancient custom among men in every contract and transaction, to touch, as a more efficacious sign of our heart and will, with our own right hands the right hand of him with whom the pact is made, and commonly it is done when peace is restored after some war and related injury. Similarly, when in such cases or in others someone takes an oath, the right hand is its instrument and officer. I believe such a custom as this to have been introduced from the cause that we shall next explain. Whatever peace or similar pact and promise has been given that was interrupted or not observed must have been broken by some new injury that, most of the time usually is begun and administered by the right hand, for it is that which strikes and in most men is very quick and ready to give offence. And therefore, the right hand is used in the above mentioned covenants as a witness and confirmation of that which is performed, for it seems to put under obligation the thing that can first and most easily violate the pact. Love therefore had given me this pledge of his promises on that day he disdained my liberty, that is on that day when he bound me. And here one must note that this seemed counter to the truth, because that day when those eyes bound me, I had not yet touched this most noble hand.

---

[77] The javelin of Peleus and Achilles, according to legend, had the power to heal the wounds that it produced.

[78] Ital. *vocobolo*.

de' dua modi, cioè o che quel dì che Amore mi legò, in sé medesimo fece questo proposito di darme in pegno questa mano, ancor che per qualche tempo differissi lo effetto; o vero, ch'io fui interamente legato e al tutto fuori di libertà come toccai quella mano, perché, come dicemmo nel precedente sonetto, quella legò il mio cuore con mille nodi. E questo mostra che il cuore allora stava per forza di legame, e, se avessi forse potuto, volentieri si saria sciolto: e però riteneva ancora qualche parte di libertà; ma poi che fu riformato di nuovo, e levato e lacci, stando di sua volontà sempre con la donna mia, allora si poteva interamente chiamare fuori d'ogni sua pristina libertà. E quel dì Amore ebbe a sdegno la libertà sua, cioè la libertà che prima aveva el cuore inanzi che conoscessi questa nuova libertà dove lo misse Amore; perché «libertà» si può chiamare quando alcuno può disporre a suo arbitrio, come poteva il cuore mio, sendo sciolto e libero da ogni legame; e di questa parte diremo più ampliamente nella exposizione del sonetto che comincia *Chi ha la vista sua* etc. Subiunge dipoi che questa mano veramente dolcissima indora li strali di Amore, questa tira l'arco di Amore e ferisce tutti e cuori gentili che s'inamorono, che sono segno e berzaglio alli strali amorosi: come certifica il nostro Petrarca, quando dice: «Amore, che i cuori gentili suave invesca, né degna di provare sua forza altrove». Qui è da notare che tutti questi sono officii che si fanno per mezzo delle mani. E, oltre a questo, dicendo che questa mano indora le saette amorose, bisogna intendere che questa mano prepara ad Amore li strali li quali inamorano, che si dicono essere aurei, e non quelli di piombo, e quali sogliono cacciare Amore e fare nascere odio. E come tutti questi sono officii della mano, similmente è officio suo medicate le ferite, perché la cerusica, la cura della quale si extende a simili medicine, non vuole dire altro che opera di mani. Ferisce adunque e sana, cioè accende il desiderio, dipoi l'adempie, come si dice faceva il telo, cioè la lancia d'Achille figliuolo di Pelleo, la quale avendo due punte, dicono e poeti che con l'una feriva, con l'altra sanava le ferite. Di questo nasce convenientemente che, potendo questa mano e ferire e sanare, può ancora uccidere e vivificare; adunque convenientemente è detto che quelle dita

But one must understand this in one of two ways, that is either that on that day when Love bound me, on that same day he made this proposal of giving me this hand in pledge, although for some time he deferred that effect; or truly, that I was entirely bound and utterly deprived of liberty as soon as I touched that hand. Because, as we say in the preceding sonnet, that lady bound my heart with a thousand knots. And this shows that my heart then remained tied perforce, and, if it had perhaps been able, it would willingly have freed itself. And therefore it still retained some part of liberty. But after it was refashioned again and its bonds undone, of its own will it stayed with my lady, when it could be called utterly without its original liberty. And on that day Love had disdained its liberty, that is the liberty that the heart enjoyed before it knew this new liberty in which Love had placed it. For something can be called at "liberty" when it can be at the disposition of its own free will, as my heart could after being untied and freed from every bond. And of this part we shall speak more amply in the exposition of the sonnet that begins "Whoever's blessed with sight so strong ...," etc.[79] It [the sonnet] says next that, after this truly most sweet hand gilds the arrows of Love, it draws Love's bow and wounds all the noble hearts that fall in love, which are a target and a mark for amorous arrows, as our Petrarch certified when he says:

> Love, who only birdlimes noble hearts,
> Nor elsewhere condescends to test his strength.[80]

Here it must be noted that all these are offices that are performed by means of hands. And beyond this, by saying that this hand gilds the amorous arrows, one must understand that this hand prepares for Love the arrows with which he makes people fall in love—arrows that are said to be golden, and not those of lead, which usually drive love away and cause hate to be born. And as all these are offices of the hand, similarly it is the hand's business to heal wounds, because surgery, whose charge extends to similar healing, can be called nothing other than a work of the hands. It wounds then and heals, that is, it kindles desire and then fulfills it, as is said of the spear, that is the javelin of Achilles son of Peleus, which had two points, one that wounded, so the poets say, and one that healed the wounds. From this it fittingly follows that, as this hand was able both to

---

[79] This is the first of two sonnets which do not appear in the text as we have it. See poem 64 in "Rime," in Simioni 1:207, and see "Appendix A" for text and translation. Cf. *Rvf.* 19, 1–2: "The world has creatures with such lofty sight/ That it holds steady though it braves the sun. . . ."

[80] *Rvf.* 165, 5–6: Amor, che solo i cor leggiadri invesca. . . . L.'s quotation, apparently from memory, is inexact.

eburnee, cioè quelle dita di colore d'avorio, tengono la vita e morte mia. E ancora questo è proprio officio delle dita, perché quello che strigne la mano, lo fa per mezzo delle dita. Tiene ancora questa mano el mio gran disio, e questo molto veramente, per quello che nel precedente sonetto è detto; perché, tenendo il cuore mio, nel quale è la virtù concupiscibile, cioè il desiderio, tiene el mio disio, el quale io nascondo dagli occhi degli uomini, a' quali al tutto è invisibile. Perché, se gli è vero quello che abbiamo detto, che questa mia donna sia gentilissima e il cuore mio da lei sia fatto gentile, perché altrimenti non poteva conoscere o amare tanta bellezza, gli occhi degli altri uomini non possono vedere el mio gentilissimo disio, ‹perché›, non sendo fatti gentili da lei, non sono sufficienti.

Ora, per non lasciare in confusione chi ha letto nel precedente comento nostro qualche cosa che pare *prima facie* contratia, a maggiore declarazione diremo come apresso. Abbiamo detto questa mano tanto da me lodata e amata essere suta la sinistra, e tutti gli essempli che abbiamo dato (e della fede che per suo mezzo ebbi da Amore, e dello indorare li strali, tirare l'arco e medicate etc.) si referiscono più presto ana mano destra. Per levare adunque questa confusione bisogna intendere che naturalmente la mano sinistra è più degna e più forte che la destra, perché è più propinqua al cuore, el quale è datore della virtù e della potenzia. È vero che lo uso umano, come molte altre cose, ancora questa naturale potenzia ha depravato, e però se la destra ha più degnità o forza è più tosto per consuetudine che per natura; né debbe lo uso obstare che non sia più degno quello che per natura è più degno. E però li buoni intelletti, come è quello della donna mia, non obstante la perversa consuetudine, volle in questa come nell'altre cose essere excellente tra gli altri; e avendo a fare fede al cuore mio della pietà e disposizione del cuore suo, lo fece per quel mezzo a cui era più naturale e che meritava più fede, come più vicino al cuore. Oltre a questo, lo indorare le saette, tirare l'arco d'Amore e medicare le piaghe amorose è officio della mano sinistra, perché, se bene le bellezze legano molto, el cuore della cosa amata strigne molto più, e così molto meglio medica; e tutte queste opere manuali, che hanno a essere a significazione del cuore, molto meglio convengono alla mano sinistra per la propinquità già detta. E però è più tosto errore quello che comunemente usano gli uomini, che la elezzione in questa parte della donna mia.

wound and to heal, it could also kill and give life. It is appropriately said, then, that her ivory fingers, that is her fingers the color of ivory, held my life and my death. And this also is the proper office of the fingers, because what the hand presses is pressed by means of the fingers. This hand furthermore holds my great desire, and does so very truly for that reason that the preceding sonnet recounted. Because, by holding my heart in which is [located] the concupiscible power, that is, desire, it holds my desire, which I was hiding from the eyes of men, to all of whom it was invisible. Because, if what we have said is true—that this my lady is most noble and that my heart was made noble by her, because otherwise it could not know or love such great beauty—then the eyes of other men cannot see my most noble desire, [because,] not having been made noble by her, they were inadequate.

Now, in order not to leave in confusion whoever has read something in our preceding commentary that seems *prima facie* a contradiction, we shall next make a grand declaration. We have indicated that this hand so much praised and loved by me was the left one, yet all the examples that we have given (either of the pledge that I had from Love by means of it, or of the gilding of the arrows, or drawing the bow or healing, etc.)—[all these] more aptly refer to the right hand. To alleviate this confusion, then, one must understand that the left hand is naturally more worthy and stronger than the right because it is nearer the heart, which is the author of its power and of its force. It is true that human use, as with many other things, has indeed corrupted this natural power, and therefore, if the right hand has more worth or power, it is owing rather to custom than to nature. And custom ought not to prevent that from being worthier which by its nature is more worthy. And therefore good intellects, like my lady's, perverse custom notwithstanding, wish in this as in other things to be most excellent among others. And having to demonstrate to my heart the pity and disposition of her heart, she did so by that instrument that was more natural and that, by being nearer the heart, merited more faith. Beyond this, gilding the arrows, pulling Love's bow, and tending the amorous wounds are offices of the left hand because, if indeed its beauties bind tightly, the heart of the beloved binds much tighter, and so heals much better. And all these manual works, which have to symbolize those of the heart, are much more fitting to the left hand because of its aforesaid propinquity. And therefore what men commonly do is in error rather than the choice of this member by my lady.

XV

Quanta invidia ti porto, o cuor bëato,
che quella man vezzosa or mulce or stringe,
tal che ogni vil durezza da te spinge!
E poi che sì gentil sei diventato,
    talora il nome, a cui te ha consecrato
Amore, il bianco dito in te dipinge,
or l'angelico viso informa e finge,
or lieto, or dolcemente perturbato;
    or li amorosi e vaghi suoi pensieri
ad uno ad un la bella man descrive,
or le dolce parole accorte e sante.
    O mio bel core, oramai più che speri?
Sol che abbin forza quelle luci dive
di transformarti in rigido adamante.

Abbiamo di sopra concluso e più volte diffinito "gentile" potersi chiamare quella cosa che, secondo la umana perfezzione, fa perfettamente e con grazia l'officio a che è ordinata; et essendo giunto a questa perfezzione el cuore mio per mezzo di quella mano bellissima, el presente sonetto fa menzione del modo come fu fatto gentile, e ancora di alcuni affetti di beatitudine e dolcezza che per questo sente il cuore: perché questa tale menzione e memoria non altrimenti è grata al cuore, che a' naviganti il raccontare qualche loro pericolosa fortuna, poi che hanno conseguita la sicurtà del porto. Parla adunque il presente sonetto al cuore mio, mostrando portarli invidia: non perché gli dispiaccia il bene suo, ma più presto per desiderio di potere conseguire il medesimo bene. E chiamandolo cuore beato, mostra assai manifesto la cagione della invidia, la quale se è, come abbiamo detto in questo luogo, desiderio del medesimo bene, la invidia necessariamente è maggiore e più manifesta quanto è maggiore il bene che si vede in altri; e nessuno è maggiore bene che lo essere beato, e quella cosa è

15

O how I envy you, my blessed heart,[81]
Because that charming hand now presses, now
Caresses you, expunging every hardness low,
And you are thereby made so noble that
　The name to which Love consecrated you,
That finger white portrays in you, and now
Imprints her face angelic, represents
It joyful now, now troubled tenderly.
　Now one by one her amorous, winsome thoughts
The lovely hand sets down, now it records
Her blessed and sagacious words so sweet.
　O my fine heart, what more then can you hope?
Only that those divine lights have the power
To change you to unyielding diamond.[82]

We have above many times defined what can be called "noble" and concluded it is that which, according to human perfection, perfectly and with grace performs the office for which it is destined. And as my heart had arrived at this perfection by means of that most lovely hand, this sonnet makes mention of the way in which it was made noble, and also of some effects of beatitude and sweetness that my heart felt as a result of this—for such a mention and memory as this is no less pleasing for the heart than it is for sailors to recount some of their perilous adventures after they have achieved the safety of the harbor. This sonnet then speaks to my heart, showing that the sonnet envies it—not because the heart's welfare displeases the sonnet, but rather because of the sonnet's desire for the same good. And calling it a blessed heart, very clearly shows the cause of its envy, which is, as we have said in this place, a desire for the same good, [for] envy is necessarily as much greater and more manifest as the good that one sees in others is greater. And nothing is a greater good than being

---

[81] See *Rvf*, 300, 1: "How much I envy you, o greedy earth...."

[82] See *Rvf*, 23, 23–5: "And frozen thoughts had hardened round my heart/ To make an almost adamantine glaze...." In Petrarch, the glazing of the heart produces ill effects, presumably because the heart cannot vent its heat. In Ficino, by contrast, one objective of a program of spiritual cleansing is to make the spirit (which, as Lorenzo tells us is what he means by the heart), "more subtle and harder.... And celestial to the highest degree ... [by being] much exposed to the influence of rays and above all to the Sun, which is dominant among celestial things" (*Vita coel.* 4 in *Opera* 1:535–36 (565–6)). See Couliano, 131. The rays of the eyes of the lady, who is an emblematic sun, may be capable of producing this salutary effect.

veramente beata che è gentile; e però, dicendo cuore beato, già si presuppone la gentilezza. Narra dipoi il modo che tenne quella mano a riducere il mio cuore dalla durezza e viltà sua naturale alla perfezzione della gentilezza, cioè mulcendolo e stringendolo: che si può interpetrare che quella mano usasse qualche volta seco cose piacevoli e dolce, qualche volta aspre e forte. Perché, avendo a combattere con due inimiche, cioè durezza e viltà, bisogna opporre due virtù contrarie, cioè forza contro alla durezza e dolcezza contro alla viltà. Perché, chi pensa bene che cose obstano a qualunque vuole andare alla perfezzione, troverrà essere solamente due. Prima una naturale inezia e contraria disposizione alla beatitudine che si cerca; e questo nasce e per difetto di complessione e di organi del corpo e per le naturali concupiscienzie e inclinazione a molti errori, conciosiacosa che la via della perfezzione sempre fu laboriosa e difficile. E però queste cose contrarie sono spesso di tale impedimento, che non lasciono, non che altro, qualche volta conoscere la beatitudine; e questa si può chiamare «durezza». L'altro obstaculo è che, ancora che qualche volta questa beatitudine in confuso si conosca, e conoscendosi si desideri, gli uomini hanno una naturale viltà e diffidenzia, per la quale spesso si disperono di conseguirla; né tentando la via per andarvi, possono già mai adiungervi. Bisogna adunque, contro a quella prima durezza la forza, contro alla viltà la mollificazione e dolcezza, usando or l'una e or l'altra secondo che si truovono potenti gli inimici, perché l'una rompe la durezza, l'altra contro alla viltà dà speranza. Questi due affetti mostra il presente sonetto dicendo or mulce or stringe, e con queste due cose trae del cuore ogni durezza e viltà, le quali remosse si fa gentile, cioè diventa subietto atto a ricevere ogni degna forma e gentile impressione. Séguita di questo che, subito che il cuore è diventato materia gentile, tanto può stare sanza la forma gentile quanto può la materia sanza ‹la› forma; e perché lo amore congiugne la materia e la forma, cioè un naturale desiderio che ha l'uno dell'altro, così Amore, che mosse quella mano a fare gentile il mio cuore, fa ancora che di nuovo si muove a darli tanta gentile impressione. E, trovando il mio cuore sanza durezza, cioè mollificato e atto a ricevere ogni impressione, comincia col dito a scrivere in lui il nome della donna mia: quel nome, dico, al quale Amore consecrò il mio cuore, perché «consecrare» s'intende un tempio a uno iddio o una chiesa a uno santo, dandoli il titolo di quel

blessed, and that thing is truly blessed which is noble. And therefore, by saying blessed heart, one already presupposes its nobility. The sonnet then recounts how that hand holds my heart to lead it away from its natural hardness and meanness to the perfection of nobility, that is by caressing it and pressing it—which must be understood to mean that the hand sometimes treated it kindly and gently, and sometimes sternly and firmly. Because, having to contend with two enemies, that is [with] hardness and meanness, it had to oppose two contrary virtues, that is, force against hardness and sweetness against meanness. Because, whoever thinks well about what things stand in the way of any desire to reach perfection will find them to be two only. First [there is] a natural ineptitude and disposition contrary to the beatitude that one seeks. And this springs both from the defect of one's constitution and bodily organs, and from one's natural concupiscence and inclinations to many errors, since the way of perfection was always laborious and difficult. And because these contrary things are often such an impediment that they will not admit of nor even sometimes recognize beatitude, this [obstacle] can be called "hardness of heart." The other obstacle is that, even if sometimes beatitude is recognized in the midst of confusion and, being recognized, is desired, men have a natural meanness and diffidence on whose account they often despair of achieving it. Nor, if they do attempt the path for going there [to perfection], they can never arrive at it. Force then is required against that first hardness, and mollification and sweetness against meanspiritedness, using either the one or the other as the adversaries are found to be powerful, because the one breaks hardness, the other gives hope against meanspiritedness. The present sonnet demonstrates these two effects by saying, "now presses, now caresses," for with these two things it drew every hardness and meanness from my heart. And, when these were removed, it became noble, that is it became an object capable of receiving every worthy form and noble impression. It follows from this that, as soon as my heart became noble matter, as long as the matter could be without noble form, the longer the matter could be without form.[83] And because Love joins matter and form together, that is a natural desire that the one has for the other, so Love, who moved that hand to ennoble my heart, also moved it again to give my heart a very noble impression. And finding my heart without hardness, that is softened and fit to receive every impression, with its finger the hand begins to write in the name of my lady—that name, I say, to which Love consecrated my heart, because "consecrate" means giving a temple to a

---

[83] See Guido Guinizelli, *Amor'e'l cor gentile*, where love and the noble heart are one in the same.

nome perché perpetuamente si conosca quel tal tempio o chiesa. Adunque il cuore mio fu veramente consecrato, perché Amore ne fece un tempio e abitaculo per sempre, dove si celebrassi e stessi quel nome della donna mia. Dipinge ancora quel candido dito l'apparenzia del viso della donna mia e quelle perturbazioni e passione che a gentile donna si convengono, come è qualche modesta letizia e qualche dolce perturbazione. E perché pare cosa impossibile quello che apresso si scrive, cioè che si possa descrivere o depingere e pensieri, che non sono sottoposti agli occhi, bisogna intendere che le passioni che convengono alla donna mia sono tre, cioè le due che abbiamo dette della modesta letizia e dolce perturbazione, e quella che si gli aggiunge al presente è l'amore, el quale include di necessità una dolce speranza; e si exclude, delle quattro perturbazione, il timor solamente, perché questo non si conviene a si gentile donna, ancora che sia comune a tutti gli uomini. Volendo adunque fare menzione di questa gentilissima passione dello amore, et essendo il vero nutrimento dello amore e pensieri, abbiamo detto nel mio cuore essere dipinti e suoi pensieri amorosi; e volendo referire questa pittura agli occhi, bisogna intendere che 'l medesimo viso della donna mia, che prima era dipinto or lieto or dolcemente perturbato, fussi dipinto ancora qualche volta amoroso. Perché, come conosciamo la letizia e 'l dolore e ridendo e piangendo e per altri segni, così e pensieri amorosi per molti segni si conoscono, anzi dagli occhi inamorati difficilmente si nascondono; e tra gli altri segni, come adviene ancora delle altre perturbazioni, per le parole molto meglio si conoscono, le quali sogliono essere el più delle volte expressioni di pensieri. E però subiunge che la medesima mano descrive ancora le parole della donna mia, come nunzii veri de' pensieri e testimoni exteriori di quello che il cuore fa dentro. Debbesi adunque presupporre che degnissima pittura fussi quella della quale era ornato il cuore mio. Perché tre cose, secondo il giudizio mio, si convengono a una perfetta opera di pittura, cioè il subietto buono, o muro o legno o panno o altro che sia, sopra 'l quale si distenda la pittura; el maestro perfetto e di disegno e di colore; e oltre a questo, che le cose dipinte sieno di loro nature grate e piacevole agli occhi. Perché, ancora che la pittura fussi perfetta, potrebbe essere di qualità quello

god or a church to a saint, giving them the title of that name, because by that name such a temple or church will perpetually be known. My heart then was truly consecrated, because Love made of it a temple and dwelling place forever, where my lady's name was [written] and was celebrated. That white finger also drew the likeness of my lady's face and those perturbations and passions that are fitting to a noble lady, as some measured gaiety is and some sweet perturbation. And because what next was written seems a thing impossible, that is that thoughts that are not submitted to the eyes could be described or printed, one must understand that the passions that are fitting for my lady are three, that is the two that we have mentioned of measured gaiety and sweet perturbation, and that which at the present love has added thereto, which of necessity includes a sweet hope. And of the four perturbations,[84] fear alone is excluded because this is inappropriate to such a noble lady even though it is common to all men. Wishing then to make mention of this most noble passion of love, and thoughts' being love's true nutriment, we have said that her amorous thoughts were depicted in my heart. And wishing to refer this picture to the eyes, one must understand that the same face of my lady that was first pictured now joyful, now sweetly perturbed, was also sometimes depicted as amorous. Because, as we know joy and sorrow both [through] laughing and weeping and through other signs, so through many signs are amorous thoughts known, indeed they are with difficulty hidden from amorous eyes. And among the other signs, as happens also with the other disturbances, they are much better known through words, which are most of the time the usual expressions of thoughts. And therefore, it [the sonnet] adds that the same hand sets down also the words of my lady as true messengers of her thoughts and as external witnesses of what the heart is doing within. It must then be presupposed that the picture that had ornamented my heart was a most worthy one. Because three things, according to my judgment, are fitting for a perfect painting, that there be a good medium, either a wall or wood or cloth or something else upon which the picture extends; a perfect master both of design and of color; and beyond this, that the things depicted be by their nature welcome and pleasing to the eyes. Because, although the picture were perfect, it could be that the quality of

---

[84] L. here follows the stoic distinction among the four disturbances of the mind: joy, sorrow, hope and fear, which Cicero discusses in his *Tusculan Disputations* 4, 6, trans., J. E. King (Cambridge, Mass.: Harvard Univ. Press, 1971), 339: "They [the stoics] hold ... that there are divisions of disorder originating in two kinds of expected good and two of expected evil, with the result that there are four in all: *lust* and *delight*, in the sense of delight in present good and lust in future good, originate in what is good; *fear* and *distress*, they consider, originate in what is evil, fear in future and distress in present evil."

che è dipinto, che non sarebbe secondo la natura di chi debbe vedere, conciosia che alcuni si dilettano di cose allegre, come è animali, verzure, balli e feste, ⟨e⟩ simili; altri vorrebbono vedere battaglie o terrestre o marittime, e simili cose marziale e fere; altri paesi, casamenti e scorci e proporzioni di prospettiva; altri qualche altra cosa diverse; e però, volendo che una pittura interamente piaccia, bisogna adiungervi questa parte, che la cosa dipinto ancora per sè diletti. Era il mio cuore materia e subietto molto atto a ricevere ogni impressione; mai non fu mano tanto gentile e dotta a tale pittura quanto quella della donna mia, né più grate cose potevono essere expresse nel mio cuore che i dolcissimi accidenti e il viso e il nome della donna mia: e però, quanto al iudicio del mio cuore, era tanto perfetta questa pittura, che desiderava si perpetuassi e che etternalmente così in esso si conservassi. E questo è molto naturale desiderio e séguita da' principii già detti, conciosiacosa che si va per la via della perfezzione, molto dura e laboriosa, per venire alla beatitudine, e chi ha grazia di condurvisi non gli resta altro desiderio che stabilirsi e fermarsi in essa, come ancora desidera il mio cuore. E, credendo che questo fussi el modo a potersi perpetuare in tanto bene, desiderava che gli occhi della donna mia avessino quella forza e virtù che si legge ebbe già il viso di Medusa, e che, come l'aspetto suo convertì gli uomini in sassi, così gli occhi della donna mia, così dipinto il mio cuore e così bello, convertissino in un duro adamante. Bisogna adunque intendere, per la pittura di tante belle e dolcissime cose nel mio cuore, i pensieri ch'erano in lui e la inmaginazione di quelle tali cose; li quali pensieri essendo pieni di somma dolcezza, el cuore desiderava si conservassino in lui e durassino a guisa della durezza d'uno adamante, e che nuovi e molesti pensieri non succedessino e cacciassino quelli che erano dolci: come spesse volte adviene negli amanti, e quali comunemente brieve tempo si preservano nel medesimo stato.

that which is depicted might not be suited to the nature of whoever might be obliged to see it, for the reason that some are delighted by joyful things, like animals, orchards, balls and feasts, and the like. Others would wish to see battles, either on land or at sea, and similar fierce and martial matters. Others [prefer] towns, casements, views, and the proportions of perspective; others, something different. And therefore, if a person wants a picture entirely pleasing, he must add thereto this requirement: that the thing painted be in itself delightful. My heart was a very suitable material and medium to receive every impression. Neither was there ever a hand so noble and expert in [forming] such a picture as that of my lady, nor could a thing more pleasing be expressed in my heart than the sweetest sayings and the face and the name of my lady. And therefore, in the judgment of my heart this picture was very perfect, for my heart wanted it to be perpetuated and thus be preserved in it eternally. And this is a very natural desire and follows from the principles already mentioned, since one goes on the way of perfection, which is very hard and laborious, to reach beatitude. And, there remains for whoever has the grace to be led there, no other desire than achieving [beatitude] and abiding in it, as my heart still desires to do. And, believing that this was the way to be able to perpetuate itself in such good, it desired that the eyes of my lady might have that power and virtue that one reads about, indeed that the face of Medusa possessed, and that, just as the sight of her turned men into stone, so the eyes of my lady thus painted in my heart and so lovely might change it into a hard diamond.[85] One must understand then the picture of such great beauty and of the sweetest things in my heart to be the thoughts that were in it and the imagination of such things as those. Since those thoughts were full of the highest sweetness, my heart desired that they might be preserved in it and that they might endure in the fashion of the hardness of a diamond, and that new and troubled thoughts would not succeed them and drive away those that were sweet, as many times occurs with lovers, who ordinarily are preserved in the same condition for but a brief time.

---

[85] L. differs markedly from Dante and Petrarch in his handling of the Medusa myth. The Pilgrim Dante flees the threat of the coming of Medusa in *Inf.* 9 lest he be turned to stone. In *Rvf.* 23, Petrarch's encounter with Laura as Medusa turns him to stone and dehumanizes him. L. wants his heart made immutable by Medusa to preserve her likeness there as a model for his own quest for perfection.

XVI

    Belle, fresche e purpurëe vïole,
che quella candidissima man colse,
qual piaggia o qual puro äer produr volse
tanti più vaghi fior' che far non suole?
    Qual rugiada, qual terra o ver qual sole
tante vaghe bellezze in voi raccolse?
Onde il süave odor natura tolse,
o il ciel, che a tanto ben degnar ne vuole?
    Care mie vïolette, quella mano
che vi elesse intra l'altre, ove eri, in sorte
vi ha di tante excellenzie e pregio ornate!
    Quella che il cor mi tolse, e di villano
lo fe' gentile, a cui siate consorte:
quella adunque, e non altri, ringraziate!

    Fu non solamente la donna mia sopra tutte l'altre bellissima e dotata di degnissimi modi e ornati costumi, ma ancora piena d'amore e di grazia; e puossi veramente di lei affermare che era tanto excellente in tutte le parte che debba avere una donna, che qualunque altra donna che fussi suta così perfettamente dotata di una parte sola di tante che n'aveva la donna mia, sarebbe suta tra le altre excellentissima. E che fussi, come abbiamo detto, tutta piena d'amore e di grazia, oltre a molti altri evidentissimi segni mi accade nel presente sonetto fare menzione d'uno singularissimo e a me gratissimo. E questo fu che essendo io stato per qualche tempo, per alcuno accidente, sanza potere vederla, questo era diventato cosa insopportabile, né potevo, sanza pericolo della vita mia, stare per qualche altro tempo, ancora che brieve, così sanza vederla. Di che essa accorgendosi, non per visibili segni, ché questo era impossibile, ma per esserli noto lo amore grande che io li portavo, e provando forse in sé medesima quanto fussi difficile e insopportabile la privazione degli occhi suoi agli occhi miei, né potendo a questo per allora rimediare, soccorse alla mia afflizione in quel modo che per allora si poteva. Dilettavasi di natura, come di molte altre cose gentili, ancora di tenere in casa in alcuni vasi bellissimi certe piante di vïuole, alle quali lei medesima soccorreva e d'acqua per li excessive caldi e d'ogni altra cosa necessaria al nutrimento loro. Elesse adunque tre vïuole tra molte altre che ne aveva, quelle alle quali o la natura volse meglio, per averle produtte più belle che l'altre, o la fortuna, che prima all'altre le fece venire a quella candidissima mano; le quali vïuole così còlte mi mandò a donare: che veramente, da lei in fuora, nessuna cosa poteva meglio mitigare tanto mio dolore.

16

    O lovely, fresh, and purple violets,
You whom that whitest hand has gathered up,
What hill or what pure air wished to produce
So many more fair flowers than usual?
    What dew, what soil, or what sun truly has
Assembled in you beauties that so charm?
That sweet aroma, whence has Nature brought?
Or Heaven that wants it worth so great a good?
    Dear violets mine, that hand that chose you from
Among the others there, by luck enriched
You with esteem and with great excellence.
    She took my heart and from a low thing made
It noble, for you now consort with it;
Give thanks to her and to no other, then.

    My lady was not only above all the others most lovely and endowed with most worthy manners and elegant habits, but she was also full of love and grace. And it could truly be affirmed of her that she was so excellent in all the attributes that a woman ought to have, that any other woman would have been most excellent among the others if she had been perfectly endowed with only one portion of what my lady so thoroughly had. And that she was, as we have said, all full of love and grace, it occurs to me in this sonnet, beyond many other most evident signs, to make mention of one most singular and, to me, most pleasing sign. And this was that, because of some accident, I had been unable to see her for some time. This became almost unendurable, nor was I able to remain thus without seeing her for very much time, even a brief time, without danger to my life. She had become aware of that, not by visible signs, for this was impossible, but by her being aware of the great love that I bore her, and perhaps feeling in herself how difficult and unbearable being deprived of her eyes was for my eyes, and as this for the time being could not be remedied, she succored my affliction in the manner that she was able to at that time. She used to take great delight in nature, as in many other noble things, also in keeping in the house in some very lovely vases certain violet plants, which she tended herself both with water against excessively hot weather and with everything else necessary for their nourishment. She selected then three violets from among many others that she had, which either Nature had wanted to be better, since she made them better than the others, or Fortune had, who made them come to this white hand before the others. These violets thus gathered she sent me as a gift, and truly, herself excepted, nothing could have better relieved my heavy sorrow.

Parla adunque el presente sonetto alle sopra dette tre viuole, le quali, et essendo per loro medesime di maravigliosa bellezza et essendo dono della donna mia e còlte da quella mano candidissima, ragionevole cosa era che mi paressino molto più belle che non suole produrre la natura; e per questo convenientemente si domanda pel presente sonetto, come si suole fare di tutte le cose maravigliose, della cagione di tanta excellenzia. E perché il presente sonetto per sé pare assai chiaro, brievemente diremo che nel domandare della cagione per che erono sì belle, si tocca tutti e mezzi per li quali la natura produce le piante, li arbusti, l'erbe e i fiori. E perché tutte queste cagioni insieme non parevono ancora sufficienti alla nuova bellezza, al colore, alla forma e allo odore di quelle bene adventurate viuole, bisognava che qualche nuova cagione et extraordinaria potenzia le avesse produtte; e impossibile era intendere qual cagione fusse, se non da chi avesse in altre cose veduta experienzia d'una simile virtù e potenzia. Avendo io adunque in me provato la virtù e forza di quella candidissima mano, che, secondo il precedente sonetto, di vile e durissimo aveva fatto il mio cuore gentile, potevo credere e affermare quella medesima mano potere avere fatto quelle viuole di tanta excessiva bellezza, perché maggiore cosa era fare gentile una cosa rozza e villana, che bellissima una cosa bella, come di natura sono le viuole. Per questo si conclude quella mano avere fatto quelle viuole di tanto pregio et excellenzia, che aveva fatto il cuore mio di villano gentile, e per questo meritamente queste viuole essere consorte del mio cuore, perché «consorti» si chiamono quelli che sono sottoposti alla medesima sorte. E però di tanta loro bellezza quelle viuole non dovevono ringraziare né il sole, né la terra, né l'aria, né la rugiada, né il luogo aprico, né qualunque altra naturale potenzia che concorressi a simile produzzione, ma solo la virtù e potenzia di quella candidissima mano.

Non è forse inconveniente vedere se la bellezza di queste viuole o era in oppinione mia o era possibile in fatto. E benché io non possa iudicare se fussi vera in fatto, perché non posso referire se non quello che pareva a me, secondo che i sensi raportavono al giudicio, e quali se erano depravati e corrutti, o se pure mi portavono il vero, a me è difficile a intendere, perché bisogna el giudicio giudichi quello che portono e sensi e in quel modo che lo pottono, nondimeno confesso essere possibile che la forte inmaginazione sia cagione di corrompere i sensi: come spesso adviene in uno farnetico, che li pare vedere quello che è; imperò che gran potenzia ha ne' sensi la inmaginazione, come faremo intendere nella exposizione di quello sonetto che comincia *Della mia donna, omè, gli ultimi sguardi*. E nondimeno

The present sonnet speaks then to the three violets mentioned above, which, both since they were in themselves of marvelous beauty, and since they were a gift from my lady and gathered by her surpassingly white hand, it was reasonable that they should seem to be much more beautiful than those usually produced by nature. And for this reason this sonnet fittingly asks, as is customarily done of marvelous things, about the cause of so much excellence. And because this sonnet seems very clear in itself, we shall briefly say that in asking about the reason that they were beautiful, it touches upon the means by which nature produces the plants, the shrubs, and the grass and the flowers. And because all these reasons together still seem insufficient for this new beauty, for the color, the form and the aroma of these fortunate violets, some new occasion and extraordinary power must have produced them. And it was impossible for someone to understand what that occasion was, unless he had experienced a similar virtue and power in other things. Since I had tested in myself, then, the power and strength of that whitest of hands, which, according to the preceding sonnet, had ennobled my heart, once mean and most hard, I was able to believe and to affirm that this same hand could have made those violets of such surpassing beauty because it was a much greater accomplishment to ennoble a rough, low thing than to beautify exceedingly something as beautiful as violets are by nature. From this one concludes that the [same] hand had made those violets of such great worth and excellence that had made my heart noble instead of mean, and through this were those violets deservedly [called] associates of my heart, because one calls "associates" those things that are placed in the same category. And therefore those violets do not have to thank either the sun, or the soil, or the air, or the dew, or the open place, or any other natural powers that join together for similar production, but only the virtue and power of that surpassingly white hand.

It is perhaps not unfitting to see if the beauty of these violets either existed [only] in my opinion or was in fact a possibility. And although I am unable to judge if it were true in fact, because I cannot appeal to anything except to that which seemed to me to correspond with what was reported to my judgment by my senses, which, whether or not they were depraved or corrupted or even if they bore the truth to me, it is difficult for me to know because the judgment must judge that which the senses bring and in the manner that they bring it. Nonetheless, I confess it to be possible that strong imagination can be a cause of corrupting the senses—as often happens in a delirium where one seems to see what is not there. Inasmuch as the imagination has great power in the senses, as we shall understand in the exposition of that sonnet that begins: "My lady's final

questo non toglie che non possa essere vera quella bellezza, o vero che la cagione d'essa sia la virtù di quella mano. Perché si vede o per la grazia di Dio o per influsso celeste o per virtù naturale, a diverse uomini essere dato diverse potenzie e grazie. Vedesi spesso un medico dottissimo uccidere gran numero di uomini, uno più ignorante sanare quasi tutti quelli che e' cura; alcuni uomini avere qualche propria virtù, con la presenzia sanare certi mali e con uno semplice tatto di mano; ad alcuno essere giovato più, contro a chi lo assale, la presenzia che la spada. Truovasi in alcuni autori di astrologia che chi ha una certa constellazione ha virtù, solo colla presenzia, di guarire indemoniati. E non è molto maggiore forza quella delle parole, che sieno udite dagli animali bruti, dalle piante e dall'erbe, come si dice de' serpenti e d'altri animali, e che possino fare seccare le piante e l'erbe, e che solo la fascinazione facessi tanti diverse e grandi effetti, quanti si legge e in Catone e in Plinio e in altri autori antiquissimi e degni di fede e reverenzia? E che più vogliamo cercare di essempli? Non veggiamo noi che maggiore forza hanno spesso gli occhi umani, che con uno semplice sguardo uccidono quasi e vivificano, fanno fuggire e tornare el sangue, tolgono e rendono le forze, e, quello che è più, conrompono el giudizio della mente umana? Pare per questo assai possibile che possa una mano avere tanta virtù, che dia, non dico alcuna nuova qualità, ma alle medesime qualità più bellezza et excellenzia che non suole dare la nature; e *maxime* la più bella mano che forse mai facessi natura. E se io fussi di questo suspetto giudice, rispondo che prima fu giudicata da me la bellezza di quella mano, che amata excessivamente, perché di necessità la cognizione precede la voluntà. Se adunque prima mi parve bella che io l'amassi, è necessario che io vachi da colpa di passione e che quella mano veramente fussi bellissima. E, se così è, pare più tosto impossibile che con tanta bellezza non fussi coniunta una maravigliosa virtù e potenzia, che difficile a credere di lei quello che ne scrivo.

XVII

Chiare acque, io sento il vostro mormorio,
che sol della mia donna il nome dice:
credo, poiché Amor fevi sì felice,

glances only, woe."[86] But nevertheless, one must not acknowledge that this beauty could not have been real, or acknowledge as untrue that the cause of it is the power of that hand. Because one sees various powers and graces that either the grace of God or celestial influence or natural power gives to different men. One often sees a most learned physician killing great numbers of men, but one more ignorant curing almost all those whom he treats. Some men having some particular power that cures certain illnesses with its presence and with a simple touch of the hand. And the presence of some men is more useful against an assailant than is the sword. One finds in some authors of astrology that whoever has a certain constellation has the power to heal the possessed with his presence alone. And is not that power much greater of words that are heard by brute animals, by plants, and by grass, as is said of serpents and of other animals—words that can make plants and grass wither, and whose fascination alone produces many varied and great effects that one reads about in Cato and in Pliny and in other very ancient authors who are worthy of credence and reverence? And what other examples should we wish to seek? Do we not see what greater power human eyes often have, for with a simple glance they almost kill and bring to life, they make the blood flee and return, they take away and restore strength, and, what is more than that, they corrupt the judgment of the human mind? By this it seems very possible for a hand to have such great virtue that it gives, I do not say some new quality, but to the same qualities greater beauty and excellence than nature usually gives. And [it] especially [seems possible for] the most beautiful hand that nature perhaps ever made. And if I were a suspect judge in this, I would answer that I judged the beauty of that hand before I excessively loved it, because knowledge necessarily precedes the will. If, then, first it seemed beautiful to me and then I loved it, it is necessary that I be exonerated from the charge of passion and that her hand truly was most beautiful. And, if that is so, it seems impossible rather than [merely] difficult to believe of her that which I write about her—that with such great beauty there would not be conjoined such a marvelous virtue and power.

17

O waters clear, I hear your murmuring
Which utters nothing but my lady's name—
So happy, I believe, Love made you once,

---

[86] The second of two sonnets mentioned but not included in the *Commentary*. It appears as "Rime," 70, in Simioni 1:210. See "Appendix A" for text and translation.

> che fussi specchio al suo bel viso e pio.
>   La bella imagin sua da voi partio
> perché vostra natura vel disdice;
> solo il bel nome a voi ricordar lice,
> né vuole Amor che lo senta altri ch'io.
>   Quanto più fûro o fortunati o saggi
> che voi, chiare acque, gli occhi miei, quel giorno
> che furno prima specchio al suo bel volto,
>   servando sempre in loro i santi raggi!
> Né veggon altro poi mirando intorno,
> né gliel cela ombra, né dal sol gli è tolto.

Ancora che nel precedente comento abbiamo detto volere riservare alla exposizione del sonetto che comincia *Della mia donna* etc. che gran potenzia ha ne' sensi la inmaginazione, nondimeno pare che accaggia al presente dire qualche cosa più tosto dello effetto che della cagione. Interviene adunque molte volte che quando altri sente qualche continua e non articolata voce, la inmaginazione nostra si accomoda quella tale voce a quello che allora più inmagina, e, inmaginando, gli pare articolata quella tale voce, dandogli quel senso e faccendoli dire quello che più desidera; e comunemente, sonando campane, cadendo una acqua continua, pare che questo tale suono dica quella cosa che vuole colui che la inmagina. Vedesi ancora, per essemplo di questo, qualche volta nelle nube aeree diverse e strane forme d'animali e d'uomini; e, considerando certa ragione di pietre che sieno molte piene di vene, vi si forma ancora dentro el più delle volte quello che piace alla fantasia. Questo medesimo interveniva a me, che ritrovandomi in un luogo amenissimo dove era uno chiaro e abundante fonte, nel quale perpetua(b)mente l'acqua, cadendo da alto, faceva uno dolcissimo mormorio, a me pareva che quel mormorio continuamente dicesse el nome della donna mia, perché questa era quella cosa la quale più inmaginavo e quel nome che più desideravo sentire. Aiutava questo dolcissimo inganno lo essere già suta la donna mia in questo luogo amenissimo e avere guardato nel fonte, che di necessità era diventato suo specchio, perché per qualche tempo aveva pure ritenuto in sé quella chiarissima acqua la effigie bellissima della donna mia. E però non pareva impossibile alla credulità delli amanti che quella acqua, inamorata di sì bel viso, da quel tempo in qua col suo amoroso mormorio perpetualmente replicassi quello dolcissimo nome. Pareva per questo conveniente, se quelle acque erano di sì bel viso inamorate, che dovessino sempre ritenerlo in loro, né lasciarlo mai partire, come a me pareva che perpetualmente dicessino il nome della donna mia. E si può bene credere che la medesima inmaginazione che mi faceva

> In mirroring her lovely, pious face.
> From you her lovely image parted then
> Because your nature won't retain its form;
> Her lovely name alone you there recall,
> And Love wants none but me to hear it said.
> How much more wise or fortunate than you,
> Clear waters, were my eyes that day when first
> They were a mirror for her lovely face,
> And always held in them those holy rays;
> Naught else, on looking round them, did they see—
> Not hid from them by shade, nor lost in sun.

Although in the preceding commentary we have mentioned wishing to reserve to the exposition of the sonnet that begins, "My lady's [final glances only, woe] ..." etc., [the discussion of] what great power the imagination has in the senses, it nevertheless seems opportune at present to say something rather about the effect than about the cause. It happens many times, then, that when someone hears some continual and inarticulate sound, our imagination will adapt that sound to what it is then most imagining, and it imagines what seems to it to be articulated by such a voice, and gives to it that sense and makes it say that which it most desires. And commonly it seems that sounds like ringing bells or continually falling water will say what the one who imagines it wishes. As an example of this, one also sometimes sees in the clouds in the sky, various and strange forms of animals and of men. And looking at a certain stony surface that is very full of veins, one will most of the time form there within them that which pleases the fantasy. This same thing happened to me, for finding myself again in a most agreeable place where there was a clear and copious fountain, into which the water's falling perpetually from above made a very sweet murmuring, I thought that the murmuring continually repeated the name of my lady, because this was that which I imagined most and the name that I most desired to hear. The fact that my lady had already been in this most agreeable place and that she had looked into the fountain, which of necessity had become her mirror, assisted in this very sweet illusion, because for some time that loveliest and clearest of waters had even retained in itself the most beautiful likeness of my lady. And therefore it did not seem impossible to a lover's credulity that the water, enamored by such a lovely face, from that time forward in its amorous murmuring perpetually repeated that sweetest name. It seemed fitting because of this, if those waters were enamored of so fair a face, that they must always retain it in themselves, and not ever let it depart, as it seemed to me that it perpetually said my lady's name. And it can well be believed that the

sempre udire quel nome, guidata da una amorosa simplicità, mi conducessi ancora a guardare nell'acqua, per vedere se v'era dentro ancora il viso della donna mia; e non ve lo vedendo, mi accorsi dello errore, e considerai subito che l'acqua non può ricevere alcuna tale forma se non ha un simile obietto assistente, perché la natura dell'acqua è così fatta per essere corpo diafano. Ma gli è bene lecito col mormorio suo, secondo che pareva a me, ricordare el suo nome; e perché questo nasceva solamente dalla inmaginazione e desiderio mio, altri che io non lo sentiva, né permetteva Amore che sì dolce armonia pervenissi ad altri che a' miei inamorati orecchi. Cominciai dipoi a fare comparazione dalla felicità di quelle acque alla propria; e parendomi essere più felice di loro, se avevo prima concetto alcuna invidia a quelle acque, la converti' in alquanto di arroganzia, mostrando che o gli occhi miei avevono avuto migliore fortuna, o erono suti più prudenti e saggi, perché dalla prima ora in qua che 'l bel viso della donna mia si presentò agli occhi, sempre serborono in loro quella dolcissima inmagine, né poterono da poi in qua mai vedere altra cosa, né per obscurità di tenebre o d'ombra, né per lume di sole: che si può interpretare l'ombra per la notte e il sole per il giorno, che è tanto a dire come se dicessi né dì né notte toglie quelli occhi dagli occhi miei. O, interpretando più largamente, possiamo dire che due cose conrompono la vista umana e levano la potenzia agli occhi, cioè una grande obscurità (e la obscurità non è altro che ombra che nasce dalla interposizione della materia tra 'l sole e noi) o uno superchio lume, come adviene a chi guarda il sole. Adunque, quella medesima inmaginazione che mi faceva sentire il nome della donna mia per il cascare dell'acqua, mi faceva ancora vedere in ogni tempo e luogo quello dolcissimo viso. Tutto questo concetto così expresso si include nel presente sonetto, el quale parla sempre all'acque del fonte sopra detto.

Resta a chiarire meglio quella parte che dice che gli occhi miei furono specchio al volto della donna mia, la quale abbiamo riservata all'ultimo per non interrompere la sentenzia del sonetto. E, non parendo da pretermetterla, diciamo che, volendo verificare che gli occhi miei fussino specchio al suo viso, bisogna intendere naturalmente come gli occhi veggono e come la potenzia visiva si reduce in atto. Secondo e Peripatetici, la cosa che è veduta si rapresenta drento agli occhi multiplicandosi la spezie e forma di essa cosa, tanto che perviene a quella parte dell'occhio che si

same imagination that made me always hear that name, guided by an amorous simplicity, led me also to look into the water to see if the face of my lady was still there within. And not seeing it there, I perceived my error, and considered immediately that water cannot receive any such form if it does not have a like object participating, because the nature of water is created so, being a diaphanous substance. But it was entirely permissible, as it seemed to me, for it to recall her name with its murmuring. And because this sprang entirely from my imagination and desire, no one other than I heard it, nor did Love permit that such a sweet harmony might come into the possession of anyone other than my enamored ears. After this, I began to make comparisons between the happiness of those waters and my own. And I seemed to be more happy than they, if I had in the first conceit any envy for those waters, I converted it into considerable self-satisfaction by showing that either my eyes had enjoyed the greater fortune, or that they were more prudent and wise, because from the first hour that the lovely face of my lady was presented to my eyes, they always kept that surpassingly sweet image in them. Nor could they from then till now ever see anything else, either because of the darkness of shadows or shade, or by the light of the sun—for shade can be interpreted as night and the sun as the day, which is as much as to say that the sonnet said that neither night nor day were her eyes taken from my eyes. Or, interpreting more broadly, we can say that two things corrupt human sight and remove the power of the eyes, that is [either] a great darkness (and darkness is nothing other than shadow that springs from the interposition of matter between the sun and us), or an overwhelming light, like what happens when someone looks at the sun. This same imagination, then, that made me hear the name of my lady in the waterfall, made me also see that sweetest face in every time and place. All this conceit so expressed is included in this sonnet that speaks always of the water mentioned above.

There remains to be better clarified that portion that says that my eyes were a mirror for the face of my lady, which we have saved for last in order not to interrupt the content of the sonnet. And, in order not to seem to omit it, and wishing to confirm that my eyes were a mirror for her face, we say that it suffices to understand how the eyes naturally see, and how the visual faculty operates. According to the Peripatetics,[87] that which one sees is represented within to the eyes by multiplying its species

---

[87] Aristotle and his followers. On the theory of sight, Bigi, 373 cites Aristotle, *De sensu atque sensili*, 2, and *De an.*, 5, 1. But these are apposite only in the most general way, and Zanato, (*Saggio*, 75) thinks it more probable that Lorenzo knew his Aristotle indirectly, perhaps via Ficino.

chiama "cristallina," perché è transparente e diafana come il cristallo, la quale riceve quella tale forma della cosa che si vede, come fa lo specchio di qualunque cosa che gli è opposita; questa tale forma così veduta, dalla cristallina si transferisce al senso comune, che giudica per questo la qualità di quella tale cosa. Secondo gli Accademici, negli occhi nostri sono certi spiriti sottilissimi, e quali si partono dagli occhi e vanno a quella cosa che si vede, e riportonla per riflessione agli occhi, quasi informati dalla forma di quella tale cosa, la quale rapresentono pure alla cristallina già detta, come a uno specchio, e di quivi poi al senso comune. E però, secondo qualunque di queste due oppinioni, molto propriamente abbiamo detto che gli occhi miei fussino specchio al viso della donna mia, perché negli occhi si forma la inmagine di qualunque cosa si vede, come nello specchio qualunque opposita forma.

XVIII

    Io ti lasciai pur qui quel lieto giorno
con Amore e madonna, anima mia:
lei con Amor parlando se ne gia
sì dolcemente, allor che ti svïorno!
    Lasso!, or piangendo e sospirando torno
a loco ove da me fuggisti pria:
né te né la tua bella compagnia
riveder posso, ovunque io miri intorno.
    Ben guardo ove la terra è più fiorita,
l'äer fatto più chiar da quella vista
che or fa del mondo un'altra parte lieta,
    e fra me dico: «Quinci sei fuggita
con Amore e madonna, anima trista:
ma il bel cammino a me mio destin vieta!».

Quando li successi d'alcuna cosa sono prosperi e il desiderio grande, se il fruire quella tale cosa per qualche cagione è impedito, si ricorre il più delle volte a quelli remedia e quali, o per similitudine o per propinquità, meglio e più proprio la rapresentono al pensiero; e perché il principio in tutte le opere è la potissima parte, la mente nostra volentieri torna col pensiero e, potendo, co' sensi a quelle cose che concorsono al principio, come

and form until it arrives at that part of the eye that is called "crystalline" because it is as transparent and diaphanous as crystal. This crystalline substance receives such forms as those from what one sees, as a mirror does from whatever is put before it. Seen thus by the crystalline, such a form as this is transferred to the common sense, which by this [means] judges the quality of that same object. According to the Academicians,[88] in our eyes are certain most rarified spirits, which depart from the eyes and go to that object that is seen, and they report it by reflection to the eyes, almost shaped by the form of that object, which they represent even to the crystalline part already mentioned, as to a mirror, and from there to common sense. And therefore, according to either one of these two opinions, very fittingly we have said that my eyes were the mirror of my lady's face, because in the eyes are formed the images of whatever we see, as in the mirror [is reflected the image] of some opposite form.

18

I left you even here that joyful day
With Love and with my lady, Soul of mine:
So sweetly was she speaking there with Love,
That you were led astray from your right path!
　Alas! now weeping, sighing I return
To that place you first fled away from me:
But neither you nor your fair company
Can I see more, though I look all around.
　I look well where the earth most flowers bore,
Where air was rendered clearer by that sight
That now delights the world another place.
　And in myself I say: "You erring Soul,
With Love and with my lady, hence you've fled:
But that fair road my fate forbids to me.

When the results of something are propitious and the desire [for them] great, if their fulfillment is impeded for some reason, most of the time one will return to those remedies that, either owing to their resemblance or to their propinquity, represent themselves to the thought as best and most suitable. And because the beginning in all our works is the most important part, our minds willingly return with thoughts and, as it can, with the senses to those things that, like the time, the place, the words, the manners

---

[88] Plato and his successors.

è tempo, luogo, parole, modi e che altro vi fussi intervenuto. Credo sia già detto a·ssufficienzia quanto fussi grande il desiderio di fruire la sua dolcissima presenzia; della quale sendo privato in quel tempo che composi il presente sonetto, mi era necessario avere ricorso al sopra detto remedio di cercare qualche cosa e più simile e più propinqua che potevo al vero che desiderava il cuore mio. E però cominciai prima a rimembrare nel pensiero quello felicissimo principio onde sono proceduti tanti dolci successi. Da questo pensiero mi nacque uno desiderio ardentissimo d'andare in quello luogo nel quale prima l'anima mia, e con la donna mia e con Amore, assai lontano da me si partì: perché passò poco tempo, dapoi che gli occhi suoi m'ebbono legato, che la vidi e molto bella e molto amorosa e dolce in uno luogo amenissimo assai vicino alla terra nostra; dopo el quale tempo, come volle la fortuna mia, lei si partì, e io stetti per qualche spazio che mi era interdetta la sua dolcissima visione: nel quale feci il presente sonetto.

 Trovandomi adunque in questo luogo nel quale avevo lasciato l'anima mia, cercavo se ve la potevo ritrovare; ma non vi vedendo né la donna mia né Amore, pensai subito che 'l mio cercare era invano e che l'anima, insieme con Amore e madonna, fussi fuggita in altra parte, come era segno manifesto non vi vedendo né l'anima né la compagnia sua, cioè Amore e madonna, li quali tutti insieme avevo lasciati in quello bello luogo. La quale anima fu sviata da Amore e dalle parole che con Amore parlava la donna mia: perché parlare con Amore non vuole dire altro che parlare cose che piacessino all'anima, e, piaccendoli, più la legassino; e certamente fu vero che molte e dolcissime parole piene d'amore e di pietà quel giorno mi fece udire. Tornai adunque non solamente in questo luogo, ma ancora mi riducevo in esso a memoria e le parole e i modi suoi, perché maggiore conforto nella absenzia sua non potevo ricevere. Questo pensiero e il luogo, che continuamente mi rapresentava quello lieto giorno, facevono nascere in me maggiore desiderio di vedere gli occhi suoi e investigare la via per la quale si fusse partita; et essendomi incognita, nessuno migliore argumento mi occorreva a trovarla che guardare la terra e l'aere. Perché, dove avevono tocco li piedi suoi era fiorita la terra, tanta virtù e grazia da quelli piedi aveva ricevuta; quella aria, per la quale il viso e gli occhi suoi erono penetrati e l'andare suo aveva divisa e partita, essendo assai più

and whatever else occurred, came together at the beginning. I think that I have already sufficiently said how great was my desire to enjoy her very sweet presence. And since I was deprived of it at that time when I composed this sonnet, it was necessary for me to have recourse to the above-mentioned remedy of seeking something as much like and as near as I could to the reality that my heart desired. And therefore I began first to recall in thought that happiest of beginnings from which so many sweet [outcomes] proceeded. From this thought a most ardent desire was born in me to go to that place from which my soul had gone so far away from me with Love and with my lady—because only a little time had passed since her eyes had bound me, and since I had seen her both very beautiful and very amorous and sweet in a most agreeable place very near to our city. After that time, as my fortune desired, she went away, and I remained with the sweet sight of her denied to me for some time during which I composed the present sonnet.

Finding myself then in this place, where I had left my soul, I sought to discover if I could again find it there. But, as I saw neither my lady nor Love, I thought immediately that my search was in vain and that my soul, together with Love and my lady, had fled somewhere else, as was manifestly signified by my not seeing there either my soul or its company, that is Love and my lady, all of whom I had left in that lovely place together. My soul had been led astray by Love and by the words that my lady was exchanging with love. For speaking with Love means nothing other than saying those things that please the soul, and that, because it pleases it, bind it more tightly. And certainly it is true that on that day I was made to hear many very sweet words filled with love and with pity. I therefore returned not only into this place, but also I was leading myself back in memory to it and to her words and her deeds, because I could not have a greater comfort in her absence. This thought, which continually represented that joyful day to me, and that place created in me an overwhelming desire to see her eyes and to inspect the way by which she had departed. And, as it was unknown to me, no better stratagem occurred to me for finding her than to look at the earth and the air.[89] Because wherever her feet had touched, the earth bore flowers, because it had derived such great virtue and grace from those feet. That air, through which her face and her eyes had penetrated and that her passing had divided and parted, by being very

---

[89] L. here employs the Petrarchan topos of *vestigi*, of searching for signs of the lady in the earth and air. This topos, in turn, has both eupractic and Christologic overtones since its archetype is to be found both in the search for signs in nature and in the symbolic search for the footsteps of Christ. See *Rvf.* 125, 60; 162, 4; 306, 12; or 360, 127.

chiara e inlustre che l'altra, faceva in quella regione segno del passare di madonna: come la via lattea in cielo, la quale, mostrandosi per abundanzia di splendore che viene da moltitudine di stelle più spesse e serrate insieme, assai similitudine aveva con la via della donna mia, inlustrata dallo splendore delli occhi suoi. Era adunque assai noto a me il cammino onde, e con madonna e con Amore insieme, s'era da me dilungata e fuggita l'anima mia; ma il destino mio e adversa sorte non sopportava che io potessi, come aveva fatto l'anima, seguitare quel bello cammino: che non poteva essere se non bellissimo, per essere ornato di fiori novelli e inlustrato dallo splendore di quelli belli occhi.

Questi affetti amorosa vorrei fussino expressi nel presente sonetto, il quale parla sempre alla fuggitiva anima mia, e conviene presupporre che fussi composto e recitato nel proprio luogo dove furono questi amorosa accidenti.

XIX

Datemi pace omai, sospiri ardenti,
o pensiero sempre nel bel viso fissi,
ché qualche sonno placido venissi
alle roranti mie luci dolenti!
    Or li uomini e le fere hanno le urgenti
fatiche e' dur' pensiero queti e remissi,
e già i bianchi cavalli al giogo ha missi
la scorta de' febei raggi orienti.
    Deh, facciàn triegua, Amor! ch'io ti prometto
ne' sonni sol veder quello amoroso
viso, udir le parole ch'ella dice,
    toccar la bianco man che il cor m'ha stretto.
O Amor, del mio ben troppo invidioso,
lassami almen dormendo esser felice!

Sogliono comunemente tutte le infirmità corporale nel sopravenire della notte pigliare augmento e affliggere più lo infermo; e questo adviene ché, mancando la virtù del sole, el quale è propizio all'umana natura, li umori maligni prendono maggiore forza e la virtù fa manco resistenzia, perché naturalmente la notte gli è data per riposo, et essendo più inclinata

much brighter and more luminous than elsewhere, gave evidence in that region of my lady's having passed by, like the Milky Way in heaven, which, by shining forth with an abundance of glory that comes from multitudes of stars that are closely spaced and packed tightly together, very like the way my lady's path had been illuminated by the light of her eyes. The path, then, by which my soul had departed from me and fled away together with my lady and with Love was very evident to me. But my destiny and adverse fortune would not allow me to follow, as my soul had done, that lovely path—which could not have existed except as very beautiful, as it had been adorned with rare flowers and illuminated by the glory of those beautiful eyes.

These amorous feelings I would have wished to express in this sonnet, which continues to speak to my fugitive soul, and ought to be supposed to have been composed and recited in the same place where these amorous incidents occurred.

19

Give me some peace, at last, you ardent sighs,[90]
And thoughts, fixed always on that lovely face,
So that a little placid sleep may come
To these bedewed and sorrowing lights of mine!
    Now men and beasts enjoy from their hard thoughts
And pressing work remission and surcease,
The escort, too, of Phoebus' orient rays
Has yoked already both his horses white.
    Ah, let us make a truce, Love! for I swear
To see none but that amorous face in dreams,
To listen just to words she utters, and
    To touch her white hand that has pressed my heart.
O Love, too envious of my well being,
At least let me be happy when I sleep!

Ordinarily, all the infirmities of the body, by usually arriving in the night, make the infirm worse and afflict them more. And this happens because, in the absence of the virtue of the sun, which is propitious for human nature, the malign humors gain greater power, and one's vital force makes less resistance, because the night is naturally given to it for repose,

---

[90] The first line of this sonnet echoes that of *Rvf.* 274: "My unrelenting cares, oh, grant me peace."

la notte che 'l giorno a posare, non è così intenta e vigilante alla conservazione del corpo. Questo medesime adviene delle infirmità dello animo nostro, le quali sono nutrite da' maligni e malinconici pensieri, come le corporali da' maligni umori; e questo procede forse da più altre cagione, ma al presente me ne occorre due: perché, come abbiamo detto alle infirmità del corpo concorre⟨re⟩ e maggior forza di maligni umori e manco resistenzia della virtù naturale, così due cagioni hanno e morbi della mente per le quali sono più validi la notte che 'l di. La prima si è che naturalmente gli umori di che siamo composti si muovono nel corpo nostro a certe ore determinate e proporzionate alla lunghezza o brevità del dì e della notte, cioè dividendo la notte (e 'l dì), o lunga o brieve, in dodici parte e chiamando ciascuna d'esse parte un'ora, in modo che verso la sera comincia a muoversi l'umore maninconico e consuma una parte della notte, e quasi tutto il resto occupa la flemma. Conciosiacosa che, secondo e fisici, l'ultime tre ore della notte e le tre prime del giorno si muove il sangue, le seguenti sei ore la collora, l'altre ultime tre ore del giorno e le tre prime della notte l'umore maninconico, le sei seguenti della notte la flemma; e perché l'umore maninconico e flemmatico generano nella mente nostra malinconici e tristi pensieri, di necessità conviene questi tali pensieri abbino maggior forza in quello tempo che si muovono quelli umori. L'altra cagione che multiplica el male della mente più la notte che il giorno, diremo essere che la notte non si possono usare quelli remedii contro a questi mali che si può il giorno; conciosiacosa che contro alla malignità de' pensieri migliore rimedio non si può trovare che la diversione da quel tale pensiero, e questo procede da vedere, udire e praticare diverse cose che ritragghino la mente dalle moleste cogitazioni, la qual cosa difficilmente si può fare la notte. Concludesi per questo e notturni pensieri essere molto più veementi, e, quando sono maligni, molto più molesti, e per essere più potenti e per avere manco resistenzia e remedio.

and, being more inclined to rest at night than in the day, it is not as attentive and vigilant in preserving the body. This same thing happens in the infirmities of our minds, which are fed by malign and melancholy thoughts, as bodily infirmities are by malignant humors. And this perhaps proceeds from other causes as well, but only two of them occur to me at present: because, as we have said, to the infirmity of the body both the greater force of the malignant humors and the lowered resistance of the natural vital vigor contribute, just as the diseases of the mind have two causes that are stronger by night than by day. The first of these is that the humors of which we are composed and that move themselves naturally in our bodies at certain hours determined by and proportional to the length or brevity of the day or of the night, that is dividing the night (and the day), whether long or short, into twelve parts and calling each of these parts one hour. [The humors operate] in such a fashion that toward the evening the melancholy humor [black bile] begins to move itself and takes up a part of the night, and almost all the rest is occupied by phlegm. Likewise, according to the physicians, the last three hours of the night and the first three hours of the day the blood moves itself, and the following six hours the choleric humor [yellow bile]. The other last three hours of the day and the three first of the night, the melancholic humor, and the rest of the night the phlegm.[91] And because the melancholic and phlegmatic humors generate in our minds melancholy and sad thoughts, of necessity it follows that such thoughts as these have greater power in that time when these humors are moving. The other cause that increases the afflictions of the mind more at night than in the day, we shall say is that at night we cannot use those remedies against these ills that we can during the day. For one cannot find a better remedy against the thoughts' malignity than being diverted from such thoughts, and this results from seeing, hearing, and doing various things that draw the mind away from harmful reflection, which is a more difficult thing to do at night. For these reasons, one concludes that nocturnal thoughts are much more vehement, and, when they are malign, much more grievous, both from being more powerful and from [our] having less resistance and remedy.

---

[91] Bigi, 377 and Zanato (*Saggio*, 115) cite Ficino, *De studiosorum sanitate tuenda* in *Opera* 1:499–500. Ficino dedicated the *De vita*, in which this work appears, to Lorenzo. The humors are the fluids that Greek physicians perceived to flow through the body, and upon whose predominance ancient psychology was predicated. The fluids partook of the four elements of Greek science: earth, air, fire, and water, and were respectively black bile, yellow bile, blood and phlegm. The predominance of one of them in a person determined his or her temperament which might be choleric or bilious, sanguine, phlegmatic, or melancholic.

Era adunque notte, e io ero tanto afflitto da' pensieri miei amorosi, che più resistere non potevo, privato al tutto di sonno, cioè di quel poco di refriggerio ch'io potevo avere; e se cercavo porre da parte que' pensieri, questo mostra assai chiaramente ch'e pensieri erono moleste. La molestia de' miei pensieri amorosi da due cose poteva procedere: o veramente da una dubitazione e continua gelosia, la quale, ancora che non abbi cagione vera, accompagna sempre la mente come l'ombra il corpo, perché è natura de' maninconici, come dicemrno nella exposizione del terzo sonetto, mettere dubio nella chiarezza del sole; o veramente ché, pensando io alla bellezza della donna mia, se n'accendeva in me uno maraviglioso desiderio, del quale ardendo il cuore mio non poteva non avere grandissima passione, desiderando sommamente quello di che allora era al tutto privato. Quale adunque di queste due cagioni fussi, mosso da questa molestia, priego nel presente sonetto li miei ardenti sospiri, cioè e sospiri che nascevono dallo acceso desiderio sopra detto; priego ancora li miei pensieri, sempre fissi in quel bel viso, cioè che altro non vedevano o pensavano che quella; priego ancora le lacrime degli occhi miei (ché tutte a tre queste cose a uno tempo mi molestavano), che mi dieno pace, acciò che qualche sonno placido e dolce venissi alle mie luci roranti, cioè agli occhi miei lacrimosi: perché «rorante» s'interpetra quello che vulgarmente diciamo "rugiadoso". E per muovere conmiserazione in questi e quali io pregavo, mostro che tutti gli altri uomini e gli animali bruti, in quel tempo che io sospiravo e lacrimavo, si stavano quieti e in riposo, sanza fatica o sanza pensiero alcuno; e oramai avevo passato con questi affanni tanta parte della notte, che era tempo mi dovessi posare, perché già e cavalli del sole erono suti messi al giogo del carro solare per conducere la luce nel mondo, perché la scorta de' raggi febei, cioè l'aurora, che precede il sole, già faceva segno al mondo del futuro giorno. E perché forse pare impropriamente detto ch'e pensieri malinconici e flemmatici avessino tanta forza nel tempo dell'aurora, che abbiamo detto muoversi il sangue, bisogna intendere che, come dicemm ne' sonetti precedente, gli amanti il più delle volte o sono o diventano di natura malinconici; e benché in ogni tempo produchino

It was then night, and I was greatly afflicted by my amorous thought, which I was no longer able to resist, [and I was] deprived of all sleep, that is of what little solace I could have. And if I sought to put those thoughts aside, this very clearly shows that the thoughts were grievous. The trouble of my amorous thoughts could have resulted from two things: either truly [it could have arisen] from a doubtful and continual jealousy, which, although it has no true cause, always accompanies the mind as the shadow does the body, for it is the nature of melancholiacs, as we say in the exposition of the third sonnet, to be in doubt about the brightness of the sun. Or truly [my troubled thoughts could have been caused by the fact] that, when I thought about the beauty of my lady, that thought kindled in me a marvelous desire, from whose burning my heart was unable not to have a great passion, for it overwhelmingly desired that of which it had been entirely deprived. Moved, then, by this trouble, I ask my ardent sighs, that is the sighs born from the kindled desire mentioned above, which of these two causes it was. I also ask my thoughts, always fixed on that lovely face, that is, which saw or thought of nothing but her. I also ask the tears of my eyes (for all three things were troubling me at once), that they give me peace, so that some placid and sweet sleep can come to my bedewed eyes, that is, my tearful eyes, because "bedewed" [*rorante*] means that which we call "dewy" [*rugiadoso*] in the vernacular. And in order to stir pity in these and in those whom I was asking, I show that all the other men and the brute animals, in that time when I was sighing and weeping, were quiet and in repose without toil and without any worry. And until then I had passed the greater part of the night with these difficulties, for it was time that I ought to have rested, because already the horses of the sun had been placed in the yoke of the solar chariot to bring light to the world, because the guide of Phoebus' rays, that is the dawn that precedes the sun, already was giving evidence to the world of the coming day. And because perhaps it seemed inappropriately said that the melancholy and phlegmatic thoughts had such great power at dawn, for we have said that the blood [the sanguine humor] was in motion, it must be understood that, as we say in the preceding sonnets, most of the time lovers either are or become melancholiacs by nature.[92] And since they

---

[92] Following Theophrastus and Aristotle (*Problemata*, 30, 1), Couliano, 46, describes two sorts of melancholia; one sort, resulting from the natural predominance of black bile, produced persons, "thin and gloomy ... clumsy, sordid, drab, apathetic, cowardly, irreverent, drowsy, and lazy...." The other sort, however, Lorenzo's sort, is caused "by the predominance of the hot humor, ..." i.e., blood, and called, "*melancholia fumosa*," which produces a "prodigious memory," and an "extraordinary capacity for analysis" (Couliano, 47–8). Both lovers and persons of extraordinary genius are typically of the second kind.

pensieri simili alla complessione, pure questi tali pensieri multiplicano più quando alla natura si agiugne el tempo nel quale si muove l'umore. E però, ancora che succede quel tempo che pare contrario alla malinconia, interviene come d'una fornace, dalla quale ancora che si levi el fuoco, vi resta el caldo per qualche tempo, per la impressione che ha fatto el fuoco: perché naturalmente da uno extremo a un altro non si va sanza mezzo. La impressione che ha fatto l'umore malinconico è grande, e la flemma che subintra non è opposita in modo allo umore precedente che gli tolga forza, per la participazione che ha con la maninconia della freddezza; e però, giugnendo questi pensieri, così fortificati dagli umori, all'ora che si muove il sangue, bisogna che a grado a grado, per la forza dell'umore, si reduchino e pensieri alla natura del sangue. E però, all'ora già detta, veramente la forza di quelli maligni pensieri non era tanto diminuita che reducessi el sonno agli occhi miei. Non bastorono e prieghi miei a farmi essaudire da' sospiri, da' pensieri e dalle lacrime. E però, pensando quello che più potessi fare, mi accorsi che la cagione vera del male mio, quella che moveva le lacrime, e sospiri e i pensieri, era Amore; e però cominciai a voltare a lui e miei prieghi, e, avendo chiesto a quelli primi invano pace, mi ridussi con Amore a domandarli triegua: cosa che più facilmente doveva consentire, perché la pace è una perpetua quiete, la triegua temporanea. E perché più facilmente me la consentisse, promissi ad Amore che, ancora che io dormissi, non mi rebellerei dal suo regno e ne' sonni miei vederei el viso della donna mia, udirei le sue dolce parole e toccherei quella candidissima mano; e i pensieri miei, dormendo, sarebbono amorosi come erano nella vigilia, solamente con questa differenzia: che, vigilando, o per gelosia o per desiderio, e pensieri erono molestissimi e duri; dormendo, sarebbono dolci e suavi, perché adempierei quello desiderio che avevo di vedere, udire e toccare la donna mia. E questo potevo securamente promettere, perché comunemente ne' sonni si veggono quelle cose che più s'inmaginono e desiderono nella vigilia. Negandomi adunque questo bene Amore, che almanco dormendo io fussi felice, veramente lo potevo chiamare invidioso, poiché d'una falsa e brevissima dolcezza non consentiva satisfarmi.

always produce thoughts of a similar complexion,[93] such thoughts are therefore multiplied even more when one adds to them the time in which the humor is stirring. And although that time follows that seems contrary to melancholy, it happens as it does with a furnace in which, although the fire has been put out, because of the impression that the fire has made, the heat remains for some time—because naturally one does not go from one extreme to the other without a half-way point.[94] The impression that the melancholic humor has made is great, and the phlegm that replaces it, because of the effect of coldness that it shares with the melancholic humor, is not opposed to the operation of the preceding humor so that it reduces its power. And therefore, [as a result of] these thoughts' coming together, so fortified by the humors, at the hour when the blood starts moving, it must be that through the power of the humors the thoughts are reduced step by step to the nature of the blood. And therefore, at the aforesaid hour, the force of those malign humors was truly not so much diminished that sleep could be led back to my eyes. Nor did my prayers suffice to make me exhaust my sighs, my thoughts, or my tears. And therefore, thinking about what else I could do, it occurred to me that the true cause of my ill, that which moved the tears, and the sighs and the thoughts, was Love. And therefore I began to address my prayers to him, and, having asked those first in vain for peace, I was reduced to asking for a truce with Love: a thing to which he ought easily to consent, because peace is a perpetual tranquillity, but a truce only temporary. And so he might more readily agree to it, I promised Love that, even if I slept, I would not rebel against his reign, and that in my sleep I would see the face of my lady, would hear her sweet words and would touch that very white hand. And my sleeping thoughts would be as amorous as were my waking ones, only with this difference: that, waking, either because of jealousy or desire, my thoughts were most grievous and hard; sleeping, they would be sweet and soft, because my desire would be fulfilled in seeing, hearing, and touching my lady. And this I was able to promise with certainty, because ordinarily one sees in sleep those things that one most imagines and desires while waking. If Love denied me this good, that sleeping, at least, I might be happy, I could truly call him envious because he did not consent to satisfy me with a false and very brief sweetness.

---

[93] Here "complexion" is used in its technical sense, implying that the quality of the thoughts reflects the mixture of the humors.

[94] Bigi, 379, cites Ficino, *In Phil. comm.*, in *Opera*, 2:1233: "ab extremo ad extremum sine medio non est endum."

XX

O Sonno placidissimo, omai vieni
allo affannato cor che ti disia!
Serra il perenne fonte a' pianti mia,
o dolce oblivïon, che tanto peni!
    Vienne, unica quïete, quale affreni
sola il corso al disire! E in compagnia
mena la donna mia benigna e pia,
con gli occhi di pietà dolci e sereni.
    Mostrami il lieto riso, ove già ferno
le Grazie la lor sede, e il disio queti
un pio sembiante, una parola accorta.
    Se così me la mostra, o sia eterno
il nostro sonno, o questi sonni lieti,
lasso, non passin per la eburnea porta!

    Abbiamo nel precedente sonetto verificato che li pensieri della notte sono più intensi che quelli del giorno, e quando sono maligni, molto più molesti. Ma ancora che generalmente così sia, li pensieri amorosi più che gli altri, secondo la mia oppinione, prendono la notte forza, e sono molto più insopportabili quando sono molesti; né possono essere altro che molesti, presupponendo la privazione della cosa amata. Perché tutti e mali che possono cadere negli uomini non sono altro che desiderio di bene, del quale altri è privato: perché chi sente alcuno dolore o torsione nel corpo desidera la sanità, di che è privato; chi è in carcere, la libertà; chi è deposto di qualche dignità, tornare in buona condizione; chi ha perduto alcuna facultà e substanzia, la ricchezza. E di questo veramente si può concludere che chi fussi sanza desiderio non sarebbe sottoposto ad alcuno caso, e chi più desidera sente maggiore afflizzione. E, se questo è vero, certamente gli amanti sono più che tutti gli altri miseri, perché hanno maggiore desiderio, e la notte sono miserrimi, perché el desiderio è maggiore; perché, mancando le altre occupazioni che distraggono la mente, non hanno altro recorso contro il pensiero che gli affligge che il medesimo pensiero, e sono private di qualche mitigazione che potrebbe il giorno avere la loro passione: come sarebbe vedere la donna amata, parlarne con qualche amico, vedere qualche suo intimo o consanguineo o domestico, vedere almeno la casa

20

O sleep most tranquil, still you do not come
To this afflicted heart that wants you so!
Seal up my everlasting spring of woes
That pain me so, o sweet oblivion!
　　Come, peace beyond compare, you only check
The course of my desire! And guide it to
My lady's company—she kind, devout,
With eyes of pity sweet, serene and clear.
　　Show me that joyful face—the graces there
Have made their seat—and show me calm desire,
A pious countenance, a clever word.
　　If thus to me you show her, let our sleep
Forever last or let these joyful dreams,
Alas! not through the ivory portal come!

In this sonnet, we have confirmed that the thoughts of the night are more intense than those of the day, and when they are malign, much more troublesome. But even though it is generally thus, in my opinion, amorous thoughts, even more than the others, gain strength at night and are much more unbearable when they are troublesome. Neither, given the absence of the beloved, can they be other than troublesome, because all the troubles that can befall a man are nothing other than his being deprived of something he desires as a good.[95] For whoever feels some pain or torment in his body desires the health of which he is deprived; whoever is in prison, liberty; whoever is deposed from some dignity, to return to a good situation; whoever has lost some wealth or substance, riches. And from this one can truly conclude that anyone who was without desire would not be subject to any possibility [of deprivation], and whoever most desires feels the greatest affliction. And, if this is true, then certainly lovers more than any others are miserable, because they have greater desire, and at night are most miserable, because their desire is greater. For, lacking the other occupations that distract the mind, they have no recourse against the thought that afflicts them other than the same thought itself, and they are deprived of whatever remission their passion might have by day—such as seeing the beloved lady would be, or speaking about her with some friend, or seeing some of her confidants, either a relation or a servant, or to see,

---

[95] Bigi, 381, cites Ficino's commentary, "In Dionysium Areopagitam de Divinis nominibus..." in *Opera*, 1075 (2:12): "Boni privantio... quae revera 'malum' cognominatur," as the source of the conceit of love as deprivation.

dove lei abita; le quali benché non sieno altro che a uno febricitante e siziente lavarsi alquanto la bocca, che è cagione di crescere tanto più la sete, pure el tempo passa con manco afflizzione. E puossi veramente dire che gli amanti vivono di dolcissimi inganni che loro fanno a loro medesimi; de' quali essendo privati in qualche parte la notte, soli e pensosi, né consolazione alcuna né sonno amettono: come mostra el presente sonetto, molto simile di sentenzia al precedente. Il quale parla al Sonno, pregandolo che vogli venire, dopo tanti affanni e inquietudine, a serrare il fonte degli occhi miei lacrimosi, fonte perenne, cioè vivo e perpetuo, quasi dica che, se 'l Sonno non serra quelli occhi, non resteranno mai di lacrimare. Chiama dipoi il Sonno dolce oblivione e unica quiete per raffrenare il desio, perché questi due soli remedii aveva l'afflizzione mia, cioè o dimenticare, intermettendo e pensieri, o mitigare tanto desiderio. E perché a me medesimo pareva impossibile non solamente il dormire, ma il vivere sanza inmaginare la donna mia, priego il Sonno che, venendo negli occhi miei, la meni seco in compagnia, cioè me la mostri ne' sogni e mi faccia vedere e sentire il suo dolcissimo riso; quello riso, dico, ove le Grazie hanno fatto loro abitaculo, cioè che è sopra tutti gli altri grazioso e gentile: che veramente è detto sanza alcuna adulazione, tanta grazia e in ogni cosa e *maxime* in questo aveva la donna mia. Desideravo ancora che 'l sembiante suo, cioè l'apparenzia, mi fussi mostra dal Sonno pia, e il parlare accorto, e atta l'una e l'altra cosa a porre in qualche pace il mio ardentissimo desiderio; e però bisognava che il sembiante e le parole fussino amorose e piene di speranza. E, come si vede, in tutto questo sonetto non si cerca altro che raffrenare e temperare il disio corrente e ardentissimo. E credendosi il mio pensiero dovere obtenere dal Sonno questa sua petizione, come adviene alla insazietà dello appetito umano, da questo primo desiderio transcorre al desiderare ancora, o vero perpetuamente queste felicità dormendo, o qualche volta remosso el sonno. Perché dice che, consentendo el Sonno e volendo essaudire e prieghi miei di rapresentarmi la donna mia bella e pietosa etc., desidererebbe dormire etternamente, sanza destarsi mai, presupponendo sempre vedere la donna mia con le già dette condizioni; e se pure questo fussi impossibile, almeno non sieno questi sogni vani e bugiardi, come sono quelli che passono per la porta eburnea. Trovasi scritto fabulosamente per li antichi poeti essere appresso gli inferi due porte, che l'una è eburnea, cioè d'avorio, l'altra è di corno, e che tutti e sogni e quali pervengono alla umana inmaginazione nel sonno passono per queste due

at least, the house where she lives. Although to one fevered and thirsty, these are only enough to rinse the mouth, for they cause the thirst to increase much more, nonetheless the time passes with less affliction. And it can truly be said that lovers live on exceedingly sweet deceptions that they themselves produce, for, by being deprived of something during some part of the night, [they become] persons lonely and full of thought,[96] nor do they allow any consolation nor any sleep, as this sonnet, very like the preceding one in content, shows. [This sonnet] speaks to sleep, pleading that it will wish to come, after so much suffering and inquietude, to dam up the fountain of my weeping eyes, a perennial spring, that is, alive and perpetual, it almost says, that if sleep does not seal up those eyes, nothing will be left except to weep. It then calls sleep sweet oblivion and the only calm for checking desire, because my affliction has these two remedies only, that is either to forget by interrupting the thoughts, or to lessen such great desire. And because not only did sleeping seem impossible to me, but [also] living without imagining my lady, I ask of Sleep that by coming into my eyes he will lead her with him in his company, that is show her to me in my dreams, and make me see and hear her exceedingly sweet laugh— that laugh, I say, where the Graces have made their dwelling, for it is above all others gracious and noble. For truly it is said without any adulation that both in everything, and especially in this, my lady had very great grace. I also desire that her likeness, that is her appearance, be shown me in a pious dream, and her clever speech, and whatever else was likely to bring some peace to my very ardent desire. And therefore the likeness and the words needed to be amorous and full of hope. And, as one sees, this entire sonnet seeks nothing other than to rein in and temper my runaway and most ardent desire. And believing that my thought ought to obtain its petition from sleep, as happens owing to the insatiability of the human appetite, from this first desire still another desire follows on, either truly [to have] this happiness by sleeping perpetually, or sometimes by having the dream taken away. Because it says that, if sleep consents and if my prayers, flying up, are granted by representing to me my lady, lovely, pious, and so on, I would desire to sleep eternally, without ever awakening, always presupposing that I could see my lady under the aforesaid conditions. And if even this were impossible, at least these dreams are not vain and lies, as are those that pass through the ivory portal. One finds two portals near the underworld that, in fables, the ancient poets have written about, one of which is made of eburneum, that is of ivory, and the other of horn, and all the dreams that appear to the human imagination in sleep

---

[96] See *Rvf.* 35, 1–2: "Alone in thought.... I wander measuring the barren fields."

porte, con questa distinzione: che e sogni veri passono per la porta del corno, quelli che sono falsi e vani per la porta dello avorio. E però, pregando io che questi sogni lieti non passino per la porta eburnea, tanto è come pregare che quelli sogni non sieno falsi, ma verificati, e abbino quello felice effetto che sogliono avere quelli della porta cornea.

XXI

    Cerchi chi vuol le pompe e gli alti onori,
le piazze, e templi e gli edifizii magni,
le delizie, il tesor, quale accompagni
mille duri pensier', mille dolori.
    Un verde praticel pien di bei fiori,
un rivolo che l'erba interno bagni,
uno uccelletto che d'amor si lagni,
acqueta molto meglio i nostri ardori;
    l'ombrose selve, e sassi e gli alti monti,
gli antri obscuri e le fere fugitive,
qualche leggiadra ninfa päurosa.
    Quivi veggo io con pensier' vaghi e pronti
le belle luci come fussin vive,
qui me le toglie ora una ora altra cosa.

Assai copiosamente nelli due precedenti sonetti abbiamo mostro quanto sieno più veementi e pensieri notturni, e spezialmente gli amorosi; e avendo fatto menzione solamente dell'afflizzione che danno li maligni pensieri, convenientemente pare che séguiti li due precedente el presente sonetto, nella exposizione del quale accade mostrare quanta dolcezza portino li pensieri amorosi che non procedono da molesta cagione, che ragionevolmente portono maggiore dolcezza che gli altri pensieri, se è vero che li maligni amorosi pensieri portino maggiore molestia; perché le medesime cagioni che fanno el primo excesso della infelicità producono ancora più excessive felicità: come diremo d'uno avaro, el quale ha tanto dolore perdendo una quantità di danari, quanto è la letizia se guadagnassi la medesima quantità. Perché, se gli è vero, come abbiamo detto nel precedente comento, che l'appetito sia quello che ci sottometta a' casi della fortuna e alle perturbazioni, pare *necessario* bisogni che secondo la quantità dello appetito si misuri

pass through these two gates with this distinction: that true dreams pass through the gate of horn, those that are false and vain pass through the gate of ivory. And therefore, my praying that those joyful dreams not pass through the ivory portal, is as much as to pray that those dreams not be false, but genuine, and that they have the happy effect that those of the gate of horn usually do.

21

    Let search who will for honors high and pomp,
For city squares, for temples, buildings great,
For wealth and pleasures, which accompany
A thousand bitter thoughts, a thousand woes.
    A small, green meadow filled with lovely flowers,
A little brook that bathes the plants around,
A little bird lamenting for his love,
Much better these our burning ardors ease;
    The shady woods, the rocks and mountains high,
The caverns dark, and fugitive wild beasts,
Some graceful, charming, apprehensive nymph.
    Ah, there with eager, straying thoughts I see
Those lovely lights as if they were alive,
Here, this or that thing cuts me off from them.[97]

Very copiously in the two preceding sonnets we have shown how much more intense nocturnal thoughts are, and especially the amorous ones. And having made mention only of the afflictions that malign thoughts bring, it seems that this sonnet most fittingly follows the preceding two, whose exposition happens to show how much sweetness those amorous thoughts bring that do not proceed from grievous causes, for they arguably bring greater sweetness than other thoughts, if it is true that malign amorous thoughts bring greater bitterness, because the same occasions that make the first [malign thoughts] excessively unhappy produce an even more excessive happiness—as we can say of a miser, who has as much woe upon losing a quantity of money as he has joy if he earns the same amount. Because, if it is true, as we have said in the preceding commentary, that the appetite is that which subjects us to the vicissitudes and to the perturbations of fortune, it seems it must be necessary for our good

---

[97] This essentially Horatian pastoral poem is reminiscent of *Rvf* 10, "*Gloriosa Colonna.*" Its style typifies Lorenzo's later sonnets.

el bene e 'l male nostro; et essendo d'una medesima cosa el medesimo appetito, pare non solamente vero, ma necessario che la felicità e infelicità di quella tale cosa sia equale secondo equali gradi, o della privazione di quella cosa o dello adempiere l'appetito. Sono adunque gli amorosi pensieri dolcissimi e più che gli altri soavi quando procedono da dolce cagione, come mostra el presente sonetto. E perché dicemmo inanzi che la infelicità degli amorosi pensieri procedeva da privazione della cosa amata e dal suspetto che comunemente accompagna gli amanti, da due cagione similmente procede la felicità de' pensieri già detti, presupposta sempre la certezza, come possono avere gli amanti, della fede e amore della cosa amata. L'una cagione è pensando a qualche fresca e passata felicità e contento, sopra alla quale il pensiero si dilata e volentieri a cosa a cosa rimembra, parendogli, così faccendo, quasi più prolungare la passata dolcezza; l'altra procede da una speranza, assai vicina allo effetto, del futuro bene, la quale abbi in sè tale certezza che quasi lo facci parere presente. E come la prima cagione, dopo il fatto, fa più perpetuo el passato bene, così la propinqua speranza, inanzi al fatto, gli dà principio: come si vede, per essemplo, che chi aspetta una simile dolcezza o chi di fresco l'ha provata vorrebbe alienarsi da tutti gli altri pensieri; e io ho conosciuto qualcuno che, avendo una sùbita e insperata novella e certezza nel propinquo e futuro bene, ne resta quasi attonito, sanza udire alcuna cosa che gli sia detta o usare alcuno senso, essendo astratto da quel pensiero.

Questi affetti amorosi adunque mostra el presente sonetto, el quale, postponendo a simili pensieri amorosi tutte le cose che agli uomini comunemente sono gratissime e dolce, assai chiaro fa intendere quanto sia grande la dolcezza della amorosa cogitazione. Dice adunque lasciare a chi le vuole le pompe e gli alti onori e le publiche magnificenzie, come piazze, templi e gli altri edifizii publici, e per questo denota gli ambiziosi e quelli che con sommo studio cercano l'onore; dice dipoi che cerchi ancora chi vuole le civili dilicatezze, e per questo denota tutti e piaceri e lascivie umane; agiugne il tesoro, mostrando l'amore e lo studio della pecunia. Perché l'appetito nostro solamente circa queste tre cose si extende, cioè ambizione, voluttà corporale e avarizia, perché l'onore, il piacere e l'utile impedisce ogni altra nostra operazione. Séguita dipoi mostrando che cose aiutono e nutriscono e pensieri amorosi, cioè un verde praticello pieno di be' fiori, e uno rivolo che bagni l'erba intorno al luogo onde gira, e gli amorosi canti di qualche uccelletto. E qui è da notare che contro alle pompe et edifizii magni e l'altre cose descritte con parole grande e

and our ill to be measured according to the quantity of our appetite. And if the same appetite arises from the same thing, it seems not only true, but necessary that the felicity and infelicity of that same thing be equal in equal degrees, or [likewise] of the privation of that thing or of what fulfills the appetite. Amorous thoughts are therefore very sweet and softer than the others when they proceed from sweet occasions, as the present sonnet shows. And because we rather said that the unhappiness of the amorous thoughts proceeds from being deprived of the beloved and from the suspicion that commonly accompanies lovers, from two causes similarly proceed the happiness of the thoughts already mentioned, presupposing always such certainty as lovers can have about the faith and love of the beloved. The one cause is thinking about some recently past felicity and about a contentment, upon which the thought expands and willingly remembers each little thing, thereby seemingly almost prolonging the past sweetness. The other proceeds from a hope, very similar in its effect, for future good, about which the thought has in itself such certainty that it almost makes it appear present. And as the first cause, after the fact, makes the past good more enduring, so the next hope, before the event, gives it a beginning: as one sees, for example, that whoever awaits a similar sweetness or whoever has recently experienced [a similar] one would want to separate himself from all other thoughts. And I have known someone who, because of sudden and unhoped for news, and [because of] certainty about a proximate and future good, remained almost thunderstruck by that, without hearing anything that was said to him or using any [of his] senses, being carried away by that thought.

These amorous effects, then, the present sonnet demonstrates, for, by placing below similar amorous thoughts all the things that are ordinarily very pleasing and sweet to men, it makes very clearly evident how great the sweetness of amorous reflection is. It then says to leave pomp and high honors and public magnificence, like squares, temples, and the other public buildings to whoever wants them, and by this means it denotes the ambitious and those that with supreme effort seek honor. It then says also to let those who will seek civic refinements, and by this it denotes all human pleasures and licentiousness. It adds treasure, indicating the love and the zeal for money. For our appetite only extends itself to include these three things, that is ambition, corporeal pleasure and avarice, because honor, pleasure and profit interfere with our every other action. The sonnet continues then by showing what things assist and nourish amorous thoughts, like a green meadow full of lovely flowers, and a freshet that bathes the grass around the place where it meanders, and the amorous songs of some little bird. And here one should note that against pomp and great buildings and the other things described with grand and magnificent words, are

magnifiche, si oppone tutte cose piccole e chiamate per vocabuli diminutivi, come praticello, rivulo e augelletto, per provare meglio che se le predette cose grande sono accompagnate da mille duri pensieri e da mille dolori, queste piccole *a contrario* debbono indurre più tranquilli e quieti pensieri. Séguita dipoi che le selve, ‹e› monti, e sassi, le spelonche, le fere silvestre e qualche timida ninfa sono cose propizie a questi pensieri d'amore, per mostrare in effetto che la solitudine e il dilungarsi dallo umano consorzio riduce la mente più quieta e non forza e pensieri; e però, non sendo forzati, facilmente tornono alla natura e si profondono tanto più nella inmaginazione di quello che più desiderano e amano. E allora ha tanta forza la inmaginazione, che mostra agli occhi quello che vuole; e a me mostrava in modo me luci, cioè gli occhi della donna mia, come se vedessi lei viva e vera. Ma nella città, quando una cura, quando un'altra mi toglieva questa dolcezza, la quale veramente è grandissimaE, quando non si provassi per altra ragione, si prova per questa: che la dolcezza della inmaginazione ha qualche similitudine con la vera beatitudine, cioè quella che consegue l'anima a cui è data la gloria etterna, la quale in altro modo non si fruisce che inmaginando e contemplando la bontà divina. E benché questa contemplazione sia differente assai dalla contemplazione umana, perché quella contempla el vero e questa una inmaginazione vana che forma l'appetito mortale, nondimeno l'una con l'altra ha qualche poco di similitudine nel modo; e così imperfetta come è, questa mortale è aprovata per la prima felicità del mondo quando ha per obieto la vera perfezzione e bontà, secondo che si può conseguire nella mortale vita. Per questo si può dire che la contemplazione di qualunque cosa non molesta abbi in sè grande dolcezza, perché ha qualche parte di similitudine con la somma dolcezza e perfetta felicità.

Bisogna nel presente sonetto presupporre che fussi composto nella città, perché dicendo «qui me la toglie» etc., come si legge nell'ultimo verso, è necessario s'intendi «qui», cioè nella città, presupponendo ancora qualche fresco piacere o di contemplazione o d'altro ricevuto in luoghi alpestri e solitarii, per la quale comparazione si appetischino le ville e s'abbi in odio la città.

XXII

—Ponete modo al pianto, occhi miei lassi,
presto quel viso angelico vedrete!

opposed all things small and described by diminutives, like "a small meadow," a "little brook," and "little birds," to better prove that if the aforesaid great things are accompanied by a thousand hard thoughts and by a thousand sorrows, these small ones, on the contrary, must lead to calmer and more tranquil thoughts. It continues then [by saying] that the woods, [and] mountains, and rocks, the caves, the forest beasts and some timid nymph are things propitious to these thoughts of love, by showing in effect that solitude and distancing oneself from human contact leads the mind to be calmer and the thoughts not turbulent. And therefore, not being turbulent, they easily return to nature and absorb themselves much more in imagining what they most desire and love. And then the imagination has such force that it shows to the eyes what it wishes to. And to me it thus showed those lights, that is the eyes of my lady, as if I had seen her alive and real. But in the city then, first one care and then another took me away from this sweetness, which truly is very great. And, if it is not proved by any other argument, it is proved by this one. For the sweetness of the imagination has some likeness to true beatitude, that is to what is pursued by the soul to which is given eternal glory, which cannot be enjoyed in any other manner but by imagining and contemplating the divine goodness. And although this contemplation is very different from human contemplation, because that contemplates the truth and this a vain imagination that forms the mortal appetite, nonetheless the one has some little likeness with the other in this fashion. And as imperfect as this mortal [contemplation] is, it is approved as the premier happiness of the world when it has as its object true perfection and goodness, insofar as that can be achieved in mortal life. In view of this, it can be said that the contemplation of whatever does not harm has in itself great sweetness, because it has some part of likeness with supreme sweetness and perfect felicity.

One must suppose that the present sonnet was composed in the city, because by saying, "Here, this ... cuts me off," etc., as one reads in the last line, it is necessary to understand "here," that is, in the city, presupposing still some recent pleasure or some contemplation or other, received in a rustic and solitary place, by which comparison we long for the country and hold the city in contempt.

22

[Sonnet:]   "Temper your weeping, eyes of mine, leave off;
That face angelic very soon you'll see!

>   Ecco, già lo veggiam. Perché piangete?—
>   Perché nel petto il cor pavido stassi?
>   —Miseri noi, che se fiso mirassi,
>   fermando in noi le vaghe luci e liete,
>   il nostro bavalischio, o faria priete
>   di noi, o converria l'alma expirassi!—
>   —Dunque, qual disio face a voi, qual sorte,
>   e temere e voler quel vi disface?
>   Chi muove o scorge il passo lento e raro?—
>   —Natura insegna a noi temer la morte,
>   ma Amor poi mirabilmente face
>   süave a' suoi quel ch'è ad ogni altro amaro.—

Leggesi in Omero, antiquo et excellentissimo poeta greco, che Giove, quando vuole mandare agli uomini nel mondo la sorte che a ciascuno si conviene, ha due grandissimi vasi, delli quali l'uno è pieno di sorte adverse e infelice, nell'altro sono sorte felici e infelici insieme confusamente miste. E volendo mandare ad alcuno cattiva sorte, toglie di quelle del vaso el quale solamente contiene le sorte adverse; volendo fare alcuno felice, gli manda dell'altro vaso nel quale sono le adverse e prospere sorte mescolate: per denotare che facilmente gli uomini possono essere infelici sanza participazione d'alcuna felicità, ma non possono già essere felici sanza participazione di miseria. E se alla confermazione di sì vera sentenzia non fussi abastanza l'auttorità d'uno poeta tanto excellente che fu chiamato "divino", la experienzia dell'umane cose ne rende assai abundante testimonianzia.

Questa verità seguitiamo ancora noi nel presente sonetto; e avendo nelli tre precedente verificato due sentenzie, cioè la felicità e infelicità degli amorosa pensieri, non pare che sanza vera cagione accaggia nel presente sonetto mostrare che la felicità e infelicità amorose bene spesso sono congiunte e complicate insieme, anzi quasi sempre sono in compagnia, se bene tra loro or l'una or l'altra abbia maggior potenzia. Né adviene questo solamente nelle cose amorose, ma ancora nelle naturali, e comunemente in tutti e casi che advengono agli uomini. Perché, quanto alle naturali, veggiamo tutte le cose che vivono al mondo constare d'oppositi e vivere per contrarietà d'umori, et essere composte di cose che ciascuna per sé offende molto la natura di quella tale cosa; e se non fussi la repressione degli umori

> We see it here already. Why, then, weep?[98]
> Why does your heart stay fearful in your breast?"
> [Eyes:] "Poor us, for if she gazes fixedly,
> By resting on us those sweet, joyful lights,
> Our Basilisk will either make us stone,
> Or else will summon forth our dying soul!"
> [Sonnet:] "So, this is what desire will do to you?
> This how fate ruins you, how fear and will?
> Who moves or guides that footstep slow and strange?"
> [Eyes:] "To fear death, Nature teaches us, but then,
> How wondrously, to your eyes Love makes sweet
> What bitter is to every other man."

One reads in Homer, the ancient and very excellent Greek poet, that Jove, when he wishes to send to men in the world the fate that suits each one, has two great vases, one of which is full of adverse and unhappy fate, in the other are happy and unhappy fates, all mixed together confusedly.[99] And when he wishes to send ill fate to someone, he takes it from the vase that only contains adverse fortune. When he wishes to make someone happy, he sends it from the other vase in which adverse and prosperous fates are mixed. [Homer wrote this] to show that men can easily be unhappy without participating in any happiness, but that they cannot indeed be happy without participating in misery. And if the authority of such an excellent poet who was called "divine" were insufficient to confirm this very true pronouncement, human experience gives abundant witness to it.

This truth we still pursue in the present sonnet. And, having in the preceding three examined two subjects, that is the felicity and infelicity of amorous thoughts, it seems that with a true argument this sonnet undertakes to show that amorous happiness and unhappiness very often are joined and twisted together; rather they are almost always in company, if indeed either the one or the other of them can have the greater power. Neither does this occur only in amorous matters, but also in natural ones and ordinarily in all the cases that befall men. Because, regarding the natural ones, we see that everything living in the world is composed of opposites and lives by the opposition of the humors, and is composed of things each of which by itself much offends the nature of the other constituents.[100] And, if it were not for the restraint of the opposing humors,

---

[98] The "we" of the third line seems to allude to the verses of the sonnet.

[99] See *Iliad*, 2,4, 527–33.

[100] On the theory of contraries see Aristotle, *Physics*, 5. Zanato, (*Saggio*, 82) observes

contrarii, non viverebbe alcuna cosa in questo mondo inferiore. E però si può dire tutti gli animali mortali, vegetativi, sensitivi e razionali, non vivere per benificio degli umori de' quali sono composti, ma a dispetto d'essi e contra alla voglia loro, perché ciascuno umore naturalmente appetisce vincere e contrarii suoi, e sùbito che questo tale naturale appetito in qualunque d'essi ha effetto, e che l'uno vinca l'altro, di necessità viene la morte; e la vita si conserve mentre che dura la potenzia equale e la guerra tra l'uno e l'altro. E però diremo la vita nostra constare d'opposizione, contrarietà e diversi mali, e la morte procedere dalla pace. Pruovasi adunque per questo la vita, che appresso e mortali è stimata tra' primi beni, avere sempre in compagnia questo conflitto delli elementi. Quanto a' casi del mondo e a quello che 'l più delle volte adviene agli uomini, è assai manifesto o essere male puro sanza participazione di bene, o bene misto con molto male. E benché non mi paia questa proposizione abbi bisogno d'alcuna confirmazione, tuttavolta, distinguendo le operazioni umane in mentali e corporali, credo sia facile ad intendere che sempre la mente e intelletto ha oppositi e inimici e sensi e le passione corporali: che così conviene che sia, essendo di natura molto contrarii lo intelletto e il corpo; le passioni e gli appetiti corporali sempre hanno per obstaculo el rimordimento della conscienzia, che procede dallo intelletto; e oltre a questo, spesso, anzi quasi sempre, una passione è contraria all'altra e l'uno appetito all'altro: che così conviene che sia, procedente le passioni umane in gran parte dagli umori delli quali siamo composti, che, come abbiamo detto, sono *de directo* contrarii l'uno all'altro. Veggiamo ancora nelle civili, proprie e domestiche operazioni la difficultà del pigliare qualche partito nascere dal concorrere in ogni partito qualche inconveniente, né si trovare di mille volte una vera diliberazione alla quale non si possa contradire. E però quelli che sono più prudenti indugiono più a pigliare partito, e per questa tardità si chiamono "uomini gravi"; e il tempo si chiama "sapientissimo," perché la sapienzia vera consiste nello aspettare e usare la occasione, e questa non sarebbe necessaria se non per la molta difficultà che portano seco le occorrente deliberazioni. Verificasi adunque ogni umana azzione non essere absolutamente buona, né dolce sanza participazione di miseria.

nothing in this lower world could live. And therefore it can be said that all mortal creatures, those with powers of vegetative growth, with sensory powers, and with rational ones,[101] do not live by the benefit of the humors of which they are composed, but in spite of them and against their will, because each humor naturally desires to overcome its opposites, and as soon as this natural appetite of theirs has its effect in someone, and one conquers the other, death of necessity comes. And life is preserved while equal power and the war between the one and the other endures. And therefore we say that our life consists of opposition, contrariety and mutually repellent ills, and death proceeds from their peace. It can be proved then by this that life, which among mortals is esteemed among the highest goods, has always in its company this conflict among the elements. Not very often in the chances of the world, and in that which most of the time happens to men, is clearly manifest either pure evil without any admixture of good, or good unmixed with much evil. And although it does not seem to me that this proposition has need of any confirmation, separating human operations, as always, into the mental and the corporeal, I think it is easy to understand that our minds and our intellects always have as their opposites and enemies the senses and the bodily passions. For it is fitting that it be thus, since the body and the intellect are very opposed by nature. The passions and the bodily appetites always have as an obstacle the remorse of conscience, which proceeds from the intellect. And beyond this, often, rather, almost always, one passion is contrary to another and one appetite to another. For it is fitting that it be thus, since human passions to a great extent proceed from the humors of which we are composed, which, as we have said, are *directly* opposed to one another. We see, moreover, in civil, commercial and domestic affairs the difficulty of taking one side born from the convergence on every side of whatever is an obstacle, nor in a thousand times can a true decision be found that cannot be contradicted. And therefore those who are most prudent longest postpone taking sides, and by this tardiness are called "serious men." And the time [so spent] is called "very wise," because true wisdom consists in awaiting and in seizing the occasion, and this [prudence] would be unnecessary if not for the great difficulty that [taking] needful decisions brings with it. Every human action is proved then to be neither absolutely good nor

---

that Lorenzo's view of the operation of the natural world is not always consistent. Though here he proposes the theory of contraries, L. also propounds the theory of harmony in the prologue and in the commentary on sonnet 33. But, as Zanato points out, this contradiction was already present in Ficino.

[101] Only human beings were possessed of all three powers, animals with the first two, and plants with the vegetative only.

E questo molto più si conosce nelle cose che la passione e l'appetito governono: come sono e casi amorosi, perché dicemmo nel comento del sonetto che comincia *In qual parte andrò io* etc., amore non essere altro che una gentile passione.

Questa medesima sentenzia conferma el presente sonetto, el quale è composto per dialago: perché nel primo quadernario parla el sonetto agli occhi miei lacrimosi; el secondo quadernario, che comincia *Miseri noi,* rispondono gli occhi; dipoi il primo ternario, che comincia *Dunque, qual disio,* parla pure il sonetto agli occhi; l'ultimo ternario, che comincia *Natura,* rispondono pure gli occhi. Ritornando adunque al principio, è necessario presupporre che gli occhi miei da grave e continuo pianto erono occupati; e questo pareva maraviglia, essendo loro molto vicini e avendo quasi presente l'angelico viso della donna mia, nella visione del quale pareva consistessi la loro felicità, come dicemmo nel sonetto che comincia *Occhi, io sospiro* etc. Per questo pareva ragionevole prima confortare gli occhi a porre fine al pianto, perché presto vedrebbono la donna mia, la quale si poteva dire essere quasi presente. E perseverando pure gli occhi nel pianto, molto convenientemente si domanda perché pure piangono e per che cagione el cuore sta nel petto tutto pavido e pieno di sospetto. Rispondono a questa proposta gli occhi, mostrando el pianto loro procedere per il dubbio che hanno della forza degli occhi della donna mia, la quale chiamano bavalischio, il quale si dice avere per natura d'uccidere solamente con lo aspetto degli occhi; e però, come con li occhi solo lui uccide, così dubitano gli occhi miei non potere sopportare lo sguardo della donna mia, la quale, se fiso gli mirassi, o farebbe priete degli occhi come del resto del corpo, o converria l'alma expirassi e la vita si partissi. Vedesi questi due dubbi che mostravano gli occhi miei essere fondati nella experienzia di cose già sute, perché, quanto al diventare priete, si legge di Medusa (come abbiamo detto), quanto alla morte, similmente abbiamo lo essemplo del bavalischio. Absoluto adunque el primo dubio e mostra la cagione giusta del pianto, ne nasce uno altro, e questo è che, dato che tale sospetto sia giusto, gli occhi dovevono fuggire lo aspetto della donna mia come cosa mortale, e, seguitando pure el cammino per vederla, era necessario che giustificassino se desiderio o sorte menassino gli occhi miei, desiderando loro e temendo una medesima cosa; e in questo desiderio e timore si mostra l'amistione sopra detta della amaritudine con la dolcezza, perché el timore presuppone la amaritudine e il desiderio la dolcezza. Dice disio o sorte perché gli uomini qualche volta sono mossi da uno proprio e

sweet without the admixture of misery. And we recognize this much more clearly in those things governed by passion and by appetite—like amorous occasions—because as we say in the commentary on the sonnet that begins, "Where shall I go," etc. [4], Love is nothing other than a noble passion.

The foregoing sonnet, which is composed in dialogue, confirms this same judgment. For in the first quatrain the sonnet speaks to my weeping eyes. In the second quatrain, which begins, "Poor us," the eyes answer. Afterward, in the first tercet—"This is what desire, then,"—the sonnet speaks to the eyes. And in the last tercet, which begins: "To fear death,"[102] the eyes answer. Returning then to the beginning, it is necessary to suppose that my eyes were occupied by heavy and continual weeping. And this seemed a marvel, since they had very near to them and almost present [before them] the angelic face of my lady, in the sight of whom their felicity seemed to consist, as we say in the sonnet that begins: "O eyes, I sigh [9]," *etc*. Because of this it first seemed reasonable for the eyes to take comfort and put an end to their weeping, because they would soon see my lady, who could be said to be almost present. And as the eyes still continued to weep, it very fittingly asks why they are still crying and for what reason my heart stays in my breast all fearful and filled with suspicion. The eyes answer this question by showing that their weeping proceeds from the fear that they have of the power of the eyes of my lady, whom they call a "basilisk," which, it is said, had by nature the power of killing with only a glance of its eyes. And therefore, as it kills with its eyes only, thus because my eyes doubt their ability to endure the glance of my lady, which, if it looked intently on them, either would make the eyes stone as it did the rest of the body, or would require that the soul die and life depart. One sees that these two doubts that my eyes reveal are founded on things already experienced, because, as regards becoming stone, one reads of Medusa (as we have said). As regards death, likewise we have the example of the Basilisk. The first doubt is resolved, then, and it shows the just cause of the tears, one of them born from the other, and it is the case that, given that such a fear is just, my eyes must flee the sight of my lady as [they would] a mortal stroke, and, even following the road to see her, it was necessary that they judge whether desire or fate menaced my eyes, which both desired and feared the same thing. And in this desire and fear is shown the above-mentioned mixture of bitterness with sweetness, because fear presupposes bitterness and desire sweetness. It [the sonnet] says "desire" or "fate" because men are sometimes moved by a proper and

---

[102] The Italian line begins with, "*Natura*."

naturale desiderio, qualche volta sforzati quasi dal destino: perché si legge: «Fata volentem ducunt, nolentem trahunt», e per experienzia spesse volte si vede gli uomini per elezzione fare molte cose contro alla proprio voluntà. Qual disio, adunque, o qual sorte muove el passo lento e raro? E in questi due epiteti del passo si mostra a un tempo e voglia e timore nello andare; perché, se fusse voglia sanza timore, el passo sarebbe presto et expedito, se fusse timore sanza voglia, non sarebbe el passo nè alcuno movimento verso quella cosa che si temessi, perché el timore di natura fa fuggire, conciosiacosa che quello che si teme s'ha in odio e quello che s'ha in odio si fugge. A questo obieto rispondono gli occhi, mostrando la cagione del timore essere molto naturale, conciosiacosa che per natura ciascuno teme la morte; la cagione dello andare pure inanzi essere Amore, el quale non per alcuna naturale ragione, ma mirabilmente fa parere suave nelli amanti quello che in tutti gli altri è amaro e durissimo. E veramente è detto «mirabilmente», perché «mirabile» è ogni cosa la quale è contro all'ordine della natura; né potrebbe essere più opposito all'ordine della natura quanto è el desiderio della morte, de' pianti, de' sospiri e dell'altre amorose passione. Concluderemo per questo gli amanti essere di tutti gli uomini miserrimi, non solamente per una sorte comune che abbiamo detto avere tutte le cose umane, per avere sempre l'amistione del male, ma ancora per una particulare cagione: che gli amanti non hanno mai bene alcuno, né per proprietà (come l'altre cose), né per participazione, conciosiacosa che le maggiore dolcezze amorose non pare che consistino in altro che in quello che gli altri uomini chiamano "sommo male". Pure è assai agli amanti gustare una felicità che paia a·lloro propria, perché il contento umano consiste più tosto nel parere che nell'essere; e se a·lloro pare essere felici, sono, non però sanza ammistione sempre di ⟨n⟩felicità, pure amorose. E per questo io giudico che la dolcezza degli amanti sia rara, e qualche volta assai grande, ma le infelicità loro essere quasi continue e il dolore sanza comparazione maggiore, conciosiacosa che 'l dolore è spesso sanza dolcezza e la dolcezza non mai sanza dolore. E così conviene che sia, dove è infinita passione e insaziabile appetito.

natural desire, sometimes almost forced by destiny because one reads: "Aye, the willing soul Fate leads, but the unwilling drags along,"[103] and by experience men are often seen doing many things by choice against their proper wills. What desire, then, or what fate moves the footstep slow and hesitant?[104] And in these two epithets about the footstep are shown at one time both a desire to go and a fear in going. For, if there were desire without fear, the footstep would be quick and speedy, if there were fear without desire, there would be no footstep nor any movement toward the thing feared, because by nature fear makes one flee, so that what one fears one hates, and what one hates one flees. To this proposition the eyes respond, showing the cause of the fear to be very natural, since by nature everyone fears death. The cause of their going on, however, is Love, which not from any natural cause, but miraculously makes seem sweet in lovers that which in all others is bitter and most unendurable.[105] And "miraculously" is truly said, because everything is "miraculous" that is contrary to the order of nature. Nor could the desire for death, for weeping, and for sighs and for the other amorous passions be more contrary to the order of nature. We conclude from this that lovers are the most miserable of men, not only because of a common fate that we have said all human things suffer, by always having an intermixture of evil, but also for one particular reason—that lovers never enjoy any good, neither through ownership (as do others), nor through participation, so that the greatest amorous sweetnesses do not seem to consist in anything else except in that which other men call the "highest evil." Very much to lovers' taste, however, is one felicity that seems to them their own, for human happiness consists more in seeming rather than in being. And if they seem to be happy, they are—not, however, without some admixture always of [un]-happiness, even though amorous. And by this I judge that the sweetness of lovers is rare, and sometimes very great, but their infelicity is almost continual and their sorrow beyond comparison greater, so that the sorrow is often without sweetness and the sweetness never without sorrow. And it is fitting that it be so, wherever there is infinite passion and insatiable appetite.

---

[103] Lorenzo apparently quotes from memory: "Fata volentem ducunt nolentem trahunt," or more exactly: "Ducunt volentem fata, nolentem trahunt," in *Seneca ad Lucilium Epistulae Morales*, trans., Richard M. Gummere (New York: G. P. Putnam's Sons, 1925), 228–29. Gummere notes that Epictetus assigns this verse to Cleanthes, but St. Augustine thought it Seneca's.

[104] "Hesitant:" Ital. *raro*.

[105] Because the lover wishes to refashion himself by *becoming* the beloved, the lover emblematically seeks his own death.

XXIII

Sì dolcemente la mia donna chiama
morte nelli amorosi suoi sospiri,
che accende in mezzo alli aspri miei disiri
un süave disio, che morte brama.
 Questo gentil disio tanto il core ama,
che scaccia e spegne in lui gli altri martìri;
quinci prende vigore e par respiri
l'alma contr'a sua voglia, afflitta e grama.
 Morte, dalle dolcissime parole
di mia donna chiamata, già non chiude
però i belli occhi, anzi sen fa piatosa.
 Così mantiensi al mondo il mio bel Sole,
a me la vita mesta e lacrimosa,
 per contrario disio, che morte exclude.

Perché nel precedente sonetto abbiamo fatto qualche menzione de' miracoli d'Amore, vorrei avere tale facultà che gli potessi fare credibili apresso di qualunque, come sono certi apresso alli gentilissimi ingegni delli inamorati. E veramente, come si può imputare a gran difetto il credere leggermente quelle cose che *prima facie* paiono impossibile, così non mi pare da aprovare la oppinione di quelli che non prestono fede ad alcuna cosa, quando exceda in qualche parte o l'uso comune o l'ordine naturale, perché spesso si è veduto nascere grandissimi inconvenienti presupponendo una cosa falsa, per parere quasi impossibile, e nondimeno pure essere vera. E, oltra questo, come el credere presto pare officio di uomo leggiere, così absolutamente el non credere dimostra grande presunzione; perché, chi dice: «Questa cosa non può essere», presumme di sapere tutte le cose che possono essere e quanto sia la potenzia della natura; e nondimeno si vede molti effetti naturali diverse e quasi incredibili, se non fussino notissimi quasi a ogni persona. E chi crederrebbe che d'uno piccolo acino d'uva, nel quale non si vede colore, odore o sapore certo, si generassi la vite, con tante degne qualità? Questo medesimo degli altri semi, che tutti servano diversamente la propria spezie; né paiono mirabile queste cose perché si veggono a ogni ora. E a me pare che sieno maggiore maraviglie quelle che a ogni ora si veggono degli effetti naturali, che quelle di alcune altre cose le quali, per essere molto rare e lontane dalla cognizione nostra, paiono mirabile: come sono alcune spezie d'animali, che, per essere ignote a noi, giudichiamo quasi impossibile che possino essere, e forse in quelli paesi che le producono sono così comune, come a noi cani, cavalli e altri simili animali. Leggonsi quelle sei maraviglie, che mette el poeta nostro Petrarca

23

    So sweetly does my lady call on Death
With her sighs amorous, that kindled midst
The bitterness of these desires of mine,
There is a sweet desire that yearns for death.
    My heart this noble passion dearly loves,
Which quenches and drives out all torments else;
Hence strength it seems my soul takes and relief
Against its wretched and afflicted will.
    Yet Death, called by my lady's sweetest words,
Does not, indeed, on that account seal tight
Her lovely eyes, but rather pities her.
    Thus my fair sun in this world is preserved,
In me my sad and tearful life is saved
By contrary desire, which keeps Death out.

Because in the preceding sonnet we have made some mention of the miracles of Love, I should like to have some capacity for being able to make them as credible to someone else as they are certain to the most noble understandings of the enamored. And truly, just as one can find a great fault in lightly believing those things that seem *prima facie* impossible, so the opinion of those who will not believe in any thing that in some measure exceeds either the common usage or the order of nature does not, therefore, to me seem warranted. For often we have seen a thing occur that has most wrongly been supposed false because it seemed almost impossible, and nevertheless has been true. And, beyond this, just as quick credulity seems the office of frivolous men, so does absolute unbelief reveal great presumption. For whoever says, "This thing cannot be," presumes to know all things that can be and how great the power of nature is. And nevertheless, one sees many various and almost incredible natural effects, even if they are not widely known to every person. And who would believe that from the little seed of a grape, in which one discerns no color, odor or certain flavor, a grapevine would be brought forth with such worthy qualities? This same [is true] of the other seeds that all variously serve their own species. Nor do these things seem miraculous because one sees them at every hour. And it seems to me that what one sees at every hour as the result of natural effects are greater marvels than some of those other phenomena that, by being very uncommon and distant from our thinking, seem miraculous—just as there are some species of animals whose existence, by being unknown to us, we judge to be impossible, though perhaps in those countries that produce them, they are as common as dogs, horses, and other similar animals are to us. One reads of those six marvels,

in quella canzona che comincia *Qual più diversa e nuova,* appresso gli autori antique e autentici. E chi considera bene e quelle e l'altre cose che per mirabile si prèdicono, vedrà, se si può così dire, molto maggior fatica della natura in queste cose che a ogni ora abbiamo inanzi agli occhi, che in quelle le quali ammiriamo più tosto per essere rare che impossibile. Debbonsi adunque ancora gli amorosi miracoli, se non al tutto credere che sieno, almanco credere che sieno possibili.

E a me è paruto dovere fare questa preparazione nella exposizione del presente sonetto, avendo a narrare una cosa che forse pare impossibile, e nondimeno è vera, perché il sonetto non intende altro che provare come el desiderio della morte è cagione *inmediate* della vita. E, per venire allo effetto, bisogna intendere che la mia gentilissima donna aveva per uno suo costume spesso in bocca la morte e mostrava nelle parole sue bramarla, credo conoscendosi tanto gentile, che li pareva questa vita noiosa non fussi degna di sì bella cosa. Et essendo io suto presente qualche volta quando lei dolcissimamente chiamava la morte, mi veniva tanta amaritudine e dolore, quanto darebbe a ciascuno el dubbio della privazione d'ogni suo bene, perché mi pareva che lei la chiamassi sì dolcemente e con parole tanto efficace, che la morte non si gli potesse negare; agravando più el dolore mio la cagione di questo suo desiderio, la quale era Amore, chiamando lei morte negli amorose suoi sospiri. E per questo bisognava che fussi cagione di questo desiderio o una grande amaritudine e passione o una somma dolcezza; perché ambodue questi affetti causano negli uomini simili desiderii, perché la morte si brama o per uscire di doglia, o perché non sopravenga amaritudine che contamini una somma dolcezza e felicità, seguitando quella sentenzia, «tunc pulchrum esse mori» etc. Quale adunque fussi di queste cagione, a me dava grandissima afflizzione, *maxime* per quello di che io potesse essere suto imputato, poiché Amore era cagione di questo desiderio. E, combattuto da questa passione, in fine mi risolvevo a

which our poet Petrarch, following ancient and reliable authors, puts in that canzone that begins: "The strangest, rarest thing that ever was."[106] And whoever considers well both those and other things that are put forward as marvels, will see, if one can put it thus, much greater labor of nature in those things that we have at every hour before our eyes, than in those that we rather admire for being rare than impossible. Of amorous miracles, then, one must, if not believe in all there are, at least believe that they are possible.

And to me it has seemed necessary to make this preparation for the exposition of the preceding sonnet, having to recount a thing that perhaps seems impossible, and that is nevertheless true, because the sonnet means to demonstrate nothing other than how the desire for death is the *immediate* cause of life.[107] And, to achieve that effect, one must understand that my most noble lady often used to speak of death and she showed in her words her yearning for it, [and] knowing her so noble, I believe that this vexing life seemed unworthy for so lovely a person. And, as I was sometimes present when she most sweetly invited death, just as much great bitterness and sorrow came to me, as the fear of losing one's every good must bring, because it seemed to me that she invited death so sweetly and with such efficacious words, that it would not be able to deny her. It increased my sorrow more that Love was the cause of this desire of hers to invite death to her with her amorous sighs. And as a result of this it was necessary that the cause of this desire be either a great bitterness and suffering or a supreme sweetness. For both these effects cause similar desires in men, because one yearns for death either as a release from suffering, or because one is not overcome by the bitterness that contaminates a surpassing sweetness and felicity, according to that maxim: "Then it would be lovely to die."[108] Whichever of these causes it was, then, it gave me very great affliction, especially because I could have been implicated in one of them, since Love was the cause of this desire. And, assailed by this passion, finally

---

[106] *Rvf.* 135, 1. The six marvels include the phoenix which dies and rises from its own ashes; a magnet in the Indian Ocean so strong that it draws nails from the hulls of ships, causing them to disintegrate and sink; the basilisk whose look turns men to stone; a fountain that boils by night and is cold by day; another which ignites burnt-out torches and quenches flaming ones; and two fountains in the fortunate isles, one of which makes anyone drinking from it die laughing, and the other of which slakes thirst.

[107] As one rises up the steps of the *scala amoris*, one "dies" to a lower condition as one is "born" to a higher.

[108] "*Tunc pulchrum esse mori.*" Bigi, 394, thinks that Lorenzo is here quoting from memory *Aen.* 2, 317: "... pulchrumque mori succurrit in armis:" "how glorious to die in arms." The sentiment, however, was surely topical.

uno unico rimedio, d'accompagnare ancora io la donna mia in questo durissimo desiderio della morte. E però si accendeva tanto in me questo desiderio, che cominciava a parermi dolce in modo, che addolciva tutte le altre mie passione. E perché naturalmente si appetisce e si seguita quello che piace più, el cuore mio abbandonò tutti gli altri pensieri e pose da parte ogni altro desiderio e cura per seguire questo dolcissimo e gentile desio della morte. E benché tutti e pensieri d'alcuna cosa, essendo intensi e veementi, faccino postporre comunemente tutte l'altre cure, pure quello della morte fa molto meglio questo effetto. Perché ogni altro pensiero mette da parte gli altri pensieri minori non per sempre, ma per qualche tempo, perché, vivendo, possono tornare, anzi è necessario che tornino, e almeno quelli che induce la necessità della vita; ma el pensiero della morte debba alienare la mente da ogni altra cosa, perché dopo la morte non v'è che pensare quanto pel corpo e pel mondo. Per questo si dice che ogni altro desiderio e passione e tutti e martirii e affanni che si sentono, erono spenti nel cuore sopravenendo questo dolce desiderio della morte. Et essendo «spente» tutte queste passioni e restando solo el dolce pensiero della morte, la vita ne pigliava vigore e respirava alquanto: che così necessariamente conveniva che fussi, essendo spenti gli inimici suoi e restando in lei solo quello dolcissimo desiderio, cioè uno desiderio che gli piaceva, e, piaccendogli, dava forza all'anima e contra a sua voglia prolungava la vita; non «contra a sua voglia», quasi contro alla sua naturale voglia, ma contra al desiderio della morte. E benché questo gli dovessi arrecare qualche molestia, sendo opposito alla dolcezza di quello desiderio, pure, vivendo madonna (come faremo intendere) e mantenendosi viva, per questa medesima cagione non gli dava molestia alcuna, anzi maggiore contento, perché el desiderio vero del mio cuore era la vita della donna mia. Provasi adunque che del desiderio della morte, che chiamava spesso la donna mia, si conservava in me la vita. Questo medesimo desiderio suo conservava ancora la vita in lei, conciosiacosa che 'l desiderio faceva che lei con le dolcissime sue parole chiamasse la morte, la quale, sentendosi chiamare, non chiudeva per questo però e belli occhi della donna mia, ma per pietà di lei gli prolungava la vita. E così e in lei e in me si conservava la vita; e questa conservazione era causata da uno desiderio contrario alla vita, cioè della morte, el quale excludeva la morte, cioè, ne' modi che abbiamo detto, faceva scostare la morte. Questo miracolo e molti altri abbiamo veduti d'Amore, e crediamo appresso e gentili cuori sarà assai credibile, el testimonio de' quali ancora appresso degli altri doverrebbe avere fede.

I settled upon the singular remedy of also joining my lady in this most cruel desire for death. And therefore this desire was greatly kindled in me, for it began to appear so sweet to me that it sweetened all my other passions. And because one naturally hungers for and pursues that which pleases most, my heart abandoned all its other thoughts and put aside every other desire and care in order to follow this most sweet and noble desire for death. And although when all one's thoughts are about a single thing, being intense and forceful, they defer all other cares, the thought of death certainly achieves this effect much better. Because any other thought puts other minor thoughts aside for some time but not forever, because, while one lives, they can return—rather it is necessary that they return, at least those produced by the necessity of life. But the thought of death ought to drive everything else from the mind, because after death there is no one who any longer thinks about the body and the world. For this reason one says that every other desire and passion and all the sufferings and troubles that one feels were extinguished in the heart, overcome by this sweet desire for death. And as all these passions had been [spent] and as there remained only the sweet thought of death, life took strength from that and somewhat was relieved. And it was necessarily fitting that this be so, since my heart's enemies were exhausted and there remained in it only that sweet desire, that is a desire that pleased it, and, by pleasing it, gave strength to the soul and, against its will, prolonged its life—not "against its will," that is not against its natural will,[109] but against its desire for death. And although this, by being opposite to the sweetness of that desire, should have resulted in some suffering, nevertheless, by my lady's living (as we shall make clear) and by the desire's sustaining life—for this same reason it did not cause my heart any suffering, but rather greater happiness, because the true desire of my heart was the life of my lady. It is proved then that in the desire for death, upon which my lady very often called, my life was preserved in me. This same desire also preserved her life in her, since that desire made her call with her very sweet words on death, which, upon hearing itself called, did not for that reason, however, close the lovely eyes of my lady, but, through pity for her, prolonged her life. And so both in her and in me was life preserved. And this preservation resulted from one desire contrary to life, that is for death, which kept death away—that is, in the manner we have described it kept death away. These miracles of love and many others we have seen, and we believe that they will be very credible among noble hearts, whose testimony must yet make the others have faith.

---

[109] By nature the soul wishes to continue living.

XXIV

    Allor ch'io penso di dolermi alquanto
de' pianti e de' sospir' miei teco, Amore,
mirando per pietà l'afflitto core
l'imagin veggo di quel viso santo.
    E parmi allor sì bella e dolce tanto,
che vergognoso il primo pensier more;
nascene un altro poi, che è uno ardore
di ringraziarla, e le sue laude canto.
    La bella imagin che laudar si sente,
come dice il pensier che lei sol mira,
sen fa più bella e più pietosa assai.
    Quinci surge un disio nuovo in la mente
di veder quella che ode, parla e spira:
e torno a voi, lucenti e dolci rai.

Ero soletto e sanza alcuna compagnia, se non delli miei amorose pensieri, li quali molestandomi come el più delle volte sogliono fare, cominciai meco medesima a fare pensiero di volerne fare doglienza con Amore, come cagione de' miei pianti e sospiri e dell'altre amorose pene; e, volendo ad una ad una narrargliene, mi era necessario cominciare da quella parte che e prima e più era offesa, la quale era il cuore. Volendo adunque narrare l'afflizzione del cuore, pareva necessario di guardare nel cuore, e, guardando, considerare, per potere narrare lo stato suo. E se bene nel cuore erano dipinte molte passioni e tormenti, pure maggiore impressione aveva fatto in esso la inmagine del viso della donna mia; el quale, essendo bellissimo e, sì come era il vero, molto lucente e chiaro, e per la bellezza e per la luce tirò gli occhi miei e gli sforzò a rimirare quella inmagine, levando loro la visione delle pene del cuore: parendo molto conveniente che una cosa bella e lucente e levi la visione dell'altre cose, come è natura della excessiva luce, e tragga gli occhi a sè, come sempre suole fare la bellezza. Mirando adunque gli occhi miei questa inmagine in luogo delle pene, parve loro molto bella e dolce, cioè piena di pietà; e però, se prima era intenzione degli occhi vedere l'afflizzione del cuore, cosa molesta e deforme, per dolersi, veggendo il viso della donna mia bello e pietoso, e *de directo* opposito a quelle afflizzioni, ne doveva nascere ancora uno affetto tutto contrario al dolersi. Per la qual cagione il primo pensiero di dolersi vergognoso morì e in tutto si spense, e un altro ne nacque contrario di ringraziare e onorare la donna mia; la quale era sì bella e tanto gentile, che,

24

    When I think of complaining somewhat, Love,
To you about my tears and of my sighs,
When I for pity look on my vexed heart,
I see the image of that holy face.
    And then it seems so sweet and fair to me,
That, filled with shame, the first thought dies away;
A new thought's born from that, an ardent wish
To thank her, and to sing aloud her praise.
    Her lovely image, when it hears the praise
Sung by that thought that looks on her alone,
Grows thence more fair and much more merciful.
    Hence surges in my mind a new desire
For seeing that which hears, and speaks, and breathes;
And I return to you, sweet, shining rays.

    I was alone and with no other company except my amorous thoughts, which were troubling me as they usually did most of the time, [and] within myself I began to think of wishing to complain to Love, as the cause of my tears and sighs and my other amorous torments. And, wishing to recount them one by one in the sonnet, it was necessary for me to begin from that part that was both first and most seriously harmed, which was my heart. Wishing then to recount the afflictions of my heart, it seemed necessary to look into the heart, and, while looking, to think about it by being able to report its condition. And although in the heart were clearly depicted many passions and torments, an even greater impression had been made in it by the image of my lady's face, which, being most beautiful and, just like the real face, very shining and clear, it attracted my eyes because of its beauty and its light, and it forced them to look again upon that image, drawing them away from the spectacle of my heart's torments. For it seemed very fitting that [I look on] one lovely and shining thing and that I avoid the spectacle of the other things, as it is the nature of excessive light to do, and it seemed fitting that the image draw the eyes to itself, as beauty usually is accustomed to do. When my eyes, then, gazed upon this image in the place of the torments, it seemed to them very lovely and sweet, that is, filled with mercy. And therefore, if, in order to complain, it was first the intention of my eyes to see the affliction of my heart, a thing troubled and deformed, on seeing the lovely and pitying face of my lady, the precise opposite of those afflictions, there also necessarily sprang from it a feeling entirely opposed to complaining. For this reason, my first thought of shamefully complaining died and vanished altogether, and from it was born another opposite thought of thanking and honoring

solamente essendomi concesso di vedere sì bella cosa, quando mai non vi fussi suto pietà alcuna, non potevo avere cagione a dolermi, ma più tosto di ringraziarla. Mosse el pensiero di dolersi la passione, che acciea la mente e obumbra lo intelletto di una tenebrosa ignoranzia; ma sopravenendo la luce della verità, e fugate queste tenebre, non sanza vergogna si rimira lo errore passato; e però muore vergognoso el primo pensiero e nel suo luogo succede l'altro pensiero, più vero e più laudabile, di ringraziare la donna mia e d'essaltarla e laudarla. Le quali laude, sendo portate alla inmagine sua che è nel mio cuore, la fanno parere assai più bella e più pietosa: che così pare al pensiero mio, che non vede alcuna cosa se non questa inmagine. E perché di sopra abbiamo detto gli occhi vedere il cuore e le cose che sono in lui, le quali sono invisibili, al presente si dice che il pensiero, el quale non ha potenzia di vedere, mira la inmagine della donna mia. E per solvere l'una e l'altra obscurità, bisogna intendere, dove si dice «occhi» e «vedere», "pensieri" e "inmaginare", perché gli occhi, gli orecchi e la lingua e ogni senso che s'atribuisce al cuore non sono altro che pensieri, per mezzo de' quali el cuore, cioè la mente nostra, inmagina e opera, come el corpo per mezzo de' sensi; e però tutte le altre operazioni corporali, come è parlare e sentire, che fa quella inmagine, si debbono referire a inmaginazioni. E, così intendendo, si verifica quello abbiamo detto, che, sentendosi quella inmagine laudare, si fa più bella e più pietosa; perché quanto la inmaginazione è più forte, più gli pare vedere quello che allora inmagina, e inmaginando la donna mia pietosa e bella, pare necessario che, quanto più la inmagina così, più diventi bella e pietosa nel pensiero. Da questa tale inmaginazione di tanta bellezza e dolcezza nasce uno desiderio ardentissimo e nuovo nella mente di vedere la donna mia viva e vera; né dice disio nuovo perché questo sia nel cuore mio el primo desiderio che avessi mai di vedere la donna mia, ma dice nuovo a quelli altri pensieri, quasi rinato allora di nuovo. Questo nuovo disire, adunque, mi muove a vedere la donna mia viva e vera, perché il parlare, udire e spirare sono officio d'animale vivo, e non di cosa che sia inmaginata. Con questo desiderio, adunque, torno a vedere li lucenti e dolci raggi degli occhi della donna mia; e dicendo torno, mostro el desiderio non essere nuovo, cioè il primo che avessi mai di vederla, perché tornare a vederla presuppone altre volte essere ito per vederla; e dicendo raggi e lucenti e dolci, si mostra la bellezza e pietà che prima era in quella inmagine, la quale, per similitudine del vero, mi mosse a vedere quella bellissima cosa della quale ella era un dolcissimo essemplo.

Notasi nel presente sonetto tre pensieri e uno detto. Prima el pensiero

my lady—she who was so beautiful and so noble that, if it had been granted me only to see such a lovely thing, when such pity had never before existed there, I could not have reason to complain, but rather to thank her. The thought had been moved to complain by that passion that blinds the mind and darkens the intellect with a shadowy ignorance. But when the light of truth had overcome it, and those shadows had fled, not without shame did it behold past error. And therefore the first shameful thought died and its place was taken by the other truer and more laudable thought of thanking my lady and of exalting and praising her. Those praises, upon arriving at her image that is in my heart, made it appear very much more beautiful and merciful—for so it seems to my thought, which sees nothing except this image. And because above we have spoken [about] the eyes' seeing the heart and the things that are in it, which are invisible, in the present sonnet we say that the thought, which does not have the power of seeing, gazes on the image of my lady. And to resolve the one obscurity and the other, where it says "eyes" and "seeing," one must understand "thoughts" and "imagining," because the eyes, the ears and the tongue and every sense that is attributed to the heart are nothing other than thoughts, by whose means the heart, that is our mind, imagines and works, as the body does by means of the senses. And therefore all the other bodily operations, like speaking and hearing, which create that image, must be ascribed to imaginings. And, understanding it in this way, one confirms what we have said, for, hearing itself praised, that image, makes itself more lovely and more merciful. For the stronger the imagination is, the more it seems to see that which it then imagines, and in imagining my lady merciful and lovely, it seems necessary that the more it imagines her, the lovelier and more merciful she becomes in thought. From such an imagination as this of great beauty and sweetness is born in my mind a most ardent and new desire to see my lady alive and real. The sonnet does not say "new desire" because this desire in my heart is the first for seeing my lady that my heart ever had, but it says "new" with respect to those other thoughts, almost then born anew. This new desire, then, moves me to see my lady alive and real, because speaking, hearing and breathing are functions of a living creature and not of a thing imagined. With this desire, then, I return to see the sweet and shining rays of my lady's eyes. And by saying, "I return," I show that the desire, which is the first that I ever had of seeing her, is not new, because returning to see her presupposes having been to see her other times. And, saying "sweet, shining rays," shows the beauty and pity that first was in that image, which, by its resemblance to the truth, moved me to see that most beautiful thing of which it was a very sweet example.

Three thoughts and one effect are to be noted in the present sonnet.

di dolersi; el quale vergognoso morendo, nasce el secondo di ringraziare e laudare la donna mia, inmaginandola bella e pietosa; quinci nasce el terzo dello andare a vedere la vera, per similitudine della inmaginata. Dopo questi tre pensieri séguita l'effetto di mettere ad essecuzione quello che propose l'ultimo pensiero.

XXV

  Madonna, io veggo ne' vostri occhi belli
un disio vago, dolce et amoroso,
che Amore a tutti li altri tiene abscoso,
a me benignamente lo mostra elli.
  Questo gentil disio par che favelli,
promettendo al mio cor pace e riposo:
questo afferma un sospir caldo e piatoso,
che Amore in compagnia per fede dielli.
  Questo sospir porta al mio cor novelle
della pietà, che fuor del bianco petto
lo manda messagger del vostro cuore.
  Giunto alla bella bocca, e pie e belle
parole forma, di sì dolce effetto,
che fa stupido star, non che altri, Amore.

Di tutti e sensi nostri, sanza alcuna controversia, el più degno è reputato il vedere; e questo non è solamente giudicio degli uomini, ma ancora della natura, conciosiacosa che ha posto gli occhi e più alti che alcuno altro senso e più vicini al luogo dove sta lo intelletto. Conoscesi manifestamente gli occhi essere più necessarii alla vita umana che alcuno degli altri sensi, perché pare che per la notizia delle cose visibile si proceda agli altri sensi molto più facilmente. Sono cagione ancora gli occhi di farci conoscere la più bella cosa che possino conoscere e sensi, cioè la luce, perché né odore, né sapore' né alcuna voce o altra cosa sensitive si può comparare alla luce. Hanno ancora gli occhi questo previlegio et excellenzia negli altri sensi: che il cuore per alcuno altro mezzo sensitivo non si manifesta, ma tiene a tutti gli altri quasi secreti e suoi concetti, e solo per li occhi gli manifesta; perché di letizia e dolore, ira e amore, e di tutte l'altre passioni del cuore,

First [comes] the thought of complaining—which, by dying shamefully, gives rise to the second of thanking and praising my lady, when it imagines her beautiful and merciful. From that one springs the third of going to see the truth, because of its resemblance with her whom I imagined. After these three thoughts there follows the effect of putting into practice that which the last thought proposes.[110]

25

>My lady, in your lovely eyes I see
>A wandering, sweet, and amorous desire,
>Which Love keeps secret from all other folk,
>But which he graciously reveals to me.
>   It seems that this desire so noble speaks,
>And promises my heart repose and peace:
>A hot and piteous sigh affirms it so,
>Which Love in public utters as a pledge.
>   This sigh brings news of pity to my heart—
>The sigh she sends forth from her breast so white,
>From it and from her heart a messenger.
>   On coming to her lovely mouth, it forms
>Such piteous, lovely words of sweet effect,
>That Love, not only others, stands amazed.

Indisputably, of all our senses, the one most worthy and valued is the sight. And this is not only the judgment of men but also of nature, inasmuch as it has placed the eyes both higher than the other senses and nearer to the place where the intellect is situated. The eyes are manifestly known to be more necessary to human life than any of the other senses, because it seems that through the knowledge of visible things the other senses function much more easily. The eyes are also the cause of making known to us the most beautiful thing that the senses can know, that is, light, because neither odor, nor flavor, nor some voice nor other perceptible thing can be compared with light. The eyes also have this privilege and excellence among the other senses—that the heart does not make itself evident by other sensory means, but keeps its notions almost secret from the others, and only through the eyes does it make them evident. Because the eyes very often give very clear indications of joy and sorrow, wrath and

---

[110] Given L.'s own Neoplatonic exposition of the allegory of these sonnets, one hardly needs to supply more elaborate speculation.

gli occhi bene spesso danno assai chiaro indizio. È tanto vicino questo senso del vedere alla qualità dello animo nostro, che, secondo Plinio, chi bacia gli occhi ad alcuna persona, gli pare quasi baciare l'animo suo. E benché questo advenga in tutte le passioni, pure molto meglio si conosce negli affetti amorosi, nelli quali gli occhi hanno grandissima parte; perché il principio onde esce e onde entra Amore sono gli occhi, e quali e per loro medesimi sono la più bella cosa che abbi el corpo umano, e hanno per obietto la bellezza; e però, essendo la più bella cosa che abbi una donna bella, credo el più delle volte sieno la prima cosa che cominci dagli occhi dello amante a essere amata. Esce adunque Amore dagli occhi della cosa amata e per li occhi dello amante entra nel cuore: che si verifica che gli occhi *active et passive* sono principio d'amore. Faccendo adunque Amore la prima impressione negli occhi e aprendo per loro la strada al cuore, molto più facilmente comunica el cuore le sue passioni amorose agli occhi che le altre. E ha Amore dato questo rimedio all'afflizzione degli amanti, che, essendo tolto di mezzo el parlare e ogni altra via d'intendere el cuore l'uno dell'altro, per li occhi spesso e amorose sguardi s'intendono.

Era la donna mia, come abbiamo detto, sopra tutte le altre bellissima, e però si può pensare quanto fussino belli gli occhi suoi, che, secondo abbiamo detto, vincono qualunque altra corporale bellezza; e perché l'appetito nostro sempre cerca più quello che gli pare migliore, ancora che tutta la donna mia da me fusse amata, pure gli occhi miei erono tirati a guardare gli occhi suoi, come maggior bellezza. Guardavo adunque fiso e suo belli occhi e pareami vedere in essi uno desiderio amoroso pieno di pietà e dolcezza, che così per mezzo loro mi voleva fare intendere el suo gentilissimo cuore. E questo dolcissimo desiderio Amore non lo mostrava se non agli occhi miei, nascondendolo dagli altri, credo perché gli altri così fiso non gli miravano; né era tanto expedita la via tra la donna mia e loro da Amore per mezzo degli occhi, come tra 'l cuore suo e 'l cuore mio, secondo che di sopra abbiamo detto; e oltra questo, essendo Amore quello che mi mostrava questo desio della donna mia, che era mezzo tra lei e me, gli altri non lo potevano vedere, perché tra loro e lei non era Amore che lo mostrassi. Parevami quello gentile desiderio parlassi al mio cuore e gli promettessi, dopo tanti affanni e amorose persecuzione, pace e riposo, presup-

love, and of all the other passions of the heart. And this sense of seeing is very close to the quality of our mind, for, according to Pliny, whoever kisses the eyes of some person seems almost to be kissing his mind.[111] And although this happens in all the passions, it is even much better known in the amorous feelings, in which the eyes play a very great part. For the eyes are the principle by which Love exits and by which he enters, and they are themselves the most beautiful thing that the human body possesses, and they have beauty for their object. And therefore, being the most beautiful thing that a lovely lady has, I believe that most of the time they are the first thing to be loved by the eyes of the lover. Love then issues from the eyes of the beloved and through the eyes of the lover enters into the heart—for it is proved that the eyes are both the *active* and the *passive* principles of Love.[112] By Love's then making the first impression in the eyes and by its taking through them the road to the heart, the heart communicates its amorous passions much more easily to the eyes than to the other senses. And Love has given this remedy for the affliction of lovers. For, since speech and every other method of understanding each others' hearts have been taken away, they are often understood through the eyes and amorous glances.

My lady, as we have said, was beyond all others beautiful, and therefore one can imagine how beautiful her eyes were, which, as we have said, surpassed every other bodily beauty. And, because our appetite always seeks that which seems best to it, though I still loved everything about my lady, my eyes all the same were drawn to look at her eyes, as at a surpassing beauty. I looked intently then upon her lovely eyes, and I seemed to see in them an amorous desire filled with mercy and sweetness, for thus by their means did she want me to understand her most noble heart. And Love did not reveal this very sweet desire except to my eyes, hiding it from others, I believe, because the others did not so intently gaze on them. Nor was the way between my lady and those others by means of the eyes as direct for Love as [was the way] between her heart and my heart, as follows from what we have said above. And beyond this, since it was Love who had shown me this desire of my lady, which was between her and me, the others could not see it, because, between them and her, Love was not there to show it. It seemed to me that the noble desire spoke to my heart and promised it, after many torments and amorous per-

---

[111] See *Natural History* 11:146, trans., H. Rackham (Cambridge: Harvard Univ. Press, 1940), 3:523, "when we kiss ... [the eyes] we seem to reach the mind itself."

[112] Active because they send forth the rays which enamor, and passive because they are the medium through which the beloved's image enters the heart.

ponendo per la futura pace la passata guerra e pel riposo e quiete le fatiche e affanni amorosi: perché tutti questi affetti dolcissimi mostravano quelli occhi. E dubitando la donna mia che per li passati essempli io non prestassi forse interamente fede alle parole che gli occhi suoi mi dicevano, accompagnò questo pietoso desiderio d'uno amoroso sospiro; el quale, sendo mandato nunzio al mio cuore, uscì fuora del bianco petto della donna mia, testimonio della pietà ch'era in essa, la quale pietà aveva messo nel cuore quello sospiro amoroso. E avendo detto la cagione naturale de' sospiri nella exposizione di quello sonetto che comincia *Se 'l fortunato core* etc., non pare necessario qui dirne altro, ma bisogna intendere che questo sospiro nacque nel cuore, el quale contrasse a sé, per mezzo dello alito, l'aere per refrigerarsi; e prima che essalassi e spirassi fuora, formò nella bocca della donna mia certe parole dolcissime e amorose, per modo che e le parole e il sospiro pareva che a uno tempo di quella bella bocca uscissi. Perché, parendo alla donna mia non fussi forse sufficiente, a testificazione della sua pietà e amore, né il segno degli occhi, né la testimonianza de‹l› sospiro, vi aggiunse quella delle parole, molto più efficace testimonio che li due precedenti, acciò che il cuore mio, e per la efficacia del testimonio e pel numero sufficiente, essendo tre, avessi maggiore certezza. Furono le parole della donna mia tanto pie e belle e di tanto dolcissimo effetto, che Amore ne restò obstupefatto: e per questo si debbe pensare quello intervenisse a me; né si debbe maravigliare alcuno che crede questo, se non sono per me narrate formalmente le parole, perché, vinto dal medesimo stupore che vinse Amore, non solamente le parole, ma quasi dimenticai me stesso.

È, a mio giudizio, el processo del presente sonetto assai naturale e secondo el vero. Perché, chi ama, prima ne fa qualche segno con li occhi; dipoi di necessità nasce il sospiro, perché el piacere del vedere la cosa amata e quella ferma intenzione del vedere genera ‹il› sospiro, per le ragione dette nel sonetto preallegato; e mostra più veemenzia d'amore el sospirare che il guardare. Seguitano el sospiro le parole, tanto più efficace quanto più si riducono alla certezza della cosa; conciosia che e li sguardi e li sospiri potrebbono essere per altre cagione che non paiono, ma le parole mostrano più chiara la verità e sono spinte da maggiore forza d'amore. E così fa la natura di grado in grado gli effetti suoi.

XXVI

Quando la bella imagine Amor pose
drento al mio cor, per sua grazia o virtute,
se per altri disir' v'eran venute,

secutions, peace and repose, presupposing for past war future peace, and for amorous pains and torments quiet and repose—because those eyes revealed all these very sweet feelings. And because my lady feared that owing to past precedents I might not perhaps entirely credit the words that her eyes spoke to me, she accompanied this pitying desire with an amorous sigh. Being sent as a messenger to my heart, that sigh issued forth from my lady's white breast as a witness to the pity that was in her—the pity that had put that amorous sigh in her heart. And having explained the natural cause for sighing in the exposition of that sonnet that begins "If close to you my heart so fortunate" etc., [11] it does not seem necessary to say more about it here, but one must understand that this sigh was born in the heart, which by means of a breath had drawn into itself the air for cooling it. And before it ascended and breathed forth, it formed in my lady's mouth certain very sweet and amorous words, in such a fashion that both the words and the sigh seemed to issue from that lovely mouth at the same time. Because, since it seemed to my lady that neither the signal of her eyes nor the testimony of her sigh would perhaps be sufficient witness to her mercy and love, she added thereto that of words, a much more effective witness than the preceding two, so that my heart, both through the effectiveness of the witness and the sufficient number of them, being three, had greater certainty. The words of my lady were very merciful and lovely and of such sweet effect, that Love was amazed by them. And on this account one must imagine what happened to me. Neither ought anyone to marvel who believes this, if the words are not formally recounted by me, because, overcome by the same stupor that overcame Love, not only did I forget the words, but almost myself.

To my judgment, the process of this sonnet is very natural and truthful. Because whoever loves, first gives some sign of it with the eyes. Next of necessity a sigh is born, because the pleasure of seeing the beloved and the firm intention of seeing her generates [the] sigh for the reasons explained in the sonnet included earlier on. And sighs reveal more extremity of love than glances do. The words follow the sigh, as much more effective as they lead to a fuller certainty about something. For both glances and sighs can result from causes other than the ones they seem to, but words more clearly reveal the truth and are impelled by a greater force of love. And so step by step nature achieves its effect.

26

When, in my heart, both for its virtue and
Its grace, Love that lovely image had emplaced,
It drove out and extinguished all things else,

  spense e scacciò da·llui tutte altre cose.
  Lasso or, se con le luci lacrimose
invan cerco le luci che ho perdute!
Dalli occhi al pensier fuggo, e mia salute
a·llui domando, a cui già mai si ascose.
  El mio pensier allor benignamente
sola in mezzo del cor la donna mia
mi mostra, e intorno tutti e miei disiri.
  Allor di novel foco arder si sente
il tristo cor, che già cener saria,
se non fusse la forza de' sospiri.

 Avendo nel precedente comento mostro quanto sieno excellenti gli occhi tra gli altri sensi e quanta degnità ha dato loro Amore, volendo che sieno la porta onde egli entri e faccendogli spesso ministri suoi e nunzii de' pensieri del cuore, bisogna confessare che grandissima dolcezza traggono gli amanti dagli occhi. E, se questo è vero, *a contrario* è quasi insopportabile tormento, in chi ama, la privazione d'essi, anzi sarebbe al tutto insopportabile se Amore non vi avessi posto uno solo rimedio, di sovenire in questo caso il cuore mediante e pensieri; el quale rimedio però non è fatto altrimenti che l'altre amorose subvenzioni, le quali sono più presto fomento e legno allo amoroso fuoco che refrigerio al cuore. Questa sentenzia mostra el sonetto presente, nel quale in principio si denota l'amorosa providenzia; perché, essendo antiveduta da Amore, come le altre pene degli amanti, ancora questa della privazione degli occhi amati, ha preparato il soccorso de' pensieri contro a questo male, avendo messo la inmagine della cosa amata drento al cuore, che la rapresenta a' pensieri quando ne sono privati gli occhi. Pose adunque Amore nel mio cuore, secondo la sua usanza, la bella inmagine della donna mia, per grazia o virtù che fusse nel cuore mio, cioè o per una particulare grazia di Amore verso di lui, che lo fe' degno di sì degna inmagine, o per virtù, essendo già fatto gentile. Quando venne questa inmagine nel cuore, spense e scacciò da lui tutte l'altre impressioni che per qualunque desire fussino nel cuore mio, e solo vi rimase la bella inmagine della mia donna. In quel giorno che io composi el presente sonetto avevo con assai passi e tempo cerco di vedere gli occhi della donna mia, e certamente invano, perché mai ebbi grazia di vederli quel dì.

If they had come there through some other yearning.
   Ah, woe is me now, if with weeping lights
I seek in vain the lights that I have lost!
From eyes to thought I flee, and ask the thought
For my well being, never from it hid.
   My thought then graciously reveals to me
My lady in the center of my heart
Alone, surrounded by all my desires.
   With new fire then my heart disconsolate,
Feels itself burn, and would indeed be ash,
Were it not for those sighs and for their power.

Having in the preceding commentary shown how excellent the eyes are among the other senses, and how much dignity Love has given them, wishing them to be the portal by which he enters and by often making them his ministers and the messengers of the heart, one must confess that lovers draw very great sweetness from the eyes. And, if this is true, it is *on the contrary* an almost unbearable torment for the lover to be deprived of [the beloved's eyes]—rather it would be entirely insupportable if Love had not placed there a single remedy for assisting the heart in this case by means of the thoughts. This remedy, however, is not constituted any differently from those other amorous expedients, which are more readily fuel and wood for the amorous flame than a relief for the heart.[113] This judgment is revealed in the present sonnet, at whose beginning Love's providence is signified. Because, since this deprivation of the lover's eyes is foreseen by Love, as also are the other torments of lovers, he has asked the help of the thoughts against this evil, and has placed within the heart the beloved's image, which represents her to the thoughts when the eyes are deprived of her. According to his custom, then, Love placed in my heart the lovely image of my lady for a grace or a virtue that would be in my heart, that is either because of a particular grace of Love's toward it, which made it worthy of so excellent an image, or because of its virtue, since it had already been made noble. When this image came into my heart, it extinguished and drove forth all the other impressions that by some desire or other had been in my heart, and only the lovely image of my lady remained there. On the day on which I composed the present sonnet I had spent many steps and much time seeking to behold the eyes of my lady, but certainly in vain, because I never had the grace to see her on that

---

[113] Cf. *Rvf.* 273, 3–4: "Despondent spirit who forever strays/And on the fire wherein you burn heaps fuel."

Cercavo adunque con le mie lacrimose luci le luci che avevo perdute, cioè gli occhi della donna mia, e quali non potevo trovare: di che certamente intollerabile tormento sentivo. Ma non sendo possibile che altrimenti fussi, ricorsi a quello unico rimedio che mi aveva concesso Amore, e, lasciato il cercare con li occhi la donna mia, rifuggi' al cercarne col pensiero; al quale domandai la salute mia, cioè che lui almeno mi mostrassi la mia donna, perché in potenzia sua era il mostrarmela, non si ascondendo ella già mai da lui, perché el pensiero la vede sempre. Furono essauditi e miei prieghi benignamente dal pensiero, e subito mi mostrò la donna mia sola; e in mezzo del cuore non erano altri pensieri, come dicemmo di sopra: ma non vi potevano essere, perché essendo el mezzo del cuore fondamento de' pensieri, come el centro fondamento della terra e di tutto el mondo, non si poteva fondare pensiero alcuno se non nella donna mia, e tutti gli altri che avessi fatto el cuore, se pure avesse potuto, sarebbono suti come sono tutte le cose sanza fondamento. Era adunque madonna in mezzo del cuore, e intorno a lei erono tutti e desiderii miei: che per questo si verifica che né li pensieri pensavono ad altro, né 'l desiderio appetiva altra cosa; e naturalmente el luogo e fonte de' desiderii è il cuore, per la concupiscibile, che è virtù e potenzia del cuore. Soccorse Amore col pensiero al difetto degli occhi; né di questo advenne altro che accumulazione di pene, perché, come dicemmo nel comento del sonetto che comincia *Allora che io Penso* etc., la inmagine della cosa amata multiplica el desiderio della vera: come advenne ancora a quel tempo, perché del vedere la donna mia drento al mio cuore s'accese uno nuovo e maggiore desiderio della donna mia. E perché pare impossibile che a tanto fuoco el mio cuore potesse resistere, che ardendo non si consumasse e divenisse cenere, si pone, per fare credibile questa maraviglia, el rimedio che non lasciava consumare el cuore, cioè la forza de' sospiri, e quali, come abbiamo detto, naturalmente sono dal cuore generati per suo refriggerio et essalazione contro alla suffocazione che l'offende, pel concorso delli spiriti vitaii.

XXVII

Più dolce sonno o placida qüiete
già mai chiuse occhi, o più belli occhi mai,
quanto quel che adombrò li santi rai

day. I sought then with my weeping lights the lights that I had lost, that is the eyes of my lady, which I could not find—and because of this I certainly felt an intolerable torment. But as it was impossible that it be otherwise, I had recourse to that single remedy that Love had granted me. And, leaving off searching for my lady with my eyes, I took refuge in searching for her with a thought. From it I begged for my well being, that is that it would at least reveal my lady to me, for it was in its power to show her to me, because, as she was never hidden from it, the thought saw her always. The thought kindly granted my prayers, and immediately it revealed to me my lady alone, and in the center of my heart there were no other thoughts, as we said above. But they could not be there, because since the center of the heart is the foundation of thoughts, as the center of the earth is the foundation of all the world,[114] thought could not be founded on anything if not on my lady, and all the other thoughts that my heart would have created, if indeed it had been able, would have been like things without foundation. My lady then was in the center of my heart, and around her were all my desires. For this proves that my thoughts did not think of anything else, and my desires did not hunger for another. And naturally the place and fountain of desires is the heart because of the concupiscible, which is the virtue and the power of the heart. Love came to the aid of the eyes' incapacity with thought. But from this nothing resulted except the accumulation of torments, because, as we said in the commentary on the sonnet that begins: "When I think of complaining" etc. [24], the image of the beloved increases the desire for the reality—as also happened at that time, because seeing my lady within my heart kindled a new and greater desire for her. And because it seems impossible that my heart could withstand so great a fire, or that its burning would not consume it and turn it into ashes, to make these marvels more credible, I include the remedy that did not permit the heart to be consumed, that is the power of sighs that, as we have said, the heart naturally generates to cool itself and to vent it against suffocation that, because of the assembling of the vital spirits, endangers it.

27

No sweeter sleep nor quiet more serene
Has ever closed an eye, or eyes more fair,
Than sleep that shaded once the sacred rays

---

[114] Lorenzo subscribes to the Renaissance view that the human being was a microcosm of the macrocosmic universe.

 delle amorose luci, altere e liete.
  E mentre stiêr così, chiuse e secrete,
Amor, del tuo valor perdesti assai,
ché lo imperio e la forza che tu hai
la bella vista par ti presti e viete.
  Alta e frondosa quercia, che interponi
le frondi tra' belli occhi e ' febei raggi
e subministri l'ombra al bel sopore,
  non temer, benché Glove irato tuoni,
non temer sopra te più folgor caggi,
da quei grati occhi consecrata a Amore.

XXVIII

 Odorifera erbetta e vaghi fiori,
che ornate il prato come il ciel le stelle,
le dolcemente fatigate e belle
membra vedesti in mezzo ai bei colori!
  Alto e dolce pensier suo, quanto onori
le cose di cui tacito favelle!
O me felice, che allor fui di quelle
(che 'l dice Amor, che ha in pegno i nostri cuori)!
  Aura süave, quale or togli or rendi
a·llei la vista del febeo splendore,
movendo i rami e insieme l'ombra intorno!
  Alla alta quercia i tuoi trofei sospendi,
o dolce sonno, e non si sdegni Amore
se trïunfasti de' belli occhi il giorno!

Se io potesse a uno a uno gli atti e amorosi accidenti della donna mia proseguire, certamente molto maggiore ornmamento ne riceverebbe questa nostra amorosa istoria e molto più laude la donna mia, perché veramente ogni atto, ancora che minimo, della vita sua è suto degno d'essere celebrato da me. E, avendone io gran parte pretermesso, ne do cagione solamente alla abundanzia e copia delle cose; perché a me è accaduto come a uno, el quale, sendo in mezzo d'uno amenissimo prato, el quale produce diverse colori di fiori, e volendo còrre de' più vaghi, non sa a qual prima porre la mano: perché la qualità della bellezza fa più difficile la elezione, essendo l'appetito nostro tirato più da quelle cose che più piacciono. Non potendo io adunque còrre tutti e fiori dello excellentissimo prato della

Of those lights, lofty, amorous, and gay.
    And while they stayed thus, closed and secretive,
A great deal of your power, Love, you lost;
That fair sight makes your empire and your force
Seem borrowed by you and seem obsolete.
    High, leafy oak, whose branches interposed
Between those lovely eyes and Phoebus' rays
And gave to them the shade for gentle sleep,
    Fear not though Jove may thunder wrathfully,
Nor fear above you more the lightning's flash,
Those graced eyes make you sacred now to Love.

28

    O fragrant little plants and lovely flowers,
Which grace the meadows as stars grace the sky,
Those sweetly weary, lovely limbs you see
Amidst the beauty of the meadow's hues.
    High thought of hers and sweet, how you revere
The things of which you silently discourse!
Oh happy me, that I was one of those
(For Love, who holds our hearts in pawn, announces it)!
    Light breeze, you now remove or give again
To her the view of Phoebus' glorious face,
Moving about both branches and the shade!
    Upon that lofty oak your trophies hang,
O Slumber sweet. And, Love, take no offense
If the day in those lovely eyes has mastered you.

    If I could in an orderly fashion go on with the acts and amorous qualities of my lady one by one, certainly this amorous history of ours would gain greater ornament, and my lady would receive much more praise from it, because truly every action of her life, even the smallest, merited my celebrating it. And, as I have for the most part already stated, I ascribe the cause of that solely to the abundance and copiousness of those acts. Because what happened to me was like what happens to someone who finds himself in the midst of a most agreeable meadow, which produces various colors of flowers, and he wishes to pick some of the lovelier ones, but doesn't know where first to place his hand because the quality of the beauty makes the choice most difficult, since our appetites are drawn most to those things that are most pleasing. I was not able then to gather all the flowers of the most excellent meadow of my lady, nor to recount in good

donna mia, né proseguire tutte le laude sue, né sappiendo eleggere qual prima meritassi essere da me còlta e celebrate, a caso errando con la mano quelli primi fiori che la sorte mi ha mostro ho còlti, faccendone più tosto giudice la fortuna che la mia elezzione.

Era, come nel precedente sonetto abbiamo detto, la donna mia absente, come mostra averla io cercata assai con li occhi e solo trovatola col pensiero. Trovandosi ella adunque in una villa non molto lontana dalla città, ma posta in luogo che non poteva vederla, mosse e passi suoi e, montando per uno monte assai alto e silvestre, pervenne in parte onde facilmente la città, dove io ero, poteva vedere, credo pensando potere dare qualche refriggerio o presente o futuro alla afflizzione la quale vedeva in me per l'absenzia sua. Era questo luogo salvatico, come abbiamo detto, e 'l terreno coperto d'erba e di fiori, il quale una vecchia quercia adombrava; et essendo pure la donna mia, pel cammino erto e difficile, alquanto affaticata, e vedendo sì bello luogo, deliberò fare degna quella erba e que' fiori che fussino letto e piuma al suo gentilissimo corpo. E dapoi che alquanto, così giacendo, contemplò la terra e luogo dove io ero, avuti alcuni dolcissimi e amorosi pensieri e mossa da quella pietà dell'afflizzione mia, vinta finalmente dal sonno, s'adormentò, aiutando el sonno l'ombra di quella quercia e una aura dolce estiva, la quale, movendo e rami della quercia e gli altri arbori vicini, con mormorio ancora quel dolcissime sonno nutriva.

Questo atto amoroso intendendo io, giudicai degno delli sopra scritti due sonetti, delli quali il primo contiene che, poi che la natura concesse sonno agli occhi umani, più dolce sonno o più quieto riposo non serrò occhio mortale, né ancora il sonno mai chiuse più belli occhi che quelli della donna mia. Quello che faceva el sonno sopra tutti gli altri dolcissimo era l'ombra, la mollizie del luogo ove giaceva lei, la dolcezza del venticello, el mormorio degli arbori che di necessità da quello nasceva e la fatica che era preceduta: che tutte sono cose che danno forza al sonno. Che quelli occhi fussino così belli come abbiamo detto, non posso assegnare altra ragione che la mia oppinione, fondata in sugli effetti che in me facevono; e se erono così belli, di necessità seguiva che Amore da loro avesse gran forza. E però, stando serrati dal sonno e celandosi quella amorosa luce al mondo, di necessità il valore e forza d'Amore ne sentiva detrimento assai, perché la vista sua gli dava e toglieva la forza. Siccome adviene ad alcuna spezie di fiori, li quali si aprono venendo il sole e dipoi nell'occaso si riserrano, in modo che quelle tali erbe il dì sono fiorite e la notte private dell'ornamento de' fiori, così diremo che i cuori gentili, pel sole degli occhi amati, si aprono a ricevere le influenzie amorose, le quali quando

order all her praises, nor did I know how to select what first merited being plucked and celebrated, by chance straying with my hand to those first flowers that Fate had shown me, I picked them, thereby making Fortune the judge rather than my own choice.

My lady, as we have said in the preceding sonnet, was absent, as my having so diligently sought her with my eyes but having only found her with my thought reveals. Finding herself, then, at a villa not very distant from the city, but situated in a place where she could not see it, my lady took her way, and ascending by a mountain very high and uncultivated, she arrived at a point from which she could very easily see the city where I was. She was thinking, I believe, that she could give either some present or future solace for my affliction, which she saw in me as a result of her absence. This place, as we have said, was uncultivated, and the ground was covered with grass and with flowers that an old oak tree shaded. And my lady, [having come there], indeed, by a steep and difficult path, being considerably fatigued, and seeing such a lovely place, decided to make worthy that grass and those flowers that were a bed and a pillow for her very gentle body. And somewhat later, lying thus, she contemplated the land and the place where I was, and had some very sweet and amorous thoughts and was moved by her pity for my affliction, and finally she fell asleep, overcome by a drowsiness assisted by the shade of that oak and by a sweet and summery breeze, which, moving both the branches of that oak and of the other trees nearby, with murmuring also nourished that exceedingly sweet sleep.

I, having knowledge of this amorous act, judged it worthy of the two sonnets written above, the first of which suggests that, since nature granted sleep to human eyes, no sweeter sleep nor quieter repose ever sealed a mortal eye, nor also did sleep ever close more beautiful eyes than those of my lady. What made the sleep sweet beyond all others were the shade, the soothing quality of the place where she lay, the little breeze, the murmuring of the trees, which of necessity sprang forth from them and the fatigue that was produced—for all are things that give sleep power. That those eyes were as lovely as we have said, I cannot attribute to any other argument than my opinion, founded upon the feelings that they created in me. And if they were so beautiful, of necessity it follows that Love took great power from them. And therefore, by their remaining sealed by sleep and concealing that amorous light from the world, of necessity one felt the power and force of Love to be greatly diminished, because the sight of her both gave and took away its force—just as it happens in some species of flowers, which the sunrise opens and sunset closes again. For just as such plants bloom by day and by night are deprived of the ornament of flowers, so we shall say that noble hearts are opened by the sun of beloved eyes to

mancassino si riserrerebbono; e acciò che mai non si serrino, fa la virtù d'Amore per mezzo di quelli occhi tale impressione, che possono dire già mai essere sanza sole. Amore adunque, che fa sentire la virtù sua per mezzo degli occhi, quando mancassi quella visione perderebbe la sua virtù.

Ora, tornando al sonno, si può facilmente comprendere che, essendo tanto suave quanto abbiamo detto, alla donna mia fussi molto grato; e però, come quella che in tutte le cose era sommamente gentile, come grata, retribuì qualche gratitudine a tutte le cose che avevano avuta parte e cagione di tanta dolcezza. E però alla erba e fiori, che sanza durezza e morbidamente avevono recevute le sue membra e fattali così ornata piuma e delicato letto, dette uno dono gratissimo, d'essere sute tocche e premute da sì pulite membra; l'aura, che aveva mosso gli arbori e rinfrescato l'aria, similmente toccò el suo bellissima corpo; l'ombre ancora, sopra a quel viso bellissimo e l'altre membra, a loro piacere errando, erano vagante. Restava solamente la quercia, non minima cagione di questa dolcezza, perché era suta cagione dell'ombre le quali aveva subministrate a quel bel sonno; e acciò che questa ancora sanza parte di premio non restassi, gli occhi della donna mia ‹la› consecrorono ad Amore, liberandola dalle percosse e impeti de' fulmini e tempestose saette: perché la quercia, essendo l'arbore di Giove, più spesso è percossa che gli altri arbori dalle sue saette; in luogo delle quali, da quel tempo in qua che soprastette a quelli belli occhi, sarà più tosto recettaculo delle saette amorose, poichè quelli occhi grati ad Amore l'hanno consecrata.

E perché nel primo sonetto non è fatta menzione alcuna del praticello sopra el quale giaceva la donna mia, né dell'aura suavissima (due cagioni, secondo abbiamo detto, assai efficace di quello bellissima sonno), perché è difficile fare capace la brevità del sonetto di molte cose, se ne fa menzione nel sequente, che comincia *Odorifera erbetta* etc., dove si vede che con somma dolcezza el mio pensiero rimembrava tutti quelli amorosi accidenti; né sanza qualche invidia di quella erba e fiori mi s'apresentò quell'atto, che fussi ricevuta da loro la donna mia così dolcemente affaticata. E però, volgendomi a quella erba e fiori, chiamandola odorifera e ponendo la varietà de' fiori simile alla distinzione che fanno le stelle nel cielo sereno, si dà quelle proprietà quasi che può avere el prato, cioè l'odore e la bellezza. E perché abbiamo detto che la donna mia, così giacendo, ebbe qualche amoroso pensiero di me, e questo era impossibile a sapere se non per chi ne ‹udisse› e pensieri, s'introduce Amore per testimonio di questa occulta visione, come quello che udì parlare tacitamente la donna mia di me, che,

receive its amorous influences, but when these are absent, they are resealed. And, in order that they might never be sealed, the power of Love makes such an impression by means of those eyes, that they can be said never to be without sun. Love, then, who makes his power felt by means of the eyes, when the sight of them is absent, would lose his power.

Now, to return to her sleep, it can be easily understood that, being as gentle as we have said, it was very pleasing to my lady. And therefore, as she was in all things incomparably noble, so, being grateful, she repaid with gratitude all the things that had had a part in and were a cause of such great sweetness. And therefore to the grass and flowers, which without hardness had so softly received her limbs and made for them such graceful pillows and a delicate bed, she gave the most welcome gift, [of] having been touched and pressed by such elegant limbs. The breeze, which had moved the trees and cooled the air, likewise touched her exceedingly lovely body. The shadows, running at their pleasure, still were straying over that incomparably beautiful face and her limbs. There remained only the oak, not the least cause of this sweetness, since it had been responsible for the shade that it had provided for that sweet slumber. And so that this oak also did not remain without part of the reward, the eyes of my lady consecrated it to Love, freeing the oak from the blows and violence of lightning and tempestuous arrows—because the oak, being the tree of Jove, is more often struck by his thunderbolts than are the other trees. Instead of that, from the time that it stood above those lovely eyes, since those grateful eyes have consecrated it to Love, it has become rather a receptacle for amorous arrows.

Because the first sonnet [27] makes no mention of the little meadow upon which my lady reclined, nor of the most gentle breeze (two very effective causes, as we have said, of that most lovely sleep), [and] because it is difficult to have room in the brevity of a sonnet for many things, I mention them in the following sonnet that begins "O fragrant little plants," [28] etc., where one sees that with consummate sweetness my thought was recalling all those amorous qualities—but not without some envy of those plants and flowers did their deeds, which my lady, so sweetly wearied, received from them, present themselves to me. And therefore, by turning to those plants and flowers, calling them fragrant and noticing that the variety of flowers resembled the constellations that the stars make in the clear sky, [the sonnet] takes on almost those characteristics that a meadow can have, that is, fragrance and beauty. And as we have said that my lady, reclining thus, had some amorous thoughts of me, [and because] this would be impossible for [me] to know except from someone who [heard] her thoughts, Love is introduced as a witness of this secret vision, as the one who heard my lady speak silently of me, for, by being worthy

per essere degno d'entrare in sì alti e dolci pensieri, felicissimo mi potevo chiamare; perché il pensare non è altro che uno tacito parlare, perché chi pensa, inmagina quelle cose ‹e› in sé medesimo le chiama per li nomi loro: onde si può dire veramente il pensare essere uno parlare tacito. Discorre poi el pensiero mio a tutte l'altre circunstanzie, come fu ancora quella dell'aura, o vogliamo dire piccolo vento, e, quasi riferendogli grazia, mostra lo effetto che faceva: perché, movendo e rami, che per la interposizione loro tra'l sole e gli occhi suoi facevono ombra, di necessità bisogna l'ombre ancora si movessino, e però quelli occhi talora potevono vedere il sole, talora no. Et essendo questi occhi di tanta perfezzione e bellezza che signoreggiavono Amore, come di sopra abbiamo detto, gloriosa vittoria fu quella del sonno quando vinse sì belli occhi; e acciò che fussi perpetua e memorabile, doveva el sonno appiccarne all'alta quercia e trofei con le spoglie degli occhi già da lui vinti: siccome solevano gli antichi Romani, e quali ebbono in consuetudine, quando vincevano qualche potente e famoso inimico, pigliare le spoglie sue e vestirne el troncone d'uno arbore per memoria della ricevuta vittoria. Bisogna vedere che fussino le spoglie di quelli belli occhi, per vedere di che cosa doveva vestire el sonno il troncone della quercia; né si può interpretrare che gli occhi della donna mia fussino vestiti d'altro che di belli e amorosi sguardi e d'una amorosa luce, che solo dagli occhi degli innamorati suole lasciarsi vedere. Questi sguardi e luce amorose, adunque, doverono certamente restare come stigmate nel tronco della quercia; e di questi spogliò el sonno la donna mia, subito che chiuse quelli belli occhi; e di queste spoglie credo sia ancora ornata quella quercia. Né Amore di questo triunfo del sonno si debba sdegnare, se è vero quello che abbiamo detto, che gli occhi suoi signoreggiassino Amore, dandogli e togliendo forza, avendo poi el sonno superati quelli belli occhi.

XXIX

  Tante vaghe bellezze ha in sé raccolto
il gentil viso della donna mia,
che ogni nuovo accidente che in lui sia
prende da·llui bellezza e valor molto.
  Se di grata pietà talor è involto,
pietà già mai non fu sì dolce e pia;
se di sdegno arde, tanto bella e ria
è l'ira, che Amor triema in quel bel volto.
  Pietosa e bella è in essa ogni mestizia,
e se rigano i pianti il vago viso,

of entering into such high and sweet thoughts, I could call myself most happy. For thinking is nothing other than a silent speech, because whoever thinks imagines those things and deep within himself calls them by their names. Accordingly, one can truly say that thinking is silent speech. My thought then passes by all the other circumstances, like that even of the breeze, or we wish to say, a slight wind, and, almost ascribing it to grace, shows the effect that it produced. Because, by moving the branches that through their interposition between the sun and her eyes made shade, of necessity the shade must also be moved, and therefore those eyes could sometimes see the sun, and sometimes not. And as those eyes were of such great perfection and beauty that they lorded it over Love, as we said above, the victory of sleep was glorious when it overcame such lovely eyes. And so that it would be forever remembered, sleep had to affix to the tall oak the trophies with the spoils of the eyes it had already overcome—just as the ancient Romans used to do who were in the habit, when they overcame some famous or powerful enemy, of taking the spoils and dressing the trunk of a tree with them as a remembrance of the victory achieved. One must see what the spoils of those lovely eyes were in order to see with what Sleep was obliged to clothe the trunk of the oak. Nor can one understand that the eyes of my lady were clothed with anything other than lovely and amorous glances and with an amorous light, which only the eyes of lovers are usually permitted to see. These amorous glances and the light, then, certainly had to remain as marks on the trunk of the oak. And of these Sleep had despoiled my lady, as soon as she closed those lovely eyes. And with these spoils I believe that oak to be still adorned. Nor could Love disdain this triumph of Sleep, if what we have said is true, that her eyes overmastered Love, giving him and taking from him his strength, when Sleep then had overcome those lovely eyes.

29

So many straying beauties in itself
My lady's noble face has gathered up,
That it collects from every new event
Much merit, and therefrom much beauty takes.
    If sometimes with kind pity it's entwined,
Pity was never so devout or sweet:
If with disdain it burns, so fair are wrath
And scorn that, in her lovely face, Love quakes.
    Pious and lovely in her every act
Is she, and if tears score her charming face,

  dice piangendo Amor: «Questo è il mio regno!».
  Ma quando il mondo cieco è fatto degno
  che muova quella bocca un suave riso,
  conosce allor quale è vera letizia.

  Grandissimo argumento mi pare di excessiva potenzia quando alcuna virtù nelle cose contrarie e diverse tra loro opera potentemente, faccendo ancora qualche volta effetti quasi fuora d'uno naturale ordine dell'altre cose; e perché questo spesse volte accade nella vita degli amanti, gli abbiamo chiamati di sopra «miracoli amorosi». Che grandissima fussi la potenzia della bellezza della donna mia intende provare el presente sonetto, per li effetti diversi et extraordinarii che in me faceva. Perché, contemplando io la bellezza del viso suo in diversi accidenti e passioni, mi pareva che tutte le passioni che apparivano o dimostravansi in quel bel viso, e ne divenissino più belle e ricevessino più forza, cioè movessino più potentemente in altri o timore o pietà o dolore o letizia; movendo non solamente potentemente, come è detto, secondo la qualità delle passioni, ma servando sempre la bellezza e la grazia, le quali in alcune passioni, come è il timore e 'l dolore, pare quasi impossibile si possino conservare. Perché, chi teme, di necessità ha in odio la cagione del timore; questo medesimo adviene a chi sente dolore, perché, potendo, fuggirebbe la cagione d'esso, e quelle cose che si fuggono non s'amano. E però grandissima potenzia era quella di questa bellezza, avendo forza, movendo timore e dolore, d'essere ancora in queste tali passioni desiderata e amata. Introduce adunque el presente sonetto quattro passioni solamente, cioè la pietà, l'ira, il dolore e la letizia, le quali dal viso della donna mia pigliano più forza e più bellezza. E, cominciando dalla pietà, mostra che quando la pietà viene in quel bel viso, non trovò mai luogo o domicilio alcuno dov'ella paressi più veramente pietà, né dove paressi più dolce e pia; et essendo per sé la pietà bella, basta sia fatta menzione solamente della forza che piglia, presuponendo la bellezza. Venendo dipoi all'ira, propriamente è detta ardere d'ira e di sdegno, perché «ira» non è altro ch'uno accendimento della collera intorno al cuore, e gli effetti dell'ira sono comunemente simili a quelli del fuoco, che presto fa gli effetti suoi; e quelli che sono di natura collerica e calda sono più disposti all'ira. Ardendo adunque quel bel viso d'ira, diventa più bello

Then, weeping, Love will say: "This is my realm!"[115]
But when the blind world grows so worthy that[116]
A gentle laugh moves that sweet mouth of hers,
Ah, then the world can know true happiness.

It seems to me a very important matter of extraordinary force when some power in different and contrary things works potently between them, sometimes producing effects almost beyond the natural order of other things. And because these things often times happen in the lives of lovers, above we have called them "amorous miracles." How very great the power of my lady's beauty was, the present sonnet intends to demonstrate through the various and extraordinary effects that it produced in me. Because, as I contemplated the beauty of her face in various qualities and passions, it seemed to me that all the passions that appeared or that revealed themselves in that lovely face, both became more beautiful because of it and from it received more strength, that is those passions more powerfully stimulated others either to fear or to pity or sorrow or gladness. And they moved them not only powerfully, as we said, according to the quality of the passions, but they were also always attended by beauty and grace, which it seems almost impossible to be able to preserve in some passions, like fear and sorrow—because, of necessity, whoever fears, hates the cause of the fear. This same thing occurs in anyone who feels sorrow, because, if one were able, one would flee its cause, and those things that one flees one does not love. And therefore this beauty's power was exceedingly great, for it had the capacity, while stimulating fear and sorrow, in the midst of these passions still to be desired and loved. The present sonnet introduces then four passions only, that is pity, wrath, sorrow and happiness, which take greater force and more beauty because of my lady's face. And, beginning with pity, the sonnet shows that when pity comes there into that lovely face, it has never [before] found a place or any dwelling where it more truly seemed to be pity, nor where it seemed more sweet and pious. And as pity is lovely in itself, it is enough to mention only the force that it takes, beauty being presupposed. Coming then to wrath, properly her face is said to burn with wrath and with scorn, because "wrath" is nothing more than a kindling of choler within the heart, and the effects of wrath are ordinarily similar to those of fire, which produces its effects quickly. And those who are by nature choleric and hot

---

[115] Cf. *Rvf.* 126, 52: "here reigns Love'."

[116] Cf. *Rvf.*, 28, 8: "this blind world," and 248, 4: "But an unseeing world's, which heeds not worth"; and Dante, *Inf.* 4, 13: "Let us now descend into the blind world here below."

e rio, cioè più da temere, come mostra lo essemplo sequente: perché, tremando Amore nel viso suo, è segno manifesto el timore della potenzia di quell'ira, e il non si partire di quel viso non obstante il tremore (che dimostra il timore essere grandissimo) mostra assai chiaro la bellezza essere quella che lo ritiene, perché, se questo non fusse, il timore caccerebbe Amore. Questo medesimo adviene nella mestizia e dolore della donna mia, la quale, movendo a lacrime ancora Amore e, così piangendo, affermando lui el viso di lei essere il regno e l'imperio suo, mostra la medesima forza e bellezza nel dolore che prima nell'ira. Nasce poi di queste premisse molto bene la conclusione del sonetto, perché, se la bellezza di quel viso ha avuto forza di parere più bella in quelli accidenti che sogliono obscurare e diminuire la bellezza, fortificando questi tali accidenti oppositi alla bellezza, molto più facilmente può crescere in bellezza negli accidenti che naturalmente subministrono forza alla bellezza, tanto più fortificando questi accidenti: come adviene nella letizia della donna mia. Era la donna mia per sé bellissima; la letizia per sé in qualunque persona è bella; se adunque quella per sé è bella e lo accidente ancora è bello, excessiva bellezza era quella quando si congiugneva insieme sì bella natura e sì bello accidente, presupposto che l'uno e l'altro pigliassi forza per tale congiunzione, come di sopra abbiamo detto dell'altre passioni, e che ancora l'accidente fussi per sé fortissimo e quasi in supremo grado: come mostra il riso, che è maggior segno di letizia che faccino gli uomini, come il pianto del dolore, il quale similmente di sopra è posto per segno d'excessivo dolore. Credendo adunque tanta bellezza e dolcezza insieme, si può dire questa bellezza essere al mondo non solamente maravigliosa, ma forse non più veduta (e però veramente il mondo potersi chiamare «cieco»), e dovere produrre in chi la vede quello che si può chiamare vera letizia e beatitudine.

XXX

Lasso!, che sento io più muover nel petto?
Non già il mio cor, che s'è da me fuggito.
Questi spessi sospir', s'ei se n'è gito,
a cui dan refrigerio, a cui diletto?
   Li alti e dolci pensier' del mio concetto
chi muove adunque, se il core è smarrito?
Amor, che'l fece al fuggir via sì ardito,
questo me ne ha con la sua bocca detto:

are most disposed to wrath. When that face burned with wrath, then, it became much more beautiful and scornful, that is more to be feared, as the following example shows. For Love's trembling in her face is an evident sign of his fear of the power of that wrath, and his not departing from that face despite his trembling (which reveals the fear to be very great) very clearly shows that it is beauty that holds him, because, if this were not the case, fear would drive Love out. This same thing occurs in the trials and sorrows of my lady, who, by her weeping even moves Love to tears, thereby revealing the same power and beauty in sorrow that she did before in wrath. And by his weeping, Love affirms her face to be his realm and empire. From these premises, then, the conclusion of the sonnet very suitably takes shape, because, if the beauty of that face has had the power to seem more beautiful in those situations that usually diminish and obscure beauty by increasing the power of these situations opposed to beauty, much more easily can that face increase in beauty in those situations that naturally strengthen beauty, even increasing its power more greatly in these latter instances—as it did when my lady was happy. My lady in herself was beautiful. Happiness by itself in any person is beautiful. When then that which in itself is beautiful and when the situation also is beautiful—then when such a lovely nature and so lovely a situation came together, they produced a surpassing beauty, presupposing that each took strength from the other because of such a joining of forces, as we have said above about the other passions, and still the situation was in itself very powerful, almost in the highest degree. This the laugh reveals, which is the greatest sign of happiness among men, just as weeping is of sorrow— [weeping] that likewise appears as a sign of excessive sorrow. When, then, one believes in such great beauty and sweetness together, this beauty must not only be said to be marvelous in the world, but perhaps not even seen, (and therefore the world can truly be called "blind"), and, in whoever sees it, [that beauty] must produce what can be called true happiness and beatitude.

30

Ah! What do I feel stirring in my breast?
Indeed, it's not my heart that fled from me.
And if these frequent sighs should send it hence,
To whom can they give refuge, whom delight?
    These sweet and lofty thoughts of my conceit,
Who'll move them if my heart is led astray?
With his own mouth has Love, who makes my heart
So boldly flee away, said this to me:

>   —Quando i belli occhi prima la via fèro,
> entrò la bianca mano e'l cor ti tolse,
> e in cambio a quello un più gentil ne misse;
>   questo in te vive, e'l tuo, fatto più altero,
> in più candido petto viver volse.
> Questo è de' miei miracoli!—Amor disse.

Ancora che in molti e diverse modi la donna mia dessi assai evidenti argumenti dello amore e pietà sua verso di me, come già in più luoghi abbiamo mostro, nessuno più efficace ne dette, né poteva mai dare, che quello el quale contiene el presente sonetto; né io da lei potevo maggiore dono ricevere, perché maggiore dono non può essere che quando altri dà e quello che è suo e quello che è carissimo al donante. Secondo Epitteto, «in nobis quecumque nostra sunt opera», però nessuna cosa possiamo chiamare nostra al mondo se non la oppinione, perché tutte l'altre cose o sono della fortuna o sono della natura. E che questo sia vero, si manifesta perché e la natura e la fortuna spesse volte contro alla voglia nostra ce ne privano. E però, sanza extendersi in molte cose, per essere tali conclusioni molto trite e provate, confesseremo essere nostra solamente l'oppinione, come è detto, la quale è sempre libera, né può da alcuna cosa essere forzata. E, a mio giudicio, chi fa menzione della oppinione, di necessità presuppone la voluntà, la quale non è altro che desiderio di quello bene che alla oppinione pare bene; e per questo si può dire, se bene la oppinione voluntà non sono una cosa, essere tanto simile e prossime, e di necessità l'una con l'altra congiunte, che a me non sia inconveniente parlare dell'una come dell'altra: perché queste mie non sono diffinizioni, ma più tosto parole largamente e liberamente dette. Se adunque sola la oppinione e voluntà è nostra, chi dona questa tale cosa dona tutto quello che possiede per suo; e chi dona tutto el suo, di necessità dona una cosa che al donante

"When those fair eyes first opened up the way,
The white hand entered in and took your heart,
And one more noble in exchange has left;
"This lives in you, and yours, made loftier,
Has gone to live within a whiter breast.
One of my miracles is this," Love said.

Although in many and various ways my lady gave very evident indications of her love and pity towards me, as I have already shown in several places, none more effective was given of it, nor ever could have been given, than that which the present sonnet contains. Nor could I receive a greater gift from her, because no greater gift can exist than when someone gives what is both his and is also most precious to the recipient. According to Epictetus, ["*Of whatever sort they are, our works are ours*"].[117] We can, however, call nothing "ours" in the world if not opinion, because all other things come either from fortune or from nature. And the truth of this is evident because both nature and fortune very often deprive us of something against our will. And therefore, without considering many matters to reach such a commonplace and tested conclusion, we shall confess only opinion to be ours, as was said, which is always free, nor can it be forced by anything. And, in my judgment, whoever makes mention of opinion necessarily presupposes free will, which is nothing other than desire for that good that seems good to the opinion.[118] And for this reason we can say that, although opinion and free will are not one, they are very similar and alike, and of necessity the one is conjoined with the other, so that it does not seem unsuitable for me to speak of the one as the other—because these words of mine are not definitions, but rather broadly and liberally spoken. If then only opinion and free will are ours, whoever gives such a thing as this gives all that he possesses for his own. And whoever gives his all, of necessity gives a thing that is most precious to the

---

[117] At this point in the mss. a textual lacuna occurs. Zanato ("Sul Testo" 134–5) argues from the punctuation of ms. Riccardiana, 2726, and from Lorenzo's fondness for epithet that L. intended to include here a brief quotation from Epictetus, perhaps: "eorum quae sunt partim est, partim non est." Though the sense of the text is clear without the interpolation, Zanato (*Comento*, 81, n. 83), has subsequently discovered grounds in the work of Poliziano and in vernacular maxim for supplying the quotation translated in brackets above: "*in nobis quecumque nostra sunt opera.*"

[118] Lorenzo's concept of the freedom of the will suggests that, despite his insistence here on the imprecision of the terminology that he employs, he is much less deterministic than, say, St. Augustine, who only posits adequate will to choose between God's will as the greater and one's own will as the lesser good for one's life. Lorenzo's quasi-identification of free will and opinion seems to give will a wider sphere of operation.

è carissima, e però non può fare maggiore dono. Intendesi largamente in questi versi amorosi per la oppinione e voluntà nostra el cuore; e però, avendo fatto la donna mia una conmutazione del suo cuore al mio, cioè tolto el mio per sé e a me donato el suo, come mostra el presente sonetto, nessuno maggiore dono mi poteva dare, né fare più evidente segno che io fussi pieno della grazia sua. E perché parrebbe, la mia, grandissima arroganzia, persuadendomi questo essere vero e faccendo me medesima auttore e degno di tanto bene, sanza el testimonio della donna mia, mi accade dire el vero di questo amoroso processo, e per fuggire la colpa della arroganzia detta e pel contento che mi reca al cuore la dolcissima memoria di quello atto amoroso.

Ero in parte che assai vicino mi trovavo al viso della donna mia, e riguardandola fisa, per la dolcezza che porgevono gli occhi suoi quasi attrito e indebilito, sostenevo col mio destro braccio la testa. Lei, pensando di darmi qualche conforto, con uno gentile modo appressandosi più a me, pose la candida sua mano sopra la sinistra parte del petto mio; e tenendola per alquanto spazio ferma, io la dimandai assai timidamente quello che intendessi fare. Lei con una onesta baldanza rispose che stava a udire muovere el cuore suo; e io a·llei: —Veramente e questa e ogni altra cosa che vive in me è vostra.—Lei, subiungendo, disse: —Io dico veramente questo essere il cuore che già viveva in me, che ora in te vive, e quello che prima era tuo conservo io nel mio petto.—Quello che mi paressino sì dolce parole e che effetto facessino in me, lascio qui giudicare a coloro a'quali è nota la fiamma e forza amorosa, perché, come dice Dante in una sua canzona, «non è di core villano sì alto ingegno, che possa inmaginare di questo alquanto». Partendomi dipoi da lei e considerando qual fussi più, o la gentilezza di quel parlare o l'amore che per questo dimostrava, diliberai fare el presente sonetto e li dui sequenti nella medesima invenzione, ancora che concludino diversamente, se bene quello amoroso parlare e quello atto gentilissimo fussino degni d'altra lingua che la mia per farne memoria.

Fingo adunque, ancora che la istoria sia sopra detta, io medesimo sentire nuovo moto nel petto mio, e con qualche ammirazione domando me

receiver, and, therefore, a greater gift could not be given. One must broadly understand the heart to stand for our opinion and free will in these amorous verses. And therefore, as my lady had made an exchange of her heart for mine, that is had taken mine for herself and given me hers, and, as the present sonnet reveals, no greater gift could she have given me, nor could she have made a more evident sign that I was filled with her grace. And because persuading myself that this was true, and making myself the author of and worthy of so great a good without the testimony of my lady would seem my greatest arrogance, it happens that I speak the truth about this amorous process, both to avoid the accusation of the afore-mentioned arrogance and on account of the happiness that the very sweet memory of that amorous act brings to my heart.

I was in a place where, almost worn out and fainting from the sweetness that the eyes of my lady put forth, I found myself very near my lady's face, and, looking intently at her, I was holding up my head with my right hand. She, thinking to give me some comfort, with a kind manner drawing nearer to me, placed her white hand upon the left side of my breast. And as she held it there firmly for some time, I very timidly asked her what she intended to do. She, with a chaste boldness, answered that she was listening to the beating of her heart. And I said to her: "Truly, both this and every other thing that lives in me are yours." Continuing, she said: "I truly declare this heart that lives now in you, to be that which once lived in me, and I preserve in my breast the one that first was yours." How sweet those words seemed to me, and I let those here who have known the amorous flames and their power judge the effect that they had on me, because as Dante says in one of his canzoni:

> The churlish heart hath never wit so high
> That can imagine aught of her....[119]

Taking my leave of her then and considering what was greater, either the nobility of that remark or the love that it demonstrated, I decided to compose the present sonnet and the two following based on the same invention, although they conclude differently, and although that amorous remark and that very noble deed were worthy of another tongue than mine to make them be remembered.

I imagine then, although the history is recounted above, that I myself feel a new stirring in my breast, and with some wonder I ask myself the

---

[119] *VN.* 32, 75–76: "Non è di cor villan sì alto ingegno, / Che possa immaginar di lei alquanto...." in *The Vita Nova and Canzoniere of Dante Alighieri*, trans., Philip H. Wicksteed (London: J. M. Dent and Sons, 1933), 118.

medesimo della cagione, *maxime* perché, essendo fuggito il mio cuore da me, come di sopra in più luoghi abbiamo detto, non poteva essere la cagione di quel moto dal mio cuore. El moto adunque, e li spesse miei sospiri, che naturalmente sono ordinate per refrigerio del cuore, mostravano pure che uno cuore dovessi essere quello che nel mio petto si moveva. Mostravano ancora questo medesimo gli alti e dolci pensieri che concepeva la mente mia, li quali dovevano essere similmente mossi dal cuore, non come luogo de' pensieri, ma come cagione; perché, essendo il cuore quello che desidera, quelli pensieri erano dal cuore, perché non erano altro che un desiderio della donna mia. Et essendo i pensieri alti e dolci, cioè più degni che a me non si conveniva, comincia' poi in me medesimo a credere che più degna cagione che non era il mio cuore gli movessi. In mezzo a questi miei dubii soccorse Amore, el quale, essendo stato quello che aveva fatto ardito il mio cuore a fuggirsi (come mostra quel sonetto che comincia *Lasso a me!, quando io sono là dove sia*), sapeva veramente il mio cuore essere fuggito, e però con la sua bocca mi manifestò questa verità: che interpetrando secondo il vero, come abbiamo detto Amore fu la donna mia, che con la bocca sua mi manifestò questo amoroso miracolo; el quale fu questo: che quando Amore prima fece la via agli occhi della donna mia, per la quale entroron al cuore, allora quella gentilissima mano entrò drieto agli occhi nel petto e ne trasse el cuore mio (come mostra el sonetto che comincia *Candida, bella e delicata mano*), e in luogo del mio cuore pose quello della donna mia; e perché questo pare cosa mirabile e inaudita, subiunse Amore questa essere opera maravigliosa della potenzia sua. E considerando veramente, Amore non è altro che una transformazione dello amante nella cosa amata, e, quando è reciproco, di necessità ne nasce la medesima transformazione in quello che prima ama, che diventa poi amato, per modo che maravigliosamente vivono gli amanti l'uno nell'altro: ché altro non vuole interire questa conmutazione di cuori.

XXXI

Quel cor gentil, che Amor mi diede in pegno
mirabilmente in cambio al mio, eletto
a maggior bene, or vuol lasciar soletto
il petto mio, di sì bel core indegno.

cause. *Especially* since my heart had fled from me, as we have said above in many places, it could not be the cause of my breast's stirring. The motion then and my frequent sighs, which were naturally generated to cool the heart, showed that there had to be one heart at least that was moving in my breast. Revealed too were those same lofty and sweet thoughts that my mind conceived, and that must likewise be moved by the heart, not as the place of thoughts, but as their cause. Because, being what the heart desired, those thoughts were from the heart, for they were nothing other than a desire for my lady. And being lofty and sweet thoughts, that is more worthy than were fitting for me, I began within myself to believe that some cause more worthy than my heart had occasioned them. In the midst of these doubts, Love brought aid. Having been the one who had emboldened my heart to flee (as that sonnet reveals that begins: "Ah woe is me! when I am in the place," [5]) he knew that my heart had truly fled, and therefore with his own mouth he uttered this truth to me. For interpreting according to the truth, as we have said, Love was my lady, for with her mouth she made manifest to me this amorous miracle: Love first made the way for the eyes of my lady by which they entered my heart, and then that most gentle hand entered my breast after the eyes did, and drew my heart forth from it (as the sonnet reveals that begins "O pure white, delicate and lovely hand," [13]) and in place of my heart he put that of my lady. And because this seems a wondrous and unheard of thing, Love added that this was a marvelous work of his power. And considering truly, Love is nothing other than a transformation of the lover into the beloved,[120] and, when it is reciprocal, of necessity the same transformation takes place in the lover who first loves, and who then becomes the beloved through that means by which lovers miraculously live in one another—for this exchange of hearts would not otherwise occur.

31

That noble heart Love gave me as a pledge
Miraculously in exchange for mine,
To greater good elect, now all alone
Would leave my breast, unfit for heart so fair.

---

[120] *FC.* 2, 8, (144): "Here, surely, is a remarkable circumstance that whenever two people are brought together in mutual affection, one lives in the other and the other in him. In this way they mutually exchange identities; each gives himself to the other in such a way that each receives the other in return." See also Petrarch, *Triumph of Love* 3, 161–62 in Wilkins 26: "and I know how / I am transformed into her I love."

> Io priego il mio che torni; egli è sì degno,
> che l'antiqua sua sede ora ha in dispetto.
> Io dico a·llui:—Se non degna il mio petto
> quel core, arà te, cor, quel petto a sdegno.
>   Misero, che farai?—E lui risponde:
> Starò in essilio in quelle luci belle,
> se pur cacciato son sanza riguardo:
>   queste non mi può tòr, né Amor le absconde.
> E tu arai di me spesso novelle
> pe' dolci raggi di quel bello sguardo.

Sogliono quelle cose che per la excellenzia e degnità loro excedono e meriti di chi le riceve parere ancora poco durabili, perché ogni excesso è di questa natura; e però si vede talora quelli temere più, che sono da infimo grado venuti in grande condizione. Oltra questo, secondo il corso delle cose umane, quelli che sono in maggiore felicità constituti debbono più che gli altri temere, essendo la felicità umana el più delle volte brieve e poco stabile. Queste condizioni erono in me, per quanto mostra il precedente comento, perché, essendo il mio petto fatto recettaculo del cuore della donna mia e il cuore mio altero e troppo nobile essendo ito ad abitare nel candida petto di quella, e mi pareva cosa molto sopra li meriti miei, e mi pareva tanto maggiore per essere di umile luogo in un tratto essaltato a tanto bene, e felicissimo sopra ogni altro per questo mi riputavo. Dovevo adunque per tutte queste cagioni temere, e parevami quasi impossibile conservarmi lungo tempo in tanta felicità; e ancora che la constanzia e fede della donna mia non mi dessi cagione alcuna di dubitare, mi pareva ad ogni ora il cuore della donna mia, el quale in me viveva perché Amore per pegno del mio me lo aveva dato, da me si volessi partire e lasciare di sé solo il mio petto. Facevami questo dubio pensare di richiamare el mio cuore a me, pregandolo che tornassi; ma essendo lui eletto a maggiore bene, cioè per stare nel candido petto della donna mia, era fatto sì degno e in tal modo insuperbito, che aveva in dispetto el petto mio, dove prima soleva stare, né tornare a me voleva. Io, credendo che di questo fussi cagione perché lui avessi oppinione di potere starsi nel petto della donna mia, proposi al cuore mio, acciò che tornassi, che quando il cuore della donna mia non degnassi di stare più nel mio petto, el petto suo similmente non degnerebbe di ricettare più el mio cuore; e di questo poteva nascere che il cuore mio, a un tempo, per elezzione sarebbe privato del petto mio e per necessità di quello della donna mia, quando da lei fussi cacciato. Risponde il cuore a questo dubio che, quando bene fussi cacciato da lei, starà in

> I beg mine to return—so haughty now
> That it disdains its former dwelling place.
> To it I say: "If my breast merits not
> Her heart; her breast, o Heart, will scorn you too.
>   Ah, wretch, what will you do?" And it responds:
> "In exile I shall stay in those fair lights,
> If I'm not driven forth with no regard:
>   "These can't be torn from me, nor Love them hide.
> And frequent news from me shall you receive
> From the sweet rays of that glance so beautiful."

Usually those things that by their excellence and worth exceed the merits of someone who receives them seem likely to endure only for a little while, because every excess is of this nature. And therefore one sometimes sees that those persons are most fearful who have come from an inferior degree into circumstances of grandeur. Beyond this, following the course of human affairs, those who have been established in greater felicity must fear more than others, being that human felicity is most of the time brief and not very stable. These were my circumstances, as a great deal of the preceding commentary shows, for my breast had become a receptacle for the heart of my lady and my proud and too noble heart had gone to live in her white breast, and that seemed to me a circumstance far above my merits, and it seemed all the more so because I had been suddenly elevated from a low place into a situation of such great good, and because of this I considered myself happy beyond every other person. For all these reasons I ought to have been afraid, and it seems almost impossible to remain for a long time in such great felicity. And although the constancy and faith of my lady gave me no occasion for fear, at every hour it seemed to me that the heart of my lady, which lived in me because Love had given it to me for a pledge, would wish to depart and leave my breast all alone. This fear made me think of recalling my heart to me, of begging it to return. But because it had been elected to a greater good, that is because it remained in the white breast of my lady, it had become so worthy and in this way had been made so proud, that my breast, where it had first dwelt, it held in scorn, and it did not wish to return to me. Because I thought that this resulted from its believing that it could remain in the breast of my lady, so that it would return, I proposed to my heart that when the heart of my lady no longer deigned to remain in my breast, her breast similarly would not any longer condescend to receive my heart. And this could mean that my heart would at some time be deprived of my breast by its own choice and, of necessity, by my lady's choice when she drove it out. To this fear my heart responded that, when it was indeed

luogo donde non potrà esser cacciato, cioè nelli occhi della donna mia, perché Amore e lei fanno che quelli occhi sieno comuni a ciascuno; e, stando in quelli occhi, non sospiri, non parole, non altro segno che proceda dal cuore diranno novelle a me del cuore mio, ma li sguardi solamente della donna mia, e quali spesso ne diranno novelle perché spesso da me saranno veduti gli occhi suoi.

È necessario intendere el naturale processo di questo sonetto, col quale queste amorose fizzioni debbono quadrare. Nasce amore allo amante e va nella cosa amata, e così prima si fugge il cuore dello amante alla cosa amata; nasce dipoi amore reciprocamente nella cosa amata, e allora si fa la conmutazione che abbiamo detta de' cuori; nasce dipoi la gelosia, vera miseria delli amanti, perché è tormento inmortale, e allora nasce il dubio che il cuore della amata non si torni a·llei, e di questo un pensiero di ritrarre lo amore suo dalla cosa amata: e questo è revocare el cuore suo a sé. Ma perché il vivace amore cresce nelli affanni, non può impetrare lo amante di ritrarre l'amore suo, ma *necessario* li bisogna continuare in esso; e benché fra sé stesso assai certo si giudichi non potere avere alcuna dolcezza, anzi affanni e tribulazioni, non sendo amato dalla cosa amata, né essendo mai libero da gelosia, si riduce infine per necessità a prendere quello che più facilmente può avere dalla cosa amata; e non potendo avere il cuore suo, non si parte però el cuore dalla amata, ma fermasi nelli occhi della amata, cioè gode le exteriori bellezze e con esse si conforta, poiché del cuore cioè amore della amata non può disporre. E allora li sguardi delli occhi amati fanno segno dello amore che è in lei, perché e la pietà e l'amore, e così lo sdegno e l'ira, qualche volta per segno delli occhi si comprendono; e di questo s'ha spesso novelle, perché la visione della amata male si può celare dalli occhi o diventare invisibile, e lo amore tanto più muove e incita l'amante a vedere spesso l'amata, quanto più mancano l'altre cose che solevano consolare la mente.

Tutti questi affetti vorrei fussino meglio expressi nel sonetto, per levare ogni difficultà a quelli intelletti che faranno degni e versi miei della loro cognizione.

XXXII

—Amorosi sospiri, e quali uscite
del bianco petto di mia donna bella,

driven forth by her, it would stay in a place from which it could not be dislodged, that is in the eyes of my lady, because she and Love have so arranged it that those eyes are accessible to everyone. And in those eyes are not sighs, not words, not some other sign that proceeds from the heart, but only the glances of my lady, which often will bring news of her to me from my heart, because I shall often see her eyes.

It is necessary to understand this sonnet's natural process, with which these amorous inventions must square. Love is born in the lover and goes to the beloved, and so first the heart flees from the lover to the beloved. Then Love is reciprocally born in the beloved, and then the exchange of hearts about which we have spoken occurs. Then jealousy is born, a true misery for lovers, because it is an undying torment,[121] and then fear is born lest the heart of the beloved return to her, and from this springs a thought of the lover's withdrawing his love from the beloved, and recalling his heart to himself. But because living love increases amidst troubles, the lover cannot be compelled to withdraw his love, but *of necessity* it must continue in him. And, although within himself the lover judges that, since his beloved doesn't love him, it is very certain that he cannot enjoy any sweetness, but rather can only undergo trials and tribulations and never be free from jealousy, he is finally reduced by necessity to take from the beloved what he can most easily have. He is unable, however, to have his own heart, because the heart won't leave the beloved, but lodges in the beloved's eyes, that is, it enjoys their external beauties and is comforted by them, since it cannot be expelled from the heart, that is, from the love of the beloved. And then the glances of the beloved's eyes give a sign of the love that is in her, for one sometimes recognizes both pity and love, and, likewise, scorn and wrath through a sign from the eyes. And for this reason, one often has news, because the sight of the beloved can hardly be hidden from the eyes or become invisible, and the more Love moves and incites the lover to see the beloved frequently, the more the other things that usually console the mind are absent.

All these effects I would wish to be better expressed in the sonnet, in order to remove every difficulty for those intellects who find my verses worthy of their knowing them.

32

"You sighs so amorous that issue from
The white breast of my lady beautiful,

---

[121] See the personification of jealousy in Lorenzo's *Selve d'amore*, 2, 39–55 in Bigi, 517–22.

> ditemi del mio cor qualche novella,
> qual voi sì dolcemente in lei nutrite.—
>   —Stassi lieto il tuo cor, quïeto e mite,
> mille dolci pensieri movendo in quella,
> co' qual' sovente e con Amor favella
> alte cose e gentil'; né voi l'udite.—
>   —Sospir' benigni, ora è ver quel che io sento
> da voi?——Sì, certo!——Almen ditemi ancora
> se là dove è starà il mio core assai.—
>   Mentre che io parlo, e lor sen vanno in vento.
> Amor sopra il suo petto giura allora
> che a me il mio cor non tornerà già mai.

Truovonsi scritte due sentenzie contrarie, e nondimeno spesso verificate nelle umane azzioni, per che si dice «e miseri facilmente credere quello che desiderano», e, contro a questo, che «a gran speranza uomo misero non crede». Io penso che la diversità delle oppinioni sopra dette nasca più presto dalla natura di quelli che sperano e desiderano alcuna cosa, che dalla ragione, presupposto che l'una e l'altra oppinione abbi cagioni equali, che non inclinino per sé più ad una parte che all'altra. E però credo che quelli uomini che di natura sono malinconici sieno di manco speranza che gli altri, e tanto più quanto nella vita loro hanno avuto la fortuna così adverse, che poche cose hanno consecute secondo il desiderio loro. Abbiamo nel principio detto ogni forte amore procedere da forte imaginazione, e questi tali amanti di natura essere malinconici: io confesso essere di quelli che con grandissima fervenzia ho amato, e però come amante ragionevolmente dovevo dubitare, più che sperare; aggiunto a questo che in tutta la mia vita, advenga che più onore e grado abbi consecuto che a me non si conveniva, pure rari piaceri e poche altre cose secondo il desiderio mio ho vedute: dico di quelle cose che per refrigerio delle publiche e private fatiche e pericoli qualche volta ammette lo animo nostro, ancora che contentissimo viva e che molto mi appaghi della mia sorte. Dovevo adunque, e per le ragioni nel precedente comento scritte e per le presente, ragionevolmente dubitare; et essendo una volta nel cuore mio nato el sospetto, grandissima e intollerabile passione, m'insegnava la natura fare ogni cosa per cacciarlo da me. E dubitando, come molto mostra el precedente sonetto, el mio cuore non fussi cacciato del petto della donna mia, né sapendo bene se quivi o altrove fussi, mi parve dovere intenderne novelle

>   Report to me some news about my heart,
>   Which you so sweetly nourish in yourself."—
>   —"Your heart is docile, glad, and tranquil here,
>   Your heart in her a thousand sweet thoughts stirs
>   And often talks with them and Love about
>   High, noble things, but you don't hear them speak."—
>   —"Kind sighs, is that which I now hear from you
>   The truth?"—"Yes, surely!"—"Tell me still, at least,
>   If where it dwells my heart will long remain."—
>   While speaking, on the wind I hear them go;
>   Then Love upon his breast swears that my heart
>   Will never more return again to me.

One finds written two pronouncements, which, though contradictory, are nevertheless often confirmed in human actions, for it is said that "wretches easily believe that which they desire," and, opposed to this, that "a wretched man does not believe in a great hope."[122] I think that the diversity of the aforesaid opinions arises more readily from the natures of those who hope for and desire something than from reason, for, presupposing that both opinions have equal causes, by themselves they do not lend more weight to one view than to the other. And therefore I believe that those men who are melancholy by nature have less hope than do others—just as much less as they have had very adverse fortune in their lives—for they have achieved few things according to their desire. In the beginning, we said that every powerful love proceeds from a powerful imagination, and that such lovers as these are by nature melancholy. I confess to being one of these, for I have loved with the greatest fervency, and therefore as a lover I should reasonably have feared more than I hoped. Let me add to this that all through my life I happened to achieve more honor and rank than I was suited for. Even so, I have rarely seen pleasures, and but a few other matters fall out according to my desire. I am speaking of those matters that are sometimes admitted to our minds as solace for public and private labors and dangers, although for the most part I am very happy and satisfied with my fate. I was rationally obliged, then, both for the reasons written in both the preceding commentary and in this one, to fear. And suspicion, that greatest and most intolerable passion, being once born in my heart, taught me the characteristic of making everything that I wanted run away from me. And fearing, as the preceding sonnet clearly shows, that my heart might be driven from the breast of my lady, and not

---

[122] Cf. *Rvf.* 150, 14: "one who's wretched credits not great hope."

da chi veniva dal luogo medesimo; e nascendo e sospiri dal proprio luogo ove sta il cuore, loro me ne potevano dire el vero. E però il presente sonetto, composto per dialago, si dirizza e parla a quelli sospiri che uscivano del petto della donna mia, e quali *inmediate* venivano dal cuore mio, se era in quel petto. E, per tòrre confusione, è da notare che li primi quattro versi parlo io a' sospiri sopra detti; nel secondo quadernario rispondono e sospiri a me; dipoi tutto el nono verso e il principio del decimo, cioè quella parola che dice *da voi,* parlo pure io ai sospiri, e la sequente parola, dove dice *Sì, certo!*, rispondono e sospiri a me; tutto el resto del sonetto parlo poi io, parte ai sospiri e parte per narrazione.

Ora, tornando al principio, è da notare che, parlando io a' sospiri della donna mia e chiamandoli amorose, cioè mossi da Amore, o era o volevo che paressi che fussi qualche speranza mescolata col dubio; come mostra ancora perché, domandandogli io che mi dicessino novelle del mio cuore, quale loro nutrivano dolcemente nel petto suo, già avevo oppinione e che el mio cuore vi fussi e che fussi bene trattato da lei. E veramente è detto che i suoi sospiri nutrivano el cuore mio, perché lui stava in quel petto dove era ancora Amore, sanza el quale el mio cuore non vi poteva stare; e però la cagione che moveva e sospiri veramente nutriva dolcemente il mio cuore e lo conservava in quel petto, perché e sospiri erano mossi da Amore. Rispondono e sospiri il mio cuore starsi lieto, quieto e pieno d'umiltà e di dolcezza, et esser cagione di molti dolci e amorosi pensieri nella donna mia, con e quali pensieri e con Amore parla spesse volte molti alti misterii amorosi e cose molto gentili. E per questo si mostra non solo il mio cuore era in quel petto, ma già vi abitava come familiare di esso e domestico, poiché intendeva tutti e pensieri della donna mia: e quali li altri non possono intendere, cioè quelli che da Amore non sono fatti degni e gentili, come era il cuore mio. Fu tanto maggiore la dolcezza che per questa desiderata novella mi venne, quanto era suta maggiore la dubitazione, come sempre adviene di qualunque sperata allegrezza. E, quasi non credendo che possibile fussi quanto avevono riferito quelli amorosi sospiri, di nuovo gli domando se è vera la loro relazione. Loro risposono in confermazione una brevissima risposta, cioè «Sì, certo!»; né potevano più lungamente rispondere, come mostra el sequente del sonetto, perché, faccendo io loro una nuova interrogazione, non bastò lo spirito a que' sospiri in modo che potessino più rispondere. E qui è da notare che tutto quello

knowing well if it were there or elsewhere, it seemed to me that I must have news from someone who came from that same place. And as sighs spring from the same place where my heart is, they could tell me the truth about it. And therefore the present sonnet, composed as a dialogue, addresses itself to and speaks with those sighs that issued from my lady's breast—sighs that came *directly* from my heart, which was itself in that breast. And then, to avoid confusion, one must note that in the first four lines I speak to the above-mentioned sighs. In the second quatrain, the sighs answer me. Then all of the ninth line and the beginning of the tenth—that is, the speech that says *From you*—I speak just to the sighs, and in the following speech where it says *Yes, surely*, the sighs answer me. In all the rest of the sonnet I speak, then, partly to the sighs and partly as narrator.

Now, returning to the beginning, one needs to note that, as I was speaking to the sighs of my lady and calling them "amorous," that is moved by Love, either there was, or I wished that there seemed to be some hope mixed with the fear. This fact is revealed when I ask them to report some news about my heart, which they are nourishing sweetly in her breast, for I already had the opinion that my heart was there and that she was treating it well. And one truly says that her sighs nourished my heart, because it stayed in that breast where also dwelt Love, without whom my heart could not have remained there. And therefore the occasion that moved the sighs truly nourished my heart sweetly and preserved it in that breast, because the sighs were moved by Love.[123] The sighs answer that my heart is glad, tranquil, and filled with humility and with sweetness, and that it is the cause in my lady of many sweet and amorous thoughts, and with those thoughts and with Love, my heart often speaks about many lofty amorous mysteries and very noble matters. And this shows not only that my heart was in her breast, but that it was already living there as its intimate and as a member of the household, since it understood all the thoughts of its lady—thoughts that could not be understood by others, that is by those whom Love had not made worthy and noble, as my heart was. The sweetness that came to me as a result of this very welcome news was as great as the fear had been, as always happens when some hoped-for joy occurs. And, almost not believing that what those sighs reported could possibly be, again I ask them if their account is true. In confirmation they return a very brief answer, that is "Yes, surely!" Nor can they answer any further, as the rest of the sonnet reveals, because, though I was asking them a new question, the breath in those sighs did not suffice so that they could answer any more. And here it must be noted

---

[123] Cf. *Rvf.* 1, 2–3: "these sighs on which I used to feed my heart...."

che parlano e sospiri predetti in questo sonetto sono tante parole, quante naturalmente potrebbe dire uno commodamente con uno spirito, cioè sanza riavere l'alito; e però, finita quella forza che portava seco lo spirito d'un sospiro, ragionevolmente più parole non doveva dire. E se bene io gli chiamo «sospiri», in plurale, cioè più d'uno, bisogna imaginare che e sospiri della donna mia fussino più, ma che uno solo contenessi la risposta. È natura di chi ha conseguito qualche gran bene fare ogni cosa per conservarlo e farlo diuturno; e però, avendo io già quello che desideravo sentito dello stato del cuore mio, desideravo ancora intendere quanto dovessi essere durabile e diuturna questa sua tale beatitudine: e però domandai li spiriti quanto fussi per stare il cuore mio in quel petto. Et essendo già, come abbiamo detto, mancato quello spirito, e li sospiri già resoluti in vento, non poterono rispondere. Amore allora, che secondo che di sopra abbiamo detto era in quel luogo donde venivano li sospiri, in supplemento loro risponde, giurando sopra il petto suo che 'l mio cuore starà sempre con la donna mia, né già mai tornerà a me, assicurandomi col giuramento, come da principio aveva assicurato el cuore mio quando prima partì da me, come mostra il sonetto che comincia *Lasso a me!, quando io sono là dove sia*.

XXXIII

Ove madonna volge li occhi belli,
sanza altro sol la mia leggiadra Flora
fa germinar la terra e mandar fora
mille varii color' di fior' novelli.
    Amorosa armonia rendon li uccelli
sentendo il cantar suo, che l'innamora;
veston le selve i secchi rami, allora
che senton quanto dolce ella favelli.
    Delle timide ninfe a' petti casti
qualche molle pensiero Amore infonde,
se trae riso o sospir la bella bocca.
    Or qui lingua o pensier non par che basti
a intender ben quanta e qual grazia abonde,
là dove quella candida man tocca.

Era del mese d'aprile, nel quale, secondo la comune consuetudine della città nostra, li uomini volentieri insieme con la loro famiglia nelle dilettevole ville a'lloro consolazione si stanno, perchè in quel tempo l'anno è tanto più bello, quanto è la prima iuventù più bella che tutte l'altre età delli uomini; e, oltre a questo, la città nostra ha vicini a sé molti e delicati e piacevoli luoghi, e quali, oltre alla naturale consuetudine, alettano

that everything that the afore-mentioned sighs say in this sonnet are as many words as one of them could conveniently speak naturally with one breath, that is without having to inhale again. And because that power that the breath of a sigh brought with it ended, according to reason the sigh ought not to speak further. And although I call them "sighs" in the plural, that is more than one, it is enough to imagine that the sighs of my lady were many, but that only one contained the answer. It is the nature of anyone who has achieved great well-being to do everything to preserve it and make it permanent. And, therefore, already having what I desired and having heard of the condition of my heart, I further desired to know how permanent and durable such beatitude as this could be. And therefore I asked the sighs how long my heart would stay in her breast. And, lacking breath already as we have said, and having already dissolved in the wind, the sighs were unable to reply. To supplement the sighs then, Love, who, according to what we have said above, was in that place from which the sighs had come, swears upon his breast that my heart will always remain with my lady, and that it will never return to me. And he assures me with an oath, as he had assured my heart from the beginning when it first parted from me, as the sonnet reveals that begins, "Ah woe is me! when I am in that place [5]."

33

Each place my lady turns her lovely eyes,
This Flora new, who needs no other sun,
Makes earth productive so that it sends forth
A thousand varied hues of flowers rare.
　The birds sound forth an amorous harmony,
Hearing her song, which makes them fall in love;
The woods and branches bare bedeck themselves
Because they hear how dulcetly she speaks.
　And Love in timid nymphs' chaste breasts instills
Some gentle thought if from her lovely mouth
Her laughter or a sigh should issue forth.
　Both tongue and thought seem insufficient now
To well express how much grace and what sort
Abounds wherever that white hand may touch.

It was the month of April, in which, according to the common habit of our city, the men willingly remain with their families at delightful villas to be at their ease, because that time of the year is as much more beautiful as early youth is more beautiful than all the other ages of men. And

qualche volta a lasciare le civili e private cure e fruire alquanto di rusticano ozio. In questo tempo, adunque, accadde alla donna mia andare, come molte altre, in una sua dilettevole villa, ove stette alquanti dì, privandomi della sua desiderata visione; nel quale tempo uno, amicissimo mio e di tanto mio amore verso di lei conscio, mi disse: —Ora si vorrebbe essere nella tale villa a vedere la tua bella donna, perché ora cantano gli uccelli, ora si rinnuovano e prati d'erbe e di fiori, ora si rivestono gli arbori di fronde; le ninfe, li uomini e tutti li animali sentono al presente più le forze amorose; e però ora sarebbe tempo che tra tanti naturali ornamenti vedessi la tua carissima donna.—Al quale io risposi che il desiderio mio di vederla né cresceva, né poteva per tempo alcuno diminuire, e che io credevo, ancora che tutto el mondo in questo tempo fussi bellissimo e ornato più che in alcuno altro, quel paese quale era intorno alla donna mia doveva essere più bello che li altri, perché dove era lei non bisognava né sole, né stagione novella, né altra virtù che la sua a fare germinare la terra, fiorire et empiersi di fronde li arbori, cantare li uccelli, e li altri effetti che suole fare primavera.

Finì il nostro parlare in simili parole. E, partito dal predetto amico mio, tutto pieno di quelli pensieri composi el presente sonetto, nel quale mi sforzai exprimere li effetti della virtù della donna mia, li quali operava in quelli salvatichi luoghi dove in quel tempo si trovava; mostrando prima che li occhi suoi avevono la virtù del sole, perché dove ella li volgeva, faceva producere alla terra diverse colori di novelli fiori, chiamandola la bella Flora in questa parte che faceva nascere e fiori, cioè la dea de' fiori. Faceva ancora cantare amorosamente li uccelli, innamorati del canto suo, quando lei sentivano dolcemente cantare; rivestiva delle loro fronde e secchi rami di quelli arbori che la vernata perdono le foglie, quando dolcemente parlava. E qui è da notare che nel cantare e nel parlare della donna mia sono comprese tre parti, che, secondo Platone, contiene la musica, le quali sono queste: el parlare, armonia e rithmo (che credo sia detta quella che vulgarmente chiamiamo "rima", perché «rithmo» non è altro che un parlare terminato da certa misura, come sono li versi e rime vulgari).

beyond this, our city has near it many both delicate and pleasing places, which, beyond the natural custom, sometimes entice them to leave their civil and private cares and to enjoy some rustic ease. At this time, then, it happened that my lady, like many others, went to one of her delightful villas, where she stayed for some days, depriving me of the longed-for sight of her. In that time, someone, a very dear friend and one who knew of my great love for her, said to me: "Right now you would want to be at that villa to see your lovely lady, because now the birds are singing, now the meadows renew themselves with grass and flowers, now the trees reclothe themselves with fronds. The nymphs, the people and all the animals at present feel most strongly the amorous forces. And therefore now would be the time that you should see your most precious lady among so many natural ornaments." To him I answered that my desire to see her could neither increase nor diminish at all with time, and that I also believed, since all the world was at this time more beautiful and more decorated than at any other, that the town that surrounded my lady must be more beautiful than the others. Because where she was no sun was needed, nor the new season, nor any virtue[124] other than her own to make the earth germinate and the trees flower and fill themselves with leaves, the birds sing, and the other effects that spring is wont to cause.

We finished our conversation in similar words. And I parted from my afore-mentioned friend, and I, all filled with those thoughts, composed the present sonnet in which I made every effort to express the effects of my lady's virtue that was at work in those uncultivated places where at that time she was to be found. [The sonnet] first reveals that her eyes had the virtue of the sun, because where she turned them, she made the earth produce various colors of rare flowers, in this part calling her lovely Flora, that is the goddess of flowers who made the blooms come forth. She also causes the birds, enamored of her song, to sing amorously when they hear her very sweetly singing. The bare boughs of the trees that lose their leaves in winter reclothe themselves when she sweetly speaks. And here it must be noted that my lady's singing and speaking are composed of three parts, which, according to Plato, comprise music, and which are these: speech, harmony, and rhythm[125] (which I believe to be what in the vernacular is called "rhyme," because "rhythm" is nothing other than a speech deter-

---

[124] In the sense of *virtù* or power. Compare *Ruf.* 12, where the virtue or power which produced the *riverdi*, the annual renewal of the earth, is ascribed to the flaming horn of the constellation Taurus, i.e., the first-magnitude star Aldeberan in the Pleiades, and where the virtue seems a mixture of warmth and rain.

[125] See Plato, *Rep.* 3, 398 c.

Chiamasi el parlare "musico", ancora che non abbi piedi certi, quando è composto in modo che diletti li orecchi, come si vede in quelli che "eloquenti" sono chiamati; l'armonia è una consonanzia di voce umane, o veramente di suoni, come è notissimo; el rithmo abbiamo detto quello sia. Vedesi la prima spezie di musica, cioè il parlare, expressa nel verso che dice: «che sentono quanto dolce la favelli»; l'altre due, cioè l'armonia e 'l rithmo, si includono nel canto della donna mia, la quale conviene presupporre che cantassi dolcemente certi versi e rime amorose, delle quali lei sopra modo si dilettava; e io molte volte li senti' cantare e delli altri e de' miei con tanta dolcezza e gentilezza, che poi in bocca d'altri non mi potevano piacere. Cantando adunque lei con suavissima melodia simili versi e rime, abbiamo tutte a tre le spezie già dette della musica. Et essendo così, manca in qualche parte la maraviglia delli effetti che faceva la donna mia, perché, essendo la musica comune a tutte le cose, che non potrebbono sanza una certa consonanzia essere, ragionevolmente per la musica si dovevono muovere: come veggiamo che, temperando due instrumenti di corde in una medesima voce e mettendo vicino l'uno all'altro, quando l'uno si suona, le corde dell'altro ancora si muovono per loro medesime, sanza essere tocche da altri, solamente per la conformità del tuono e similitudine di voce che hanno tra loro. Ora, avendo detto di sopra due potenzie della donna mia, cioè delli occhi e della armonia etc., e avendo a dire più maravigliosa operazione di lei, bisogna ancora assegnarne più potente cagione. Perché, ancora che sieno grandi effetti fare germinare la terra, cantare li uccelli e vestire li arbori di fronde, queste sono tutte cose naturali; ma mettere una impressione contraria in uno subietto è maggiore cosa, come è fare che le ninfe, timide e caste, ammettino nella durezza del cuore loro qualche molle e dolce pensiero d'amore: perché lo amore è al tutto contrario alla timidità e castità. E però maggior cagione fa questo maggiore effetto, come è il riso e il sospirare della donna mia, el quale quando viene nella bocca sua muove li pensieri amorosi, come abbiamo detto, nelle ninfe. E che sia più potente cagione questa, lo mostra che quella cagione a mio parere è più potente a muovere effetto, che mostra in sé maggiore affetto, ‹come mostra in sé maggiore affetto› il riso e il sospiro che il guardare, il cantare o il parlare, come mosterremo; e maggiore affetto mostra di tutti questi il toccare. E però conclude il sonetto che questo fa ancora maggiore effetto che li altri, mostrando che dove tocca la sua candida mano abonda tanta grazia e virtù, che non si può né referire né imaginare. E così, delle cose manco efficace per gradi si procede a quelle che sono efficacissime. Perché, presuponendo che Amore muova

mined by a certain measure, as are vernacular verses and rhymes). One calls speech "music," although it may not have a certain meter, when it is composed in a manner that delights the ears, as one sees in those who are called "eloquent." Harmony is a consonance of human voices, or truly of sounds, as is very well known. We have said what rhythm is. One sees the first category of music, that is speech, expressed in the line that says: "Because they hear how dulcetly she speaks." The other two, that is harmony and rhythm, are included in my lady's song when one fittingly presupposes that she sang sweetly certain amorous verses and rhymes, in which, in the fashion above, she took pleasure. And many times I heard her singing both others' rhymes and mine with such sweetness and nobility that afterward I could take no pleasure in [hearing them from] the mouths of others. In her singing of a most gentle melody similar to verses and rhymes, then, we have all three of the above-mentioned characteristics of music. And, being thus, it lacks in some measure the wondrousness of the effects that my lady produced. Because, as music is common to all things, since without it they could not have a certain consonance, they must rationally be moved by music. For we see that, if one tunes two stringed instruments in the same key and places them near one another, when the one is played, the strings of the other are also moved by the same without being touched by anyone, but solely by the conformity of tone and similarity of voice that the [instruments] share. Now, having explained above two of my lady's powers, that is [the power] of her eyes and [that] of harmony, etc., and having spoken of her more marvelous accomplishments, I still must assign to them their most important causes. Because, although making the earth germinate, the birds sing, and the trees clothe themselves in leaves are great effects, all are natural things. But to make an impression opposite to nature in an object is a greater matter, as is causing chaste and timid nymphs to admit into the hardness of their hearts some soft, sweet thought of love—because Love is entirely opposed to timidity and chastity. And therefore greater effects result from greater causes, like the laugh and the sighing of my lady, which, upon arriving in her mouth, stir amorous thoughts in the nymphs, as we have said. And to my way of thinking, that cause reveals itself to be most powerful that produces the strongest effect and that, as it does so, reveals its very great effect in itself. The laugh and the sigh reveal in themselves a greater effect than the glance and the song or speaking, as we shall show. And touching reveals the greatest effect of all of them. And therefore the sonnet concludes that this [touching] produces a still greater effect than the others, revealing that wherever her white hand touches, so much grace and virtue abound that one can neither report nor imagine it. And so from things that lack effect, one proceeds by steps to those that are most effective. Because, presupposing that

tutti li atti che abbiamo detto della donna mia, cioè il vedere, il cantare, il parlare, il ridere e sospirare, e ultimamente il toccare, manco affezzione mostra il vedere che il cantare, manco il cantare che il parlare, e così dico di tutti gli altri, insino al tatto. Perché, presuponendo essere uno amante innamorato di questa donna, credo che, se lei lo guarda amorosamente, li sarà molto grato; se la sente cantare versi amorosi, li parrà ancora maggior segno d'amore; se la ode parlare seco, lo giudicherà ancora più efficace testimonio dello amore suo; se la vede o ridere o sospirare per amore, li parrà maggiore augumento della grazia sua; e molto maggiore di tutti se la toccassi. E però tutte queste cose faranno maggiori o minori effetti in lui, secondo la qualità delle cagioni predette. Sono adunque comprese nel presente sonetto quelle linee, cioè gradi di amore, che pone Ovidio, poeta ingeniosissimo, in quel libro ove dà gli amorosi precetti.

XXXIV

Il cor mio lasso, in mezzo allo angoscioso
petto, i vaghi pensier' convoca e tira
tutti a sé interno; e pria forte sospira,
poi dice con parlar dolce e piatoso:
—Se ben ciascun di voi è amoroso,
pur ve ha crëati chi vi parla e mira.
Deh! perché adunque eterna guerra e dira
mi fate, sanza darmi un sol riposo?—
   Risponde un d'essi:—Come al novo sole
fan di fior' varii l'ape una dolcezza,
quando di Flora il bel regno apparisce,
   così noi delli sguardi e le parole
facciam, de' modi e della sua bellezza
un certo dolce-amar che ti nutrisce.—

Ancora che nel comento del sonetto che comincia *Ponete modo al pianto, occhi mia* etc., assai dicessimo quanto fussi misera la condizione umana, e *maxime* l'amorosa, pure, perché non se ne può dire tanto, che non sia molto più, accade nella presente exposizione farne qualche menzione nuova. Né so quale più efficace argumento possa meglio provare la verità di questa cosa, che considerando a quello in che l'umana felicità consiste,

love causes all the acts of my lady that we have described, that is the looking, the singing, the speaking, the laughing, the sighing, and finally the touching, looking reveals less feeling than singing, singing less than speaking. And so I say of all the others until the touch. Because, presupposing a lover enamored of this lady, I think that, if she looks at him amorously, it will be very welcome. If he hears her sing amorous verses, it will seem to him a still greater sign of love. If he hears her speak with him, he will consider it a yet more telling witness of her love. If he sees her either laugh or sigh for love, it will seem to him a major argument of her grace. And if she touches him, that will seem by far the greatest of all. And therefore all these things produce greater or lesser effects in him, according to the quality of the causes mentioned above. There are thus included in the present sonnet those features, that is those steps of love that Ovid, a most talented poet, put in that book where he gave his amorous precepts.[126]

34

My weary heart convoked my wandering thoughts
Amidst my anguished breast and drew them all
Around itself; and first it loudly sighed
Then spoke with words both piteous and sweet:
   "If each of you indeed is amorous,
Then he who made you looks on you and speaks.
Ah! why then do you always make grim war
On me and give me no repose at all?"
   And one responds: "As pressed by the spring-time sun
The bees from varied blooms a sweetness make,
When Flora's lovely realm comes into view,
   Thus we create from glances and from words,
And from her manners and her loveliness
A certain bitter-sweet to nourish you."

Although in the commentary on the sonnet that begins: "Temper your weeping eyes of mine" etc., [22] we have very fully discussed how wretched the human condition is, and especially the amorous one, nevertheless, because one can't say as much about it as there is to be said, the present exposition brings it up again. Nor do I know what the most effective argument may be that can prove the truth of this matter, considering

---

[126] *Ars amatoria.*

parlando largamente e secondo la depravata consuetudine delli uomini, e mettendo da parte per ora la vera felicità, la quale credo in questa vita non si truovi. E però diremo quella felicità essere maggiore alla quale procede maggiore desiderio e ardore; et essendo ogni appetito, quanto è maggiore, più veemente passione, bisogna confessare il fondamento di questa felicità essere miseria grandissima. E che lo appetito sia suo vero fondamento è manifesto perché, mancando lo appetito, manca ancora la volontà: come, per essempio, chi ha grande appetito di mangiare sente con più dilettazione e piacere el sapore di quello che mangia, la quale dura quanto dura la fame e con la fame muore; anzi, quello che è piacere mentre che è desiderato, quietato tale desiderio, diventa cosa molesta e fastidiosa. E per questo si può dire questa tale felicità consistere più presto nella privazione di quello che dà molestia, che in cosa la quale porti seco alcuno bene, et essere una medicina che solamente levi dallo infermo il male, sanza fortificare poi la natura o darli virtù alcuna. Come mostra Orazio in una sua epistola, quando dice: «Nocet empta dolore voluptas», e avenendo questo in tutte le cose umane, in nello onore, nello utile, nella voluttà, è necessario confessare tutta la vita umana, che da queste cose depende, essere una passioni, e la felicità sua sempre mista con essa, perché la passione è sola inmediata cagione di essa e l'accompagna come l'ombra el corpo.

Trovandosi adunque in me questo medesimo affetto, e ricevendo io dalli miei pensieri gravissima e continua molestia, né parendomi potere sanza questi tali pensieri vivere, composi il presente sonetto, ad expressione dello stato del cuore mio. El quale, sendo posto in mezzo del petto mio pieno d'angoscia, e stracco già dalla molestia de' pensieri, chiama intorno a sé tutti e pensieri, e quali, secondo abbiamo detto, naturalmente sono intorno al cuore come cagione di essi. Di questo adviene naturalmente che il cuore sospira, perché, concorrendo diverse passioni a un tempo, generano sospiri, e per le ragioni già dette. Dopo il quale sospirare il cuore, voltatosi ai pensieri, con dolce e pietoso parlare gli priega che debbino cessare alquanto di molestarlo e fare pace della lunga e continua guerra che sanza intermissione li fanno; mostrando che debbino satisfarli in questo, conciosiacosa che sono suoi figliuoli, creati e generati da lui: perché,

what human happiness consists in, speaking broadly and according to the depraved habits of men, and setting aside for now true felicity, which I do not believe is found in this life. And therefore we shall declare that felicity to be greater which is preceded by greater desire and love. And given that as every appetite is greater so is each torment more vehement, one must confess the foundation of this felicity to be the greatest wretchedness. And that the appetite is its true foundation is evident because, if one lacks appetite, he also lacks will. For example, one who has a great hunger tastes with greater relish and pleasure the flavor of what he eats, but the relish lasts [only] as long as the hunger does, and with the hunger it dies. Rather, that which is a pleasure dies, while what one desired, when such a desire has been appeased, becomes annoying and troublesome. And as a result of this, such happiness can sooner be said to consist in the deprivation of what gives offense than in what brings some good with it, and [such happiness can be said] to be a medicine that only relieves the symptoms of an unwell person, without strengthening his constitution or giving him any power, as our Horace reveals in one of his epistles when he says: "Despise pleasures: pleasure bought with pain is hurtful."[127] And as this is the case in all human affairs, in honor, in profit, in pleasure, it is necessary to confess all human life, which depends on these things, to be a suffering [*passione*], and its felicity always mixed with it, because suffering only is its immediate cause, and suffering accompanies happiness as the shadow accompanies the body.

As I found in myself, then, this same effect, and as I had received from my thoughts a very grave and continual offence, and as it seemed to me that I could not live without these same thoughts, I composed the present sonnet as an expression of the condition of my heart. My heart, being placed in the center of my anguished breast and worn out indeed by the offenses of the thoughts, calls around him all the thoughts that, as we have said, naturally are arranged around the heart as their cause. As a result of this, the heart naturally happens to sigh, because diverse passions running together at one time generate sighs for the reasons already given. After that sighing, the heart turns itself to the thoughts, and with sweet and pitying speech, mentions to them that they ought to cease troubling him somewhat, and to make peace for the long and continual warfare that they make on him without intermission. This shows that they ought to satisfy him in this way because they are his children, created and brought into

---

[127] Horace, "Epistle" 1, 2, 55 in *The Works of Horace*, trans., C. Smart (London: Henry G. Bohn, 1850): "Sperne voluptates: nocet empta dolere voluptas." L. quotes only the last clause.

ancora che sieno pensieri amorosi, perché d'altro non parlano che d'amore, il cuore gli ha fatti amorosi, e però altro padre che lui non debbono riconoscere, e, come figliuoli, non gli dare tanta molestia. A questa pietosa proposta risponde uno de' pensieri già detti, mostrando in effetto loro essere cagione della vita del cuore, e faccendo comparazione che, come le pecchie la primavera, quando Flora di fiori adorna il mondo, fanno di diversi fiori una sola dolcezza, cioè il mèle, così li miei pensieri, di diverse bellezze della donna mia generano nel cuore una certa dolcezza mista con amaritudine, onde il cuore si nutrisce e vive; mettendo nella donna mia li sguardi, le parole, e modi e l'altre bellezze sue come stanno fiori in un prato, ove diversamente pascendosi, e miei pensieri generano questa amara dolcezza, per le ragioni dette di sopra: che alcuna voluttà del mondo non è sanza mistione di passione (ancora che ne' pensieri amorosi si vegga più distinto lo amaro dal dolce, benché sieno misti insieme) e che grandissima dolcezza è contemplare e inmaginare tante maravigliose bellezze nella donna mia, ⟨ma⟩ grandissimo tormento e amaritudine è poi desiderarle et esserne privato. E ⟨perché⟩ il cuore, tirato dalla dolcezza detta, non può fare che non pensi alla donna sua, e li pensieri di necessità portano seco ancora el desiderio, cioè la privazione di quel bene, veramente è detto el cuore nutrirsi e ⟨vivere⟩ di questi dolci e amarissimi pensieri.

XXXV

Se io volgo or qua or là li occhi miei lassi
sanza veder quel ben che sol mi piace,
miseri lor!, già mai non truovon pace:
questo adviene a' pensier', parole e passi.

Onde pel meglio e lacrimosi e bassi
gli tengo, e la mia lingua afflitta tace,
el piè nel primo suo vestigio iace,
ciascun pensiero al cor ristretto stassi.

Allor sì bella e sì gentil la veggio
drento al mio core, ove Amor l'ha scolpita,
che altro bene, altra pace più non chieggio.

Tacito e solo il mio bel cor vagheggio:
e in quel si parte, e fugge con la vita;
né vivo resto o morto allor, ma peggio.

being by him. Because, although they are amorous thoughts since they speak of nothing but love, the heart has created them amorous, and therefore they ought not to recognize any father but him, and, as his children, ought not to give him such great annoyance. To this piteous proposal one of the thoughts already mentioned responds, revealing themselves to be in effect the cause of my heart's life by making the comparison that, just as in spring when Flora adorns the world with flowers, the honey bees make from various blossoms a single sweetness, that is, honey, so my thoughts from various beauties of my lady create in my heart a certain sweetness, mixed with bitterness, upon which the heart is nourished and lives. [For the thoughts] place in my lady the glances, the words, and the manners, and her other beauties, as flowers stand in a meadow, where, by variously grazing, my thoughts generate in my heart this bitter sweetness for the above said reasons. For no pleasure in the world is without a mixture of suffering (although in amorous thought one sees the sweet better distinguished from the bitter, since they are mixed together) and since the greatest sweetness is in contemplating and imagining such marvelous beauties in my lady, [but] the greatest torment and bitterness is then to desire them and to be deprived of them. And [because] the heart, drawn by the sweetness mentioned, can't help but think of its lady, and as these thoughts of necessity carry with them still the desire, that is the deprivation of that good, truly it is said that the heart is nourished and lives on these sweet and most bitter thoughts.

35

If here or there I turn my weary eyes
And do not see the only good I love,
They, wretched, never find their peace.
For thoughts and words and steps this is the case:
    Whence for the best both tearful and abashed
I drop my eyes, and hush my stricken tongue,
My foot in its first track still idle lies,
Each thought remains confined within the heart.
    I see her then, so noble and so fair
Within my heart, where Love has sculpted her,
That other good or peace I do not ask.
    My fine heart, hushed, alone, looks longingly,
And in that instant parts and, with life, flees—
I'm neither dead nor living, then, but worse.[128]

---

[128] Cf. *Rvf.* 23, where the lover goes through a series of dehumanizing metamorphoses,

Perché io non credo sia determinato qual sia maggiore infelicità, o lo essere infelicissimo o veramente perdere al tutto lo essere, lascerò la verità di questa cosa a maggiore iudicio che 'l mio, affermando però, per molte experienzie, alli uomini accadere molte volte cose che pigliano per elezzione più presto privarsi della vita che sopportarle; e ancora che sia cosa reprensibile, la passione in questi casi si tira drieto ogni altro migliore rispetto. Vedesi ancora molte volte li uomini eleggere più presto privarsi per qualche poco di tempo della operazione de' sensi, che sopportare la offesa loro: come diremo d'uno che serra li orecchi a qualche grande e pauroso strepito, un altro li occhi per non vedere o qualche cosa brutta o altro che movessi compassione e dolore, altri el naso per qualunque fetore; e si debbe credere questi tali terrebbono questi sensi sempre serrati, se sempre durassino le cose che offendono. E, se questo è, possono accadere molti casi che reputeremmo manco male la privazione dello essere che la offensione. E perché a' sensi mia era gravissima offesa quando erono privati del vero obbietto loro, cioè la donna mia, el presente sonetto verifica la sentenzia sopra detta, eleggendosi per me in tal caso più presto la privazione d'ogni exteriore operazione che tale offensione, stimando maggior cosa la privazione della donna mia che la privazione dello essere delle operazioni già dette; e ancora che paia che privandomi solamente dello atto, e non della potenzia, non sia intera privazione, presuposto quello che abbiamo detto di sopra, cioè che la offensione durassi sempre, si può affermare la privazione così della potenzia come dello atto.

Dice adunque il sonetto che, quando accadeva che io cercassi o con li occhi o co' passi, con le parole o co' pensieri la donna mia sanza trovarla, ne resultava grandissima miseria a tutte queste cose che lei cercavano, perché non è maggiore miseria che non trovare mai pace o quiete né fine alle passione, *maxime* quando quella cosa della quale altri è privato è assai desiderata. Nessuna cosa poteva essere più desiderata o cara che la donna mia, presuposto che la fussi quel bene che solo mi piacessi: che significa ogni altra cosa fuori che lei darmi dispiacere e molestia; e però, sendo infinite di numero l'altre cose, tanto maggiore era la molestia mia quante più cose mi si offerivano dinanzi: e però erono quasi infinite molestie, e tutte gravi, perché tutte mi appresentavano la privazione della donna mia. Inter-

Because I do not believe it has been determined whether it is a greater infelicity to be most unhappy or to lose one's existence entirely, I shall leave the truth of this matter to a better judgment than mine, affirming, however, through many experiences, that many times things happen to men that make them choose more readily to be deprived of life than to suffer them. And although suffering is regrettable, in these cases suffering overrides every other greater consideration. One also often sees men more readily choose to deprive themselves for some little time of the operation of the senses than to suffer their offence—as we say of one who blocks his ears against some frightful uproar, or of another who closes his eyes so he won't see some ugly thing or other that would stir up compassion or sorrow, or another who holds his nose against some foul odor. And it must be believed that these people would keep their senses always sealed if the things that offended them endured forever. And if this is so, many cases can occur in which we impute less evil to ceasing to exist than to the injury. And because very grave injury was done to my senses when they were deprived of their true object, that is of my lady, the present sonnet proves the judgment stated above, for I more readily choose in such a case the deprivation of every external function than such an injury. For I deem the absence of my lady a greater matter than the absence of the aforesaid functions. And although it seems that depriving myself only of the action and not of the capacity to act is not entirely privation, what we have said above is to be presupposed, that is, that the fact that an injury could endure forever can thus confirm the deprivation of the capacity as well as of the action.

The sonnet says then that, when it happened that either with my eyes or my footsteps, with words or with thoughts, I sought my lady without finding her, it produced very great wretchedness for all those attributes that were seeking her. Because there is no greater wretchedness than never finding peace or quiet nor an end to pain, especially when the thing of which someone is deprived is very much desired. Nothing could be more desired or precious than my lady, for one must understand that she was that good which alone might please me, which means that, except for her, every other thing gave me displeasure and torment. And therefore, other things being infinite in their number, my torment was as much greater as there were more things presented before me, and therefore my torments were almost infinite, and all were serious, because all reminded me of the

---

particularly lines 75–89, when, literally "disheartened" and changed to stone, the lover is suspended between life and death after the lady has taken away his heart.

viene allo animo nostro che non si quieta mai insino che non truova quella cosa che più che l'altre li piace; e ancora che molte cose li piaccino, l'appetito, che si ferma in quello che li piace più, mette da parte tutte l'altre quando può conseguire il suo primo desiderio. Come, per essemplo, uno si diletta di diverse cose, come è cani, uccelli e cavalli, e con queste cose insieme è avaro di natura e più tirato al cumulare che alcuna di quelle altre cose; e però, postposti li altri piaceri che ancora naturalmente appetisce, l'appetito suo solo in quello si quieta che prima e più appetisce, e ogni altra cosa li dà molestia. Molto maggiore era la molestia mia, perché solo desideravo la donna mia, né di altra cosa mi appagavo, perché il desiderio di lei non solo era el primo e maggiore desiderio mio, ma era solo, sanza compagnia di alcuna altra cosa che mi dilettassi: e però grandissima molestia era la mia, e per il numero delle molestie e per la quantità di esse. Né truovavo a queste cose migliore rimedio che la privazione sopra detta, perché serravo li occhi, coprendoli con le lacrime e tenendoli fissi a terra, fermavo e passi nel vestigio loro, cioè in quella orma nella quale si trovavano, la lingua teneva silenzio e i pensieri si ristrignevano al cuore. E qui è da notare che questi pensieri s'intendono per la industria la quale io usavo per trovare la donna mia, pensando quelli modi come più presto la potessi trovare, a differenzia de' pensieri che diremo apresso, e quali in un altro modo e in un altro luogo la cercavano; e, trovandola, di questa sedazione delle operazioni exteriori, li pensieri intrinseci e la fantasia ne pigliava tanto più forza, quanto più mancava la distrazzione de' sensi. E però quasi di necessità e pensieri miei, ristretti al cuore, contemplavano la donna mia, nel cuore da Amore scolpita, nel quale la vedevano e bellissima e gentile, come era veramente. E allora con li occhi de' pensieri io vagheggiavo il mio cuore, bello veramente, essendo in lui scolpito la bella donna mia; et era lo imaginare mio sì forte, che, imaginando, in me medesimo quel piacere ricevevo allora, che se li occhi la vera avessino veduta. E perché una forte imaginazione, se non in molti pochi et eletti, può poco durare, accorgendomi io di quel dolcissimo inganno, quasi come da un sonno svegliato, trovandomi sanza la mia donna, in grandissima passione restavo, per la quale il cuore si partiva da me e, quasi essanime e mezzo

absence of my lady. It happens that our minds are never satisfied unless they find what pleases them most.[129] And although many things please them, the appetite, which fixes upon what most pleases it, puts all else aside when it is able to obtain its primary desire. The appetite is like one who, for example, is delighted by various things, like dogs, birds, and horses, but who also is greedy by nature and more drawn to accumulate [possessions] than he is to [enjoy] something else. Therefore, the other pleasures, which he still naturally hungers for, having been deferred, his appetite is satisfied only in that which he primarily and most greatly hungers for, and every other thing gives him torment. My torment was much greater, because I desired only my lady. Neither was I satisfied with anything else, because my desire for her was not only my first and greatest desire, but was my sole desire and unaccompanied by anything else that delighted me. And therefore mine was a very great torment, both because of the number of the torments and because of their abundance. Neither did I find a better remedy for these things than the above mentioned privation, because I closed my eyes, obscuring them with tears and keeping them fixed on the earth. I stopped my footsteps in their tracks, that is in that footprint in which they found themselves. My tongue kept silence, and my thoughts restricted themselves to my heart. And here it must be noted that these thoughts must be understood to be the diligence that I employed for finding my lady, thinking of those ways in which I could more readily find her, and they differ from the thoughts that we shall next describe and that in another fashion and in another place were seeking her. And, finding her, from this sedation of external functions the internal thoughts and the fantasy took as much more force as the distracted senses lost. And therefore, almost of necessity, my thoughts, confined to the heart, were contemplating my lady, sculpted in my heart by Love, where they saw her both most beautiful and noble, as she truly was. And then with the eyes of thought I looked lovingly upon my heart, which in truth was fine since my lovely lady was sculpted in it. And my imagining was very strong, for, imagining in myself that pleasure I then received, it was as if my eyes had looked upon the reality. And because a strong imagination, except in a very few and blessed, can last but briefly, I became aware of that exceedingly sweet deception almost as if I had wakened from a dream and found myself without my lady. And I remained in great suffering, because of which my heart departed from me, and he left me thus

---

[129] Bigi, 430, cites Lorenzo's *Altercazione*, 6, 49–54, in *Scritti Scelti*, 47–88, where L. insists that our desire seeks, not things in themselves, but the good that is in them—the highest good, the Divine.

morto, così tacito e solo mi lasciava. Perché la bellezza della donna mia, che nel cuore a' miei pensieri si mostrava, faceva nascere el desiderio della vera, come dicemmo nel comento del sonetto che comincia *Allor ch'io penso di dolermi* etc.; e quel desiderio faceva non solo e pensieri, ma quasi tutti li spiriti miei partire di quella forma imaginata e ire alla vera, perché e pensieri non potevano stare se non dove era la donna mia. E però stettono tanto in me, quanto in me la vedevano, e partendosi quella imagine, loro ancora mi abbandonorno. Allora restai né vivo né morto, perché, partendo il cuore, sede della vita, morto mi potevo chiamare; ma perché pure qualche vitale forza restava, né morto mi potevo chiamare, né vivo interamente. E se sono vere quelle cose che abbiamo dette nella exposizione de' tre sonetti della conmutazione del cuore, chi vive in altri, come fanno li amanti, quanto a sé non si può chiamare vivo, né ancora morto, se vive in qualche luogo. Né si può interpretare che altra cosa fussi lo stato in che io restavo, se non el primo che mostra questo sonetto, cioè in quella molestia di cercare con li occhi, con le parole e co' passi etc., sanza trovare la donna mia. E però si verifica quello che proponemmo al principio di questo comento, la privazione dello essere parere manco male qualche volta che una gravissima molestia, poiché io restai peggio che se fussi stato o tutto vivo o tutto morto; e perché morte include questa tale privazione, così dello atto come della potenzia, a me pareva minor male che la miseria di quello infelicissimo stato.

XXXVI

—Lasso!, or la bella donna mia che face?
Ove assisa si sta? Che pensa o dice?
Chi fanno or li occhi o quella man felice?
Amor, dimmelo tu!—E lui si tace.
 Li occhi allor, per saper della lor pace,
mandan lacrime fuor triste, infelice:
qual giugne al petto, a qual più oltre ir lice,
bagna la terra, ivi s'arresta e iace.
 Manda il mio cor molti sospiri allora:
questi sen vanno in vento; onde conforta
i pensier' pronti il core al bel cammino:
 questi a·llei vanno, et ella l'innamora,
sicché alcun le novelle non riporta.
Segueli il core; io piango il mio destino.

Ancora che molte e diverse sieno le pene delli amanti, pure, chi con-

silent and alone almost lifeless. Because the beauty of my lady, which my thoughts revealed to me in my heart, created the desire for the reality, as we say in the commentary on the sonnet that begins "When I think of complaining," [24] etc. And that desire made, not only the thoughts, but almost all my spirits depart from that imagined form and go toward the true one, because my thoughts could only remain where my lady was. And therefore they only remained as long in me as they saw her in me, and in leaving that image they also abandoned me. I remained, then, neither living nor dead, because when the heart, the seat of life, departed, I could call myself dead. But because some vital force always remained, I could not call myself either completely dead or alive. And if these things were true that we have said in the exposition of the three sonnets about the exchange of hearts [30, 31, and 33], whoever lives in others, as lovers do, can neither be called alive nor yet dead insofar as he is dwelling some place. Nor can the state in which I remained be interpreted otherwise than this sonnet at first reveals, that is, in the torment of searching with the eyes, with the words and with my footsteps, etc., without finding my lady. And therefore what this commentary proposed in the beginning is proved: being deprived of existence sometimes seems a lesser evil than a very grave torment, since I remained worse off than if I had been either entirely alive or entirely dead. And, because death includes deprivation, both of the action and of the capacity to act, it seems to me a lesser evil than the wretchedness of this most unhappy state.

36

"Woe! what's my lovely lady doing now?
Where does she stay? What does she say or think?
Whom do those eyes make happy? Whom that hand?
You tell me that, Love!" But he silence keeps.
    My eyes, then, so that they can know some peace,
Send forth unhappy tears and sorrowful;
Some reach the breast; some, going on beyond,
Bedew the earth, where, checked, they idly lie.
    Then many sighs my heart sends forth; one hears
Them passing in the wind, by them the heart
Exhorts the eager thoughts to that fair path.
    These go to her, and she enamors them
So that they do not any news report;
My heart pursues them; I bewail my fate.

Although the torments of lovers are many and various, for one who

sidera bene, tutte da due cagioni procedono, cioè da gelosia e da privazione per l'absenzia della cosa amata; e bisogna di necessità così sia, perché in due cose similmente consiste la felicità loro, cioè due proprietà che sono nella cosa amata: la prima, la exteriore e apparente bellezza, l'altra lo amore, cioè il cuore della cosa amata. Perché due cose sono nello amante che si hanno a pascere e adempiere, cioè li sensi, per li quali si conosce così le bellezze visibili come dolcezza di parole e altri sensitivi ornamenti o naturali o accidentali, e il cuore, al quale piaccendo queste cose, tanto che si transforma in altri (come abbiamo detto), si pasce della reciproca transformazione del cuore amato nello amante. Se queste sono adunque le felicità delli amanti, la infelicità consiste nella privazione di queste, che non può essere se non per mezzo della gelosia e absenzia già dette. E però, trovandosi in questi nostri versi bene spesso la deplorazione della absenzia, non è maraviglia, perché, dettando la passione il verso, maggiore passione muove più numero di versi; et essendo grandissima passione l'absenzia della cosa amata, tanto più spesso ricorreva il mio cuore a·rremedio de' versi, quanto spesse volte accadde l'absenzia mia, sempre con grandissima mio dolore.

Trovandomi adunque dilungato dalli occhi della donna mia e per qualche tempo e per assai intervallo di luogo, cominciai meco medesimo a pensare, non sanza gran passione, quello che in quel punto facessi la donna mia, ove sedessi e quello pensassi, e chi fussi degno di tanto bene o tanto in grazia della fortuna, che, essendo veduto dai suoi belli occhi o tocco dalla mano sua, fussi felicissimo. Né potendo intendere quello che desideravo da altri che da Amore, lui ne domandavo; e non volendo lui darmi alcuna risposta, pensai meco medesimo chi potessi portarmene qualche novella. Né occorse alli miei lacrimosi occhi più expedito messo che le lacrime, le quali da loro uscivano: ma non potevano però aggiugnere al luogo dove era la donna mia, perché il loro cammino si finiva in sul petto mio, dove cadevano, o alla più lunga insino a terra, la quale le mie lacrime bagnavano. El cuore allora, veggendo tornare vano el disegno delli occhi e le lacrime non potere arrivare alla mia donna, deliberò mandare a·llei molti sospiri, pure per intendere qualche novella. E qui si verifica quello abbiamo detto di sopra, mettendo li occhi per tutti e mezzi sensitivi che hanno per obietto la exteriore bellezza, e il cuore che aveva per obietto il cuore della donna mia; e li occhi sono e primi che si muovono, e il cuore li segue, perché, approvata la bellezza exteriore, séguita *inmediate* il desiderio del cuore, non solo di quella bellezza, ma del cuore amato. Mandò adunque il cuore drieto alle lacrime delli occhi molti sospiri, el

considers carefully, they all nevertheless proceed from the same two causes, namely from jealousy and from that privation which is the absence of the beloved. And of necessity it must be thus, because their felicity consists in two similar things, that is in two properties that are in the person beloved. The first is external and perceptible beauty, the other love—that is, the heart of the beloved person. For there are two things in the lover that have to be fed and satisfied. [First there are] the senses, by which one knows such perceptible beauties as the sweetness of speech and other either natural or fortuitous perceivable graces. [Second there is] the heart, which finds qualities so pleasing that it is transformed into something else, as we have said, fed by the reciprocal transformation of the lover's and the beloved's hearts. If these then are the felicities of lovers, their infelicity consists in being deprived of these, which cannot exist except in the midst of the jealousy and absence already mentioned. And, therefore, finding absence very often deplored in these verses of ours is no wonder. Because suffering [inspires] verse, a greater suffering will inspire a greater number of verses. And, as the greatest suffering is the absence of the beloved, my heart had recourse to the remedy of verses as often as my absence occurred, which always occasioned the greatest sorrow in me.

Finding myself then separated from the eyes of my lady, both by a certain time and by a great distance, I began to think to myself, not without great suffering, about what my lady was doing at that moment, about where she was sitting and what she was thinking, and about who was worthy of so great a good or was so much in fortune's graces that, being seen by her lovely eyes or touched by her hand, he was most happy. And being unable to learn what I desired to know from anyone other than Love, I asked him about it. And as he did not wish to give me any answer, I considered who could bring me some news of her. Nor did there occur to my tearful eyes a more expeditious means than tears, which issued forth from them.

They, however, were unable to reach the place where my lady was, because their path ended on my breast, where they fell, or at the farthest, on the earth, which they moistened. Seeing its plan about the eyes return in vain and as the tears were unable to reach my lady, my heart then decided to send many sighs to her so it could get some news. And here is proved what we have previously said, letting the eyes stand for all the means of perception that have as their object external beauty, and [understanding] the heart [to mean] that which has as its object the heart of my lady. And the eyes are the first to stir themselves, and the heart follows them, because once the external loveliness was commended, not only did the desire of the heart for that beauty follow *instantly*, but desire for the beloved heart did as well. The heart, then, sent after the tears of the eyes

viaggio de' quali non fu molto più lungo che quello delle lacrime, resolvendosi in vento e in aria, come erono quando diventorono sospiri. Essendo adunque il cuore fraudato di questa sua speranza, ricorse a' pensieri, confortandoli che loro andassino a trovare la donna mia, ché, essendo velocissimi e pronti, ancora che il cammino fussi lungo, presto potevano andare. Li pensieri subitamente vanno a trovarla, e trovonla sì bella e piena di tanta dolcezza, che s'innamorono di lei, né possono da essa partirsi; e, non si ricordando della miseria nella quale m'avevano lasciato, non mi rendono né risposta né novella alcuna. Per la qual cosa el cuore, che, come altrove abbiamo detto, solo di questi pensieri si nutriva e viveva, con lo essemplo de' pensieri da me si parte, e piangendo mi lascia sanza lui misero e sconsolato e vassene ancora lui alla donna mia. Né io nelli miei pianti mi dolevo se non della mia sorte e destino mio averso, che non m'aveva fatto sì agile e pronto che potessi insieme col cuore e co' pensieri transferirmi alla donna mia.

E perché abbiamo molte volte fatto menzione di questa fuga e partenza del cuore e della transformazione d'esso e del fuggire della vita, pare necessario verificare come questo sia, mostrando massimamente qualche volta che 'l cuore e la vita si parta, e pure in me resti vita, come mostra il sonetto antecedente nell'ultimo suo verso. E però diremo nella anima nostra essere tre potenzie, o vogliamo dire tre spezie di vita: la prima, per la quale viviamo solamente, nutriànci e cresciamo sanza alcuno senso e nel modo che vivono gli albori e l'erbe, che si chiama "vegetativa"; l'altra, per la quale veggiamo, odoriamo e usiamo li altri sensi come fanno gli animali bruti, che per questo si chiama "sensitive"; la terza, per la quale intendiamo sopra li sensi e con ragione aproviamo che una cosa sia meglio che un'altra, discorrendo nelle cagioni delle cose, che si chiama "razionale": la quale è comune con li angioli, et è quella parte di noi che si dice essere inmortale, perché le due prime si vede che mancono e muoiono. Adunque chi s'innamora, di queste tre potenzie ne transforma dua nella cosa amata, cioè la sensitiva e la razionale, perché tutte le forze dello intelletto e quello che per mezzo de' sensi si conosce, si dà in potestà della cosa amata, et ella al suo modo ne dispone e governa; e così segue necessariamente, perché, sottomettendosi la libertà dello arbitrio volontariamente, che è principio in noi d'ogni operazione, bisogna tutte le operazione seguino el principio, sanza el quale non si farebbono. Resta adunque solamente in chi ama quella parte della vita per la quale solamente viviamo, come abbiamo detto,

many sighs, whose journey was not much longer than that of the tears, for they resolved themselves into the wind and the air, which they had been when they became sighs. Having been defrauded of this hope, the heart then had recourse to thoughts, encouraging them to go and find my lady, for, since the thoughts were extremely fast and eager, they could go quickly although the road was long. The thoughts immediately went to find her, and they found her so beautiful and full of such great sweetness that they fell in love with her and would not part from her. And, not remembering the wretchedness in which they had left me, they did not bring me any answer or news. For this reason, as we have elsewhere said, my heart was nourishing itself and living only upon these thoughts, and, taking its example from the thoughts, it departed from me, leaving me weeping, wretched and disconsolate without it, and it too went to my lady. Nor did I complain in my weeping except about my adverse fate and destiny, which had not created me so nimble and quick that I could, along with my heart and thoughts, transfer myself to my lady.

And, because we have many times made mention of this flight and departure of the heart and of its transformation, and of the flight of life, it seems necessary to confirm how this may be by revealing especially, sometimes, that the heart and the life had departed, even though life remained in me, as the preceding sonnet shows in its last line. And therefore we shall say that in our life there are three powers, or we mean to say three species of life. The first, by which we merely live, nourish ourselves and grow without any sensation in the fashion that the trees and grass live is called the "vegetative." The next, by which we see, smell, and use the other senses, as do the brute animals, for this reason is called the "sensitive." The third, by which we understand beyond the senses and with reason prove that one thing is better than another, discoursing on the causes of things, we call the "rational." This we share with the angels, and it is that part of us which is said to be immortal, because the first two are seen to be incomplete and they die.[130] Two of these three powers, then—the sensitive and the rational—in whoever falls in love, are transformed into the person beloved, because all the powers of our intellect and what we know by means of the senses, are given into the power of the beloved person, and she in her way governs them and disposes of them. And it has to be this way because, by voluntarily submitting the freedom of the will, that is the principle in us of our every function, it is necessary that all our functions follow the principle without which they would not operate. Only that part of life remains in a lover then, by which we merely live, as

---

[130] See Aristotle, *De an.*, 1, 18–19.

a guisa delle piante; e così si verifica el partire della vita e del cuore, cioè della razionale e sensitiva potenzia, sanza che manchi la vita, restando la potenzia vegetativa nello amante.

XXXVII

    Lasso!, io non veggo più quelli occhi santi,
de' miei dolenti pace e vero obietto;
e perché quel ch'io veggo altro ho in dispetto,
Amor pietoso e miei copre di pianti.
    Le lacrime, che cascan giù davanti,
destano il cor, di fuor bagnando il petto;
il cor domanda Amor qual duto affetto
fa così gli occhi madidi e roranti.
    Amor gliel dice. Allor pietà gli viene
degli occhi, e manda alla umida mia faccia,
sospirando, una nebbia di martìri.
    O dolcissimo Sole, o sol mio bene,
móstrati alquanto e questa nebbia caccia:
non han più gli occhi pianti o il cor sospiri!

Non pare conveniente dire molte cose nella exposizione del presente sonetto, essendo molto simile d'argumento alli dua precedenti, né volendo denotare altro che la miseria dello stato amoroso quando accade la privazione per absenzia della cosa amata. E perché per tre vie si sfocano comunemente le passione amorose quando procedono da absenzia, cioè lacrime, sospiri e pensieri, con qualche indulgenzia credo si replichi molte volte queste medesime cose, ancora che in diversi modi; perché, se questa passione e spesse volte accade nelli amanti e non ha altri rimedii, bisogna spesse volte le medesime cose replicare. Mostra adunque il presente sonetto che, essendo privati gli occhi miei de' dolcissimi occhi della donna mia, solo e vero loro obbietto e riposo, avevano in dispetto tutte l'altre cose che vedevano. Amore, mosso dalla pietà della miseria degli occhi, gli ricopriva di pianti, acciò che, occupati dalle lacrime, almanco fussino liberi dalla visione dell'altre cose che davano loro dispetto: perché gli occhi abondanti di lacrime difficilmente veggono. Cascando adunque queste lacrime sopra quella parte del petto, sotto la quale dentro è posto il cuore, destorono el cuore, sentendo el petto di fuora essere offeso pel cascare delle lacrime: e per questo si mostra l'abundanzia del pianto; dal quale desto el cuore, cioè svegliato quasi, d'uno dolce pensiero che prima lo teneva occupato, dalla nuova offensione delle lacrime, quasi come uno che dorma da una nuova

we have said, in the manner of the plants. And the departure both of the life and of the heart proves this—that is the departure of the rational and sensitive powers, without which life is absent as there remains in the lover [only] the vegetative power.

37

> Alas! I see no more those holy eyes,
> My sorrowing eyes' true object and their peace;
> And since what else I see, I hold in scorn,
> Love mercifully blinds my eyes with tears.
>
> Those tears, which fall cascading down my front,
> Awake my heart, from outside bathe my breast;
> My heart demands of Love what hard effect
> Has made my eyes so dewy and so damp.
>
> Love answers it. Then pity for my eyes
> Affects my heart; it, sighing, sends a fog
> Of torments to my tearful countenance.
>
> O sweetest sun, o my sole good, reveal
> Yourself a bit and drive this fog away;
> My eyes have no more tears, my heart no sighs.

It does not seem fitting to say much in the exposition of this sonnet since its argument is very similar to the two preceding, nor do I wish to point out anything other than the wretchedness of the amorous condition when deprivation occurs through the absence of the beloved person. And because in three ways the amorous passions ordinarily vent themselves when they proceed from absence, that is [through] tears, sighs and thoughts, with some indulgence, I believe these same things are replicated many times, although in various ways. For, if this passion both frequently occurs in lovers and has no other remedies, the same things must often repeat. The present sonnet reveals, then, that as my eyes were deprived of the sweetest eyes of my lady, their only true object and repose, they scorned everything else that they saw. Love, moved by the pity of the wretchedness of the eyes, covered them with tears so that, occupied with weeping, they would at least be free of the sight of the other things that vexed them, since when they are filled with tears the eyes see with difficulty. These tears then cascaded upon that part of my breast under which the heart is located. They aroused the heart, which feels the breast pelted by the cascading tears outside. And this reveals the abundance of the tears that arouse the heart, when the new assault of the tears almost awakens it from a sweet thought that had earlier kept it preoccupied. Almost as one

e orrida voce, domanda Amore, che era presente, per che cagione piangono così forte gli occhi. E narrandogli Amore la cagione del pianto, bisogna gli dica che la pietà che hanno mossa in lui li miei miseri occhi ha fatto che lui subministra loro queste lacrime, acciò che, essendo gli occhi privati della donna loro e avendo in dispetto ogni altra cosa, se non può rendere loro la disiderata visione, almanco gli aiuti di fugire quello che hanno in odio. Perché due rimedii si truovano nella miseria, cioè el fare, d'uno misero, felice (e questo è il più perfetto) o veramente levarli la miseria, cioè il male, sanza darli il bene: come sarebbe in uno mendico e d'ogni cosa necessitoso, che chi gli levassi la necessità di quelle cose sanza le quali non può fare e solamente gliele dessi a·ssufficienzia, trarrebbe questo tale della miseria e d'uno grandissima male, che è la necessità d'ogni cosa; ma chi lo facessi ricchissimo e abundante d'ogni cosa, non solo leverebbe il male della miseria, ma gli darebbe il bene, faccendolo ricchissimo. Fece adunque Amore agli occhi questo effetto, dando loro l'infimo grado del bene, levando loro quella cosa che gli offendeva, cioè la visione dell'altre cose, essendo in essi due cagione di dolore, cioè il desiderio di vedere la donna mia, come prima felicità e ultimo bene loro, e il timore della offesa procedente dalla visione dell'altre cose. El cuore, sentendo la cagione de' pianti, mosso dalla medesima compassione che mosse Amore, aiuta la occecazione degli occhi, cominciata per le lacrime, con gran numero di sospiri, e oppone la nebbia de' sospiri agli occhi, acciò che, aigunti alle lacrime, più possino difendere gli occhi e levarli la visione dell'altre cose. E naturalmente è detto «nebbia de' sospiri» che ascende e monta alla faccia, perché il sospiro porta seco una certa aria più vaporosa e grossa, a guisa quasi di fumo e di nebbia; e naturalmente vanno in sù verso gli occhi, ove gli manda l'impeto che nasce dell'ultima parte del petto. Ma perché tutti questi rimedii non bastavano a tanta miseria, perché il perdere la visione dell'altre cose non era sola e vera beatitudine degli occhi, tutti li disiderii del cuore mio si volsono a pregare gli occhi della donna mia che alquanto si mostrassino e dalli miei si facessino vedere. Et essendo le lacrime simile all'acqua che piove, e li sospiri alla nebbia, come al dissipare la nebbia e acqua non c'è più efficace virtù che quella del sole, così nessuno rimedio migliore si poteva trovare a levare le lacrime e sospiri che il lume degli occhi della donna mia. Al quale, come a unico remedia si ricorre, pregandolo (come abbiamo detto) che si mostri, perché quando indugiassi o per alquanto tempo celassi la sua luce e virtù, gli occhi si tornerebbono nella maggiore miseria, perché non solamente sarebbono privati di questo sole, vera beatitudine loro, ma sarebbono forzati a vedere le altre cose, che

who sleeps is awakened by a new and horrid voice, the heart asks Love, who was present, how the eyes came to be weeping so hard. And Love tells the heart the cause of the crying, which requires that Love tell it that the pity that my wretched eyes had stirred in him had made him provide these tears to them, for as the eyes were deprived of their lady, and as they held every other thing in scorn, if he could not grant them their desired vision, he could at least help them flee that which they hated. Therefore, one finds two remedies for wretchedness, either to make a wretch happy (and this one is the most perfect) or truly to relieve his misery, that is to relieve him of the evil without giving him good. This would be [the case of] a beggar or of any needy person whom someone freed from needing those things without which he could not function, and [if a benefactor] only gave them to him in sufficiency, he would rescue him from poverty and from a very great evil, for everyone has needs. But, whoever made him very rich and abounding in everything would not only relieve the evil of poverty, but would do him the favor of making him very wealthy. Love then produced this effect for my eyes, giving them the lesser good by relieving them of those things that offended them, that is sight of other things. For there were two causes of sorrow in them. These were the desire to see my lady, as their first happiness and ultimate good, and the fear of the offence proceeding from the sight of other things. The heart, on hearing the cause of the weeping and moved by the same compassion that had moved Love, assists in the blinding of the eyes begun by the tears, with a great number of sighs, and puts the fog of the sighs in the eyes, so that, on encountering the tears, the sighs can better defend the eyes and relieve them of the sight of other things. And naturally a "fog of sighs" that ascends and climbs to the face is mentioned because the sigh carries with it a certain very vaporous and dense air almost in the guise of smoke and fog. And naturally these go up toward the eyes, where that impetus that was born in the lowest part of the breast has sent them. But because all these remedies were inadequate for such great wretchedness, because the loss of sight of the other things was not the sole and true beatitude of the eyes, all the desires of my heart turned to beg the eyes of my lady that they reveal themselves somewhat, and that thereby they cause my eyes to see. And since tears resemble rain water, and sighs resemble fog, as there is no more efficacious power to dissipate the fog and water than the sun, so I could find no better remedy to relieve the tears and sighs than the light of the eyes of my lady. To that light as to a unique remedy I appeal, begging it (as we have said) to reveal itself. Because when it delays or for some time conceals its luminescence and power, my eyes are returned to their greatest wretchedness. For not only would they be deprived of this sun, their only true beatitude, but they would be compelled to see the

abbiamo dette essere a·lloro sommamente in dispetto; conciosiacosa che le lacrime e i sospiri non potevano lungamente occupare la loro veduta, perché pareva impossibile il fonte delle lacrime non ristagnassi e seccassi, e la sede e luogo de' sospiri ne avessi tanta copia, che non fussi qualche volta per mancare questa pietosa subministrazione.

XXXVIII

  Io torno a voi, o chiare luci e belle,
al dolce lume, alla beltà infinita,
onde ogni cor gentile al mondo ha vita,
come dal sole il lume l'altre stelle.
  Vengo con passi lenti a mirar quelle,
pien di varii pensier': che alcun ne invita
pure a speranza, da altri sbigottita
l'alma teme d'intenderne novelle.
  Dicemi in questo Amor:—Nel tuo cor mira:
vedra'vi scritte l'ultime parole
che udisti in mia presenza, et io le scrissi
  Ciascuno altro pensier, disdegno et ira
tolto ho da·llei, e in quel bel petto sole
restan le fiamme che io per te vi missi.

Grandissima miseria è quella d'alcuno, el quale si affligge per disiderio d'una cosa, la quale poi quando è di conseguirla in grandissima speranza, non manca però della sua prima miseria, dubitando, conseguendola, ancora restare misero. E perché questo spesse volte adviene negli accidenti amorosi, si può chiamare la vita degli amanti sopra tutte l'altre misera, poiché e avendo e non avendo quello che vuole, non muta mai la sua infelice sorte, ancora che si mutino le cagioni della miseria. Questo affetto exprime el presente sonetto. Perché, essendo stato, come abbiamo detto di sopra, per qualche tempo distante dalla donna mia con molta afflizzione, et essendo già in cammino per tornare al suo tanto desiderato aspetto e vicino alla visione de' sua belli occhi, come se fussi quasi presente a·lloro dirizzo le parole, mostrando che io torno a rivedere la dolcezza del loro lume e la loro infinita bellezza, dalla quale ogni cuore gentile ha da riconoscere la vita, come le stelle del cielo riconoscono la cagione del lume loro dallo

other things that we have said to be their greatest vexation. For the tears and the sighs cannot long engage their sight, because it seems impossible that the source of the tears would not cease flowing and dry up, or that the seat and place of the sighs would have such an abundance of them that it might not some time fail in this merciful provision.

38

> I turn to you, O fair and shining eyes,
> To your sweet light and beauty infinite,
> From which all noble hearts on earth take life,
> As other stars take their light from the sun's.[131]
>   With paces slow I come to gaze on these,
> With varied thoughts they're filled, and some invite
> Hope, even; but, by others terrified,
> The soul fears knowing any news from them.
>   Love speaks to me this way: "Look in your heart—
> Inscribed there you will see the final words
> You heard me say to you, and those I wrote.
>   "I've taken every other thought, all scorn
> And wrath from her, and in that lovely breast
> Burn just the flames I kindled there for you."

The greatest wretchedness is that of someone who is afflicted by a desire for something that, although he then stands in the greatest hope of obtaining it, does not therefore lessen his first wretchedness, since he fears that, even though he achieves it, he will still remain a wretch. And because often times this comes to pass in amorous misfortunes, one can call the life of the lover wretched above all the others since, in both having and not having what he wants, his unhappy fate never changes, although the causes of his wretchedness are changed. The present sonnet expresses this effect, because, as we have said above, having been for some time with great affliction distant from my lady, and being already on the road to return to the much-wished-for sight of her, and nearing the sight of her lovely eyes, as if she were almost present, [the sonnet] addresses its words to them, revealing that I return to see again the sweetness of their light and their infinite beauty, from which every noble heart takes its life, as the stars of heaven acknowledge the source of their light to be the glory of the

---

[131] See Lorenzo, *Altercazione*, 6, 1–6, in Bigi, 81. As God's goodness is reflected in his creatures, so solar light was thought to be the source of stellar fire.

splendore del sole. E a provare questa verità, che la vita delli gentili cuori proceda da questa infinita bellezza, bisogna presuporre la bellezza essere sanza fine: e però sarebbe non solo la maggiore bellezza, ma quanta bellezza può essere, perché ogni cosa infinita è tale; et essendo una medesima cosa somma bellezza e somma bontà e somma verità, secondo Platone, nella vera bellezza di necessità è la bontà e verità, in modo annesse che·l·l'una con l'altra si converte. E intendendosi per li cuori gentili gli animi elevati (secondo che abbiamo detto) e perfetti, bisogna sia vero che ogni gentile cuore viva d'infinita bellezza, perché el bello, buono e vero sono obietto e fine d'ogni ragionevole desiderio, dando vita a quelli che gli appetiscono: perché chi si parte dal bello, dal buono e dal vero si può dire non vivere, perché fuora di queste perfezzioni non si dice essere cosa alcuna. Adunque, come il sole co' raggi suoi fa risplendere le stelle sanza diminuzione della sua luce, così questa somma bellezza infonde come raggi, ne' gentili cuori, della sua grazia, cioè uno lume spirituale, per lo quale vivono e spiritualmente relucono. E se bene la materia di che parlano e versi nostri non è di tanta perfezzione, pure gli errori amorosi fanno credere potere essere in altri quello che in sé medesimo si trova; e però, vivendo io della luce di quelli belli occhi, la loro bellezza mi pareva sì maravigliosa, che pensavo a ciascuno doversi egualmente piacere sì come a me: onde affirmavo di tutti gli altri quello che in me sentivo.

 Tornando adunque a questa infinita bellezza, sanza la quale miserrimo mi giudicavo, et essendo pieno di varii pensieri, e tanto più in me confuso quanto più me apressavo ad essa, grande infelicità si debbe reputare la mia, poiché in quel bene che io cercavo dubitavo di male. La varietà e confusione de' pensieri era che una parte d'essi mi persuadeva che troverrei la donna mia piena d'amore, di pietà e di dolcezza, un'altra parte mi sbigottiva persuadendomi el contrario; in modo che in me medesimo dubitavo d'intendere le vere novelle, per la molestia che arebbe portato al cuore quando avessi inteso essere cacciato al tutto della grazia della donna mia. Questo faceva alentare e passi miei, et era potentissima cagione, poiché, desiderando io sopra ogni cosa gli occhi della donna mia, ritardavo il passo per vederla. Soccorse Amore a questa mia durissima perplessità, perché uno amoroso pensiero mi redusse a memoria alcune parole che mi aveva detto

sun. And to prove it true that the life of noble hearts proceeds from this infinite beauty, one must presuppose the beauty to be without limit, and it would therefore be not only the greatest beauty, but as much beauty as can exist, because every infinite thing is thus. And as the highest beauty and the highest goodness and the highest truth are one and the same, according to Plato,[132] in the sense that in true beauty both the good and the true are of necessity conjoined, for each is interchangeable with the other. And when one understands noble hearts to mean elevated and perfected minds, according to what we have said, it must be true that every noble heart lives by infinite beauty, because the beautiful, the good, and the true are the object and end of every rational desire, giving life to those who hunger for them. Because whoever is parted from the beautiful, the good, and the true can be said not to live, for outside of these perfections nothing can be said to exist. Then, as the sun with his rays causes the stars to shine without diminishing his own light, thus this highest beauty penetrates into noble hearts with the rays of its grace, that is, with a spiritual light, by which they live and are spiritually rekindled. And although the subject about which our verses speak is not of such great perfection, nevertheless these amorous illusions make it possible to believe in those other subjects that one finds in their midst. And as I therefore lived by the light of those lovely eyes, their beauty seemed so marvelous to me that I thought they ought to be equally as pleasing to everyone as they were to me. So I affirmed for all the others that which I felt in myself.

As I returned then to this infinite beauty, without which I judged myself most wretched, and as I was filled with conflicting thoughts, and since the nearer I drew to it the more confused I felt myself to be, one must find me very unhappy, for in that good which I sought I feared evil. One part of the variety and confusion of my thoughts persuaded me that I would find my lady full of love, of pity, and of sweetness. And another part terrified me, persuading me of the contrary in such a way that within myself I feared to know the true news because of the torment that would be carried to my heart when it had understood itself to be driven away from every grace of my lady. This made my steps falter, and it was a very powerful cause, since, although I desired above every other thing the eyes of my lady, I slowed my footsteps in order to see her. Love brought aid in this, my exceedingly cruel perplexity, because an amorous thought led me

---

[132] Noting that Plato argues for the identity of the True, the Good, and the Beautiful, Bigi, 439, cites Ficino; see *FC*, 2, 1, 2, 3, (133) [*SA* 25–30], and notes the mixture of Platonic and stilnovistic elements taken largely from Ficino. Ficino himself discusses the relationship among the good, the beautiful, and the just.

la mia donna, partendo da essa, tutte piene di speranza, affermando che in ogni luogo e tempo sarei sempre pieno della sua grazia, acertandomi della fede e constanzia sua; le quali parole mi scolpì drento al cuore Amore con le mani sue. Questa dolce memoria mi fece prestare fede a quello più che subiunge Amore, mostrando ogni altro pensiero, ogni sdegno e ira avere tratto del cuore della donna mia, né restare altro desiderio o altro fuoco che quello vi aveva messo Amore per mia satisfazione e felicità. Pieno adunque di questa speranza, si può presumere che io accelerai e passi (ancora che il sonetto di questo non faccia menzione), perché mancava el sospetto onde procedeva la prima lentezza de' passi miei.

XXXIX

    Quello amoroso e candido pallore
che in quel bel viso allor venir presunse,
fece all'altre bellezze, quando giunse,
come fa campo l'erba verde al fiore,
    o come ciel seren col suo colore
distinguendo le stelle, ornato aggiunse;
né men bellezze in sé quel viso assunse,
che fiori in prati o in ciel lume e splendore.
    Amore in mezzo della faccia pia
lieto e maraviglioso vidi allora,
così bella questa opra sua li parve.
    Come il dolce pallor la vista mia
percosse e il lume de' belli occhi apparve,
fuggissi ogni virtù, né torna ancora.

Platone, filosofo excellentissimo, pone dua extremi, cioè scienzia e ignoranzia: la scienzia, quasi uno lume che ci mostra quello che è veramente e perfettamente, e la ignoranzia come una tenebrosa obscurità, la quale ci priva della cognizione di quelle cose che sono e resta solamente in quello che non è. E perché sempre tra gli extremi debba essere il mezzo, mette la oppinione tra'lla scienzia e ignoranzia, la quale, per essere qualche volta vera e qualche volta non vera, pare che in un certo modo participi qualche volta della scienzia, qualche volta della ignoranzia: non che possa essere mai scienzia, ancora che la oppinione sia vera, delle cose

to recall some words that my lady had spoken to me, when, all filled with hope, I parted from her, affirming that in every place and time I would be always filled with her grace, and assuring me of her faith and constancy. These words Love, with his own hands, sculpted within my heart. This sweet memory lent me more faith in that which Love added, revealing that every other thought, every disdain and wrath had withdrawn from the heart of my lady, nor did there remain any other desire or other fire than that which Love had put there for my satisfaction and felicity. Filled with this hope then, one can presume that I hastened my steps (although the sonnet makes no mention of this) because the suspicion from which the first hesitation of my steps had proceeded was absent.

39

>That pale and amorous glow which even then
>Presumed to come into her lovely face,
>Compared to other beauties that may come,
>Was as a flower to a grassy field;
>　Or, as the color of the heavens serene,
>In setting off the stars, adds ornament;
>That face takes no less beauty for itself
>Than meadow flowers, or heaven's glorious light.
>　Then Love, amazed and joyful, next I saw
>Amidst that pitying countenance of hers—
>To him how lovely seems this work of his.
>　As that sweet pallor struck my eyes and from
>Those eyes so beautiful the light appeared,
>My every force fled forth—and won't return.

Plato, a most excellent philosopher, posits two extremes, that is, knowledge and ignorance. Knowledge is almost a light that perfectly and truly shows us that which is, and ignorance is like a shadowy darkness, which deprives us of the cognizance of those things that are, and remains only in that which is not. And because there must always be a midpoint between the extremes, between knowledge and ignorance he puts opinion, which by sometimes being true and sometimes not true, seems in a certain fashion sometimes to participate in knowledge and sometimes in ignorance.[133] Not that opinion, even though it be true, can ever be knowl-

---

[133] See *Rep.* 5, 478 c–d, and *Theatetus*, 194 b; though Bigi, 441, thinks L. is more likely remembering Ficino, *Theol. plat.* 18, 10 in *Opera*, 1:423: "*item in ratione inter scientam et ignorantiam opinio recta.*"

che sono, ma ignoranzia può bene essere quella oppinione di quello che non è. La scienzia comprende le cose che sono certe e chiare, la ignoranzia comprende nulla, la oppinione quelle che qualche volta sono, qualche volta non sono, e che possono essere e non essere. E per questa cagione la oppinione è sempre ansia e inquieta, perché, non si contentando l'animo nostro se non di quello che è vero, e non ne potendo avere la oppinione alcuna certezza, non si quieta, ma giudica le cose più presto per comparazione e *respective,* che secondo el vero. Come, *verbi gratia,* io dirò: «El tale è un grande uomo», perché excede d'alquanto la grandezza di tre braccia, ove comunemente termina la statura degli uomini; e se gli uomini si trovassino grandi quattro braccia, quello che fussi tre braccia e mezzo sarebbe reputato piccolo. Chiamerassi tra gli Etiopi, di natura neri, «bianco», uno che sarà manco nero che gli altri, e tra questi occidentali uno «nero», che tra gli Etiopi sarebbe candidissimo. Dirai: «El tale è buono», che, secondo Davit profeta, «non est usque ad unum», ma chiamerassi «buono» respetto alla malizia degli altri. Tale è oggi ricchissimo a Vinegia, in Firenze o altrove, che con le medesime facultà al tempo della monarchia di Roma sarebbe suto mendico, a comparazione di molte altre maggiori ricchezze. E però diremo secondo la oppinione umana non potere essere scienzia d'alcuna cosa, ma giudicarsi il meglio essere quello che più s'accosta al bene, o vero che più si discosta del contrario suo. E se, per essemplo, a uno paressi molto più bella una perla quanto fussi più chiara e candida, cioè quanto più s'apressassi alla vera e perfetta bianchezza, la vorebbe vedere in un campo nero e in qualche colore obscuro, acciò che quella comparazione del contrario suo mostrassi la perla accostarsi più alla vera bianchezza; e ancora che la prima intenzione sia questa bianchezza, vi mescola el colore nero, che gli è opposito, ingannandosi e parendogli che questo gli dia più forza, perché in fatto quella perla non è più bianca sul nero che fussi sul bianco. Quinci nasce la bellezza, che procede dalla varietà e distinzione delle cose, perché l'una per l'altra piglia forza e pare che più s'apressi alla sua perfezzione; pure, se·lla oppinione intendessi il vero, solamente quelle cose che sono più belle elegeremmo, sanza ammistione d'altre cose meno belle, e dove nella vita umana per somma bellezza comunemente cerchiamo la varietà, se intendessimo perfettamente, prima ad ogni altra cosa la fugiremmo.

 Tutto questo discorso è paruto necessario trattando nel presente sonetto della somma bellezza che venne nel viso della donna mia, per uno accidente che negli altri el più delle volte suole la bellezza ricoprire e spegnere,

edge of the things that are, but ignorance can well be that opinion about what is not. Knowledge includes those things that are certain and clear, ignorance includes nothing, opinion [includes] those that sometimes are and sometimes are not and that can exist or not exist. And for this reason opinion is always anxious and unquiet, because our mind is not contented except by that which is true, and opinion is unable to have either certainty or quiet, but very quickly judges things by comparison and *relatively* rather than according to the truth. As for example, I may say: "so-and-so is a big man," because he somewhat exceeds the length of three arms, where the height of men ordinarily ends. And if men found themselves four arms tall, one who was three-and-a-half arms tall would be considered short. Among the Ethiopians, black by nature, one is called "white" who is less black than the others, and, among these westerners, one is "black" who among the Ethiopians would be very white. I may say: "So-and-so is good," when according to the prophet David, "there is none that doeth good, no, not one,"[134] but one is called good in comparison with the evil of others. There are today very wealthy persons in Venice, in Florence and elsewhere that with the same means would have been beggars in the time of the Roman empire in comparison with many greater fortunes. And therefore we shall say that by depending on human opinion there cannot be knowledge of anything, but the best judgment is that which resembles the good, or truly, that which least resembles its contrary. And if, for example, a pearl seemed as much more lovely to someone as it was clearer and whiter, that is, as it approached true and perfect whiteness, he should want to see it against a black field and against some dark color, so that comparison with its opposite would show the pearl more nearly approached true whiteness. And although the primary objective is this whiteness, he mixes there the color black, which is its opposite, deceiving himself and opining that this gives it greater force, for in fact that pearl is no whiter on black that it was on white. Thence springs that beauty that proceeds from the variety and distinctness of things, because the one takes force from the other and it seems that it more nearly approaches its perfection. Therefore, if opinion understood the truth, we would choose only those things that are most beautiful, without any admixture of other less beautiful things, and whereas in human life we ordinarily seek out variety as the highest beauty, if we understood perfectly, we should flee it before anything else.

All this discourse has seemed necessary, for the present sonnet concerns the highest beauty that came into the face of my lady as the result of an unforeseen event, which in others most of the time covers over and

---

[134] Psalms 14:3.

e in essa la multiplicò. Andavo adunque per una via assai solitaria, solo, pieno però d'amorosi pensieri; et essendo fuori d'ogni expettazione di potere in tal luogo vedere la donna mia, subito la scontrai, e già molto vicina m'era quando la vidi. Questa insperata visione e sùbito assalto degli occhi suoi a' miei fece in un tratto partire da me quasi ogni forza e 'l colore del viso; e, rimirando la faccia sua, mi parve similmente adorna d'uno amoroso e bellissimo pallore, non però di colore smorto, ma che pendessi in bianchezza. E di principio mi parve fussi suta grande presunzione di quel colore pallido ad essere venuto in sì bel viso; ma pensando poi meglio, vidi che aveva agiunto forza all'altre bellezze, come suole fare l'erba verde più belli e fiori e il cielo mostrare più chiaro le stelle distinguendole col colore e serenità sua; ancora che e fiori sieno più belli che·ll'erba, e le stelle più belle che il campo del cielo, l'erba faceva parere più belli e fiori, che se fussi tutto il prato fiori e non fussino campeggiati dal verde dell'erba; similmente il cielo delle stelle: per la forza non solamente della varietà, ma perché gli opposti l'uno vicino all'altro pigliono maggiore forza e meglio si mostrono; né erono a me manco bellezze, in numero, quelle della donna mia, che sieno e fiori de' prati e le stelle del cielo. Erano adunque quelle bellezze in mezzo del pallido colore, come fiori in mezzo dell'erba e stelle in mezzo del colore del cielo. Tra tanti fiori era ancora, in mezzo di questo viso, Amore, bellissimo fiore, e tra tante stelle era similmente la stella d'Amore. Era Amore in un tempo medesimo lieto e maraviglioso, avendo fatto sì gentile e bella opera: lieto, perché era bellissima, e maraviglioso perché gran cosa era quella che aveva fatto e molto nuova, avendo agiunto tanto ornamento per mezzo di quello colore pallido, che, come abbiamo detto, gli altri visi suole turbare e fare brutti. Se ne era Amore pieno di maraviglia, che era suto auttore di sì bella opera, si può pensare che io ne restassi atonito e pieno di stupore, e che ogni mia virtù, superata dalla excessiva e nuova bellezza, per qualche tempo si partissi da me: che così credo sarebbe intervenuto a ciascuno che avessi avuto grazia di vederla, considerarla e amarla.

XL

Lasso!, oramai non so più che far deggia,
quando io son là dove è mia donna bella:
se io miro l'una o l'altra chiara stella,
veggo la morte mia che in lor lampeggia;
    se advien che io fugga e 'l mio soccorso chieggia

extinguishes beauty, but in her increased it. By a very solitary way, then, I went alone, filled, however, with amorous thoughts. Entirely without any expectation of being able to see my lady in such a place, I suddenly encountered her, and she was already very near me when I saw her. This unhoped for vision and the sudden assault of her eyes on mine made almost my every force and the color in my face depart from me at one stroke, and gazing again on her face, it seemed to me similarly adorned with an amorous and most lovely pallor—not, however, a lifeless color, but one inclined to whiteness. And in the beginning it seemed to me to have been a great presumption for that pallid color to have come into such a lovely face. But, thinking better of it then, I saw that it had joined forces with the other beauties, as the green grass usually makes the flowers more beautiful, and as the heavens reveal the stars more clearly by setting them off against its color and serenity. Although flowers are more beautiful than the grass, and the stars more lovely than the field of the sky, the grass makes the flowers seem more beautiful than if the meadow were entirely flowers and if they did not stand out against the green of the grass. Similarly the sky [serves] the stars, not only by the power of the variety, [but also] because the opposites next to each other take greater force and better reveal themselves. Nor were the beauties of my lady any fewer in number than were the flowers in the field or the stars in the sky. There were, then, those beauties amidst the pallid color, like the flowers amid the grass, and stars against the color of the sky. Among many flowers, too, in the middle of this face was Love, a flower most beautiful, and among so many stars was similarly the star of Love. Love was joyful and, at the same time, amazed at having made his work so noble and beautiful—joyful because she was most lovely, and amazed because he had made such a grand and very rare thing, having brought together every grace in the midst of that pallid color, which, as we have said, usually disturbs other faces and makes them ugly. If Love who had been the creator of such a beautiful work was amazed, one can imagine that I was thunderstruck and stupefied, and that my every power for some time departed from me, overcome by that rare and exceeding beauty, for so I believe everyone would have been who had had the grace of seeing her, considering her, and loving her.

40

Woe! I no longer know what I should do
When I am where my lovely lady bides:
On either of those bright stars if I gaze,
I see my death flash lightning in them there;
    If I should chance to flee and succor beg

> ora a questa bellezza et ora a quella,
> ora a' modi, ora a sua dolce favella,
> loco non truovo ove sicur mi veggia;
>   se io tocco la sua mano, ella m'ha privo
> di vita, e tiensi in un bel fascio stretto
> el core e i pensier' miei, pronti e felici.
>   Da tali e tanti dolci miei inimici
> ho mille dolci offese, e ancora aspetto
> sì dolce morte, che a pensar ne vivo.

Tutti gli affetti umani, sanza controversia, sono passione, e le cagioni che muovono gli affetti degli uomini sono due, la ira e la concupiscienzia: che, per essere passione molto diverse, secondo alcuni hanno diverso luogo e sede nel corpo nostro, perché la potenzia irascibile si genera nel cuore, la concupiscibile nel fegato, secondo alcuni altri amendue sono nel cuore. Che sieno diverse potenzie e differente, mòstranlo gli affetti che procedono da queste cagione, de' quali una parte, cioè quelli che procedono dall'ira, il più delle volte sono molesti e ⟨duri⟩ all'animo nostro, quelli che nascono da concupiscienzia più spesso grati e dolci; et essendo tutti questi affetti, come abbiamo detto, passione, di necessità si conclude che ogni desiderio, ancora che sia per cosa dolce e grata, sia pure passione. Anzi, come abbiamo detto e nel principio, nella diffinizione d'amore, e nella exposizione del sonetto che comincia *Ponete modo al pianto, occhi miei lassi,* ogni appetito mostra la privazione di quello che s'appetisce: che è somma infelicità; e però, chi non può quietare lo appetito e frenarlo, vive in continua passione. E così in un tempo medesimo una medesima cosa si cerca e fugge, perché chi desidera assai quietare uno grande appetito ha assai desiderio, e chi non desidera quietarlo ha similmente lo appetito grande. Ma quello fa maggiore errore, che cerca quietare lo appetito d'una cosa pigliando rimedii e modi atti a multiplicarlo e accrescerne la inquietudine; come aveniva a me, che, pensando alla bellezza della donna mia, ne avevo grandissimo desiderio, e, credendo quietarlo, andavo per vederla, e, cominciando a veder li occhi, mi parevano sì belli occhi, che il desiderio pure cresceva: che era il contrario di quello volevo. Non trovando adunque la pace mia nelli occhi suoi, ma vedendo in essi rilucere e lampeggiare la

>   Now of this beauty, now that other one,
>   Now of her manners, now of her sweet speech,
>   I find no place where I can feel secure;
>   And if I touch her hand, it takes my life,
>   And in a lovely bundle tightly holds
>   My heart and all my eager, happy thoughts.
>   From such foes, sweet and many, I've received
>   A thousand tender wounds, and still I wait
>   A death so sweet I live to think of it.

Indisputably, all human feelings are passions, and the causes that move the feelings of man are two, wrath and concupiscence. For, as they are very different, the other passions, according to some, have diverse places and headquarters in our body, because the irascible power is generated in the heart, the concupiscible in the liver; according to some others, both are in the heart.[135] For there are various powers and differences that reveal the effects that proceed from these causes. Among these, one sort, namely those that proceed from wrath, are most of the time troublesome and [difficult] for our mind. Those that are born from concupiscence are more often pleasing and sweet. And being that all these effects are, as we have said, passions, one of necessity concludes that every desire, although it be for a thing sweet and pleasing, is nevertheless a passion.[136] Rather, as we have said in the beginning in the definition of Love and in the exposition of the sonnet that begins: "Temper your weeping, eyes of mine, leave off" [22], every appetite reveals the deprivation of something hungered after, for hunger is the highest infelicity. Therefore, whoever cannot quiet the appetite and rein it in lives in continual suffering. And thus at the same time it [the appetite] seeks and flees the same thing, because whoever very much desires to appease a great appetite has very great desire, and whoever does not desire to appease it similarly has a very great appetite. But that one who seeks to appease the appetite makes the greater error by taking remedies and means apt to multiply it and to increase its inquietude. So it chanced with me, for, thinking about the beauty of my lady, I had a very great desire for her, and thinking to satisfy it, I went to see her, and when I began to see her eyes, they seemed to me so lovely that the desire even increased, which was the opposite of what I wanted. Not finding my peace, then, in her eyes but seeing my death, that

---

[135] See Plato Rep. 4, 440c-442b, and Ficino's *Commentary . . . in Timaeum*, 65, in *Opera*, 2:1147ff.

[136] The basic meaning of "passion" is, of course, "suffering."

morte mia, cioè Amore, fuggivo l'aspetto loro, credendo trovare la quiete, che non avevo trovato in essi, in qualcun'altra delle molte bellezze che apparivano nella donna mia. E però domandavo el mio soccorso, cioè la quiete predetta, quando ai suoi gentilissimi modi, considerandoli con grandissima attenzione, quando sentendo el suo dolcissimo parlare; e diversamente, secondo la multiplice diversità di tante bellezze naturali e ornamenti suoi, trovavo in effetto Amore armato e parato alla mia morte: perché, ‹come› è vero officio d'infinita bellezza accendere infinito desiderio, così diremo, a proporzione, d'ogni bellezza e desiderio. Desperato adunque della quiete mia dalle bellezze e ornamenti che continuamente vedevo con li occhi, pensavo quietarmi quando potessi toccare la sua mano candidissima; ma, ricordandomi ch'ella era stata quella che mi aveva tolto la vita e teneva il mio cuore e tutti li miei pensieri in sé stretti, ancora di questo mi disperai, perché, se li miei pensieri erano felici sendo in quella mano, era impossibile loro si partissino dalla felicità, ove sogliono correre tutte le cose. E io sanza pensieri non potevo quietarmi, perché li pensieri sono il principio d'ogni umana azzione, e perché procedono l'opere, né si può fare cosa che prima non si pensi; e però, mancando el pensiero, mancano l'opere. Non potendo adunque ottenere la mia salute, cioè la quiete del desiderio, anzi crescendo ogni ora più, la necessità mostrava che io dovessi sopportare queste offese dolcissime e che amassi sì dolci inimici come erano li occhi, le parole, e modi, la mano e l'altre bellezze della donna mia; e quali erano veramente dolci, perché gran dolcezza era considerare tanta bellezza, e veramente inimici, essendo cagione di multiplicare più el desiderio, cioè la passione. Godevomi adunque non solamente quella presente bellezza, ma ancora la speranza di molto più dolce morte, la quale dalli inimici già detti, per mezzo di sì dolce offese, con grandissimo desiderio aspettavo, perché, quanto maggiore erono le offese, cioè el desiderio di tanta bellezza, più dolce si faceva la morte. E però la speranza di questa morte mi empieva il cuore di tanta dolcezza, che il cuore già se ne nutriva e viveva: intendendo questa morte nella forma che abbiamo detto morire li amanti, quando tutti nella cosa amata si transformono, che non importa altro che lo adempiere il desiderio, che si adempie quando l'amante nello amato si transforma. E però questa morte non solamente è dolce, ma è quella dolcezza che puote avere l'umana concupiscienzia, e per questo

is, Love, flashing and lightning in them, I fled their sight, believing that I would find the quiet that I had not found in them in one of the many other beauties that appeared in my lady. And therefore, I asked for my succor, that is for the aforementioned quiet, sometimes attending to her most noble manners, considering them with the closest attention, sometimes hearing her very sweet and varying speech. And, in keeping with the complex variety of her abundant natural beauties and charms, I found Love armed with various weapons and prepared for my death, in effect. Because it is the true office of infinite beauty to kindle infinite desire, we therefore say that desire is proportionate to every beauty. Despairing then of finding respite among the beauties and charms that I was continually seeing with my eyes, I thought that I could calm myself if I could touch her exceedingly white hand. But, it occurred to me that it was what had bereft me of life and held my heart and all my thoughts tightly in itself. Also for this reason I despaired because, if my thoughts were happy in that hand, it was impossible for them to depart from such felicity, toward which all things customarily run. And without thoughts I could not calm myself, because thoughts are the beginning of every human action, both because they precede the works, and because nothing can be done that is not first thought about. And therefore, if thought is absent, the work is lacking. As I was unable then to achieve my well-being, that is, to calm desire rather than increase it more every hour, necessity showed that I must bear these very sweet injuries and love such sweet enemies as were her eyes, her words, her manners, her hand and the other beauties of my lady. And these were truly sweet, for it was great sweetness to consider such great beauties, and truly [they were also] my foes, being the cause of increasing more my desire, that is my suffering. I was enjoying, then, not only this beauty before me, but also the hope of a much sweeter death, which from the already mentioned enemies, I awaited with the greatest desire in the midst of these amorous injuries,[137] because the greater were the injuries, that is the desire for such great beauty, the sweeter death was made [to seem]. And therefore the hope for this death filled my heart with such great sweetness that my heart indeed nourished itself and lived on it—understanding this death to mean the fashion in which we have said lovers die when they are entirely transformed into the beloved, for nothing matters besides satisfying the desire, which is satisfied when the lover is transformed into the beloved. And therefore this death is not only sweet, but it is also that sweetness that human concupiscence can achieve. And

---

[137] Here the ms. tradition provides equally secure grounds for reading "such sweet injuries." See Zanato, "Sul Testo," 145.

da'mme, come unico remedio alla salute mia, era con grandissima dolcezza e desiderio aspettata, come vero fine di tutti li miei desiderii.

XLI

    Non è soletta la mia donna bella
lunge dalli occhi miei dolenti e lassi:
Amor, Fede, Speranza sempre stassi
e tutti i miei pensieri ancor con quella.
    Con questi duolsi sì dolce e favella,
che Amor pietoso oltre a misura fassi,
e in quei belli occhi che il dolor tien bassi
piange, obscurando l'una e l'altra stella.
    Questo ridice un mio fido pensiero,
e se io non lo credessi, porta fede
della sua dolce e bella compagnia.
    E se non pur che ad ora ad ora spero
li occhi veder che sempre il mio cor vede,
per la dolcezza e per pietà morria.

Come molte altre volte accadde, secondo abbiamo detto, ero assai dilungato dalli occhi della donna mia nel tempo che composi el presente sonetto; e, tra molti duri pensieri che facevano molestissima questa absenzia, uno maravigliosamente offendeva il cuore mio: e questo è che, considerando quante diverse passione generava in me la privazione dello aspetto suo, entrai in pensieri che quelle medesime cose dovessino similmente assai offendere lei. E però, al dolore che del mio proprio male sentivo, si aggiunse ancora questo, presentandosi al cuore mio la pietà e il dolore suo per essere sola e sanza me. E perché la natura e ogni buono medico, della natura imitatore, prima pone remedio a quello che principalmente e più offende la vita, li miei amorosi pensieri, sola medicina di questo dolcissimo male, prima pensorno el remedio ‹a quello› che più mi offendeva, cioè la pietà della solitudine della donna mia, mostrando in effetto che sola non era, ancora che fussi di lungi dalli occhi miei dolenti e lacrimosi, perché in compagnia sua era Amore, Speranza e Fede, e insieme tutti e miei pensieri. Non era adunque sola, ancora che in sua compagnia non fussi alcuna persona e fussi destituta dalla conversazione delli altri, come testifica la sentenzia di Catone, dicendo «mai essere meno solo che quando era solo», e chiamandosi ancora da Ieremia la città di Ierusalem «sola», ancora che

because of this, with very great sweetness and desire, I awaited it as a unique remedy for my health and as a true end of all my desires.

41

> My lovely lady is not all alone
> Far from my sorrowful and weeping eyes;
> Love, Faith, and Hope and all my thoughts besides
> Forever with my lady have remained.
> With these so sweetly she laments and speaks
> That Love becomes past measure pitying,
> And in her lovely eyes, with grief cast down,
> He weeps, obscuring both those lovely stars.
> A faithful thought of mine repeats this, and,
> Lest I not credit him, he bears a pledge
> From her sweet, beautiful companions there.
> And if I do not hope from hour to hour
> To see those eyes my heart forever sees,
> For sweetness and for pity I shall die.

As on many other occasions, as we have said, it chanced that I was very distant from the eyes of my lady at the time when I composed this sonnet. And among many cruel thoughts that made this absence most tormenting, one wondrously injured my heart. And this is that, considering how many diverse sufferings the deprivation of the sight of her generated in me, it occurred to me that those same things must similarly very much injure her. And therefore to the sorrow that I was feeling owing to my own ills was added also this, [of a thought's] suggesting to my heart her pity and her sorrow at being alone and without me. And, because nature and every good physician, who is an imitator of nature, first applies the remedy to that which principally and most endangers life, my amorous thoughts, the only medicine for this sweet illness, first thought of the remedy for what injured me most, that is the pity of my lady's solitude, revealing in effect that she was not alone, although she was distant from my sorrowing and weeping eyes because in her company were Love, Hope and Faith,[138] and together with them all my thoughts. She was not then alone, although in her company there was no other person, and she was deprived of the conversation of others, as the saying of Cato witnesses that says: "I am never less solitary than when I am alone."[139] And Jeremiah also called

---

[138] That is, the three cardinal Christian virtues.
[139] See Cicero, *The Republic* 1, 17, 27, trans., Clinton Walker Keyes (London: William

fussi piena di popolo: perché la vera solitudine è essere destituto da quelle cose che piacciono. E dicesi uno essere «solo» in mezzo di molti inimici, perché, mancando il vero fine per che è ordinata una cosa, di necessità quella cosa non è più quella: come, per essemplo, chiamiamo uno uomo «razionale» perché è ordinato a·ffine della ragione, dal quale quando lui manca non si può più chiamare uomo. La società e compagnia delli uomini l'uno con l'altro dalla natura fu ordinata acciò che tutte le commodità necessarie alla vita umana, che non si possono trovare in un solo, si abbino da molti; e se questo è il fine della compagnia, ogni volta che fussi grandissimo numero per offendere uno, quella non si può chiamare «compagnia», anzi «inimicizia». Se adunque alla donna mia la conversazione delli altri era molesta e solo li piaceva Amore, Speranza, Fede e·lli miei pensieri, sanza questi tra molti era in extrema solitudine, e con essi, quando fussi suta ne' deserti della arenosa Libia, si poteva chiamare accompagnata; e che non fussi sola, si dimostra ancora parlando lei e dolendosi con questa compagnia. Dolevasi adunque sì dolcemente, che Amore maravigliosamente si faceva pietoso di lei, e, constretto da questa compassione, nelli occhi suoi piangeva; e avendo detto che la sede d'Amore e il vero suo luogo era ne' suoi bellissimi occhi, di necessità in quelli occhi piangeva. E di questo pianto, e perché da loro medesimi, vinti dal dolore, bassi si stavano, alquanto si rimetteva lo splendore loro; non che li occhi per questa obscurazione ne diventassino manco belli, ma splendevano alli altrui occhi come suole il sole interponendosi qualche nube: dico, secondo pare alli occhi nostri, non che il sole perda parte alcuna della sua luce. E perché pareva cosa maravigliosa e quasi incredibile quanto è detto, bisognava fare autore di questo chi fussi suto presente, come era suto uno de' mia pensieri; el quale, essendovi tutti li miei pensieri, di necessità vi era ancora lui, perché, come dicemmo in principio, questo rimedio venne dai pensieri amorosi. E per confermazione di questa verità ne portò seco fede della compagnia sua, cioè delli altri pensieri, d'Amore, della Fede e della Speranza, veramente dolce e bella compagnia, perché altro bene non ha la vita umana, né maggior dolcezza. E se Amore e Fede erano veramente nella mia donna, di necessità vi era la compassione della absenzia mia, e il pensiero, con questi testimoni, doveva essere creduto. Questo fido nunzio, con queste novelle, da un canto mi empié el cuore di dolcezza, pensando che non solo non era sola la mia donna, ma di sì bella compagnia accom-

the city of Jerusalem "solitary,"[140] although it was full of people, because true solitude is being deprived of those things that please one. And one is said to be "alone" in the midst of many enemies, because, lacking the true end for which a thing is ordained, of necessity that thing no longer exists—as, for example, we call man "rational," because he is ordained for a rational end, lacking which he can no longer be called man. The society and companionship of men with one another was ordained by nature so that all the necessary commodities of human life that one would be unable to find alone may be had by many. And, if this is the purpose of company, every time that a great number are injuring one, that is not what one can call "companionship" but rather "enmity." If, then, the conversation of people was annoying to my lady, and only love, hope, faith, and my thoughts pleased her, without these, [though] among many, she was in extreme solitude, and with them, though she had been in the deserts of sandy Libya, one could call her "accompanied." And that she was not alone was further revealed by her speaking and lamenting to this company. She lamented, then, so sweetly, that Love was made wondrously pitying by it, and, constrained by this compassion, he wept in her eyes. And having said that the seat of Love and his true dwelling was in her most lovely eyes, of necessity he wept in those eyes. And with this weeping and because they themselves were overcome by sorrow and were lowered, their splendor was somewhat diminished—not that her eyes by this darkening became less beautiful, but that they shone among the eyes of others as the sun usually does when some clouds interpose themselves. I speak according to the way it seems to our eyes, not that the sun loses any part of its light. And, because what I have said seems an amazing and an almost incredible thing, as has been said, someone who was present had to be the author of this, as one of my thoughts was. That one, since all of my thoughts were there, necessarily had to be there too, because, as we say in the beginning, this remedy came from amorous thoughts. And, for confirmation of this truth, from there it carried with it a pledge of her companions, that is of the other thoughts, of Love, of Faith, and of Hope, truly a sweet and lovely company, because human life has no other good and no greater sweetness. And if Love and Faith were truly in my lady, of necessity there was compassion for my absence, and with these witnesses the thought had to be believed. This faithful messenger by this news filled my heart with a song of sweetness, for I thought that not only was my lady

---

Heinemann, 1928), 49, where Scipio Africanus the younger quotes Cato's attribution to Africanus the elder. The same saying appears somewhat differently in *De officiis* 3,1.

[140] See Lamentations 1:1, "How doth the city sit solitary, *that was* full of people!"

pagnata; da altra parte, sentendo pure che la donna mia si doleva e piangeva, mi accese il cuore di grandissima pietà: tanto che veramente per quella dolcezza e per la pietà sarei morto, se la Speranza non mi avessi soccorso di vedere presto li occhi suoi, e quali sempre vedeva el mio cuore. E perché li occhi del cuore sono e pensìeri, si verifica che e pensieri sempre erano con la donna mia.

[XLII]

. . . .

not alone, but I thought of what lovely companions accompanied her. On the other hand, feeling also that my lady lamented and wept, my heart was kindled with a very great pity—so great that, truly, I would have died for that sweetness and that pity if I had not been rescued by the hope of seeing soon her eyes, which my heart forever looked upon. And because thoughts are the eyes of the heart, it is proved that my thoughts were always with my lady.

42

. . . .

[Here Lorenzo's text breaks off.]

Index of First Lines of Poems

Ah! What do I feel stirring in my breast? 211
Ah woe is me! when I am in the place 81
Alas! I see no more those holy eyes 249
Each place my lady turns her lovely eyes, ... 227
Eyes, you are certainly within my heart 89
Give me some peace, at last, you ardent sighs, ... 155
How often to my mind returns—or yet 85
If here or there I turn my weary eyes 237
If when my heart so fortunate sometimes 107
I left you even here that joyful day 151
I turn to you, O fair and shining eyes, ... 253
Let search who will for honors high and pomp 167
My lady, in your lovely eyes I see 191
My lady's final glances only, woe, ... 145
My lovely lady is not all alone 267
My weary heart convoked my wandering thoughts 233
No sweeter sleep nor quiet more serene 199
O brilliant star, which with your rays make fade 59
O eyes, I sigh as Love wants me to do 97
O fragrant little plants and lovely flowers, ... 201
O how I envy you, my blessed heart, ... 133
O lovely, fresh, and purple violets, ... 141
O sleep most tranquil, still you do not come 163
O waters clear, I hear your murmuring 145
O my own gentlest, loveliest of hands! 125
O pure white, delicate and lovely hand 119
So many straying beauties in itself 207
Sometimes among the sighs that from my breast 43
So sweetly does my lady call on Death 181
Temper your weeping, eyes of mine, leave off 171
That noble heart Love gave me as a pledge 217
That pale and amorous glow that even now 257
The sweet light of my life has fled away 67
What folly to hope for or desire to have 93
When after my lucky heart was overcome 111

When, from the far horizon, sinks the sun, ... 61
When, in my heart, both for its virtue and 195
When I think of complaining somewhat, Love, ... 187
Where shall I go that I don't find you there 71
Whoever's blessed with sight so strong that he 129
Woe! I no longer know what I should do 261
Woe! what's my lovely lady doing now? 243
You sighs so amorous that issue from 221

Appendix A

Sonnets 64 and 70 from the "Rime"

64

    Chi ha la vista sua cosí potente,
che la mia donna possi mirar fiso,
vede tante bellezze nel suo viso,
che farien tutte l'anime contente.
    Ma Amor v'ha posto uno splendor lucente,
che niega a'mortal occhi il paradiso:
onde a chi è da tanto ben diviso
ne resta maraviglia solamente.
    Amor sol quei c'han gentilezza e fede
fa forti a rimirar l'alta bellezza,
levando parte de'lucenti rai.
    Quel, che una volta la bellezza vede
e degno è di gustar la sua dolcezza,
non può far che non l'ami sempre mai.

64

    Whoever's blessed with sight so strong that he
Upon my lady fixedly can look,
Will see such wondrous beauties in her face
That they delight the souls of everyone.
    But Love has put a shining glory there
That cuts off paradise from mortal eyes:
And so to one denied so great a good,
Only the marvel of it can remain.
    Just those who have nobility and faith
Love strengthens to regard that beauty high,
By lessening a bit those shining rays.
    A person who regards that beauty once
And who its sweetness worthy is to taste,
Cannot but love it ever afterward.

70

 Della mia donna, omè, gli ultimi sguardi
il pensier mio sol sempre e fiso mira:
gli occhi miei prima n'hanno invidia ed ira,
ché sono al giugner de' lor ben piú tardi.
 Ma poi, se ben diverse cose io guardi,
il mio forte pensier, che a sé le tira,
tutte in lei le converte, e quinci spira
breve dolcezza agli occhi miei bugiardi.
 E come il sol, senza accidenti o forma
di caldo, prende poi nuova virtute
per la reflession, e'l mondo accende;
 cosí, poi che al pensier mio son venute
varie cose per gli occhi, Amor le informa,
e sol la donna mia agli occhi rende.

70

    My lady's final glances only, woe,
My thought forever looks on, fixedly:
For that thought first my eyes felt envy, wrath,
Since they arrived too late for their own good.
    But then, if I should look on other things,
My thought so strong, which pulls them to itself,
Transforms all into her, and thus inspires
Brief sweetness in those lying eyes of mine.
    And even as the sun, without mischance
Or form of heat, receives new power from
Reflection and sets all the world alight,[1]
    Just so, when through my eyes to my thought come
Things various, then Love refashions them—
Shows nothing but my lady to my eyes.

---

[1] This is a difficult conceit, but as I understand it, the lady's death has caused Lorenzo's metaphorical sun to be extinguished and without heat. But the thought of her final glances for him converts the entire world into her. Reflecting that conversion, the sun is rekindled, and without the sort of mischance that occurred when Phaeton attempted to drive the solar chariot, the reflection of Lorenzo's thought is so powerful that it set alight the world, either by bringing light to it or by burning it. In either case, this refashions the world, and similarly Love refashions whatever Lorenzo looks at so that he only sees his lady.

Bibliography

Aquinas, St. Thomas. *Sancti Thomae de Aquino Expositio super librum Boethii de Trinitate.* Ed. Bruno Decker. Leiden: E. J. Brill, 1955.

Alighieri, Dante. *De vulgari eloquentia.* Trans. A. G. Ferrers Howell. London: K. Paul, Trench, Trubner & Co., 1880.

Il Convivio. Eds. G. Busnelli and G. Vandelli, 2nd ed. 2 vols. Florence: Le Monnier, 1964.

The Convivio. Trans. William Walrond Jackson. Oxford: The Clarendon Press, 1909.

The Divine Comedy. Trans. Charles S. Singleton. Princeton: Princeton Univ. Press, 1977.

The Vita Nuova and Canzoniere of Dante Alighieri. Trans. Thomas Okey. London: J. M. Dent, 1933.

Aristotle, *The Politics.* Trans. H. Rackham. London: W. Heinemann, 1932.

The Generation of Animals. Trans. A. L. Peck. London: W. Heinemann, 1963

The Physics. Trans. Philip H. Wicksteed and Francis M. Cornford. 2 vols. London: W. Heinemann, 1929–34.

Problemata. Trans. E. S. Forster. Oxford: The Clarendon Press, 1927.

Bigi, Emilio, ed. *Scritti Scelti di Lorenzo de' Medici.* Turin: Unione Tipografico-Editrice Torinese, 1965.

Boccaccio, Giovanni. *The Decameron.* Trans. John Payne. Berkeley: Univ. of California Press, 1982.

Brown, Alison. "Guicciardini and Lorenzo." Paper delivered at Warburg Institute, Univ. of Warwick conference on Lorenzo. Warwick, May 30, 1992.

Cicero, Marcus Tullius. *De Re Publica.* Trans. Clinton Walker Keyes, 12–285. London: William Heineman, 1928.

De Officiis. Trans. Walter Miller. London: W. Heinemann, 1951.

Tusculan Disputations. Trans. J. E. King. Cambridge, Mass.: Harvard Univ. Press, 1971.

Couliano, Ioan P. *Eros and Magic in the Renaissance.* Trans. Margaret Cook. Chicago: Univ. of Chicago Press, 1987.

Ficino, Marsilio. *Commentary on Plato's "Symposium,"* trans. Sears Reynold Jayne, in *The University of Missouri Studies,* 19, 1. Columbia Mo.: Univ. of Missouri Press, 1944.

Opera omnia. Turin: Bottega d'Erasmo, 1962.

Sopra lo Amore. Ed. G. Renzi. Carabba: Lanciano, 1919.

Garin, Eugenio. *Prosatori latini del Quattrocento*. Milan: Riccardo Ricciardi, 1952.

Garsia, Augusto. *Il Magnifico e La Rinascitá*. Florence: Luigi Battistelli, 1923.

Guinizelli, Guido. *The Poetry of Guido Guinizelli*. Trans. and ed. Robert Edwards. New York: Garland Publishers, 1987.

Hankins, James. "Lorenzo and the Invention of the Platonic Academy." Paper delivered at Lorenzo il Magnifico and his World International Conference, Florence, June 13, 1992.

Homer, *Iliad*. Trans. Richard Lattimore. Chicago: Univ. of Chicago Press, 1962.

The Works of Horace. Trans. C. Smart. London: Henry G. Bohn, 1850.

Hook, Judith. *Lorenzo de' Medici: An Historical Biography*. London: H. Hamilton, 1984.

Kraye, Jill. "Lorenzo and the Philosophers." Paper delivered at The Warburg Institute, Univ. of Warwick Conference on Lorenzo. London, 28 May 1992.

Jayne, Emily. "A Choreography by Lorenzo in Botticelli's *La Primavera*." Paper delivered at Brooklyn College, City Univ. of New York Conference, "Lorenzo de' Medici: New Perspectives." Brooklyn, May 1, 1992.

"Tuscan Dancing Figures in the Quattrocento." Ph. D. Diss., Princeton Univ., 1990.

Kennedy, William J. "Petrarchan Figurations of Death in Lorenzo de' Medici's Sonnets and *Comento*." *Life and Death in Fifteenth Century Florence*. Ed. Marcel Tetel, Ronald G. Witt, and Rona Goffen, 46–68. Duke Univ. Press: Durham and London, 1989.

Kent, William. "Lorenzo the Magnificent: Culture and Politics in Medicean Florence." Paper delivered at Warburg Institute, Univ. of Warwick Conference on Lorenzo. Warwick, May 29, 1992

Landino, Cristofero. *Comedia de divino Poeta Dante Alighieri, con la dotta et leggiadra sposititone di Christophoro Landino*. Vinegia: ad instantia di M. Giovanni Giolito da Trino, 1536.

Lipari, Angelo. *The Dolce Stil Novo According to Lorenzo De' Medici*. New Haven: Yale Univ. Press, 1936.

Lowell, Robert. *History*. New York: Farrar Strauss and Giroux, 1973.

Mallett, Michael M. "Horse Racing and Politics: The Role of Lorenzo's Stable." Paper delivered at Warburg Institute, Univ. of Warwick Conference on Lorenzo. Warwick, May 31 1992.

Marshall, M. L., trans. *The Comment of Lorenzo de' Medici, the Magnificent on some of his sonnets*. Washington: The Marshalls, 1949.

Martelli, Mario. "Il Sonetto del cavallo perfetto." *Rinascimento* 2, 6 (1966): 57–77.
    "L'autografo laurenziano del "Comento dei Sonetti." *La Bibliofilia* 68 (1966): 233–71.
    "La cultura letteraria al tempo di Lorenzo." Paper delivered at Warburg Institute, Univ. of Warwick conference on Lorenzo. London, May 27, 1992.
    "Questioni di cronologia laurenziana," *Lettere italiane* 18 (1966): 249–61.
    Studi laurenziani. Florence: Olschki, 1965.
Massacurati, Giancarlo. "Storia e funzione della poesia lirica nel *Comento* di Lorenzo de' Medici." *Modern Language Notes* 104, 1 (Jan. 1989): 48–67.
Medici, Lorenzo de'. *Comento de' Miei Sonetti*. Ed. Tiziano Zanato. Florence: Olschki, 1991.
    Simposio. Ed. Martelli, Mario. Florence: Olschki, 1966.
    Opere, 2 vols. Ed. Attilio Simioni. Bari: Laterza, 1913.
Newbigin, Nerida. "The Politics of the 'sacra rappresentazione' in Lorenzo's Florence." Paper delivered at Warburg Institute, Univ. of Warwick Conference on Lorenzo. Warwick, May 31, 1992.
Ovid, Publius Naso. *The Art of Love and Other Poems*. Trans. J. H. Mozely. Cambridge, Mass.: Harvard Univ. Press, 1947.
    Metamorphoses. Trans. Frank Justus Miller. New York: G. P. Putnam's Sons, 1916.
Palmarocchi, Roberto. *Lorenzo De' Medici*. Turin: UTET, 1941.
Petrarca, Francesco. *Rerum vulgarium fragmenta: Petrarch's Canzoniere*. Trans. James Wyatt Cook. Binghamton, N. Y.: Center for Medieval and Renaissance Texts, forthcoming.
    Letters on Familiar Matters. Trans. Aldo S. Bernardo. 3 vols. Baltimore: The Johns Hopkins Press, 1985.
    Triumph of Death. The Triumphs of Petrarch. Trans. Ernest Hatch Wilkins. Chicago: Univ. of Chicago Press, 1962.
Plato. *Laws*. Trans. R. G. Bury. London: William Heinemann, 1926.
    Republic. Plato with an English Translation. Trans. R. G. Bury. 2 vols. London: William Heinemann, 1926
    Symposium. Plato with an English Translation. Trans. R. G. Bury. London: William Heinemann, 1925.
    Theaetetus. Trans. F. M. Cornford. New York: Liberal Arts Press, c. 1959.
    Timaeus. Plato with and English Translation. Trans. R. G. Bury. The Loeb Classical Library, vol. 7, 1–254. Cambridge, Mass.: Harvard Univ. Press, 1926.

Pliny, the Elder. *Natural History*. Trans. H. Rackham. Vol. 11. Cambridge, Mass: Harvard Univ. Press, 1949.

Proclus, Diadochus. *The Elements of Theology*. Trans. E. R. Dodds. Oxford: The Clarendon Press, 1933.

Rochon, Andre. *La Jeunesse de Laurent de Medicis (1449–1478)*. Paris: Les Belles Lettres, 1963.

Rowden, Maurice. *Lorenzo the Magnificent*. London: Weidenfeld and Nicolson, 1974.

Rubinstein, Nicolai, Riccardo Fubini and Michael Mallett, eds. *Lorenzo de' Medici: Lettere 1–7*. Florence: Giunti-Barbèra, 1977.

The Government of Florence under the Medici, 1434–1494. Oxford: Clarendon Press, 1966.

Seneca ad Lucilium Epistulae Morales. Trans. Richard M. Gummere. New York: G. P. Putnam's Sons, 1925.

Shawcross, John T., ed. *The Complete English Poetry of John Milton*. Garden City, N. Y.: Doubleday and Company, 1963.

Sturm-Maddox, Sara. *Lorenzo de' Medici*. New York: Twane, 1974.

Thiem, Jon, trans. *Lorenzo De' Medici: Selected Poems and Prose*. University Park, Pa.: Penn State Univ. Press, 1992.

Varro, Marcus Terrentius. *On the Latin Language*. Trans. Roland G. Kent. Cambridge, Mass: Harvard Univ. Press, 1951.

Virgil. *Aeniad*. Trans. Allen Mandelbaum. Berkely: Univ. California Press, 1971.

Von Reumont, Alfred. *Lorenzo De' Medici the Magnificent*, 2 vols. Trans. Robert Harrison. London: Smith, Elder & Co., 1876.

Weintraub, Karl J. "Autobiography and Historical Consciousness." *Critical Inquiry* 1 (1975): 821–48.

Welliver, Warman. *L'Impero Fiorentino*. Florence: La Nuova Italia, 1957.

Williamson, Hugh Ross. *Lorenzo the Magnificent*. New York: G. P. Putnam's Sons, 1974.

Young, George Frederick. *The Medici*, 2 vols. London: John Murray, 1920.

Zambrini, *Scelta di Curiosità letterarie inedite or rare*, vol. 31. Bologna: 1873.

Zanato, Tiziano. Ed. *Lorenzo de' Medici, Comento de' Miei Sonetti*, Florence: Leo S. Olschki, 1991, and Turin: Einaudi, 1992.

Saggio sul "Comento" di Lorenzo de' Medici. Florence: Leo S. Olschki, 1979.

"Sul Testo del 'Comento' Laurenziano," *Studi di Filologia Italiana* 38 (1980): 71–152.

"Un Nuovo Codice del 'Comento' Laurenziano, *Studi di Filologia Italiana* 39 (1981): 29–55.

List of Abbreviations

Aen. = Virgil, *Aeneid*.
Bigi = Bigi, Emilio ed. *Scritti Scelti di Lorenzo de' Medici*. Turin: UTET, 1965.
Canz. = canzone.
Comento = Zanato, Tiziano, ed. *Lorenzo de' Medici, Comento de' Miei Sonetti*, Florence: Leo S. Olschki, 1991.
Comento a Inf. = Landino, Cristofero. *Comento a Inferno*.
Conv. = Alighieri, Dante. *Il Convivio* 2d. ed. 2 vols. Ed. Antonio Enzo Quaglio, G. Busnelli, and G. Vandelli (Florence: Le Monnier), 1964.
De an. = Aristotle, *De animalium generatione*.
Dec. = Boccaccio, Giovanni. *Decameron*. Trans. John Payne Berkeley: Univ. of California Press, 1982.
De vulg. elo. = Alighieri, Dante. *De vulgari eloquentia*.
Ep. Rac. = Poliziano, Agnolo. "Epistola," in Medici, Lorenzo de'. *Raccolta aragonese*.
FC = Jayne, Sears Reynolds, trans. "Marsilio Ficino's Commentary on Plato's *Symposium*," in *The University of Missouri Studies* 29, 1, 1944 (119–247).
Inf. = Alighieri, Dante. *Inferno*.
In Phil. com. = Ficino, Marsilio. "Commentary on the 'Philebus'," 44 and 45, in In Platonem, *Opera*.
Jackson = *Dante's Convivio*. Trans. William Walrond Jackson. Oxford: Clarendon Press, 1909.
L. = Lorenzo de' Medici
Met. = Ovid, *Metamorphoses*, 2 vols. Trans. Frank Justus Miller. New York: G. P. Putnam's Sons, 1916.
Par. = Alighieri, Dante. *Paradiso*.
Pol. = Aristotle, *Politics*
Problematum = Aristotle, *Problematum ineditorium*. Ed. Didot.
Rep. = Plato, *Republic*. In *Plato with an English Translation*, 2 vols, trans. R. G. Bury, London: William Heinemann, 1926
Rvf = Petrarch, Francesco. *Rerum vulgarium fragmenta: Petrarch's Canzoniere*. Trans. James Wyatt Cook. Binghamton, N. Y.: Center for Medieval and Renaissance Texts. (Forthcoming).
SA = Ficino, Marsilio. *Sopra lo amore*. In *Opere*.

Saggio = Zanato, Tiziano. *Saggio sul "Comento" di Lorenzo de' Medici.* Florence: Olschki, 1979.

Som. Scip. = Petrarca, Francesco. *Somnium Scipionis.*

Sul Testo = Zanato, Tiziano. "Sul Testo del 'Comento' Laurenziano," *Studi di Filologia Italiana* 38 (1980): 71–152.

Theol. Plat. = Ficino, Marsilio. *Theologiae Platonicae* IV, in *Opera Omnia*, 2 vols. Turin: Bottega D'Erasmo, 1962.

Tr. M. = Petrarch, Francesco. "Triumph of Death." In *The Triumphs of Petrarch*. Trans. Ernest Hatch Wilkins Chicago: Univ. Chicago Press, 1962.

Tusc. Disp. = Cicero, Marcus Tullius. *Tusculan Disputations.* Trans. J. E. King. Cambridge, Mass.: Harvard Univ. Press, 1971.

Un Nuovo Codice = Zanato, Tiziano. "Un Nuovo Codice del 'Comento' Laurenziano, *Studi di Filologia Italiana* 39 (1981): 29–55.

Vita coel. = Ficino, Marsilio, *Vita coelestis.* In *Opere* 1.

VN = Alighieri, Dante. *The Vita Nuova and Canzoniere of Dante Alighieri.* Trans. Thomas Okey and Philip H. Wicksteed. London: J. M. Dent and Sons, 1933.

Index

Academics 8, 151
Achilles 127, 129
Aldeberan 229
Alighieri, Dante 5, 6, 26, 77, 87, 117, 125, 215
   Canzoniere 215
   Commedia 47, 49, 51
   Convivio 6, 33, 43, 49, 77, 87, 117, 119, 125
   De vulgari eloquentia 6, 51, 53
   Inferno 139, 209
   La Vita Nuova 6, 43, 69, 215
   Paradiso 33, 75, 88
Angels 247
Antipodes 63
Apollonius 65
Aragon, Don Federigo of 26
Aristotle 11, 19, 33, 57, 103, 149, 159, 173, 247
   De animalium generatione 11, 19, 33, 149, 247
   De sensu atque sensili 149
   Physics 57, 173
   Politics 33
   Problematum 159
   Problematum ineditorium 103
Basilisk 177, 183
Bernardo, Aldo 55, 277
Bibbiena, ser Piero da 26
Bigi, Emilio 43, 49, 73, 81, 83, 95, 99, 103, 109, 117, 157, 161, 163, 221, 241, 253, 255, 258
Boccaccio, Giovanni
   Decameron 43, 49, 63
Botticelli
   Birth of Venus 7, 55
   Primavera 55
Brown, Alison 13, 19
Bryce, Judith vii

Busnelli 77
Careggi 5
Cato 268
Cattaneo, Simonetta 7, 25
Cavalcanti, Guido 37, 43, 49
Christian virtues 267
Christology 153
Cicero
   De officiis 268
   On the Dream of Scipio 95
   The Republic 268
   Tusculan Disputations 137
Cleanthes 179
Colonna, Egidio 43
Concupiscible power 131, 263
Concupiscible spirits 99
Couliano, Ioan P. 133, 159
   Eros and Magic in the Renaissance 67
Dini, Dino di Piero
   Horsemanship 119
Dolce stil novo 115
Donati, Lucrezia 3
Elysian Fields 57
Ennoblement, process of 125
Epictetus 179, 213
Exchange of hearts between lovers 215
Eyes, role in love 193
Ferrante, King of Naples 26
Ficino, Marsilio 17, 149, 174
   Commentary in Timaeum 263
   Commentary on the "Philebus" in In Platonem 95, 161
   Commentary on Plato's "Symposium" 35, 37, 39, 57, 83, 109, 113, 115, 217, 255
   De Amore 17, 255
   De studiosorum sanitate tuenda 157
   De vita 157

In Dionysium Areopagitam de Divinis nominibus... 163
Opera Omnia 55
Theolgiae Platonicae 55, 75, 258
Vita coelestis 133
Flora 227, 229, 237
Florentine empire 51
Fra Silvestro 5
Free will and opinion 213
Garbo, Dino del 43
Garin, Eugenio
   Prosatorie latini del Quattrocento 35
Guinizelli, Guido 26
   Al cor gentil repara sempre Amore 35
   Dolce stil novo 39
Gummere, Richard M. 179, 278
Hankins, James 16
Happiness 69, 73, 167, 193 ff., 219 ff.
Harmony 229, 231
Homer
   Iliad 173
   Ulysses 57
Horace 167
   Epistle 235
Humors 67, 161, 175
Ignorance 257
Imagination, power of 143, 147
Irascible power 263
Ivory portal 163, 165
Jayne, Emily 125
Jayne, Sears Reynolds 35
Jealousy 221
Jeremiah 268
Jerusalem 269
Joy and sorrow, effects 103
Kennedy, William J. 25, 26
Kent, William 15
Knowledge 257
Kraye, Jill 17, 18
Lamentations 269
Landino, Cristofero 49
   Comento a Inferno 117
Language, question of 49
Language, question of (la questione della lingua) 43
Left hand, superiority of 131

Leo X, Pope 26
Lipari, Angelo
   The Dolce Stil Novo According to Lorenzo de' Medici 8
Love, definition of 99
Lowell, Robert
   History 23
Lucifer 81
Mallett, Michael M. 12
Marshall, M. L.
   The Comment of Lorenzo de' Medici... 1, 13
Martelli, M. 119
Marvels 183
Medici
   Clarice Orsini de' 3, 25, 26
   Cosimo de' 3, 25
   Giovanni de' 26
   Giuliano 4, 25, 43, 55
   Lucrezia Tornabuoni de' 3, 25
   Piero di Cosimo de' 3, 25
Medici, Lorenzo de'
   Altercazione 241, 253
   Giacoppo 3
   Ginevre 3
   Raccolta Aragonese 26, 43
   Rime 129, 145
   Selve d'amore 221
Medusa 139
Melancholy 159
Milton, John 23, 278
Neoplatonism 10, 191
Newbiggin, Nerida 17
Nobility, characteristics of 115
Nobility, definition of 133
   etymology 117
Noble hearts, definition of 255
Opinion 257
Ovid
   Ars amatoria 233
   Metamorphoses 63
   Phaeton 53
Passions, source of 103
Paul II, Pope 26
Pazzi 4, 43
Pazzi conspiracy 105
   Salviati, Archbishop 105

Sixtus IV, Pope 105
Peleus 127, 129
Perturbations, according to the stoics 137
Peripatetics 8, 149
Petrarca, [Petrarch] Francesco 25, 26
  Laura 139
  Letters on Familiar Matters 55, 277
  Rerum vulgarium fragmenta 39, 63, 69, 71, 75, 77, 95, 129, 133, 139, 153, 155, 165, 167, 183, 197, 209, 223, 225, 229, 238
  Triumph of Death 59, 67
  Triumph of Love 217
Physiology of love
  vital spirits 83
Pico della Mirandola, Giovanni 26
  letter of 15 July 1484 35
Pisa, University of
  Endowment by Lorenzo 25
Plato
  Diotima 99
  Laws 51
  Platonists 97
  Republic 51, 87, 231, 259, 263
  Socrates 99
  Symposium 99, 277
  Theatetus 258
  Timeus 100
Pleiades 229
Pliny
  Natural History 193
Poliziano 5
Poliziano, Agnolo 25
Poliziano, Angelo
  epistola 43
Powers
  vegetative, sensitive, rational 175, 247
Psalms 259
Pulci, Luca 25
Pulci, Luigi
  La Giostra di Lorenzo de' Medici 25
  Morgante 119
Rhyme 230
Rhythm 230

Riccardiana Library
  Codex 1684 119
  Codex 2726 213
  Codex 2934 119
Riverdi 229
Rowden, Maurice 5
Ruffo, Giordano 119
Savonarola 5
Scipio Africanus the younger 268
Seneca 179
  Ad Lucilium Epistulae Morales 179
Sforza family, Dukes of Milan 26
Sighs, causes of 109
Sighs, effects
  cooling the heart 111
Sight, phenomenon of 149
Simioni, Attiliâ, 145
Scrittori d'Italia 3
Sixtus IV, Pope 26
Solitude, effects of 171
Spenser, Edmund
  translations from Petrarch 23
Spheres, celestial 95
St. Augustine 179, 213
Taurus 229
Tears, source of 103
Terza rima
  tercets 51
Theophrastus 159
Theurgy 153
Vandelli 77
Varro
  De lingua latina 73
Venus, 81
Virgil
  Aeneid 183
  Aeneas 57
Vital spirits 107, 109
Volterra, sack of 25
Wicksteed, Philip H. 215
Wilkins, Earnest Hatch 67, 217, 277
Wretchedness 253
  remedies against 251
Zanato, Tiziano 7, 25, 33, 73, 103, 117, 119, 149, 157, 173, 213, 265

James Wyatt Cook's translation and edition of *The Autobiography of Lorenzo de'Medici: A Commentary on My Sonnets* makes available in English for the first time a document central to the understanding of Lorenzo's view of his own place in the emergent Italian vernacular literary tradition. In this work, Lorenzo sets forth forty-one sonnets with his own commentary on them and a lengthy prefatory statement. He reveals his thinking on a number of literary, political, philosophical, religious, amatory and scientific issues. Most importantly, Lorenzo's text gives his readers an idealized view of the interior person.

Based on Tiziano Zanato's 1991 critical text, also included in this bilingual volume, Cook's translation renders gracefully and accurately both Lorenzo's text and its tone. Cook's editorial apparatus and notes trace Lorenzo's insights to their sources in both the ancient world and the world of his Italian contemporaries. The introduction to the volume sets Lorenzo's work in the context of modern autobiographical theory and relates the work to Lorenzo's life and times, his view of himself, and his thinking on Florentine statecraft.

The work will be especially useful to anyone concerned with Italian Renaissance history and letters, with autobiography as genre, or with Lorenzo as a central figure in Florentine political and intellectual affairs.

James Wyatt Cook is Professor of English at Albion College, Albion, Michigan. He has been a summer fellow of the National Endowment for the Humanities and a Fellow of the Centre for Reformation and Renaissance Studies and of the Pontifical Institute for Mediaeval Studies at the University of Toronto. His verse translation of Petrarch's *Canzoniere*, which received an NEH translation award, will be published by MRTS.

MRTS

MEDIEVAL AND RENAISSANCE TEXTS AND STUDIES
is the major publishing program of the
Arizona Center for Medieval and Renaissance Studies
at Arizona State University, Tempe, Arizona.

MRTS emphasizes books that are needed —
texts, translations, and major research tools.

MRTS aims to publish the highest quality scholarship
in attractive and durable format at modest cost.